This guide to business problem solving provides readers with a broad array of tools they can use to solve everyday business problems. I appreciate the need for sound business decision making and this book will help employees at all levels of their organizations and business students do just that.
Richard M. Heins, former CEO of the CUNA Mutual Group

These faculty authors have created a very useful guide to organizational decision making. Starting with commonly asked questions, they introduce and plainly explain tools that private and public sector managers and supervisors can use to make better business decisions.
John Baldacci, former Governor of Maine

A great resource in solving business problems. See how others face similar issues-what works and what doesn't work.
Thomas F. Gilbane, Jr. Chairman and Chief Executive Officer, Gilbane Inc.

T0361014

Dedication

To Alexa King Bolland – Eric Bolland

To Devon and Aliya – Frank Fletcher

Solutions

Business Problem Solving

Edited by
ERIC BOLLAND and FRANK FLETCHER

Managing Editors:
LAURA D'ANTONIO
LINDA ELDRIDGE

Routledge
Taylor & Francis Group

LONDON AND NEW YORK

First published 2012 by Gower Publishing

Published 2016 by Routledge
2 Park Square, Milton Park, Abingdon, Oxfordshire OX14 4RN
711 Third Avenue, New York, NY 10017, USA

First issued in paperback 2016

Routledge is an imprint of the Taylor & Francis Group, an informa business

British Library Cataloguing in Publication Data
Solutions : business problem solving.
1. Problem solving. 2. Decision making. 3. Business.
4. Management.
I. Bolland, Eric J. II. Fletcher, Frank.
658.4'03-dc23

Library of Congress Cataloging-in-Publication Data
Bolland, Eric J.
Solutions : business problem solving / by Eric Bolland and Frank Fletcher.
    p. cm.
Includes bibliographical references and index.
ISBN 978-1-4094-2687-5 (hardback)
1. Decision making. 2. Strategic planning. 3. Industrial
management. 4. Leadership. I. Fletcher, Frank. II. Title.
HD30.23.B665 2011
658.4'03--dc23

2011042702

ISBN 13: 978-1-138-25688-0 (pbk)
ISBN 13: 978-1-4094-2687-5 (hbk)

Contents

List of Figures

List of Tools

Acknowledgments

A successful business relies on teamwork. A successful book relies on teamwork as well. This book was definitely a team effort. The editors would like to thank all those who collaborated on this book and who worked diligently to make it a success. The team could not have come together without the support of Midway College. The college itself fosters an academic atmosphere that encourages creativity and teamwork among the faculty. The President of the college, Dr William Drake provided the support and encouragement needed to launch and complete the book, as did Provost Sarah Laws and Dean of the School for Career Development, William Brown. Joan Dillard provided invaluable assistance in formatting figures.

Special thanks goes to Corinne Farneti who devoted many volunteer hours to the editing effort as well. The following is a list, no doubt incomplete, of those who helped with this book:

Karen Damrell
Rosy Covarrubias
David Wolfhanger
Anne Cockley
Vonda Melton
John Higdon
Joe Clancy
Garry Garvey
Cindy Fogg
Carlos Lopes
Midway College Business Advisory Council

About the Authors

Marla Ashe has been a member of the Midway College business faculty since 2009. Prior to coming to Midway, she taught at several universities while conducting executive training and development in marketing, corporate communications and internal/external organizational communication throughout the United States. Marla has shared her significant experience in global and domestic marketing with several Fortune 500 consumer packaged goods corporations. She has a DBA from Argosy University and an MBA from Keller Graduate School of Business.

Laura Barthel joined Midway College's business faculty in 2009. Previously, she held the position of Internal Auditor for Tempur-Pedic International leading efforts for post Sarbanes-Oxley compliance improvement and internal assistance to Ernst & Young's integrated external audit. Her experience also includes public accounting, governmental accounting, and secondary education. Laura is a CPA and has a Masters in accounting from University of Kentucky and a BS from Eastern Kentucky University.

Rik Berry joined Midway College's MBA faculty in the fall of 2008. Previously, he held teaching positions at the University of Arkansas /Fort Smith, Morehead State University, Brenau University, and Virginia Military Institute. His current research interests include operations management in healthcare, interdisciplinary teaching requirements and methodologies, sustainable services and operations, constraint identification and management, quality control and basic statistics. He has a PhD from the University of Georgia and an MA in accounting from James Madison University.

Eric Bolland was appointed Chair of the Midway College MBA Division in 2009, a year after he joined the faculty. He has more than twenty years teaching experience and over twenty-five years of business experience. His business experience encompasses managing strategic market information for a Fortune 500 company (TDS Telecom), product promotion management for CUNA Mutual Insurance Company and strategic marketing consulting for Alliant Energy. He served as the executive director of the State of Wisconsin Board on Aging. He has published two major books and over twenty articles or proceedings on various business topics. Eric has a DBA from Nova Southeastern University and an MA in Public Administration from the University of Wisconsin at Madison.

Karen Clancy joined the full-time faculty of the Midway Business Division in 2010. With over thirty years of experience in healthcare, she has held leadership positions including Assistant Dean of Finance and Administration for the University of Kentucky College of Pharmacy, Associate Director of University of Kentucky Health Service, Director of Consulting and the Center of Learning at Cardinal Hill Healthcare System, Administrator of the Lucille Parker Markey Cancer Center and Director of Communications for the

University of Kentucky Chandler Medical Center. Karen has an MBA from Morehead State University and a BA in Health Care Administration from the University of Kentucky.

Laura D'Antonio joined the Midway Faculty in 2010. Prior to joining the faculty, she enjoyed a successful Banking career with a focus on Commercial Banking, Private Banking and Mortgage and Construction Lending eventually reaching middle management levels at Wells Fargo and Citigroup. Her areas of academic interest include Strategic Management, Entrepreneurship, Leadership Development and Communication. She holds an MBA from New York University's Stern School and a BA from Yale University.

Glenn Dishman has been a faculty member in the Business Division at Midway College since 1989. In 2010, he was recognized by the Midway College Board of Trustees for Outstanding Teaching. Col. Dishman USAF (Ret.) has more than fifty years of experience in the United States Air Force and in the education field. In the past he has held various aviation, staff and command assignments of increasing responsibility in the Air Force. He is also a graduate of the Command and Staff College and the National Defense University. Glenn has an MPA from Auburn University and a BS in Economics from the University of Kentucky.

Linda Eldridge has been a member of the faculty of the Business Division at Midway College since 1989. She has more than thirty years of experience working in education and computer-related business. In the past, she has held teaching and administrative positions at Kentucky State University. Additionally, she has worked for the Council on Higher Education and other areas in Kentucky State government. In spring of 2011 she was appointed Midway College's Registrar. Linda's MPA and BS are from Kentucky State University.

Corinne Farneti joined the Midway College business division faculty in August of 2009 as the Coordinator of the Sport Management program. Corinne previously held a teaching and academic counseling position at the University of Kentucky. She also has several years of experience working in collegiate athletics. She has published and presented nationally in areas of sports personnel management, media representation of gender, fantasy sport and team dynamics. She has a PhD from Ohio State University and her Masters in Education from the University of Georgia.

Frank Fletcher has served as Professor and Chair of the Business Division at Midway College since 2003. He has more than twenty-five years of experience working in education, business, and nonprofits. In the past he has held teaching and administrative positions at the University of Texas/El Paso, Husson College (Bangor, ME) and the University of Massachusetts/Boston. Frank has also earned professional certifications for both fundraising and marketing: Certified Professional Fundraiser (CFRE) and Certified Professional Marketer (CPM). Frank has his EdD from the University of Massachusetts and his MS from Fitchburg State College.

Wendy Hoffman has been a faculty member in the Business Division at Midway College since 1995 following a financial management career in the telecommunications industry. She has earned professional certifications for cash management (CCM) and treasury management (CFM). Her current areas of academic research and writing are in the areas of strategic management of businesses, stock market performance and investment management. Wendy is the Athletic Director and Head Tennis Coach for Midway College. She has an MBA from Drexel University and a BS from St Joseph's. She earned a Doctorate of Higher Education Management from the Institute of Higher Education at the University of Georgia.

Teresa Ann Isaac is the former mayor of Lexington, Kentucky and has been a member of Midway College's business faculty since 2009. A University of Kentucky Law School graduate, she served for three years as a prosecutor in the Fayette County Attorney's office and five years as Associate Professor in the Eastern Kentucky University Department of Government and Law. The US Department of State sends her to cities around the world as part of a democracy project to train government leaders. Teresa has earned a JD at the University of Kentucky and a BA at Transylvania University.

Sal Mirza has more than twenty-eight years of international business experience and joined the Midway College business faculty in 2010. His business experience covers the industry segments of research & development, technical service, production, sales and marketing for several global organizations. He has held managerial positions as global market manager, business development manager, project leader and research scientist. He has international experience in Asia, Europe, North America and the Southern Cone, having extensive work time in countries such as China, Indonesia, Malaysia, Singapore, South Korea, Japan, Pakistan, Australia, Brazil, Mexico and Poland. Sal has a PhD from Capella University and an MBA from the University of Phoenix.

Bobby Ricks is a member of the Midway Faculty and Coordinator of Midway College's Public Safety Administration Program. His law enforcement career began as a law enforcement specialist with the United States Air Force Security Forces. He has also worked as a patrolman and then director of Crime Prevention of the Richmond, Kentucky Police Department, and Special Agent with the Federal Bureau of Investigation. He was also Lead Instructor and Senior Instructor in the Legal Division at the Federal Law Enforcement Training Center. Bobby earned a JD at the University of Memphis and a BS at Eastern Kentucky University.

Jerry Wellman joined Midway College's MBA faculty in 2010. Previously, he was an executive at Honeywell where his last assignment was Vice President of a 1,800-person services business that supported various Department of Defense (DOD) and government systems around the world. These included satellite monitoring and control, pre-positioning of war readiness assets, nuclear test ban treaty compliance monitoring systems, earthquake detection and monitoring systems, rapidly deployable portable hospitals and others. Jerry earned a PhD and an MS from Fielding Graduate University.

Introduction

The purpose of this book is to be a guide for executives, managers, supervisors and students in solving the most common business problems. The unique aspect of this book is that readers will be able to quickly locate, understand and use appropriate tools to solve a problem or make decisions leading to solutions. Instead of having to uncover a decision making tool buried within a textbook, search for just the right employee who has the answer locked in their mind alone or plow through a lengthy search of partial and unproven tools on the Internet, the reader can now go directly to a book chapter that will have tools and solutions in close alignment. The book can be considered an owner's guide to business, providing a focused source of information on how businesses operate. Readers will find out what can be done to fix problems and help businesses perform better.

Readers who encounter business problems or challenges will be able to immediately locate a set of remedies that are accessible, practical, meaningful and reliable. Just by knowing the general category of the issue such as strategy, human resource management, accounting or information technology, readers can turn to the chapter dealing with that subject and get introduced to a host of tools that can be used to understand and solve problems.

The chapters are organized in the usual functional areas of business, and this is the best way to get the search started. It also serves as a framework for organizing the myriad of business problems into separate areas. At the same time, each chapter makes cross references to other chapters. Different functional areas of business may make use of the same tools. It is important that readers know how the tools may work for more than one business issue. In writing this book, considerable attention was paid to having an integrated volume that avoided duplication of tools and repetition of thought.

Every chapter is built around commonly occurring questions which managers, business owners and students ask. The questions came from business practitioners and were screened by the chapter authors and editors of this book. More specifically, the Midway College Business Advisory Board, a group of Lexington, Kentucky area business professionals, contributed questions. The chapter authors and their business associates also suggested questions.

A major objective of the book was to connect a proven tool to a related business question. The authors introduce the question, provide a context for it and make sure the question can be answered adequately. A tool or tools will then be introduced and explained. Often, examples of the usage of the tool are provided. In this book, a tool is considered to be an accepted way of understanding an issue or problem and coming up with a way of making a decision that leads the way to a solution. Our tools, some fifty in total, tend to be data driven because data drives business. Tools range from simple checklists to much more quantitative tools like cost-benefit analysis. In addition to tools for business problems, the book contains numerous tips and figures. The tips are highlighted as quick and handy reminders aimed at helping readers execute management practices. The figures help shed light on the various concepts discussed.

Fifteen Midway College full-time business faculty members, virtually the entire business faculty, are the chapter authors. They teach in both the undergraduate and MBA business programs. The authors have extensive experience in the subjects they write about. They are also very familiar with the full array of tools that business professionals use. Faculty authors are scholar-practitioners. All the authors possess both academic qualifications and real world business experience.

Using many authors is necessary for this broad-scope book. No single author has enough expertise to produce a book of this extent by themselves. While all the authors were focused on a main direction for the book, they also were able to enliven their topics with their own writing styles, avoiding a cookie-cutter approach to our main theme. That theme is business solutions. This book is a primary source compendium of solutions, organized so the reader can step right from issue to practical resolution without extraneous theory or unnecessary background that may interfere with the match of solution to problem.

The reader will be able to use the book many different times, not just for a single problem in a single functional area of the organization. Consequently, it is an encyclopedic reference for answers to organizational problems. As such, the book should retain its usefulness for managers who will assume increasing responsibilities in business and who need to learn more about the issues and practices of other business areas. For those who may just want to know more about business and for those who are business students, this book will help show the breadth and depth of how businesses can solve problems.

There are two different sections of this book. The first, which is comprised of chapters one through six, deals with subjects that span the entire business organization: problems, decision making, leadership, communications and strategy. The second section, chapters seven through nineteen, deals with functional areas of the business. Together, the chapters cover the great majority of issues and problems the reader has faced or will face.

As a final part of this introduction, the following table shows what major tools are presented in each chapter.

Chapter Number	Chapter Subject	Tool(s)
1	Problems and Decision Making	1.1 Problem Solving
2	Decision Making Problems and Pitfalls	2.1 Group vs. Individual Decision Making Guide
3	Leadership	3.1 Applying Intellectual Standards: Questions to Ask 3.2 Organizational Culture Evaluation 3.3 The Change Process
4	Communications	4.1 Communication Transaction Tool 4.2 Presentation Tool
5	Strategy	5.1 External Analysis Tool 5.2 Value Chain 5.3 Growth-Share Matrix 5.4 SWOT Analysis 5.5 Decision Tree

Chapter Number	Chapter Subject	Tool(s)
6	Organizational Design	6.1 Current Assessment of Organizational Resources 6.2 Integration Strategies 6.3 Four Phases of Linking Strategy to Structure
7	Human Resource Management	7.1 Recruiting Methods Comparison 7.2 Selection Methods Comparison 7.3 Appraisal Methods Comparison 7.4 Employee Performance Improvement Plan 7.5 Incentive Program Comparison
8	Promotion	8.1 Budgeting Approaches 8.2 Ad Agency Selection Questions 8.3 Sample Creative/Communications Brief 8.4 Communication Objectives 8.5 Advertising Appeal Options 8.6 Trade Promotion Options 8.7 Message Evaluation Methods
9	Competitors and Competition	9.1 Competitor Encounter Tracking Device 9.2 Competitor Analysis Tool 9.3 Competitor Profile Tool 9.4 Competition Self Appraisal
10	Pricing	10.1 Pricing Strategy Objectives 10.2 Pricing Self Audit 10.3 Marketing Strategy Comparison 10.4 Economic Valuation Estimation 10.5 Customer Price Sensitivity Survey
12	Production and Operations	12.1 Seven Tools of Quality Selection Guide 12.2 Outsourcing Readiness Guide
13	Suppliers and Distributors	13.1 Distribution Preparedness Checklist 13.2 Supplier Selection Questionnaire 13.3 Supply Chain Management Mapping Tool
14	Project and Process Management	14.1 Guide to Project Management 14.2 Guide to Process Management
16	Finance and Budgeting	16.1 Budget Process Success Ideas
17	Organizational Performance	17.1 Guide to Financial Ratios 17.2 IRR Calculator 17.3 Advantages and Disadvantages of Debt and Equity
18	Government and Legal	18.1 Contract Basics 18.2 UCC Summary
19	Information Technology	19.1 Choosing a Financial Analysis Tool 19.2 Buy or Outsource Tool Example

1 *Problems and Decision Making*

WENDY HOFFMAN

There are some events in life that are inevitable, and the emergence of problems in the workplace is one. Problem solving is the domain of the manager. Fortunately, skill in finding optimal solutions to problems can be developed. Such skill stems from understanding the nature of problems and utilizing a basic process to address the problem.

The simplicity and profundity of the last sentence should not be overlooked. First, consider "understanding the nature of the problem." What does this entail? It can be a greater challenge than it may first appear. For example, problems are subjective. A problem to one individual might be a godsend to another. If your competitors have problems, isn't that good news for you? Also, problems are deceptive. Often an acknowledged problem is discovered to be a signal of more complex problems lurking below the surface. Finally, even when fixed, the same type of problem might recur.

Second, consider the idea of utilizing a basic process to address the problem. Simply going after a solution willy-nilly may or may not solve the problem. Time, money and patience may be expended unnecessarily. A systematic approach to solving the problem brings about a deliberate and potentially more valid course of action.

Problem solving skill relies on judgment and perceptual acuity—the ability to recognize and evaluate the situation at hand. In the presence of multiple solutions, the selection from a purely egotistical position might solve the problem. At the same time, it may create a stream of new issues of increased consequence. Understanding the nature of the problem at hand and deliberately approaching the problem enhances the manager's insight and judgment leading to more successful solutions.

This chapter will familiarize you with the nature and types of common problems. It will explain the importance of deciphering the type of pending problem. A decision making model is explained that guides the manager to effective problem solving. The role of stakeholders in the problem scenario and the impact of solutions on them will be examined.

Finally, several factors that can be managed to increase the effectiveness of a problem's solution will be reviewed. In this, a discussion of the nature of the problem-solver is provided. Lastly, this chapter, because it focuses on defining and understanding problems, forms a natural segue into chapter two on decision making challenges and pitfalls. Problems and decisions are not synonymous. A problem creates an opportunity for or forces a decision. Consequently, these two chapters work in tandem to provide a more complete context for both problem solving and decision making.

Throughout this chapter, inserts will highlight useful tips as guidance to the practical decision-maker. By keeping your problem-solving toolbox handy, you may confidently approach the most complex problems and lead the way to an effective solution.

What is a problem?

As noted by William F. Pounds (1969), a problem can simply be defined as a difference between an actual state and an expected or, often, a desired state. Presented in this way, problems do not have to represent a negative condition. They instead represent the existence of a discrepancy, and the discrepancy requires attention and response, even if that response is no action at all. Here is an example:

> *Actual State: A private aircraft manufacturer produces small, four seat aircraft which use aluminum fuselages, tails and wings.*
>
> *Desired State: A lighter weight aircraft is desired which has the same or better flying performance and can be manufactured using as many current production processes and materials as possible.*

Notice that the actual state is a very simple, factual statement. There is nothing overt or even implied about the deficiencies of the actual state. That is your starting point. The desired state is a statement that is infused with something better. It is a dream or step above what is actually happening. Notice too, that the desired state is phrased in such a way that there is a cost effective transition to the desired state. In the example, this is stated as, "the same or better flying performance" and "using as many current production processes and materials as possible." Sometimes, if these conditions for a solution are not stated, they are not met. When business problems are posed this way, they not only clearly depict a future state, they lead to an analysis of the gap between what is and what ought to be.

The definition of the problem is critical. Einstein is said to have observed that if he had one hour to save the world, he would spend fifty-five minutes defining the problem and five minutes finding the solution. Business managers may not be given such Herculean problems as Einstein pondered but the essential point is that problems need to be defined and measured. There is a problem with problems if we do not structure them, fit them into classification systems and divide them into their component parts.

When managers address problems, they engage in problem-solving and make reasoned decisions among alternatives as they progress toward a final resolution. Thus, the series of decision-making steps as a practical matter is considered synonymous with problem solving.

What can I do to get a handle on a problem?

To come up with a solution to a problem, the problem has to be managed down to a reasonable level. The problem cannot have such an immense scope as, "how can we achieve world peace?" This is certainly far too much to ask of any person and of any single organization. The problems we solve have to be manageable in scope. Organizational problems also need to be framed in time. They need to be responsive to the application of organizational resources. The problems organizations face tend to be complex but they also tend to be solvable.

Consider your own reaction when you were asked to solve a major problem at work. You may have thought, "Can I do this?" That element of self-doubt is a valid reaction to most problems when the solutions are not obvious. The reaction may have been precipitated from the nature of the problem itself and this section deals with that issue. The problem may be ambiguous such as, "how can our business situation improve?" Or it may be stated as a symptom rather than a cause such as, "our customers are not happy." It may not even be an actual problem such as, "what kind of landscaping is preferred for our new corporate office?"

The first step to solving problems is to examine the problem statement itself. Here, the tried and true expression of divide and conquer applies. Look at the problem statement and slice and dice it until you come up with a clearly stated problem that lends itself to an actionable solution. Here are some ways of doing that:

1. Clarify the language of the problem. Words are powerful and have a major role in how a problem is understood. You want to state the problem in a neutral way so that it is not directed toward a specific solution before the problem analysis occurs. As an example, the statement "how can we replace our outdated copy machine" is already skewed toward a replacement instead of an upgrade. Using the term outdated indicates a judgment before the problem is analyzed. You should rephrase your problem several times until you are satisfied with the language. The word changes may be subtle but the impact substantial. To increase sales is much more meaningful than to enhance sales. Make sure your chosen words are judgment free.

2. Once you have reworked the language, you should check out the problem statement with those who are not working on its solution. Have them respond to your problem statement and ask if they understand it. The better the problem is understood, the easier it will be to solve it with the understanding and commitment of organizational members.

> **Problem Solving:**
>
> 1. Clarify the language of the problem.
>
> 2. Consider the "who" in the "what" of the problem.
>
> 3. Check problem assumptions.
>
> 4. Expand and contract the problem.
>
> 5. Look at the problem from other perspectives.
>
> 6. Make it a question.
>
> 7. Go to the root of the problem.
>
> 8. Research your problem statement.
>
> 9. Use multiple authorship of the problem statement.

Tool 1.1   Problem Solving

3. Consider the "who" in the "what" of the problem. Problems are solved if their human impact is considered. Who does it fall on (or who does it elevate) to have the problem solved? Problem statements mostly succeed in defining what the problem is but they can be improved by stating who will be affected, meaning which departments or work units.

4. For most of us, it is more difficult to relate to higher-level organizational goals than goals for our own areas. Commitment to solutions is facilitated when names are named. For instance, if a problem concerning increasing sales is framed as making jobs

easier to improve throughput which improves sales, then people are more willing to participate in problem solving. However, it is also important not to make a potential solution part of the problem statement because the problem statement itself should be solution free and not lead problem analysts toward a certain path.

5. Check problem assumptions. Every organization's situation is a result of preceding causes or what are assumed to be causes. We always make assumptions about the circumstances of the problem. Many of these assumptions are based on the notion that what happened in the past will continue in the future. These assumptions may be inaccurate, although they are natural for us to fall back on.

6. Assumptions based on past events can fool us. Organizations do not usually go through abrupt and fundamental changes. Nevertheless, it is important to dispose of incorrect assumptions before formulating the problem statement. To do this, make a list of assumptions. Each assumption should be explicit and should be evaluated. Certain assumptions may be so broadly stated (the sun will produce light tomorrow to run solar batteries) that they need not be named but others (photocell manufacturers will grow in number) should be assessed. Your listed assumptions should be challenged for their appropriateness and the actual working assumptions should then be identified and recorded as part of the problem statement creation process.

7. Expand and contract the problem. The problem you are exploring may have critical links to a larger problem that needs to be addressed at a different organizational level by different people. This possibility needs to be considered. On the other hand, the problem may have a series of smaller but related component problems that need to be sorted out and addressed before problem statement formulation. It may even be the case that one of the component problems needs to be solved before the main problem can be stated.

8. Look at the problem from other perspectives. CEOs have been known to say that customers are not interested in our problems. This is short sighted. Customers have a stake in an organization's success or failure because they have reliance on the organization. Looking at the problem from the customer's perspective does not require their perspective be incorporated into the problem statement. It does mean the customer's perspective as well as the perspectives of other stakeholders such as suppliers, distributors, citizens, investors and government entities should at least be considered in the problem statement formulation stage of problem solving.

9. You may also want to consider how non-stakeholders would look at this problem. For example, what would a competitor say about the problem? If you raise this as a question, it gives you the opportunity to look at the consequences of the solution on someone who is not your friend in the market.

10. Make it a question. Phrasing the problem as a question gets right to the heart of the matter. Ask who, how, when or what can be done. Answering the question demands action not contemplation. It leads to the formation of a team to implement a solution. If you start your problem statement with something like "the issue is..." then the language loses its power. Ask a question and the question format will lead more easily to a solution.

11. Go to the root of the problem. The Total Quality Management movement popularized in the 1980s in an effort to improve product quality and customer satisfaction, led managers to consider root causes. This approach can be adopted in problem

formulation as well. Even after a problem statement has been devised, it is entirely appropriate to ask if this is the fundamental question that cannot be pushed back to another question. A problem of Somali pirates is not a piracy problem but a problem of dysfunctional government in Somalia.

12. Research your problem statement. Once you have your problem statement composed, you can do an internet search to find out what other organizations have done to solve the problem. Most problems are not unique. A carefully crafted problem statement can get you directly to another organization that encountered and perhaps solved a similar problem.

13. Use multiple authorship of the problem statement. Writing the problem statement is the initial and most critical part of problem solving. To count on a single individual to do it is risky. The problem statement may not lead to a feasible solution. The problem statement might not be realistic or it might not even be true. The solution that emerges may be worse than the problem itself if the problem statement is poorly fashioned. These and other consequences can happen from single authorship. Having a small team to work on the problem statement alleviates the chances of this because of the wider diversity provided by others. The achievement of this diversity is, of course, dependent on open and honest communications by group members and that is your responsibility as the manager.

What are some key questions to ask before moving on to the problem-solving phase?

Before formalizing the problem solving process, it is important to ask some basic screening questions about your problem solving effort. As screening questions, these should be answered in the affirmative to the extent possible before proceeding to the search for a solution. These questions include:

1. Is this our organization's problem? (Having successfully implemented the nine steps in Tool 1.1, the answer should be a resounding "yes.")
2. Has this problem happened before? If so, how was it solved?
3. Do we have the resources (capabilities, funds, skills, etc.) to solve this problem?
4. Are the benefits of solving the problem greater than the costs?
5. Does the problem need to be solved now? Serious problems need urgency.
6. Is it dangerous to ignore the problem?
7. Is there a good chance that the problem will go away on its own?

Not all these questions can be answered at the outset but raising them will at least be a means of discovering any show-stoppers before going ahead. This tool will enable you to think broadly about your apparent problem which in and of itself is important.

PROBLEM SOLVING TIP # 1

Some problems need a short-term fix—a band-aid to bridge conflict, plaster to patch a leak, or a splint to hold together parts—until an appropriate solution can be developed.

However, don't let the short-term fix become the long-term solution or you may see that problem again.

What is important to know about the nature of organizational problems?

Organizational problems that managers deal with are not usually routine and minor. They are more often non-routine and complex. As a result, the problem itself has to be dissected, as Einstein might advise.

The solutions to organizational problems are also not perfect because the business world does not deal with certainty or ultimate truth. It is just not possible, feasible or cost efficient to consider every alternative and every variable. More often, the answers *satisfice* or are good enough. The first available and adequate solution is generally adopted. That is because organizations do not have the resources to come up with the ultimate truth, however scientific that may be.

What is the role of communications in problem solving?

As mentioned in the introduction, problems are subjective. It may be evident that a problem exists. But as stated earlier, problems are in the eye of the beholder. A problem for one person may be a welcome event for someone else. Effective communications (covered in more detail in chapter four) are vital to effective problem solving. A manager must learn to look at a problem from different angles and discuss the problem with other individuals who are involved. Seeking input upfront in the process will minimize conflict and produce a solution from a better informed platform. This point builds on the earlier idea of looking at the problem from different perspectives by communicating what these perspectives might mean for the problem solver. Through communication you are also building early consensus for buy-in to the eventual solution.

PROBLEM SOLVING TIP # 2

Just like movie producers shoot with different cameras and analyze the frames in 2D and 3D, problem-solvers need to view a problem from different dimensions to consider all of the angles and produce the best solution.

Problems make themselves known in different ways. However the problem manifests itself, the situation might not be as plain as it seems. Consider this idea from two vantage points. In the first case, realizing a problem, a manager may begin to respond to the problem—only to find that another or several more problems exist. So, in solving the first problem, another is uncovered or created by the first, and so on. Problems may be linked in a linear fashion or tangentially. Thus, more time and resources are required to solve the problem, more than what was originally expected.

In the second case, the manager realizes a problem and capably resolves it. Later, the manager discovers that what was thought to be the problem was merely a symptom of, or a signal to, the actual problem. Take the very simple situation of a ceiling light fixture burning out. The manager arranges for the bulb to be replaced. The next day, the lights are on. The following day the fixture is again dark. Once again, the bulb is replaced and, once again, after a brief time, the fixture will not light. The assumed problem of the bulb was not the real problem at all. The real problem uncovered was a loose electrical connection. The initial problem—no light—was a symptom of another problem all together. As stated in the introduction, problems can wear disguises.

Thus, as these two cases indicate, managers must note if there is only one problem or a series of problems to address. Likewise, managers must be wary and watchful so that the problem they are solving is indeed the real problem.

How do we discover the most important aspects of the problem?

As noted earlier, a problem can be entwined with other problems. Using a figurative approach, different parts of the problem can be illuminated to find the specific source of the trouble. Tiny gas leaks on the shuttle's fuel tank (which could have doomed an entire mission) were only uncovered in an inch-by-inch inspection of the entire tank surface.

PROBLEM SOLVING TIP # 3
A flashlight aids the use of tools, by shining on the work area and then centering on the key point. Use the flashlight approach to survey the problem and its borders and determine where the key trouble spot really is.

How can we classify problems and how does this help?

Organizational problems can be classified or divided into broad problem-type categories. This can help in dealing with them. Problems can be classified as routine or non-routine. Routine problems are unsurprising and perhaps anticipated. They are easily defined and termed "structured problems." Programmed decisions, something that managers often have on hand, can be used to address structured problems. The solution is known and can be applied again and again. For example, a customer returns to a grocery store and tells the store manager that she forgot to present her coupons to the cashier. The store manager knows to take the coupons and adjust the receipt for the customer. Programmed decisions accelerate the problem solving process.

Rule, procedure, or policy — which one?

Solutions to programmed decisions are often formalized in the business world as rules, procedures, or policies. In this way, the next time the problem occurs, an approved and acceptable solution is readily available. Generally, a rule is an absolute direction of behavior that is to be followed when a prescribed situation arises. Employees accept and follow rules as part of their workplace.

Procedures refer to activities that should be followed in a defined manner to achieve a desired outcome. It is the business' chosen way of going about certain tasks. Policies are governance statements that guide employees and possibly affect internal and/or external stakeholders. All three build consistent and uniform behavior in the workplace and reduce the need for management involvement in problem solving. Employees' commitment to rules, procedures, and policies is increased when they are clearly understood and managers have explained the benefits of adhering to them.

As an example, consider any large retailer. Merchandise returns are common problems that go along with a retail business. A store's policy might be to accept all store returns within ninety days of purchase. A rule might be that no returns are accepted without a receipt. The procedure might be that the cashier needs to complete a form, have the customer sign it and then put the returned merchandise back in a particular queue to be replaced in inventory.

How do I solve more complex problems?

Non-routine or unstructured problems represent new territory for managers. The cause of the problem, the size of the problem, the elements of the problem, and/or the implications of the problem may be unfamiliar, and the solution is not readily at hand. Therefore, it is best to follow a deliberate and systematic approach to solving the problem. The benefit will be a well-researched and rational solution with a good probability for success.

Also, if there is the possibility that the non-structured problem might recur, the solution can be retained for the next time. Translating the solution into a programmed decision and maintaining it by way of a rule, procedure, or policy will save manager and employees time and alleviate the stress of the situation.

PROBLEM SOLVING TIP # 4

Problems come in different sizes and shapes; some require delicacy while others require a hands on approach. Choose the right tool to fit the problem at hand. Otherwise that small leak could end up as a broken pipe.

What accepted problem solving process can I use?

Even simple problems in the workplace can prove challenging to the manager. For non-routine problems, the ability to make sense of the problem can be lost without a model to lend structure to the circumstances. A model or conceptual procedure organizes thoughts,

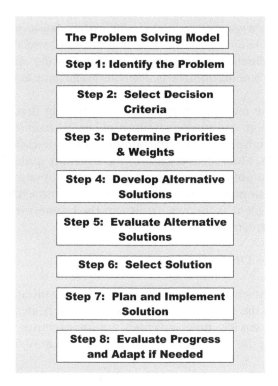

Figure 1.1   The Problem Solving Model

prioritizes data, leads to hypotheses and points to a logical progression for evaluation. There is a generally accepted process, described below, that many organizations have found to be very useful.

Some managers give little thought to following such a model and dismiss the idea out of hand. Why is this? An immediate objection to following a formal process might be the assumption of time and resources needed for following the steps of a model when faced with the immediacy of an out-of-sync situation. However, as you will see by the following discussion, there is a balance between using the model described below and using spontaneous judgement. Most good decision making has elements of both. The following model, adapted from Robbins and Coulter (2009), illustrates the steps in the general problem-solving process. The following sections will describe each step and within these descriptions, a scenario will be developed and used to illustrate the step.

STEP 1: IDENTIFY THE PROBLEM

Managers must be observant and alert. Some problems boldly make themselves known, while others may be present and persist with little fanfare. Once a problem is identified, the manager needs to assess the seed of the problem. Is the appropriate problem the real problem or a signal of another situation? As discussed earlier in the chapter, theorists commonly discuss symptoms of problems being misconstrued as the actual problem. Consider the following scenario:

A marketing manager for a new retail chain is reviewing market information reports. The results are favorable but, at the same time, problematic. The data shows that product demand is increasing rapidly but customer dissatisfaction is rising. A significant number of current and potential customers have commented that the store locations are too far away for their convenience.

In the scenario, the manager might begin by thinking that the obvious problem is that the retail locations are inadequate in number. Further consideration might be that the locations are misplaced. Without jumping to these conclusions, the manager continues to deliberate. More ideas regarding the situation spring forward. Finally, the manager identifies the problem. The marketing strategy is not satisfying the need to place the products where customers want to transact the purchase exchange. The marketing manager states the problem as follows; "How can the business improve accessibility of their products to satisfy demand?"

STEP 2: SELECT DECISION CRITERIA

A good solution must fit with the overall mission of the organization. It must satisfy the priorities and goals of the business. Such goals might be related to employee morale, production, customer service, time, revenues and/or expenses. Many solutions may address the problem but the outcome of the chosen solution must focus on the businesses' preferred goals.

Therefore, the second step in the problem solving process is to identify the key factors that the selected solution will support. Decision criteria drive the problem solving process. It is important to be accurate in the choosing these factors.

Going back to our scenario, the marketing manager considers the overall objectives and organizational strategies of the company and department goals. He knows that certain obvious solutions will not be acceptable to senior management. Therefore, with regard to the problem he is facing, the manager lists four criteria to which the ultimate solution must align:

1. Organizational Objective: Superior customer service as indicated by a 98% satisfaction rate on customer surveys.
2. Company Policy: Absolute freeze on new retail locations.
3. Department Objective: Six-month growth targets for the number of customers and revenue.
4. Organizational strategy: Minimize expense.

STEP 3: DETERMINE PRIORITY OF AND ALLOCATE WEIGHTS TO CRITERIA

Decision criteria may range from one to several factors. More than five is not advisable. The process becomes cumbersome when attempting to evaluate solutions relative to criteria.

Decision criteria do not carry equal significance. While each is important, one factor generally takes precedence over another or several others. Therefore, in this step, the first task is to determine a priority order of the decision criteria and then to rank them.

Once the criteria are prioritized, incorporate them in the problem solving process in a deliberate and systematic manner by assigning weights to each factor. The greater the assigned weight, the higher the priority level of the decision criterion. Any scale can be designed for weights. A simple approach is to assign a value of five for the most important element down to a one for the least important.

In the evaluation and selection of alternative solutions (steps five & six), criteria and their weights are meant to guide, pinpoint or suggest adherence to solutions according to their value. Criteria will not always be known or certain. Thus in some instances, a weighted score is used merely for insight and guidance versus an indication of the absolute choice of solution.

Returning to the scenario, our marketing manager orders his decision criteria from one to four. He then assigns weights to the identified criteria as follows:

Weighting of Decision Criteria

Criteria	Weight
Absolute freeze on new retail stores	5
Superior customer service as indicated by a 98% satisfaction rate on customer surveys	4
Achievement of six-month growth targets for the number of customers and revenue	3
Expense control	3

Note that the marketing manager has concluded that criteria three and four are of equal importance. This is fine. Find a weighting system that works for you.

STEP 4: DEVELOP ALTERNATIVES

Developing alternatives is the brainstorming part of the process. When feasible, development of alternatives should involve more than one individual. Creativity generally increases when several employees offer input. Also, the number and variety of possible alternatives increases. Often, the interplay of ideas from several individuals leads to refined alternatives of greater efficiency and/or effectiveness.

One tendency for the manager or group to avoid is the desire to leap at the first solution that looks reasonable. Deciding too quickly might limit the generation of possible strategies and preclude the best alternative from coming to light. Business situations are complex and warrant careful consideration.

Our marketing manager brings together key personnel from marketing, production and finance to consider the problem and generate possible courses of action to resolve it in a brainstorming session. The group takes some time to discuss the framing of the problem and the identification of the decision criteria. Different perspectives based on the employees' positions and personalities quickly come to light. While different, these perspectives aid the overall understanding of the problem by the group. The group is able to generate a wide variety of alternatives. Four representative alternatives are shown below:

1. Increase customer use of electronic retailing
2. Open additional locations at three regional malls
3. Do nothing for the next six to twelve months
4. Rent kiosks at major metropolitan malls in the sales regions.

STEP 5: EVALUATE ALTERNATIVES

Once a number of alternatives are identified, each needs to be analyzed for its ability to solve the problem and support the decision criteria. Rigorous consideration should be given to each alternative. However, managers cannot study all the data. Also, the degree of certainty surrounding an alternative varies. How clearly can the risks of each alternative be identified? Thus managers must satisfice as described earlier in the chapter.

In the analysis of alternatives, objective and subjective evaluations are important to predict as accurately as possible how well each alternative will satisfy the decision criteria. Objective evaluation generally relies on metrics, research findings and measurable observations though a certain amount of guesswork does happen.

Subjective assessment is made through evaluative statements based on experience, expertise, analogy and intuition. Often a manager faces strong feelings about the likely success or failure of a possible strategy. The basis for his or her intuition may not be clear but likely comes from past learning and knowledge of current conditions and constituents. Intuition and judgment are acceptable, even necessary means of evaluating alternatives.

The problem solving manager and team should discuss objective and subjective information regarding each alternative. Then, to capture the assessment of alternatives, scoring can be continued by assigning a rating to the ability of each alternative to support each of the decision criteria. A rating scale needs to be chosen for this task. Numeric ratings are generally easier to manipulate and provide clearer understanding.

Our scenario's marketing manager and team now sit down and analyze the alternatives and rate the alternatives versus the criteria. The team sets a rating of ten for fully satisfying with the criteria down to zero for no satisfaction of the criteria. The following table summarizes the team's assessment of alternatives:

Table 1.1   Rating of alternatives

	No new store required	Supports customer service targets	Supports achievement of growth targets	Minimizes operating expenses
Increase electronic retailing	10	6	5	5
Open additional stores	0	9	9	0
Do nothing	10	0	0	10
Rent kiosks	8	9	8	5

STEP 6: SELECT SOLUTION

Once alternatives are identified and evaluated, a solution should be selected. If a scoring system is followed, the numerical weight of the criteria should be multiplied by the alternative's rating. The products for each decision criteria are summed to provide a total score for each alternative. The alternative with the greatest score is the preferred solution based on the identified decision criteria. When addressing problems of significant complexity or impact, a final discussion surrounding the leading solutions and the preferred solution is advisable.

In our example, the problem solving team has discussed and evaluated the alternatives on objective and subjective bases. Now, the alternatives are scored by multiplying the criteria weights by the ratings and summed. The following chart illustrates the calculations of scores and displays the final score for each alternative. Based on the scoring, the fourth alternative, "rent kiosks at major metropolitan malls in the sales regions" should be selected.

Table 1.2   Scoring of alternatives

	No new store required (5)	Support customer service targets (4)	Support achievement of growth targets (3)	Minimize operating expenses (3)	Total score for alternative
Increase electronic retailing	5 x10 = 50	4 x 6 = 24	5 x 3 = 15	5 x 3 = 15	104
Open additional stores	5 x 0 = 0	4 x 9 = 36	3 x 9 = 27	3 x 0 = 0	63
Do nothing	5 x 10 = 50	4 x 0 = 0	3 x 0 = 0	3 x 10 = 30	80
Rent kiosks	5 x 8 = 40	4 x 9 = 36	3 x 8 = 24	3 x 5 = 15	115

One final time, looking at the problem subjectively, the group reviews their process and confirms that the kiosk rental alternative supports the objectives of the business, fits with other initiatives of the business and can gain the support of the company executives.

The group agrees but inserts a necessary caveat. Given the successful development of an implementation plan, the company will rent kiosks at major metropolitan malls using data available from customer surveys. Only if they can draw up an effective and efficient implementation plan can the strategy be adopted.

STEP 7: PLAN AND IMPLEMENT THE SOLUTION

Once the manager reaches this step, there is no time for complacency. The best decision if not implemented or not implemented well could bring the problem, and many more, full circle. A well-laid plan to implement the solution is needed.

Implementation plans involve policies, procedures, personnel, resources and effective communication. The specific goals of the solution are identified in clear and measurable statements. Most important, one individual should be assigned to coordinate the overall activity with input from a supporting team. In this manner, the plan will be put into action by the appropriate employees and will be coordinated with accountability to an overall project director.

Returning to our scenario, our group's deliberations conclude that the marketing manager should now continue to direct the solution. The team believes that he is in the best position to lead an implementation team and manage the progress and outcome of the solution. The group sets a schedule to develop the implementation plan and its goals.

STEP 8: EVALUATE PROGRESS AND ADAPT IF NEEDED

Here again, the process of problem solving cannot be abandoned prematurely. Too many times, the attention of managers is diverted once a solution is underway. As a result, the solution is not monitored and progress goes awry. The final step of the problem solving model requires that the manager monitor the implementation and on-going effectiveness of the solution. If the implementation plan and its goals are not being met, the manager needs to take corrective action.

Going back to the decision criteria, it is advisable to acknowledge that not all solutions satisfy the problem to its fullest. Trade-offs sometimes must be accepted. Thus, the solution must be evaluated with regard to the priority of criteria it was meant to satisfy and the goals stated in the implementation plan. Finally, if a solution is performing well, the manager might consider codifying the solution as a formal rule, procedure or policy in the event the problem occurs in the future.

To conclude our scenario, our marketing manager has followed the establishment of the kiosks along a planned timeframe and has set up a system of financial and marketing reports to provide data on the success of the solution. As data becomes available and customers have had time to learn of the kiosks, the solution will be assessed and further action taken as necessary.

PROBLEM SOLVING TIP # 5

No matter how good a solution looks, if it does not conform to the organization's culture, the going will be tough. Present unwelcomed solutions with the perspective of the audience (employees, customers, suppliers, etc.) in mind; show the audience how they can succeed with the results of the solution in place.

What if my "sixth sense" contradicts the top scoring alternative?

Over the years, managers develop a gut-feel or sixth sense based on their accumulated experiences, education and technical know-how. This is called intuition. Some people are better at it than others. Some personality types require more information, some less. Intuition plays a significant role in decision making no matter how systematic and scientific we'd like to be. Studies show that managers use intuition to solve problems at least 50% of the time.

One of the major benefits of intuition is speed. One of the major objections to a problem solving model is time requirements. Your competitor may have already implemented a new technology while you are still assigning weights to your decision criteria. In today's rapidly changing environment, managers often don't have the luxury of time. And the above process is time consuming.

In Malcolm Gladwell's 2005 book, *Blink*, he explores the concept of rapid cognition. He describes this as the decision making process that occurs in the first seconds of evaluating a situation. Consider the thought process of a driver on a highway. The driver sees brake lights flashing on vehicles ahead of him. In a matter of seconds, the driver takes in the status of the traffic beside him, in front of him and approaching him in the emergency lanes, then considers potential courses of action. He immediately acts on the best and safest choice. The process happens all subconsciously. The driver perceives the problem, evaluates, chooses, and then acts very rapidly.

Another instance when intuition comes into play is when the data surrounding the problem is incomplete, changing rapidly or when the question itself is poorly defined. While it is important to use the techniques described in the early part of this chapter to clearly define the problem, sometimes this just is not possible. At that point, using the model to give direction is a great step but in the end, you might just have to go with your sixth sense. Finally, if your intuition and the model are suggesting different outcomes as the best solution, you may need to revisit the assumptions you used in the model.

If we already have a problem solving process, how can we improve its effectiveness?

As managers learn to make decisions using the problem solving process, they can also increase the effectiveness of their decisions by considering several factors. First, as mentioned earlier in the chapter, all problems have stakeholders—parties who have an interest in the situation and who are potentially affected by the outcome. Stakeholders can be internal to the company such as employees or the board of directors. Stakeholders may be external groups associated with the company such as customers, suppliers and members of the local community, to name a few.

First, in their deliberations, managers should take time to look at the problem and possible solutions from the various perspectives of the stakeholders or involve some of these stakeholders in the solution finding process. Some stakeholders are more important than others. And managers must determine which stakeholders and stakeholder demands should get priority. Consequences to stakeholders can bear significant influence on the choice of problem solving strategy.

Second, the participants in the problem solving process each bring a variety of personal biases to the process. This is explored in detail in the next chapter. Unchecked biases can lead to inferior decisions. Realistically, biases cannot be totally eliminated but should be recognized and controlled according to the situation. By keeping the focus on the decision criteria, undue influence can be minimized. Finally, the characteristics, personality, and style of the individual affect his approach to problem solving.

PROBLEM SOLVING TIP # 6

Information technology can be the backbone for problem solving success. In all steps of the problem solving process, IT (information technology) can play a vital, supporting role. Develop information systems that gather, manipulate and respond to managers' inquiries. Inflexible data collection methods are seldom worth their ongoing expense.

How does the human element factor into the process?

In addition to the biases discussed above, people are people and this impacts decision making. All problem solvers bring strengths and weaknesses to the process. For example, some managers find creativity flows easily while others struggle to formulate an innovative alternative. Some are able to analyze detail quickly while others must put extensive, diligent effort into making sense of complicated data. Some managers approach problems from a primarily financial standpoint while others look to the behavioral outcomes and effects.

Managers are best served by recognizing their weaknesses and taking steps to counteract them. This can be achieved through training, inviting an individual with complementary strengths to assist with problem solving, incorporating technology as an aid, or simply learning from past mistakes and avoiding them. The point is not to be complacent about areas that can be improved.

There are many cases where managers claim not knowing the problem existed to excuse their inaction. As stated by Bolman and Deal (2008), "Cluelessness is not a defense of inadequate response or avoidance of solving a problem." Managers must practice perceptual skills. They need to view, evaluate and react appropriately. Asking questions and soliciting input from employees helps in developing this ability.

All managers have personality traits that influence their problem solving style. The optimist and the pessimist will often arrive at different conclusions given the same information. Overconfident or self-righteous managers might insist that they are right, even when off-track, and bully their way to an ultimately poor decision. Solving problems is difficult. There is no doubt that often the needed information to make a decision is not available. Even when information is accessible, interpreting that data can be difficult. Still, personality traits should be harnessed by the manager through self-discipline or structure to enhance and not detract from the problem-solving process.

The turn of events at Home Depot, as described by Bohlman and Deal, illustrates the vulnerability of business results when personality is left unchecked. After a successful career at General Electric, Bob Nardelli was tapped by Home Depot in 2000 to take the reins as CEO. Nardelli's structured and measured approach to business management was at first hailed as far superior to the less formal structure that had been in operation at

Home Depot. Soon however, customers rebelled against the new, all-business stance, and employee morale dropped. Nardelli stuck with his militaristic approach and refused to listen to critics. Critics included the Home Depot's Board of Directors and the stockholders who voiced concern at the 2006 annual shareowners' meeting. Amid criticism and plummeting company results, Nardelli continued to lead through the use of metrics and rigid policy—until, in 2007, he made a sudden and forced departure from Home Depot. In all, over eight years, Nardelli stubbornly stuck to his own single counsel and his own distorted picture of reality, regardless of the chaos that emerged from it.

In their research, Feinberg and Tarrant (1995) observe that, in some cases, very smart people act stupid; they label this as "self-destructive intelligence syndrome." As a result of personality traits, including pride, arrogance and defensiveness and perhaps a lack of self-discipline, managers may miss the actual problem and adhere to courses of fruitless activity. Knowing your tendencies in advance of approaching a problem can help a manager to avoid perilous mistakes.

Some managers just go for it, but I'm pretty cautious. How can this impact my decision making?

Finally, individuals bring to the process a personal profile toward risk. There are extreme risk-takers and extreme risk-avoiders, and many other types in-between. As there is no absolute certainty to the outcome of a problem-solving strategy, a manager's tolerance for risk may interfere with the best choice of problem solving solution. Rather than the individual's risk tolerance, the degree of risk acceptable by the business should bear on the choice of problem solving strategy. The organizational culture of the business, past behavior, and senior management leadership should be the guide for assuming an appropriate level of risk in adopting solutions.

PROBLEM SOLVING TIP # 7

Auto mechanics run diagnostic tests of the electronic software center of cars to ensure that all sensors and synapses are in sync. Similarly, managers should run a self-test to be sure that emotions, biases and personality traits are working together to support a reasoned, rational solution.

Additional Resources

Problem solving by managers is a continual need in all facets of business. Thus, development in organizational knowledge, interpersonal skills and leadership styles is supportive of effective approaches to problems. Consider reviewing literature associated with emotional intelligence, risk management, and stakeholder relationships to broaden your knowledge and better understand and manage problem situations. Webb's "Why Emotional Intelligence Should Matter to Management" (2009—SAM: *Advanced Management Journal*, Spring) is a helpful survey.

Two recommended books are:

Bolman, L. and Deal, T. (2008). *Reframing Organizations*. San Francisco: John Wiley & Sons Inc.

Brad, G. (2008). *Five Steps to Build a Winning Corporate Culture*. Supervision, March, 2008.

These can be perused by subject or in-depth to gain insight. Finally, Saxe's poem, "The Blind Men and The Elephant" is perhaps a whimsical but nonetheless clever illustration of inaccurate results due to narrow perspectives.

References

Bolman, L. and Deal, T. (2008). *Reframing Organizations*. San Francisco: John Wiley & Sons Inc.

Feinberg, M. and Tarrant, J. (1995). *Why Smart People Do Dumb Things*. New York: Simon & Shuster.

Gladwell, M. (2005). *Blink: The Power of Thinking Without Thinking*. New York: Little, Brown.

Hill, C. and Jones, G. (2009). *Essentials of Strategic Management*. Mason: South-Western Cengage Learning.

Kurtz, D. (2008). *Contemporary Marketing*. Mason: South-Western Cengage Learning.

Pounds, W. (1969). *The Process of Problem Finding*. Industrial Management Review, Fall, 1969, 1–19.

Robbins, S. and Coulter, M. (2009). *Management* (10th ed.). Upper Saddle River: Pearson Prentice Hall.

Taylor, Ronald (1984). *Behavioral Decision Making*. Glenview, IL: Scott, Foresman and Company.

Williams, J. D. (1954). *The Complete Strategist*. New York: McGraw-Hill.

2 Optimizing Decision Making and Avoiding Pitfalls

CORINNE FARNETI and GLENN DISHMAN

Each day we make hundreds of decisions. What should I eat for breakfast? Which way should I drive to work? Should I hire another employee? Whether simple or complex, private or public, decisions are an essential part of all areas of our lives. When you understand the inherent psychological, social and emotional components of a smart decision, you can examine errors that you might have made in past decisions and avoid potential future mistakes.

Making a good decision or avoiding a bad one is not a chance act; it is a skill that can be learned, developed and even perfected. This chapter suggests that bad decisions are usually made because of a poor decision making process. It is our contention that the decision making process can be enhanced by controlling personal biases, gathering pertinent information and using intuition appropriately.

In this chapter we will explore how individuals, groups and organizations make effective decisions. Further, we will offer you tips and techniques to enhance the effectiveness of your own decision making efforts.

What are some famous decision making blunders?

You are probably reading this chapter because you either just made a bad decision or you want to avoid making a bad decision. You are not alone. Professionals all around the world have made mistakes in their decision making. For example, let's consider the 1996 Mount Everest Tragedy. As Dr Michael Roberto (2009) notes, this tragedy occurred when two expedition teams got caught in a storm, high on the mountain, on May 10–11, 1996. Both expedition team leaders, as well as three team members, died during the storm. Despite knowing all the risks and preparing thoroughly for the trip, the two leaders obviously made grave errors. These errors were caused namely by the cognitive biases of overconfidence, the sunk-cost effect, and the recency effect (all of which will be explained in detail later in the chapter).

Another example of a horrible error in judgment occurred in 1986, when NASA decided to launch the Challenger space shuttle despite engineers' concerns about possible O-ring erosion due to cold temperatures on the morning of the launch. How could such intelligent people ignore such prudent advice? Finally, why did Coca-Cola's CEO, Roberto Goizueta, decide to introduce New Coke to the world in 1985, when their current formula was an obvious hit with the public?

One more blunder occurred in 1961, when President Kennedy decided to invade Cuba in the Bay of Pigs fiasco. With hopes of overthrowing Cuban communist dictator Fidel Castro, Kennedy asked the Joint Chiefs of Staff to look at the plan proposed by the CIA. They concluded that it could work, but only with certain caveats. The CIA argued that the time was right to invade. The process went wrong because there was no candid dialogue, and debate did not take place in the meetings between the CIA, the President and his staff. The group spent most of its time tweaking the proposal rather than analyzing other options. Groupthink (also discussed later in this chapter) was the major downfall. In other words, the group felt it could do no wrong. The result of the invasion included a significant loss of life, a tarnished United States reputation and it may have led to the Soviets putting missiles in Cuba the following year. The above-mentioned scenarios demonstrate that bad decisions are made even by experienced, intelligent professionals and are not limited to the everyday layperson.

What are some common decision making myths?

According to Professor Michael Roberto, there are five distinct myths about how decisions are made in organizations. By identifying these myths, we can improve our decision-making capabilities.

Myth #1: The chief executive decides.
  Reality: Strategic decision making entails simultaneous activity by people at multiple levels of the organization (refer to chapter five for more on strategy). We can't always blame or credit the head executive for all the decisions.
Myth #2: Decisions are made in the conference room.
  Reality: Much of the real work occurs off-line, in small groups or in one-on-one conversations. Usually, formal meetings are used to simply approve decisions that have already been made.
Myth #3: Decisions are largely intellectual exercises.
  Reality: High-stakes decisions are complex emotional, social and political processes.
Myth #4: Managers analyze and then decide.
  Reality: Strategic decisions occur in a non-linear fashion, with solutions often arising before managers define problems or look at other alternatives.
Myth #5: Managers decide and then act.
  Reality: Strategic decisions often evolve over time and proceed through a repetitive process of choice and action.

There are several ways to make a decision. Although some issues may seem complex and confusing, the process below is one that will help make the decision-making process a little bit easier.

What should we do about risk in decision making?

With all decisions comes some level of risk. Risk exists when the outcome of a chosen course of action is not certain. Keep in mind that *some risk is okay*. A decision wouldn't be a decision without it. In life (and in business) there are low risk takers and high risk takers. There are benefits and drawbacks to both styles of decision making.

While low risk takers may collect and evaluate more information, trying to obtain and consider too much information may also paralyze them. High risk takers, on the other hand, do not waste time agonizing over small details. But on the flip side, they may make their decisions based on too little information. As a decision maker, you should evaluate your current risk-taking profile. It is virtually impossible to know all of the information there is to know. At some point, there needs to be a level of information that is good enough. This point will differ by individual based on risk tolerance. Are you a person who jumps into things head first? Or are you someone who gets caught up in the details and ends up always making the safest decision?

Believe it or not, there is a happy-medium. Some risk is a good thing, and that is where you should strive to be. Look at the average performance level of others. Where do you stand in comparison to them? Is everyone around you taking more decision-making risks than you? Or are you the one always making the high-risk/high-reward decisions? As a decision-maker, your optimum level should probably be right in the middle, making educated, researched decisions that do in fact have some associated risk.

Why do we make bad decisions?

According to Dr Michael Roberto, decisions are complex emotional, social and political processes that often evolve over time. Sometimes we think too deeply, ignore our intuition, or make biased judgments that can lead to errors in the decision making process.

COGNITIVE BIASES

A cognitive bias is a distortion in the way we perceive reality a trap that affects us all as we try to make decisions. In other words, we do not examine all options and often take shortcuts when we make choices. What makes cognitive biases unique is that they are predictable and consistent, fooling you over and over again. There are several biases to which decision makers fall victim. Below is a description of some of the more common biases and how to avoid them.

- *Ease of Recall/Recency Effect*: The ease of recall/recency effect occurs when decision-makers rely too much on information that is easy to recall from recent memory.
  - Example: When doing a yearly evaluation of an employee, a manager usually recalls the last few months prior to the evaluation much more easily than the employee's performance ten months prior. This can work for or against the person being reviewed.
  - How to Avoid the *Ease of Recall/Recency Effect* Bias: First, being aware of the problem in and of itself can help. Second, keep good notes. Whatever the situation may be, reviewing previous notes or records is a great way to analyze all information, not just the most recent. This will help you get the big picture and make the best decision possible.
- *Confirmation Bias*: According to the University of Southern California's Levan Institute (2010), people tend to look for information that will confirm their pre-existing views,

to interpret information in ways that support their own view and to selectively remember the information that supports their view.

- Example: Your organization is looking to put out a new product line. You've paid to have some market research done and the results are finally in. Some of the data indicates just what you had hoped, that your new product line is highly desired by the public. However, portions of the results suggest that some small changes may be necessary to appease the public. Despite the mixed findings, your company decides to launch the product as-is solely because they received some indication that their initial thoughts were correct.
- How to Avoid the *Confirmation Bias*: Write down all possible reasons why your decision (or original thought) might not be the best option. Think of as many alternatives as possible, even bringing in outside analysts to help objectively look at the situation. If you have data available, remind yourself to include all relevant information when making the decision.

- *Sunk-Cost Bias*: The more we invest in something (financially, emotionally or otherwise), the harder it is to give up that investment. This leads to making poor decisions based on invested capital. Psychologists believe this is because we are unwilling, consciously or unconsciously, to admit to a mistake.
  - Example: You are serving on a hiring committee and looking to bring in a high-ranking employee to your organization. You fight very hard for one candidate, and even convince the rest of the committee to give him the signing bonus that he requested. As time goes on, the new employee struggles and is even costing the company money. Since you are his direct superior, you are responsible for reprimanding, disciplining or firing him. Because you put so much effort (and money) in the hiring of this employee, you keep him on board just so you don't look like you made a bad recommendation to hire him and spent all that money up front for nothing.
  - How to Avoid the *Sunk-Cost Bias*: Stop spending resources (time and money) on a bad move and cut your losses immediately. Quickly admit your mistakes—in fact, be proud of them and of the fact that you were able to cut off a problem before it became that much worse. Try to detach yourself emotionally from your past decisions. Finally, always be mindful of long-term objectives.

- *Anchoring Bias*: Per Robbins and Coulter (2008), the anchoring bias involves putting too much emphasis on the first piece of information encountered and failing to adjust for subsequent information.
  - Example: A person buying a used car may focus excessively on the odometer reading and model year of the car, and may subsequently use those criteria as a basis for evaluating the value of the car, rather than considering how well the engine or the transmission has been maintained.
  - How to Avoid the *Anchoring Bias*: Make a physical list of your thoughts or statistics regarding the decision. Do *not* rank the list and make sure all aspects of the decision are considered. This will allow you to assess all information equally. In fact, if you have time, take a day or so away from the decision and come back to the list you made. Your initial anchor may disappear when you step away from the issue for a bit.

- *Bandwagon Effect*: The bandwagon effect occurs when people do and believe things merely because many other people do and believe the same things, regardless of underlying evidence.
  - Example: Your company is thinking about buying out a smaller, rival company and all of its factories. All of your fellow executive staff members think it is a great idea because it will not only eliminate a competitor, but it will also increase product reach to markets in which you hadn't had a presence before. Privately, you have misgivings about the deal because you aren't sure your company can handle all of the overhead costs. But, because all of your co-workers and fellow managers believe it is a fantastic idea, you decide that they must be right and you must be wrong. Therefore, you go along with the deal, despite your initial trepidation.
  - How to Avoid the *Bandwagon Effect*: Have confidence in yourself and your initial feelings. Any decision requires thorough research and should never be made just because several people like the idea. If you are afraid to speak up about your doubts or even suggest alternatives, perhaps approach a co-worker or superior individually. This will help you avoid any potential groupthink that may arise in a group setting. Your co-workers will appreciate the thought and effort you put in, especially if you save the organization from making a grave error.
- *Framing Effect*: People's decisions are altered when the same option is presented in different contexts or formats.
  - Example: Faced with a decision between two packages of ground beef, one labeled 80% lean, the other 20% fat; which would you choose? Based on the work of Miller (2006), the meat is exactly the same, but most people would pick 80% lean because of an emotional reaction to the word "lean" versus the word "fat."
  - How to Avoid the *Framing Effect*: It is important to remind yourself that information is often presented in a way solely to trigger an emotional reaction. If, for example, you are reading a proposal, be aware that the person who wrote it had a vested interest in getting it accepted. They may frame all of their data to trigger a positive emotion in the reader. Do your best not to be fooled. Look at the data for what it is. Even if it means writing down statistics, facts or thoughts separate from the original format to be sure you are analyzing them independently.
- *Overconfidence Bias*: From the writing of Robbins and Coulter, overconfidence bias occurs when decision makers hold unrealistically positive views of themselves and their products or performance.
  - Example: Product A has been selling like hotcakes after a strong marketing campaign. It is time to decide how much of Product A to manufacture for the next sales period. Without looking at any hard data you decide to double the quantity, solely going on the fantastic sales from last quarter. Unfortunately, you are way off the mark and the market has cooled off. Apparently, your product was just a fad and now you are stuck with thousands of units of Product A on your warehouse shelves.
  - How to Avoid the *Overconfidence Bias*: Find someone who can act as your voice of reason. Present them with all the relevant facts and data and allow them to give their unbiased opinion. Also, be cognizant of your optimism. While it's great to think positively, make sure thinking positively doesn't outweigh reality.

With decision making biases, half the battle is knowing they exist. The fact that you are aware that these pitfalls are out there will help you make better decisions if you actively look for and respond appropriately to your own biases.

What is the role of intuition?

Intuition is a process dominated by your subconscious mind which somehow finds links between your current situation and various patterns of your past experiences. This subconscious activation is often experienced as a gut feeling. In many cases, your gut feeling is correct. Unfortunately, it doesn't ring true for all cases and we may not trust our intuition merely because we've been trained not to.

When we use our intuition, we do not evaluate a whole set of alternatives. Instead, we assess a situation and instinctively spot certain cues. From these cues we recognize patterns based on our past experiences. We then subconsciously match the current situation to these past patterns. Intuition becomes a major problem when you solely rely on your instincts and ignore or fail to seek additional information. Our subconscious mind isn't correct 100% of the time. Sometimes, it does not make the right match to past situations. Therefore, we draw the wrong lessons from those perceived parallel situations and end up making poor decisions. Another issue with intuition is the fact that it's very hard to communicate our intuitive choices to our fellow employees. How can you explain the choice of your subconscious mind when your conscious mind doesn't even know why or how you made it?

Some jobs require employees to not only be experts about the information in their field but also to be able to act intuitively. Nurses and doctors use intuition all the time. For example, consider the case of a patient who is both showing and describing signs of a pulled or torn calf muscle. The doctor knows that the patient gets little exercise as they've talked about this in the past. However, having seen several similar cases in the past the doctor is able to recognize and compare the situations with a greater eye for detail. As it turns out, the pulled muscle is not a pulled muscle at all, but is a blood clot. The doctor had a feeling that such an inactive person could probably not pull their muscle that badly, so he ordered further tests. In this case, the doctor's intuition saved a potentially deadly situation.

Communicating our intuition more effectively is one key to making good decisions. Organizational scholar Karl Weick (1995) has proposed a five-step process for communicating intuitive decisions and for garnering feedback so as to ensure clear understanding on the part of the group. His process is as follows:

Step 1—Describe the situation. "Here's what I think we face."
Step 2—Describe your idea. "Here's what I think we should do."
Step 3—Tell the group your reasoning. "Here's why."
Step 4—Advise of potential pitfalls. "Here's what we should keep our eye on."
Step 5—Garner feedback. "Now, talk to me."

Following these five steps will at least expose your inner thoughts and feelings to a second party, lessening the chance of a hasty decision based solely on intuition.

What is *Escalation of Commitment* and how can it be avoided?

Poor decisions are made every day and we as decision-makers have to accept that. However, once a bad decision is made, we need not compound the damage by sticking with the decision. In other words, if you've just steered your ship into an oncoming storm, it is never too late to try and change course. Unfortunately, people oftentimes feel an escalation of commitment when they happen to make one of these decision making blunders. This is similar to the sunk-cost bias mentioned earlier.

People do not want to admit to themselves or to others that they have made a mistake. They may even believe that an additional commitment of resources is justified, given how much has been spent in hopes of recouping some of the losses. According to Michael Hitt and colleagues (2006), the process of escalation of commitment goes something like this:

1. A decision maker initially makes a decision that results in some kind of loss or negative outcome.
2. Rather than change the course of action from the initial decision, the decision maker commits more time, money, and/or effort to the course of action.
3. Further losses are experienced because of this escalation of commitment to a failing course of action.

Since you now know this phenomenon exists, be sure to check yourself and your motives after any poor decision to make sure you are not just sticking to your guns because of pride.

How can we decide between individual and group decision making?

When making an individual decision you must be an expert on the subject, confident your co-workers will accept your decision and willing to take the blame if the decision turns out to be wrong. It is important to remember that the decision making process is affected by four factors:

1. The decision-making approach
2. The type of problem
3. Decision-making conditions
4. Your individual decision-making style.

As a guide, you should follow the general eight-step process outlined in chapter one in most decision-making situations. However, make sure you keep in mind that there are both internal and external factors playing a role in your decision making process.

Groups tend to follow the same decision making process that individuals do. However, there are dynamics and interpersonal processes that make group decision making very different from decisions made by an individual. For example, the group may be composed of individuals at different levels within the organization. Not only will these people have different perspectives, they may also have conflicting goals or expectations

Figure 2.1   Group Decision Making Phenomena

for the organization. Because of the varying group dynamics, there are several different techniques that a team of employees may use to arrive at a decision.

BRAINSTORMING

Brainstorming is a technique used to generate a large number of ideas while deferring the evaluation of the ideas. Evaluation of the ideas is postponed until group members can no longer think of any new ideas. In this setting, imagination is a good thing, with no idea being deemed too unique or different. Building on the ideas of others is also encouraged. When using brainstorming, the group should nominate a person to record all ideas from the session. Another individual may be assigned the duty of task master, to ensure the group stays on the topic and remains focused on the issue at hand. The major caveat of group brainstorming is to never criticize any idea, no matter how bad it may seem at the time. Criticism introduces an element of risk for group members when putting forward an idea. This suppresses creativity and cripples the free running nature of a good brainstorming session.

NOMINAL GROUP TECHNIQUE

With this technique, individuals silently write down their ideas on a piece of paper. As described by Hitt and colleagues, when everyone is finished writing down their thoughts, each member presents one idea at a time, until all ideas are presented, without discussion. Ideas (from all group members) should then be recorded on a whiteboard or large flip chart. Discussion is used to clarify any details. After all ideas are explained, a silent and independent vote is done to develop a ranking of the group's choices.

DELPHI TECHNIQUE

The Delphi Technique, developed at the Rand Corporation, consists of a highly structured anonymous survey of group members regarding their opinions or judgments on a topic. It is imperative that the group has a facilitator who is willing to gather and redistribute all of the members' opinions and ideas. The success of this process depends upon the members' expertise and communication skills. Also, each response requires sufficient time for reflection and analysis. The four major merits of the Delphi process are:

1. The elimination of interpersonal problems
2. The efficient use of experts' time
3. It generates a diversity of ideas
4. Solutions and predictions tend to be very accurate.

DIALECTICAL INQUIRY

This method is intended to overcome the tendency of a group to avoid conflict when they evaluate alternatives. To employ this technique, the leader should come prepared with at least two very different sets of recommendations and assumptions. The leader must force the group to fully discuss all options, even if members came into the session with preconceived notions. While the conflict of options and ideas will be brought to the forefront, it is more likely to result in a quality decision this way.

DEVIL'S ADVOCACY

As with dialectical inquiry, devil's advocacy overcomes the tendency of groups to avoid conflicts when trying to come to a decision. With this technique, an individual or sub group is assigned to argue against the recommended actions put forth by other members of the group. This allows for an in-depth critique of the possible decision, ensuring that it is indeed the best solution for the organization.

What are some group decision making pitfalls?

According to Hitt and colleagues, groupthink occurs when group members maintain or seek consensus at the expense of identifying and debating honest disagreements. In other words, groupthink occurs when a group makes faulty decisions based on group pressure to conform and avoid disagreement at the expense of reason. Groups tend to be more vulnerable to groupthink when their members have similar backgrounds and when the group is insulated from outside opinions. Highly cohesive groups, with strong pressure to conform tend to fall prey to groupthink.

Groupthink was coined by social psychologist Irving Janis in 1972. Janis has documented eight symptoms of groupthink:

1. *Illusion of invulnerability*—creates excessive optimism that encourages taking extreme risks.

2. *Collective rationalization*—members discount warnings and do not reconsider their assumptions.
3. *Belief in inherent morality*—members believe in the rightness of their cause and therefore ignore the ethical or moral consequences of their decisions.
4. *Stereotyped views of out-groups*—negative views of out-groups as the enemy make effective responses to conflict seem unnecessary.
5. *Direct pressure on dissenters*—members are under pressure from other members not to express arguments against any of the group's views.
6. *Self-censorship*—doubts and deviations from the perceived group consensus are not expressed.
7. *Illusion of unanimity*—the majority view and judgments are assumed to be unanimous.
8. *Self-appointed mindguards*—some members protect the group and the leader from information that is problematic or contradictory to the group's cohesiveness, views and/or decisions.

FAMOUS EXAMPLES OF GROUPTHINK INCLUDE:
- Failure to protect forces at Pearl Harbor in 1941
- Bay of Pigs fiasco in 1961
- US escalation of the Vietnam War
- Failed rescue attempt of hostages at US Embassy in Iran

What are some ways to avoid groupthink?

The following is a list of ideas designed to help avoid the pitfalls of groupthink:

- The leader should assign the role of critical evaluator to someone.
- The leader should avoid stating preferences and expectations at the outset.
- Each member of the group should routinely discuss the group's deliberations with a trusted associate and report back to the group on the associate's reactions.
- One or more experts should be invited to each meeting on a staggered basis and should be encouraged to challenge views of the members.
- The leader should make sure that a sizeable block of time is set aside to survey warning signals.
- The leader and group members should challenge others to think.
- The group may consider using dialectical inquiry or devil's advocacy (discussed in more detail earlier in this chapter) to avoid unquestioned consensus.

What are some common group decision making challenges beyond the pitfall?

Common information bias occurs when group members overemphasize information held by a majority, failing to heed the information or viewpoint held by one or more members of the group in the minority. When a team ignores alternate information too often, members will start to hold back their thoughts and opinions over time. Eventually this could lead to groupthink.

- Example: A group of five top-level executives meets to discuss the tardiness problem of one of their middle managers. Four of the five executives bring up how many times in the past month the employee has come in late to work, all the while complaining that they pay him too much to be taken advantage of like that. Because his ideas have been ignored in the past, the fifth executive decides not to mention all of the late nights the tardy employee has been working to communicate with a business partner overseas. The employee in question ends up wrongly accused.

Have you ever been in a group where individuals feel so strongly about their varying ideas that the group fractures into subgroups or verbal altercations occur? If so, you have experienced diversity-based infighting. According to Hitt and colleagues, this phenomenon usually takes place when individuals have strong feelings about their ideas and no mechanisms exist to channel the disagreement in a productive way. Remember, diversity of ideas is a good thing. It should be used to create rich discussions and insight but if no mechanism exists to do so, diversity of ideas may have the opposite effect.

- Example: An organization is deciding whether or not to eliminate the childcare program it has for its employees. One group of workers feels that it is an unnecessary cost to the company while another group currently utilizes the program on a weekly basis and is passionate about retaining it. As tempers flare, the arguments escalate and may turn personal. Unfortunately, leadership fails to keep things focused on making a quality decision.

When people are in groups, they make decisions about risk differently from when they are alone. In a group, they are likely to make riskier decisions, as the shared risk makes the individual risk less. In other words, if you had to make a multi-million dollar decision for your company, you'd probably feel more comfortable moving ahead if you had the input of others. In your mind, you most likely feel that if you happen to make the wrong decision, you can say "Hey, I'm not the only one responsible."

- Example: Your company forms a committee on whether or not to buy from an up-and-coming vendor. The vendor has a lot of hype surrounding it, but no proven relationships as of yet. If you take the leap and spend the money, it is possible that you could be their flagship partner. If the vendor doesn't live up to the hype however, your company could lose its money and tarnish its reputation. The committee openly discusses how great it would be to have the deal be a success and start pumping out new products. Ultimately, the committee takes a huge risk and purchases from the new vendor—something that the majority of the committee members wouldn't have done if they had to make the decision on their own.

What is the value of individual vs. group decision making?

According to Hitt and colleagues, there are several important considerations for judging the overall value of individual versus group decision making:

- Time—it is generally more time consuming to make a group decision. Therefore, if time is of the essence, an individual decision may be preferable.
- Cost—because of the time factor and logistical issues (getting everyone together), the out of pocket cost of group decision making is generally higher although conference calls and teleconferencing mitigate this concern somewhat.
- Nature of the problem—if there is one right answer to a problem, it's generally not worth investing the time and money that a group decision requires.
- Satisfaction and commitment—a by-product of group decision making is a higher level of employee satisfaction and commitment to the solution/outcome.
- Personal growth—another by-product of group decision making is the personal growth experienced through participation in the group process and through exposure to the ideas of others in the group.

Due to these considerations, individual and group decision making have both positive and negative aspects and should be used accordingly.

It is important to remember that if you do decide to make a group decision, evidence indicates that groups of five or seven individuals are the most effective. Any larger and the group becomes unwieldy. Any smaller and the group loses the benefit of diverse opinions and insights. Also, having an odd number of group members helps avoid decision deadlocks. According to Robbins and Coulter, this size group is large enough for

Advantages of Group Decision Making/ Disadvantages of Individual Decision Making	Advantages of Individual Decision Making/Disadvantages of Group Decision Making
Groups generate more complete information and knowledge than individual decision making.	Group decisions almost always take more time to reach a solution than would an individual.
Groups lead to more diverse alternatives than individuals.	A dominant and vocal minority can heavily influence a group's decision.
Group decision-making can result in growth of group members.	Groupthink can undermine critical thinking in a group and lower the quality of the decision.
Group decisions lead to a higher level of acceptance and satisfaction than would individual decisions.	Group members share responsibility, but the responsibility of any single member is ambiguous.
Group decisions are perceived as more legitimate than ones made by an individual.	Managers may rely too much on group decisions, leading to a loss of their own decision and implementation skills.

Tool 2.1   Group vs Individual Decision Making Guide

members to shift roles and withdraw from unfavorable positions but still small enough for quieter members to participate actively in discussions.

When the time comes to make a decision, a leader must first decide if associate/co-worker involvement is necessary. The Vroom-Yetton Decision-Making Model (1973) poses, questions to determine the level of associate involvement in decision making. The questions are:

- Is there a quality requirement such that one solution is likely to be more rational than another solution, or will any number of solutions work reasonably well?
- Is there sufficient information to make a high-quality decision without the group meeting?
- Is the problem adequately structured (do I know the question to ask and where to look for the relevant information)?
- Is acceptance of the decision by associates critical to effective implementation?
- If I were to make the decision myself, is it reasonably certain that my associates would accept it?
- Do the associates share the organizational goals by solving this problem?
- Is there likely to be conflict among subordinates over alternative solutions?

The Vroom-Yetton method defines five different decision procedures. Two are autocratic (A1 and A2), two are consultative (C1 and C2) and one is group based (G2):

A1: The leader takes known information and then decides alone.
A2: The leader gets information from followers, and then decides alone.
C1: The leader shares problems with followers individually, listens to ideas and then decides alone.
C2: The leader shares problems with followers as a group, listens to ideas and then decides alone.
G2: The leader shares problems with followers as a group and then seeks and accepts consensus agreement.

In general, a consultative or collaborative style is most appropriate when:

- You need information from others to solve a problem.
- The problem definition isn't clear.
- Team members' buy-in to the decision is important.
- You have enough time to manage a group decision.

An autocratic or individual style is most efficient when:

- You have more expertise on the subject than others.
- You are confident about acting alone.
- The team will accept your decision.
- There is little time available.
- The problem is clearly defined.

Mastering the art of successful decision making is fundamental to improving your life at home, at work or in your community. According to Robbins and Coulter, in order to make effective decisions in today's fast-paced world you should follow some general guidelines:

- *Understand cultural differences.* People in both your organization and around the world are very diverse. Different beliefs, values, attitudes and behavioral patterns are present. Keeping this in mind, you should make the best decision possible based on the people involved.
- *Don't be afraid to call it quits.* Although it is tough to swallow your pride, you can save yourself and your company lots of time and resources if you admit your initial decision was the wrong one. Because we live in a dynamic work environment, scenarios are constantly shifting, which may force you to change your mind after a decision has been made.
- *Use an effective decision-making process* that has the following characteristics:
  1. It focuses on what's important.
  2. It's logical and consistent.
  3. It acknowledges both subjective and objective thinking and blends analytical with intuitive thinking.
  4. It requires only as much information and analysis as necessary to resolve the problem.
  5. It encourages the gathering of relevant information and informed opinions.
  6. It's straightforward, reliable, easy to use and flexible.
- *Build an organization that can identify and adapt to unexpected changes in the environment.* Organizational psychologist Karl Weick says that highly reliable organizations share five habits:
  1. They are not tricked by their success.
  2. They defer to the experts on the frontline, those who have day-to-day contact with the customers.
  3. They let unexpected circumstances provide the solution.
  4. They embrace complexity.
  5. They anticipate but also recognize their limits.

As previously mentioned, creativity and successful brainstorming can lead to more diverse alternatives and ultimately a higher success rate when it comes to decision making. IDEO, one of the world's leading product design firms, is well known for their creative processes in making decisions. They have been the subject of several case studies due to their high success rate in making risky decisions. Some key items that make IDEO unique and successful in their creative processes are:

1. Everyone becomes an ethnographer. In other words, everyone in the company goes and observes how people are using their products in their natural settings. These observations are crucial in determining people's needs, habits, etc.
2. They have a work environment that is fun and encourages free-flowing ideas.
3. They do not have much formal hierarchy or many symbols of status.
4. The ground rules for brainstorming sessions are written on the walls to serve as a reminder.

5. There are plentiful materials so that people can think visually and so that basic prototypes can be built.
6. They keep old failures around to remind people that you have to take risks to be creative and that you have to accept some rate of failure.
7. Leaders openly tell employees to disagree with them and do not tell people what to design.

In order to be successful in decision-making, creativity is vital. According to Roberto (2009), there are three important steps in this creative process. First, you must use experts and expert knowledge in the appropriate matter. Next, you have to wipe away old assumptions and beliefs, and unlearn old ways of working before you can creatively generate something new. Last, you have to frame problems in ways that do not constrict the debate or range of solutions that will be considered.

Additional Resources

Numerous books can provide insight on decision making:

How We Decide by J. Lehrer gives you the decision-making tools you need, drawing on cutting-edge research as well as the real-world experiences of a wide range of decision-makers from airplane pilots and hedge fund investors to serial killers and poker players. Lehrer shows how people are taking advantage of the new science to make better television shows, win more football games and improve military intelligence. His goal is to answer two questions that are of interest to just about anyone, from CEOs to firefighters. How does the human mind make decisions? And how can we make those decisions better?

M. Roberto's book, *Know What You Don't Know: How Great Leaders Prevent Problems Before They Happen*, shifts the focus from problem solving to the problem-finding capabilities of effective leaders. Roberto examines how leaders can unearth the small problems that are likely to lead to large-scale failures in their organizations and how leaders need to shift from fighting fires to detecting smoke, so that they can detect and interrupt the chain of errors that often precedes a major failure.

And finally, *Winning Decisions: Getting it Right the First Time* by E. Russo and P. Schoemaker provides an extensive discussion of many of the cognitive biases that affect individuals and provides some simple prescriptions for overcoming these traps.

An organization that can provide decision making resources is The Society for Judgment and Decision Making. It is an interdisciplinary academic organization dedicated to the study of normative, descriptive, and prescriptive theories of judgments and decisions. Its members include psychologists, economists, organizational researchers, decision analysts, and other decision researchers. The Society's primary event is its Annual Meeting at which Society members present their research. It also publishes the journal *Judgment and Decision Making*.

References

Custer, R. L., Scarcella, J. A. and Stewart, B. R. (1999). The modified Delphi technique – A rotational modification. *Journal of Vocational and Technical Education*, 15(2).

Gilovich, T., Griffin, D., and Kahneman, D. (2002). *Hueristics and Biases: The Psychology of Intuitive Judgment*. Cambridge, England: Cambridge University Press.

Hitt, M. A., Miller, C. C., and Colella, A. (2006). Decision making by individual or groups. In J. Heffler (ed.) et al., *Organizational Behavior: A Strategic Approach* (pp. 354–91). Hoboken, New Jersey: John Wiley & Sons, Inc.

Janis, Irving L. (1972). *Victims of Groupthink*. New York, NY: Houghton Mifflin.

Miller, G. (2006). The emotional brain weights its options. *Science*, 313(5787), 600–01.

Psychologists for Social Responsibility. (2010). *What is Groupthink?* Retrieved from http://www.psysr.org/about/pubs_resources/groupthink%20overview.htm.

Robbins, S. P. and Coulter, M. (2008). *Management*, (10th ed.). Upper Saddle Ridge, New Jersey: Pearson Education, Inc.

Roberto, M. A. (2009). *The Art of Critical Decision Making*. Chantilly, VA: The Teaching Company.

Tversky, A. and Kahneman, D. (1974). Judgment under uncertainty: Heuristics and biases. *Science*, 185(4157), 1124–31.

USC Levan Institute Ethics Resource Center. (2010). *Obstacles to Good Ethical Decision Making and Behavior, and Some Things You Can Do to Overcome Them*. Retrieved from http://college.usc.edu/overcoming-obstacles-to-ethical-behavior/.

Vroom, V. H. and Yetton, P. W. (1973). *Leadership and Decision-Making*. Pittsburgh, PA: University of Pittsburgh Press.

Weick, K. (1995). *Sensemaking in Organizations*. Thousand Oaks, CA: Sage Publishing.

3 *Leadership*

SAL MIRZA and FRANK FLETCHER

At its core, leadership is about working through others to achieve objectives. Organizational leaders have many tough challenges, especially leading organizations through complex changes in turbulent times. Business consultant David Maister (1997) explains: "leaders do not build business, but leaders build organizations that build business." Today's leaders must focus on influence rather than power or control.

These turbulent times demand constant innovation and leadership. Leadership nowadays can come from any direction within an organization. Organizations are increasingly flexible and unstructured. This is especially true for the organization without boundaries (discussed in more detail in chapter six of this book) which is made up of rapidly changing subgroups that come together only for a limited purpose. Leadership is no longer a solitary or a one-time act limited to the top players.

Managers at all levels are expected to take the role of leadership to motivate, arouse enthusiasm, and develop an environment of respect that encourages participation. Managers of departments or divisions are expected to lead for success in their area of responsibility. As expressed by Dossenbach (2004) leadership from the bottom up empowers employees and managers alike to support the success of the organization.

This chapter explores the topic of leadership by first defining it, then by examining the relationship between leadership and the organization's mission and vision. Next, we look at the relationship between critical thinking and decision making. Topics include feedback, leading change and leading knowledge workers. Finally, we look at assessing leadership and leadership development.

What is leadership?

Noted management theorist Warren Bennis (2009) believes that "... leadership revolves around vision, ideas, direction, and has more to do with inspiring people as to direction and goals than with day-to-day implementation ..." According to Bennis, a leader has to help form a vision which provides a bridge to the future. A leader communicates that vision, gives it meaning, and builds trust. A leader must also understand their own skills and abilities. Most importantly Bennis believes that leaders are made and not born.

Like Bennis, Peter Drucker believed that leaders have to think through the mission of their organization, communicate it and then set goals and priorities with total clarity. Drucker believed that everyone needs to learn and to exhibit leadership. Today, leaders need to uncover new knowledge and know how to share it with others. More than ever before, knowledge truly is power. While hierarchies will continue to exist, the best organizations will be those that empower their members to be leaders. Authority, according to Drucker, comes from what one says, not who one is. The best leaders will be the ones who are best at developing, listening and empowering.

According to Brian Dive (2008), regardless of the circumstances, leaders are accountable for:

1. Deciding who comes into the team, negotiating and managing a budget for that team and being held to account for its expenditures.
2. Deciding who will work where, in which jobs and when.
3. Securing employee commitment to attain the relevant goals and providing them with the means they need to deliver their goals.
4. Giving constructive feedback and deciding upon individuals' performance and appraisal ratings, agreeing on their training and development needs, and ensuring that these are acted upon.
5. Ensuring that the members of the team meet all their obligations and, if necessary, changing the goals, obligations or team members, as appropriate.
6. Providing solutions when confronted with problems. Accountability entails finding a new solution.
7. Making change happen.
8. Achieving results from peers and colleagues over whom the manager does not have direct control.
9. Achieving results with and through external agencies, such as consumers, customers, suppliers and shareholders.
10. Setting timelines and establishing goals, which then need to be achieved in terms of quality, quantity and service.

As you can see from the above, leadership requires a good deal of analysis and decision making. See chapters one and two for more on decision making. Organizational leaders make decisions every day, which is what they get paid to do. They get evaluated on the quality of those decisions, and their decisions impact others either intentionally or unintentionally. Professor Paul Nutt (2002) of Ohio State University has studied many organizational decisions and why they didn't work out as planned. He notes that two out of every three decisions use failure prone practices. Poor decisions are made because of a rush to judgment resulting in premature commitments and wrong-headed investments. This often happens to carry out and support an idea someone is wedded to, trying to show it will work.

> **TIP: DECISION MAKING TRAPS:**
>
> 1. Failure to uncover concerns and reconcile competing claims
> 2. Overlooking people's interests and commitments
> 3. Leaving expectations vague
> 4. Limiting the search for remedies
> 5. Misusing evaluations
> 6. Ignoring ethical questions
> 7. Failing to reflect on results to learn what works and what does not.
>
> Adapted from Paul Nutt's book, *Why Decisions Fail* (2002)

The first step in being an effective decision maker is to figure out the goals for the decision-making process. Professor Nutt said one needs a clear direction for the decision process. This means being able to address: Where is the decision going? What is it meant to accomplish? Throughout the process you must continually re-articulate your goals and purposes. You need good information to make a good decision, so the second step is to seek out and uncover stakeholder concerns. This requires hearing opposing concepts and fully understanding each party's concerns and ultimately finding a common theme in making a diagnosis of the problem.

The third step is carefully analyzing the information you receive. From your analysis you can construct solid inferences. Then you figure out your options and evaluate the pros and cons of each. Next, you can adopt a strategic approach and follow through on your strategy to address the problem. Last, monitor results, and when necessary, change the strategy based on thorough evaluation.

What is critical thinking and why it is important?

It is essential that leaders are also critical thinkers. According to the Foundation for Critical Thinking, a well-cultivated critical thinker will:

1. Raise vital questions and problems, formulating them clearly and precisely.
2. Gather and assess relevant information, using abstract ideas to interpret it effectively to come to well-reasoned conclusions and solutions, testing them against relevant criteria and standards.
3. Think open-mindedly within alternative systems of thought, recognizing and assessing, as need be, their assumptions, implications, and practical consequences.
4. Communicate effectively with others in figuring out solutions to complex situations.

Being an effective critical thinking decision maker requires working the process while being aware of the traps and pitfalls described above. Most of all, the process needs to adhere to the universal intellectual standards described by Elder and Paul (2008) of clarity, accuracy, precision, relevance, depth, breadth and logic.

Critical thinking and decision making are very human activities and as such these activities will never be perfect. They can however, be made better through practice and application of standards. As noted, we live in a complex and fast-changing world, and even the best processes cannot anticipate every contingency and possibility. Using critical thinking throughout the process will certainly make it a better decision.

How important is leadership?

While much of the attention in the past has been on the development of leaders at the upper levels of the organization, a change in organizational paradigms has shifted this focus. The new paradigms, including the sharing of information, decentralization, and use of teams, have made the development of leaders across all levels of organizations increasingly important. A leader's effectiveness in a network organization is determined by his or her ability to build high performance teams.

Effective leaders play a defining role in organizational performance outcomes and employee job satisfaction. The effective leader acts as a means for change and provides employees the opportunity to exert some control over their futures. Leader behaviors,

---

CLARITY, ACCURACY, and PRECISION
Could you elaborate further on that point? Could you express that point in another way? Could you give me an illustration? Could you give me an example?

RELEVANCE:
How is that connected to the question? How does that bear on the issue?

DEPTH:
How does your answer address the complexities in the question? How are you taking into account the problems in the question?

BREADTH:
Do we need to consider another point of view? Is there another way to look at this question? What would this look like from a conservative standpoint? What would this look like from the point of view of . . .?

LOGIC:
Does this really make sense? Does that follow from what you said? How does that follow? But before you implied this, and now you are saying that; how can both be true?

FAIRNESS:
Do I have a vested interest in this issue? Am I sympathetically representing the viewpoints of others?

Adapted from: Linda Elder and Richard Paul (2008), *Intellectual Standards.*

Tool 3.1   Applying Intellectual Standards: Questions to Ask

communication, and interpersonal relationships all combine to influence subordinate job satisfaction. Higher job satisfaction leads to lower absenteeism and turnover. More satisfied employees are more productive and less prone to workplace misbehavior.

Given the important relationship between the leader and subordinate performance, leaders need a clear understanding of the relationship between employee job satisfaction and leader style and behavior. The best results come from influencing employees and developing their participation and commitment rather than coercion.

A leader must draw on many qualities to perform effectively. A leader must have vision, be adaptable to change, develop high trust, delegate authority, communicate effectively and emphasize innovation. An effective leader must exemplify the values, goals and culture of the organization. Leaders have to energize subordinates into action, develop subordinates into leaders, and transform organizational members into agents of change.

Leaders can develop a sense of ownership in their subordinates by developing goals that subordinates can identify with. Taking time to converse with employees to develop relationships helps foster a sense of ownership as well. Effective leadership strongly depends on a complex pattern of exchanges among leaders, subordinates, and situations. Leaders have to be adaptable to change as required by the situation to increase influence and to be as effective as possible.

How can I connect my leadership style to my organization's culture?

Organizational culture is a set of shared beliefs that impact an organization's day-to-day activities. Culture answers the question of "how things are done around here." It is a social energy that moves organizations and provides meaning and direction to organizational members. Although parts of an organizational culture are unseen, it can be observed. An understanding of organizational culture will assist you to work within your organization's cultural confines.

 Organizational culture can be visualized as an iceberg with the bulk of the influencers below the water line. The easily observable elements of culture include: practices, stories, language, symbols and socialization. The hidden elements are norms, values and assumptions. Keeping an eye on what's above and below the water line will help ensure that your leadership doesn't mirror that of the captain of the *Titanic*.

1. Power Distance Index (PDI): Review your understanding and that of others of the power within your organization (including decision making). The following reflective questions will help you to learn more about your organization's PDI:
   - How are key decisions made for your department and company?
   - Is power equally or unequally distributed within the organization?
   - Who has the power?
2. Individualism versus Collectivism: Review the degree to which employees are integrated into teams or groups. In an individualist culture the ties between individuals are loose. Everyone is expected to look after himself. At the other end of the spectrum, in a collectivist culture, employees are integrated into strong, cohesive groups, looking out for and trusting each other. The following reflective questions will help you to learn more about your organization's individualism versus collectivism culture:
   - How are the organization's values positioned with respect to individualism versus collectivism?
   - How are organizational goals positioned and achieved? Are they individual or collective?
   - To what degree is there inter-dependence between group members and group decision making?
3. Uncertainty Avoidance Index: Review how leaders, managers and employees deal with uncertainty and ambiguity. Organizational cultures that tend to avoid uncertainty and ambiguity will have specific procedures, policies and requirements in place. The following reflective questions will help you to learn more about your organization's culture with respect to uncertainty and ambiguity:
   - Does the organization employ strict rules, regulations, and policies?
   - Is the organization tolerant of differences in opinions and feedback?

Tool 3.2   Organizational Culture Evaluation

The contemporary emphasis on culture has brought about a change in the functioning of organizations. There is no one set culture that should be modeled by an organization. Each person does not have the same demeanor or personality and such is the case for organizational cultures.

Hofstede's various works on national culture as just described can be applied to organizations as well. As you review these dimensions, bear in mind that the cultural dimensions are a continuum with extremes identified. Your organization may fall anywhere on that continuum.

How does leadership relate to our values, mission, and vision?

Linked to organizational culture is knowledge and understanding of the organization's values, mission, and vision usually first established by the company founder. Communicating the organization's mission, vision and values easily and simply will develop loyalty and motivation. Relate the organization's mission to the mission of your specific area. Looking for areas of value congruence (agreement and alignment) gives individuals a similar point of reference.

Value congruence between the organization, you and your employees will correlate to feelings of personal success. It's a great way to build commitment, encourage ethical behavior and impact employee job satisfaction and performance.

As you review your organization's mission, vision and values use these activities and questions to help understand and link your team's function to the organization overall:

- Analyze the mission statement to establish why the organization exists. Link the "why" to your department's purpose and objectives.
- Determine the vision the leaders have for the organization. Answering this question and then linking the answer to your team's functions/goals, lets your team know where the organization is going. This also provides them with reasons for their activities and goals.

TIPS FOR COMMUNICATING MISSION, VISION AND VALUES:
- understand what each one is;
- understand why each is important;
- link them to day-to-day activities;
- link them to the short, mid-range and long-term goals of your team.

- Identify the values that are reflected in and surround the mission. Values can come from leaders but may also be grown from the grass roots level. Staying true to your own and your organization's values is the measure of your integrity. Integrity is central to building and maintaining trust.
- In your communications and meetings emphasize:
  - Why the organization exists and what is the link to the department and individual roles.

- The impact each team member is having—provide specific examples of how projects and results tie into the organization's mission.
- Why organizational values are critical to the success of your organization.

How do I build trust?

Leadership scandals such as Martha Stewart, Enron, and WorldCom have created a crisis of trust between leaders and employees. The increasing popularity of books on leadership indicates that leaders and managers recognize that new or different approaches to leadership will be needed. This is due to the rapid changes demanded in today's global business environment. As a transformational leader, which will be discussed later in the chapter, you are consistently interacting with your team to motivate them to transcend their self-interests for those of the organization. To be able to do this you must have a position of trust within the organization and with each employee.

From your perspective, communication and trust directly relate to overall team performance. Three specific conditions promote the development of trust:

- First, your actions must be consistent and aligned with the organization's mission and values.
- Second, your communications must be clear and transmitted effectively to employees.
- Third, you must develop effective relationships with each member of your team.

Personal relationships promote a spirit of togetherness. Relationships promote trust, increase motivation and act as a glue bonding members of the organization together. A benefit of establishing relationships early in the team-forming process is that team members learn about each other, and form bonds early on.

Building trust requires consistent effort on a long-term basis, as trust earned can be quickly lost. Here are some ideas for building and maintaining trust:

- Communicate as openly as organizational polices allow. Encourage open, honest and frequent communication.
- Establish a pattern of regular communications. Communicate often using different methods.
- Encourage social interactions. Take time to get to know each employee on a personal level. Remember, you should not only go and see an employee when there are problems. Take time to socialize and bring both work and common interests into the discussions. This will lead to stronger relationships and trust levels.
- Hold face-to-face meetings that are regular and purposeful.

When carried out in a consistent manner and with integrity, these behaviors will lead to stronger relationships and trust levels.

LEADERSHIP TIPS:
- Be a role model. Be consistent in your actions as an example for others to emulate.
- When required, positively question the status quo in an attempt to lead change.
- Foster collaboration and a sense of ownership.
- Recognize and celebrate team and individual achievements and success.

Adapted from Kouzes and Posner (2003) *Leadership Inventory*

How can I provide effective feedback to my employees?

Delivered in the present, feedback is information about past behavior that influences future behavior. Feedback is fundamental in helping individuals, teams or units in your workplace to reach an objective and avoid unpleasant surprises. Timely and substantial feedback leads to higher job satisfaction. Most important, in these times of constant change, effective feedback is essential for maintaining consistent performance.

Feedback delivered ineffectively can reduce the receiver's self-confidence, lower their motivation, and cause simmering feelings of anger. The tendency will develop to attempt to resolve interpersonal conflicts through head-on confrontation rather than through compromise or collaboration.

While giving feedback is seldom easy, especially if the feedback is negative, you can learn to give effective feedback. To be effective, you must understand the process when feedback is being delivered and received. You also need to develop a strategy for being secure enough to tolerate the unpredictability of feedback. Finally, according to Edie Seashore, past president of the National Training Laboratories Institute and co-author of *What Did You Say?: The Art of Giving Feedback* (2000), you don't have to be perfect to give good feedback.

Seashore says feedback is " … an interactive process, a rapid fire and complex flow of information gathering, internal processing, and response, often with both parties being givers and receivers at the same moment." Feedback between people is a system. Many factors enter into this system and affect the quality of it.

Your feedback must be heard and understood by the receiver to be effective. It must also be devised and delivered by you so that the relationship between you and your receiver stays intact and future interactions are possible. Effective feedback provides information that can be used. Most of all, effective feedback is not criticism, because criticism is evaluative whereas feedback is descriptive.

Seashore says that productive feedback between people involves several critical factors. To complete an effective feedback process through to closure, explicitly or implicitly share your goals for the process. All parties involved in the process must manage the climate to reduce resistance. Any conflict that arises must be addressed to prevent the feedback process from being derailed. Allow time for people to digest and integrate the information you share with them, and provide them with an opportunity for them to return later for clarification. Finally, directness and openness are vital.

Communication is at the core of giving and receiving feedback. Communications are discussed in depth in chapter four of this book. In addition to general communication challenges, possible influences on the feedback process include: the context of the conversation, the parties' priorities, their self-perceptions, and the parties' affiliated needs such as the need for approval and belonging. Some of these other factors, according to Seashore, could take priority over the substance of the message. Your delivery of the feedback might reflect the power imposed by you as the sender, the emotional power of your message, and your personal style.

> **TIPS FOR GIVING FEEDBACK:**
> 1. Share your goals for the process
> 2. Reduce resistance by managing climate
> 3. Address any conflicts that arise immediately
> 4. Allow time for digestion
> 5. Schedule time for clarification and a follow up session

You should give feedback in a non-threatening environment. You may try perhaps to deliver the feedback on neutral ground (in the conference room as opposed to in your own office for example.) The feedback you offer must be apparent and concrete to the receiver, and your feedback should be dramatically presented. Humor, another key element, allows you to explore alternatives. Humor during the process also allows you to introduce new material in a safe way.

Feedback is vital to the success of all organizations as well as for teams and individuals. Keep in mind that feedback has to be shaped so that the receiver can understand it. It must also be presented openly and directly with the goals of the feedback process shared explicitly or implicitly. Conflicts that arise during the process must be addressed, and the receiver has to be given time to digest the message and be able to return later for clarification. Feedback, most importantly, must be concretely relevant.

How do I lead change?

Change management is the ultimate test of leadership since people affected by fundamental change often resist it. To bring about change, leaders need to create a sense of urgency about why the change needs to happen. Leaders need to assemble the players (or a coalition) who can get it done. They have to have a vision of how the change will happen and why it is good for the organization and the people involved. Most of all, they must communicate their vision of the change and be certain that people understand it.

Before starting the change process, managers need to understand precisely what type of change their unit is capable of by assessing three factors: resources, processes, and values. Conducting an inventory and understanding tangible and intangible resources is the vital first step. Next, understanding the patterns of interaction, coordination, communication, and decision making processes must also be accomplished. Finally, the leader must examine their organization's values, the standards by which employees set priorities.

Harvard Business School professor John P. Kotter (2007) has examined over a hundred companies (both large and small) that have gone through change. Kotter states the goal of change is "to make fundamental changes in how business is conducted in order to help cope with a new, more challenging market environment." Drawing on that experience he concludes: "that the change process goes through a series of phases that, in total, usually require a considerable length of time. Skipping steps creates only the illusion of speed and never produces a satisfying result. A second very general lesson is that critical mistakes in any of the phases can have a devastating impact, slowing momentum and negating hard-won gains..."

For you as a manager, this suggests you need to complete each of the steps in the change process. Kotter's eight steps for organization transformation cover necessary activities in the process.

Leading change is especially important in the emerging knowledge economy. What follows will provide guidance specific for leading knowledge workers.

Number	Step
1	Establish a Sense of Urgency • Examine market and competitive realities. • Identify and discuss crises, potential crises, or major opportunities.
2	Form a Powerful Guiding Coalition • Assemble a group with enough power to lead the change effort. • Encourage the group to work together as a team.
3	Create a Vision • Create a vision to help direct the change effort. • Develop strategies for achieving that vision.
4	Communicate the Vision • Use every vehicle possible to communicate the new vision and strategies. • Teach new behaviors by the example of the guiding coalition.
5	Empower Others to Act on the Vision • Get rid of obstacles to change. • Change systems or structures that seriously undermine the vision. • Encourage risk taking and nontraditional ideas, activities, and actions.
6	Plan for and Create Short-Term Wins • Plan for visible performance improvements. • Create those improvements. • Recognize and reward employees involved in the improvements.
7	Consolidate Improvements and Produce Still More Change • Use increased credibility to change systems, structures, and policies at don't fit the vision. • Hire, promote, and develop employees who can implement the vision. • Reinvigorate the process with new projects, themes, and change agents.
8	Institutionalize New Approaches • Articulate the connections between the new behaviors and corporate success. • Develop the means to ensure leadership development and succession.

Tool 3.3   The Change Process

How do I lead knowledge workers? What are some of the unique challenges?

The term "knowledge worker" was coined by Peter Drucker almost fifty years ago to describe anyone who works for a living at the tasks of developing or using knowledge. Knowledge workers are typically engaged in the tasks of: planning, acquiring, searching, analyzing, organizing, storing, programming, distributing, marketing, or otherwise contributing to the transformation and commerce of information. These workers enjoy more autonomy than other workers. It is often difficult to measure the full scope of their work since much of it involves contemplation without written record.

The essence of leading knowledge workers is an expression of the authentic self. Authenticity is largely defined by what other people see in the leader, and as such, can be controlled by the leader. Establishing your authenticity as a leader in the eyes of knowledge workers is a two-part challenge. First, you have to ensure that your words are consistent with your deeds. Second, you need to find common ground with the people that you seek to recruit as followers.

Managers must create an environment in which their knowledge workers can thrive as clever people. Clever people have one defining characteristic: they do not want to be led. They also seek a high degree of organizational protection, recognition that their ideas are important and the freedom to explore and fail. Studies have found that they expect their leaders to be intellectually on their level. They do not want a leader's talent and skill to outshine their own.

Managers have to inspire and support their unit's collective responsibility to create a better future. Effective leaders understand their role to bring out the answers in others. They must avoid the trap of assuming they are the person with all the answers.

Leaders of this type of employee also need to develop their capacity for integrative thinking. As opposed to conventional thinking which accepts the world as it is, integrative thinking welcomes the challenge of shaping a better future. Integrative thinkers have the capacity to hold several opposing ideas in their minds at once. They resolve the tension of this situation by proposing a solution that is superior to the one that contains either or both.

Leaders of knowledge workers need to be able to listen, collaborate, delegate and develop new leaders. Managers should expect their knowledge workers to stay current in their respective fields, drive their own growth, and be team players through triumph and failure. In turn, leaders should provide clarity, realistic goals, and feedback that is specific, timely, and relevant.

How can I assess my leadership effectiveness?

Linked to how you can impact organizational performance is the issue of recognizing ways to assess your effectiveness as a leader. Again the bottom line will be the ultimate measure. Ask yourself the following questions: Were our goals attained? Were budget targets achieved? Did we meet our sales growth or profitability objectives?

The answers to these questions reflect on your effectiveness as a leader. These however are task outcomes. The focus in this section will not be on the task outcomes but on people issues as related to leader effectiveness. Include in your goals and objectives measures related to employee turnover, absenteeism and job satisfaction. In other words, are you measuring and tracking how happy your employees are?

The word happy can conjure many different images, ranging from a country club leadership style where there is no direction or guidance to an autocratic style where employees are told exactly what to do and when to it. As a transformational leader you will be attempting to direct your employees to work for the greater good of the department and organization rather than their own selfish needs. The areas that influence this employee change are relationships and empowerment.

Graen and Uhl-Bien (1995) in their leader-employee exchange theory established that the quality of the leader employee relationship influences leader trust and empowerment. The quality of your relationships with your employees will affect levels of trust and empowerment.

As the leader of your department or team you will form different relationships with each employee. There are two extreme types of relationships you may have with your employees either high or low quality. These relationships are a result of communications and feelings of belonging on the part of the employee. High quality relationships tend to result in employees feeling they are part of an in-group or a feeling of belonging to the team, department or organization. Employees who are in the in-group will seek responsibility, have greater self-confidence and self-esteem, have a positive and proactive approach to their work, and are motivated.

At the other extreme of the leader-employee relationship continuum are the low quality relationships. The low quality relationships result in the employee feeling that they are in the out-group and have no sense of belonging. For employees with a low quality relationship you may offer less support and give less responsibility and empowerment as the trust level is low.

To form high quality relationships, practice the follow habits:

- Be consistent with your communication messages. Provide reasons and supporting information when direction changes.
- Practice active listening. Listen to your employees, hear what they are saying, acknowledge and try to understand their perspective.
- Project confidence. Be realistic and down to earth.
- Be honest. Be open and honest with your employees as honesty develops trust.
- Protect your team and employees. Look out for each employee and your department.
- Bond with employees. Take the time to learn what is important to each employee.
- Project positivism. Your attitudes and behaviors will be watched by others, so always lead by example.
- Create learning opportunities. Provide opportunities to employees to shine in their work efforts.

By strengthening your relationships with employees and others in your organization you will positively affect employee trust, attitudes, motivation, and performance. Thus, as a result of these high quality employee relationships, you as the leader will be able to empower your employees by delegating power, authority and control.

Which of my leadership behaviors will be most effective?

Today's changing work environment calls for you to be aware. Understand the behavioral aspect of your leadership and the resulting effects on performance and employee job motivation and satisfaction. There are many facets of leadership that can impact leadership effectiveness and if you are able to adapt and manage a multitude of these factors you will positively impact employee satisfaction and productivity. As established in prior research, leadership competencies can be taught and learned. However, the capacity to learn depends on the person themselves. Some people have an inclination to learn some competencies better than others. New learning must be internalized and applied to be effective.

Aspects that impact your observable behaviors and actions include your beliefs, values, attitudes, and personality. The organizational culture and the beliefs, values, attitudes, of your co-workers, management and senior leaders of your organization also impact your behavior.

Your beliefs and values are central to your attitudes, assumptions and the conclusions you make about yourself and about others in the world. The clearer you are about what you value and believe in, the more effective you will be as a leader. You demonstrate and model your values in action in your personal and work behaviors, decision making, contribution and interpersonal interaction.

Values are linked to your upbringing (family, friends, religious affiliation, education, and culture). They reflect how you have learned to value how people should behave, especially in terms of qualities such as honesty, integrity and openness. As an effective person, manager and leader, you will recognize these environmental influences. Identify and develop a value statement for yourself that is clear and concise, with a set of values, and priorities. Once defined, these values impact every aspect of your life.

Identify the values that are most important to you, the values you believe in and that define your character, then live them visibly every day at work and at home. Living your values is one of the most powerful tools available to you to help you accomplish goals and to help you lead and influence others.

From an organizational perspective, values have been frequently cited as reasons for organizational success. The concepts of value congruence and organizational fit are closely tied. By identifying your values and those of each team member you can start to work towards alignment between personal and organizational values.

Studies have demonstrated that some traits are more important than others in determining leadership effectiveness. Kirkpatrick and Locke (1991) proposed that key traits are a necessary precondition for effective leadership. The identified traits are:

- drive (including motivation and energy);
- desire and motivation to lead;
- honesty and integrity;
- self-confidence;
- intelligence and;
- knowledge of the business.

Kirkpatrick and Locke further suggested that leaders are not born with all the key traits; traits like knowledge and self-confidence can be acquired with time and experience.

Fiedler's leadership model (1987) leads the modern theme that there is no one best way to perform the leadership function, suggesting that a number of leadership behavior styles may be effective depending on the situational characteristics. Your leadership effectiveness will depend on using the appropriate behavior to match the situation.

We referred to the concept of transformational leadership earlier and expand on it here by linking it with the concept of transactional leadership. The transactional-transformational paradigm incorporates aspects of trait theory and is also a systems approach to leadership. Transactional leadership is based on a contractual exchange process between leader and subordinate. This is, in effect, a reward for performance approach. Transformational leadership, on the other hand, goes beyond performance exchanges by developing, stimulating, and inspiring subordinates to transcend self-interests for a higher collective purpose. This approach engages the employee at a deeper level to rise above self-interests. Most leaders actually display some combination of transactional and transformational leadership styles.

As a leader you have to decide which leadership behaviors and processes to apply in various situations. As a leader you have to reach a balance between task leading (focus on scheduling, completion of task, production/output) and socio-emotional leadership or people leadership (focusing on building confidence, self-esteem and self concept). To assess your range of effectiveness of your leadership behaviors you can use Hersey and Blanchard's (1996) Leader Effectiveness and Adaptability Description (LEAD) instrument. The LEAD instrument measures task and relationship behavior through a set of situations. You then respond to one of four alternative actions. Each of the alternatives reflects one of the four combinations of task and relationship behavior:

1. Telling: High task/low relationship (S1)
2. Selling: High task/high relationship (S2)
3. Participating: Low task/high relationship (S3)
4. Delegating: Low task/low relationship (S4)

By selecting your preferred actions in each of the situations the tool will provide four scores that describe your leadership range of styles. The more your score reflects an equal distribution among the four combinations of leader behaviors, the more effective you are as a leader.

Kouzes and Posner offer an alternative perspective to what it is that leaders do when they are leading. They identify five fundamental practices that enable leaders to affect subordinates and organizations:

1. challenging the process;
2. inspiring a shared vision;
3. enabling others to act;
4. modeling the way;
5. encouraging the heart.

The behavioral approach emphasizes leadership behaviors in practice—what you actually do on the job. Kouzes and Posner developed the Leadership Practices Inventory (LPI). The LPI is a thirty-item instrument designed to measure five leadership practices. The Participant's Workbook will help you appreciate how others see your leadership behavior, and to understand how to use that information to become the most effective leader possible. This short, ten-step workbook guides you through the process of understanding your LPI feedback report. Using the Participant's Workbook will help you:

- examine self perceptions;
- explore consistency within your behaviors;
- identify patterns to your behaviors;
- identify your developmental areas;
- plan towards your future leader self.

It is common to think of personality as providing one kind of explanation for behaviors in a variety of situations. Faced with the same situation, you may behave differently from someone else. Understanding your personality will allow you to engage your strongest personality traits towards successful leadership. There are many tools to help you assess you personality types. One instrument is the Briggs Myers-Briggs Type Indicator® (MBTI®) personality inventory. The results from the MBTI® instrument help you become aware of your personality preferences. The four preferences are:

Extraversion (E) or Introversion (I): This provides information on the direction of your focus—is it internally or externally directed. For example when faced with a decision, do you do you talk to other people or do you think on your own about the problem to arrive at a decision.

Sensing (S) or Intuition (N): This refers to how you focus on information. Do you take the information at face value or do you add your own interpretation.

Thinking (T) or Feeling (F): This refers to how you make decision: Do you only consider the facts or do you incorporate the human aspect as well.

Judging (J) or Perceiving (P): This applies to how you live your life on a daily basis. For example, do you plan ahead or do you do things at the last minute.

Myers and Briggs identified sixteen personality types that result from the interactions among the preferences. Expansion and description of each of the personality types can be obtained at the Myers and Briggs Foundation website.

It's important to remember that there is no single best personality type for leadership. One purpose of learning your personality type is to understand and value differences between people. Another way to gain personal insight is the 360 degree feedback evaluation. In addition to being a performance management tool as described in chapter seven, a 360 degree feedback evaluation can be a way of developing your leadership effectiveness. You should obtain feedback from different perspectives: your direct reports, peers, and upper management. From the feedback analysis you can create a development plan to address identified weaknesses.

Competencies for feedback consideration may include: development and growth, motivation and drive, self-awareness, ethics, communications, influencing others, teamwork, empowerment, mentoring and coaching, change leadership, and problem solving. Other competencies may be added to a 360 degree feedback evaluation as they pertain to your organization.

How can I better manage my emotions?

When you think of an effective leader, you first think of the various behaviors and competencies that you can learn and employ when interacting with your employees and peers. Another aspect of being an effective leader is having knowledge and understanding of your emotions. Are you prone to getting agitated, excited or angry? Can you identify triggers for getting excited or angry? Are you stoic, keeping your emotions under tight control? Our emotions can lead us to certain actions and behaviors that can enhance or handicap relationships. Consider and reflect on the following everyday situations you may have come across:

> *Situation 1:* As you are driving, you are cut off by another driver causing you to brake and slow down. How do you react? Some folks would tend to let their emotions and feelings surface through a series of verbalizations and gestures to express their displeasure. While others may just accept the occurrence, slow down and continue without another thought to what had taken place. Then there are some folks who will let the situation bother them internally but not be outwardly expressed.

> *Situation 2:* You are in discussions with employees or your co-workers trying to explain your needs. However, they do not appear to fully grasp your meaning and message. You may continue to use different approaches to communicate your needs with patience and understanding. Or, you may become impatient and just tell them what to do. The third alternative is to give up, leave and do what was needed yourself.

The above two scenarios demonstrate the gamut of possible reaction options to a certain situation or person. You can manage the option that is observed by others. You have the control and the ability to manage how you react and behave. If you are emotionally adept, that is you know and manage your feelings and can read and deal with other people's feelings, then you have a leadership advantage.

Goleman (2004) says that most effective leaders have high emotional intelligence and that self-awareness is the first component of emotional intelligence. Self-awareness is an emotional intelligence skill that allows leaders to know how they are feeling and why, and the impact feelings have on their behavior. Leaders often get caught up in focusing on results and may pay little attention to their own behavior.

An example is the behavior of a manager who is solely focused on delivering results to the CEO. The manager's subordinates have started complaining about the lack of contribution and collaboration within the team. The manager was oblivious to the fact that his actions to please the CEO were causing him to micromanage his team. In doing so, the manager was undercutting the team member's independence and confidence. The lack of self-awareness impacted the performance of team members.

Caruruso and Salovey's model (2004) identifies four emotional skills that you can leverage to become an effective and emotionally intelligent manager. They are:

1. Identify Emotions: Become aware of your feelings and express them appropriately. Identify the feelings of those you are working with.
2. Use Emotions: Understand your feelings to manage and guide your thinking and problem solving.
3. Understand Emotions: Understand that feelings will and do change as the circumstances change and develop.
4. Manage Emotions: Emotions can dictate thinking and decisions, so be open to the information derived from yours and others emotions.

In their book *The Emotionally Intelligent Manager*, Cauruso and Salovey have developed a tool that can assist in developing self-awareness. The Assessing Your Emotional Style tool provides a means for you to develop insight into your emotional style.

Your behavior is the external appearance that is observed by others (your employees, peers and superiors) and that can be modified with training. By learning more about yourself and those around you through the tools in this chapter, you will be able to understand how to develop yourself as a leader and discover the best ways of working with others. The ultimate benefit to you and your organization and department is that you will learn how to develop and realize your leadership potential in an effective and rapid way.

This chapter has pointed out that leaders are made and not born and that leadership is no longer exclusively a role of top executives in an organization. Authority comes from what you say. The best leader will be the one who is best at developing, listening and empowering.

The ultimate test of leadership is managing change since fundamental change is most resisted by the people affected by it. In order to bring about change, a leader has to have a vision, create a sense of urgency and assemble a team who can get it done. Most of all, they must communicate a vision of the change and be certain that people understand it. The more leadership you can demonstrate through your actions and communications to employees the greater the buy-in.

Effective leaders play a defining role in subordinate performance outcomes and job satisfaction. Leaders have to appreciate and respect the diversity of their colleagues since effective leaders play a defining role in subordinate performance outcomes and job satisfaction. Norris (2009) points out that 50% of the causes of a leader's lack of success have to do with poor working relationships and communication failures. Therefore leaders need to develop their social intelligence including social awareness.

Being a critical thinker and lifelong learner is also necessary to being an effective leader. As Bennis points out, leaders need to understand their own skills and abilities and constantly work at improving them. Your beliefs and values are the core that leads to the attitudes, assumptions and conclusions you make about yourself and about others in the world. This is demonstrated in action in your personal and work behaviors, decision making, contribution, and interpersonal interaction. Most of all, leaders need to be around talented people. Don't be afraid to hire people who might be more intelligent or talented than you, because being around people who are better than ourselves has a tendency to make us stretch to improve.

Additional Resources

During the leadership development process, personality may be used to help identify the best fit between the candidate and the organization. Two sources of commonly used personality testing are HumanMetrics: Identify Your Type with Jung Typology™ Test and Myers-Briggs Type Indicator® (MBTI®) personality inventory. More information on Myers Briggs can be found through the Myers & Briggs Foundation.

Since 1948, the Society of Human Resource Management (SHRM) has been providing resources for managers and leaders across the globe. Their website provides extensive information on a variety of related topics (www.shrm.org).

References

Bennis, W. G. (2009). Avoiding the Mistakes That Plague New Leaders. *Harvard Management Update*, 14(5), 3. Retrieved from EBSCO*host*.

Cauruso D. R. and Salovey, P. (2004). *The Emotional Intelligent Manager*. San Francisco, CA: Jossey-Bass Publishers.

Dive, B. (2008). *The Accountable Leader*. Concordville, PA: Soundview Executive Book Summaries.

Dossenbach, T. (2004). Is your leadership AWOL? *Wood & Wood Products*, 41 (2), 23–24.

Elder, L. and Paul, R. (2008). *Intellectual Standards*. Tomales, CA: Foundation for Critical Thinking.

Fiedler, F. (1987). *New Approaches to Effective Leadership*. New York, NY: John Wiley & Sons.

Goleman, D. (2004). What makes a leader? *Harvard Business Review*, 82 (1), 82–91.

Graen, G. B. and Uhl-Bien, M. (1995). Relationship-based approach to leadership: Development of leader-member exchange (LMX) theory of leadership over 25 years: Applying a multi-level multi-domain perspective. *Leadership Quarterly*, 6(2), 219–47.

Hersey, P. and Blanchard, K. (1996). Revisiting the life-cycle theory of leadership development. *Training & Development*, 50(1), 42–47.

Hofstede, G. (2001). *Culture's Consequences; Comparing Values, Behaviours, Institutions, and Organizations Across Nations*, 2nd. Ed. Thousand Oaks, CA: Sage Publications.

Kirkpatrick, S. A. and Locke, E. A. (1991). Leadership: Do traits matter? *Academy of Management Executive*, 5, 48–60.

Kotter, J. P. (2007). Leading Change. *Harvard Business Review*, 85(1), 96–103. Retrieved from EBSCO*host*.

Kouzes, J. M. and Posner, B. Z. (2003). *Leadership Practices Inventory – Participants Workbook* (3rd ed.). San Francisco, CA: Jossey-Bass Publications.

Maister, D. H. (1997). *True Professionalism*. New York, NY: Touchstone.

Norris, E. (2009). LEADERSHIP: CULTIVATING PEOPLE SKILLS. *Review of Business Research*, 9(4), 67–83. Retrieved from EBSCO*host*.

Nutt, P. C. (2002). *Why Decisions Fail*. San Francisco, CA: Berrett-Koelher.

Seashore, C. N., Seashore, E. W. and Weinberg, G. (2000). *What Did You Say?: The Art of Giving and Receiving Feedback*. Columbia, MD: Bingham House Books.

4 *Communications*

KAREN CLANCY and LINDA ELDRIDGE

Effective communication is essential to business strategy and success. Without it, companies cannot prosper. Communication forges important linkages between the mission and goals of an organization and its internal and external constituents. Successful managers must develop effective communication skills and processes to exchange information and build linkages with important stakeholders such as customers, workers, suppliers, distributors, financiers, boards, communities and many others.

Written, verbal and non-verbal communications are at the heart of effective information exchanges but there are often many barriers and challenges. This chapter is dedicated to identifying the most common communication problems that managers face and to providing solutions to each. Specific problems are identified and diagnosed, and a set of possible alternatives is offered so the reader can quickly and effectively arrive at a solution.

What are the basic components and common barriers of business communication?

Have you ever had difficulty understanding someone? Was the meaning of the message difficult to interpret? Or, have you felt like people just didn't understand your messages? Examining the basic steps of a specific communication process enables you to identify potential barriers or diagnose existing ones. Analyzing and preparing a communication transaction helps to avoid misunderstandings, misalignment of resources and loss of productivity.

Let's review the basic components of a communication transaction. The communication process involves senders, messages and receivers. That sounds simple enough. However, upon closer examination, there are many factors that influence senders, messages and receivers. These influences often determine the effectiveness of the information exchange and ultimately impact the outcome of the communication transaction process. Therefore, it is important to consider the spheres or context of the sender, message and receiver when examining a communication transaction.

The figure below reveals the basic components of a communication transaction. There are many variables that can interfere with the effectiveness of a simple communication process. Be aware of these variables when preparing or analyzing your messages.

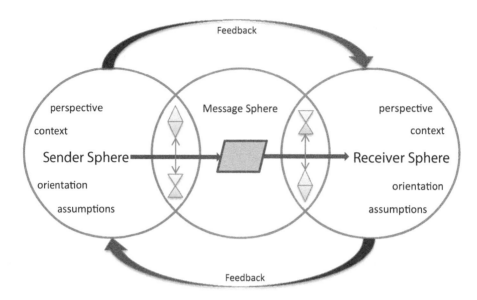

Figure 4.1   Communication Transaction Process

I'm the sender, what do I need to know?

The sender is the person who initiates the information transaction. Often, the sender owns the message. He may construct the message or have someone else construct it. The perspective, context, orientation and assumptions of the sender can create sender bias. The sender needs to be aware of his own personal bias and the potential effects on the communication process. The goal of the sender is for the receiver to receive and understand the message. Perception of sender trustworthiness and credibility are beneficial. The sender may send written, verbal and nonverbal messages. The messages should be consistent regardless of their format. The sender must also consider factors within the sphere of the receiver that influence understanding the message.

What should I know about my receiver?

The receiver is the person or persons for whom the message is intended. The ease with which the receiver accurately interprets the message determines the effectiveness of the communication. Factors within the sphere of the receiver such as personal and professional perspectives or filters, the context of the message, orientation to the message, assumptions about the purpose of the communication, and the work environment affect receiver bias. Personal and professional perspectives include education, professional socialization, culture, emotions and even social circumstances. Orientation includes prior familiarity with and personal attitudes about the message. The receiver's personal trust in the sender is an important factor.

How about the message itself?

The message is constructed and encoded by the sender and decoded by the receiver. The spheres of the sender and receiver influence the creation, encoding, decoding and reception of the message. However, the construction of the message itself is also vital to effective understanding of the communication. The message should be clear, concise and grammatically correct. Key message points should be easily identifiable. Messages that are congruent or aligned with the values of the sender are easier for the sender to effectively

COMMUNICATIONS TRANSACTION TOOL	
SENDER	**DATA**
Sender - name/s	
Perspective - sender's position, professional and personal influences	
Context - situation	
Orientation - sender's orientation to the receiver/s	
Assumptions - of the sender about the receiver/s and the message	
Sender bias - that may influence the communication transaction process	
RECEIVER	**DATA**
Receiver/s - name/s	
Personal perspective - culture, emotions, social circumstances	
Professional perspective - education, professional viewponts	
Orientation to the message - prior familiarity and personal attitudes	
Assumptions - of the receivers about the purpose of the communication	
Work environment - conditions	
Perception - of sender trustworthiness and credibility	
MESSAGE	**DATA**
Key messages	
Context (Situation)	

Tool 4.1   Communications Transaction Tool

construct. Messages that are congruent with the values of the receiver are easier for the receiver to receive. Those that are not congruent are more difficult for both.

A communications transaction tool will help you to analyze, evaluate and plan crucial messages at the transaction level. The tool will help you to identify potential communications barriers that should be considered when developing effective communications strategies. If you are completing the tool as the sender, it is important to remember that your own bias may skew the analysis. You should complete the tool as honestly and objectively as possible. Asking an individual or groups of people such as anonymous focus groups to complete the tool may yield different but valuable results. The more you understand in advance about potential barriers in the spheres of the sender, receiver and message, or in the feedback loop, the more equipped you will be to develop effective communications that are received and understood.

What's the role of feedback in the communication process?

Communication is a two-way process. Feedback from the receiver to the sender verifies the message has been received and understood. Feedback may be verbal, non-verbal (smiling and nodding for example), written, or no feedback at all (which in and of itself is feedback). If the message is not understood, feedback can help to clarify the meaning of the message. It is important to solicit feedback in order to ensure effectiveness of the message.

TIPS FOR GIVING FEEDBACK:
1. Ask clarifying questions.
2. Paraphrase to demonstrate understanding.
3. Pay attention to the non-verbal feedback you might be already giving.

A sender may pilot-test the message before distribution to the target audience by asking select individuals or focus groups to provide feedback. Creating an environment that allows receivers to feel comfortable asking questions facilitates understanding of the message. Feedback between the sender and receiver is also a way to further enhance the meaning of the message.

Why is active listening important?

We think of our employees or stakeholders as the receivers of most messages. However, communication is a two-way process. In the sender-receiver feedback loop, the sender is simultaneously delivering and receiving messages. One of the most vital business strategies of a successful manager is active listening. In The Seven Habits of Highly Effective People, Stephen Covey (1989) recommends "Seek first to understand, then to be understood." A good manager minimizes his personal bias and actively listens to the messages of his employees and other stakeholders. Active listening includes providing feedback to the sender that the message has been received and understood.

What are the basic forms of communication?

Within organizations, communication is usually conducted in written, verbal or nonverbal forms. Selection of written, verbal, and/or nonverbal messages is driven by the purpose, audience and chosen communications distribution channels. These forms are often

> **TIPS FOR ACTIVE LISTENING**
> 1. Talk less – listen 80% of the time and talk 20% of the time
> 2. Ask sincere (not leading) questions
> 3. Paraphrase to demonstrate interest and understanding
> 4. Watch for the speaker's non-verbal cues
> 5. Evaluate the speaker's data and evidence
> 6. Give your undivided attention.

used together to support and enhance communication. Phillip Clampitt, in his book *Communicating for Managerial Effectiveness* (2000), suggests asking the following questions as you chose a communication method:

1. Feedback—How quickly can the receiver respond to the message?
2. Complexity capacity—Can the method effectively process complex transactions?
3. Breadth potential—How many different messages can be transmitted using this channel?
4. Confidentiality—Can communicators be reasonably sure their messages are received by the intended audience only?
5. Encoding ease—Can senders easily and quickly use this channel?
6. Decoding ease —Can receivers quickly and easily decode messages?
7. Time-space constraint—Do senders and receivers need to communicate at the same time and in the same space?
8. Cost—How much does it cost to use this method?
9. Interpersonal warmth—How well does this method convey interpersonal warmth?
10. Formality—Does this method have the needed amount of formality?
11. Scanability—Does this method allow the message to be easily browsed or scanned for relevant information?
12. Time of consumption—Does the sender or receiver exercise the most control over when the message is dealt with?

Written communication includes emails, letters, memorandums, reports, facsimiles, publications and web pages. Written communication provides a permanent hard copy of the message. This can be good or bad especially when it comes to email. Internet publishing and visuals (discussed later in this chapter) that are used to enhance verbal presentations are also forms of written communication. Written messages should be easy to read and visualize. Final versions should be clear, concise and grammatically correct. Accurate spelling is essential. Given the plethora of writing aids on the market, there are no excuses for poor grammar and spelling.

Summarization and supporting details should be appropriate to the target audience and the channel of communication. Proofreading written communications before distribution improves the credibility of the sender and understanding by the receiver. This includes email messages. Email messages should be carefully reviewed for clarity, tone and etiquette. Many times, it is too easy to fire off an angry or emotional email that is easily misinterpreted.

Verbal communication is used in one-to-one interactions, group meetings, presentations, video-conferences and on the telephone. Clear and concise messages that are grammatically correct are just as important in verbal as in written communication. Voice volume, pitch and tone, word pronunciation, language inflection, and timing are also important to effective verbal communications. Even the simplest messages can be misunderstood if the sender is speaking too quickly or the sound of his voice is not supportive of the message.

Non-verbal communication is an important part of both written and verbal communication and it can be considered a communication medium in its own right. Body language, posture, eye contact, and facial expressions clue receivers to the subconscious thoughts of the sender. For example, managers who use good posture, appear relaxed but confident, make good eye contact, and smile occasionally, appear to be authoritative and sincere.

It is important for written, verbal and nonverbal messages to be consistent and harmonious. Listening to a concert with one of the choir members singing off key detracts from the experience. Similarly, the message can get lost if the sender's written, verbal, and nonverbal signals are dissonant. For example, if the sales manager's written message introduces a new service line, but his voice and nonverbal communication suggests doubt about its potential, the sales force may come away from the meeting less than motivated. The resulting impact of incongruent messages may be disastrous for the company.

What are the channels of business communication?

Business messages are distributed through communications channels or media. Development of information technologies in recent years has given managers more channel options than ever before. Channels have unique characteristics that meet specific communications needs. For example, interpersonal communication offers more opportunities for face-to-face exchange, while web-based channels allow communication en masse—with potentially millions of people all over the world. Selection of appropriate channels is driven by the purpose of the communication and the size and needs of the organization.

Face-to-face interactions provide the best channels for interpersonal communications. These types of interactions may be one-to-one, in small or large group settings, via the telephone, or over the Internet in the form of video-conferencing. Effective interpersonal communications are best achieved in one-to-one or small group settings. Factors that determine the platform for interpersonal communication include purpose of the communication, location of the target audience, time, convenience and budget, many of the same factors described above by Clampitt. Face-to-face communication includes public speaking and in-person presentations. Written, verbal and nonverbal messages may be exchanged via interpersonal communication.

In recent years, creation and development of Internet and web-based technologies have dramatically expanded communications capabilities. Managers can conduct meetings and exchange information with individuals or groups who are physically located anywhere that has an Internet connection or wireless network access. Methods of electronic communication include:

- informational web pages
- web-based presentations
- databases with web-page interfaces
- secure virtual private networks
- intranets
- video-conferencing
- social networking
- email.

The power of social networking technologies such as Facebook, Twitter, LinkedIn and Myspace have recently been in world news. The ability to send messages to millions of people with one click of the mouse mobilized thousands of people to protest and depose government leaders in 2011. Managers can effectively use these same technologies to communicate and develop a sense of community within their organizations.

How can I make my oral presentations better?

Think about a successful presentation that you have attended. Chances are that the speaker was confident, energetic, knowledgeable and comfortable talking about the topic and the content was well organized and easy to understand. As a result, the audience was attentive, motivated and engaged. Although the presenter may have appeared to be a natural public speaker, most likely his secret weapon was his effective preparation. You can achieve the same success in your presentations by preparing and practicing.

The first step is to identify the goals and learning objectives of the presentation. What do you hope to accomplish? What do you want the audience to learn and how do you want them to respond? Each goal is a broad statement of what you plan to achieve. You may have more than one goal for a presentation. However, identifying fewer goals allows you to provide a more focused presentation. Learning objectives define specifically how you plan to achieve your goals. Objectives may be stated at the beginning of your presentation. They should be used as a road map to organize your presentation.

The next step is to develop primary messages for your presentation. Primary messages are brief talking points that you want your audience to remember. They are typically stated throughout the presentation and re-stated in the conclusion. They may also be incorporated into the presentation objectives. Always end by summarizing the presentation with your primary messages. The messages should be simply stated and easy to understand. Having fewer central messages (three to five is a good number) allows you to emphasize their importance and improves the odds that your audience will retain them.

Next, you should evaluate and define your target audience. Consideration should be given to culture, demographics, professions, the environment and the ability of your audience to receive the message. Successful presentations connect with and engage the audience. That means you should use communication strategies that will help them

Presentation Tool
Presentation Demographics
Title
Date
Location
Start Time
End Time
Key Messages 1) 2) 3)
Target Audience
Handouts 1) 2) 3)
Other Information
Presentation Storyboard
Learning Objectives 1) 2) 3)
Sequence of Ideas 1) 2) 3) 4) 5)

Tool 4.2   Presentation Tool

to hear, understand, and receive your presentation. A review of the Communications Transaction Process (Figure 4.1) described earlier will be helpful at this stage.

Once you have identified goals, objectives, and key messages and analyzed your audience, you are ready to outline the presentation. Creating a written outline will help to keep the presentation organized and focused. It also helps you to prioritize information to accomplish your objectives. Details and tangents not supportive of your goals, objectives, and key messages should be left out. Simple storyboarding is a useful method of outlining. Storyboarding is a visual method that allows you to tell a story in sequence. Arranging your information in an outline format, in such a way that it tells a story, will be useful when you begin developing the presentation. Use a tool, like the one on the preceding page, to help plan your presentation.

This presentation tool will help you to outline, plan, and develop your presentations. The tool includes sections for presentation demographics including title, location, time, purpose, primary messages and target audience. Sections are also included for storyboarding and sequencing of your ideas. The main messages should be stated at the beginning, throughout the sequencing of ideas, and summarized once again at the end of the presentation.

Once you have prepared the draft of your presentation, practice, practice, practice! The best public speakers invest time in their presentations. Practicing your presentation may help you to discover areas that need to streamlined, moved or left out altogether. You may find that you need to clarify or add ideas. Practicing helps you to keep your presentation within the allotted time. It also helps you to feel at ease when the big day finally arrives.

Getting started is my biggest challenge. What can I do to get my presentation off to a great start?

Some of the most memorable points of successful presentations are delivered in the form of storytelling. An effective story, strategically placed at the beginning of a presentation, helps to engage the audience. Opening stories serve as icebreakers and attention grabbers. They relieve speaker anxiety by helping the speaker get rolling and they build audience desire and anticipation for the remainder of the presentation. Descriptive language in stories can help the audience to visualize important points of the message.

Stories that involve situations familiar to the audience help them to hear new information. Storytelling is an effective tool, but it must be used carefully. Stories should be clear, easy to understand, simple, brief and most important, pertinent to the presentation. They should connect to the audience and the message. Pausing to allow time for your audience to absorb the meaning of the story is as important as the story itself.

Audio-visual aids such as PowerPoint presentations (discussed next), videos, signage, props and written materials can serve to enhance your presentation. The use of audio-visual aids should be adapted to the learning styles of your audience. Learning styles may be grouped into three categories: auditory, visual and interactive. Auditory learners benefit most from hearing the message. They learn in situations where the presenter is talking. Visual learners prefer aids such as handouts, reports, images and visual outlines.

Interactive learners prefer situations where they are collaboratively working through exercises to receive and understand the messages.

Whether you are presenting to small or large audiences, the use of your voice is important. Delivery of the oral presentation should be done using a relaxed but steady tone. Proper pronunciation is important. Before your presentation, look up unfamiliar words, proper names of people and places, and learn how to pronounce them. Make pronunciation notes as a reminder. Summarize your main messages and learning objectives in the beginning. Tell your audience what you are going to talk about. Stay focused and avoid going off on tangents. Don't rush or read through the presentation. Talk about your points.

Relate to your audience by talking to them rather than through or at them. Maintain eye contact with a few individuals randomly located around the room. Visually monitor for audience engagement. Be sure to provide time for questions and feedback at the end. If a question is asked that you cannot answer, recognize the value of the question and be honest about the answer. Perhaps you can research it for them and communicate your findings at a later date or direct them to another resource. Each presentation is a learning experience, even for the best presenters. The most important things are to be prepared, sincere, and knowledgeable about your key messages.

TIPS FOR AUDIENCE ENGAGEMENT STRATEGIES

1. Refer to someone in the audience by name during your talk.
2. Arrive early. Engage other early audience members in a brief discussion. Use points from the discussion in your talk.
3. Ask someone in the audience a question.
4. Include a few interactive questions in your slides. People enjoy being quizzed.

How do you use technology as a tool to create both informative and engaging presentations?

Regardless of how large or how small your business, there will be ample opportunities for product or service presentations. Whether you are presenting to a board of directors or to a prospective customer, you want your presentation to leave a positive impression on your audience. Many times, this impression can determine the birth or the early death of an idea or a product line. So how do you, as a presenter, make the most of your presentation?

Microsoft PowerPoint is quickly becoming the accepted standard in business settings for presentation graphics. However, there are other software packages available such as Lotus's Freelance Graphics, Adobe Persuasion, Corel Presentations and more. All of the packages are very similar and the same guidelines can be applied. For the sake of simplicity, this chapter will refer to PowerPoint for illustration purposes.

How do you create a PowerPoint slide to hook your audience?

The first step in a presentation is to secure your audience's hunger to want to hear what you have to say. Audience involvement is a must to keep their interest and hopefully win their support. Most audiences rush to conclusions in the first two minutes of a presentation. If you fail to develop that strong introduction, then chances are you have failed to get their interest and consequently the rest of the presentation may fall on deaf ears. This is why the first slide in a PowerPoint presentation is so important. It should serve as a hook or bait for the audience to want to hear what follows.

How do you spark that interest? Creativity must come to the forefront. Many of you will say that you have no imagination or cleverness, but that is never the case. Some of us just have to work at it a bit harder than others. But everyone can be inventive enough to generate interest. Consider the following example. You are giving a sales pitch for a new electronic doorbell that has different chimes based on the time of day. Before you even approach the new doorbell, you spark the audience's interest by negating their opposition to something new. Examine the two slides below. Which one would entice you more to listen to the presentation?

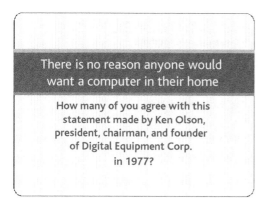 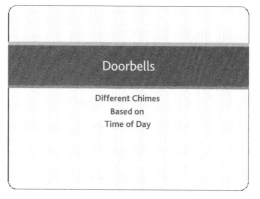

Figure 4.2 Attention Grabber Comparison

I think that you would agree that the home computer statement will get more response from your audience. People will start to voice their opinion (whether audibly or silently) that there are several reasons for home computers and this statement made by Mr. Olson has definitely proven not to be true. So then you follow up with a similar slide.

You want to make sure that you make the most of that first impression. Engage them with a relevant story (as mentioned

Figure 4.3 Alternate Attention Grabber

above), an appropriate humorous illustration or an alarming statistic. Once you have grabbed their attention, the hook is set. It is just a matter of reinforcing and maintaining that interest throughout your presentation. So, your first couple of slides should facilitate that process. Get the audience thinking about your product or idea before they even know all the details that will follow.

What is meant by the "Less is More" Principle?

The PowerPoint slides that follow that initial attention hook can also make or break your presentation. The key to remember when creating your slides is "less is more". You want your audience to listen to you and not read your slides. This is one of the few times when your English teacher's "always use complete sentences" rule is not to be followed. Audience members read at different speeds so slides that are packed with words can become an obstacle to them actually listening to your presentation. Compare these slides:

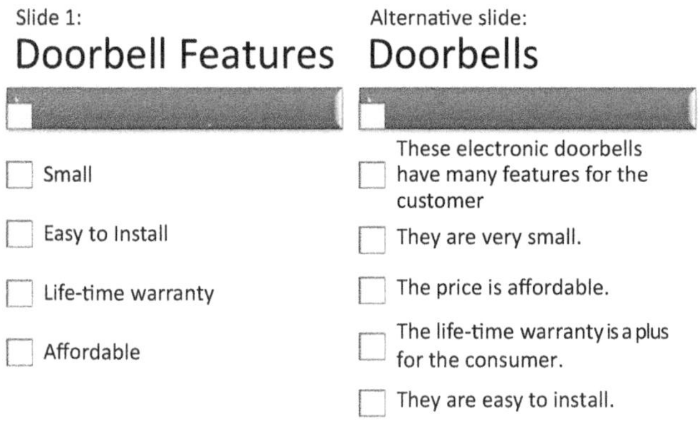

Figure 4.4   Less is More Principle

Both slides convey the same information to the audience. However, the slide on the left is much more concise and easy to read. The audience is made aware of the four features of the doorbells in one quick glance at the slide and then the attention is returned to you as the presenter to elaborate and give details about the various features. This supports the principle to remember, "less is more" when developing the slides' content. A rule of thumb is to follow the 6x6 rule (six or fewer words on six or fewer lines per slide) when possible.

Should I use the latest and greatest technology features in my presentation?

Always remember your overall purpose is to sell or promote your product or idea, not to sell PowerPoint software. Many times presenters think that they need to use the latest and greatest features of PowerPoint in their presentation. The members of your audience that are not familiar with PowerPoint might be impressed, but the majority of audience members in today's society have used PowerPoint and will probably not be the least impressed and might even bemoan your attempt to be a PowerPoint geek.

A slide packed full of graphics, sound effects or animations flying in from all directions demonstrates a lack of professionalism and seriousness about your presentation. On the other hand, a single doorbell chime sound accompanying the doorbell introduction slide would be very appropriate and would serve as a icebreaker to get the audience's attention and spark their interest in the upcoming presentation. So a simple word of caution would be to refrain from getting carried away with the PowerPoint software and stick to the basics of your content.

Should tables and charts be used in PowerPoint presentation slides?

Another pitfall to avoid is to show a slide and immediately say, "I know that this might be a little hard to read, but …" First of all, why is it difficult to read? You created the slide so if you knew that the content was not easy to see then make it a larger font so that it is readable from the audience's position. If this involves making your slide's content into two or three slides, then that should be done. Again, use as few words as possible. Avoid using charts and spreadsheets if the content becomes small on the slide. These can always be placed in a handout that can be distributed after your presentation. As was stated earlier in the chapter, the slide presentation should not be a reproduction of the presenter's content, but merely a tool that will keep the audience engaged and interested in what you, the presenter, are saying. Details and particulars should not be on the slides.

How do you use color and slide design to enhance your presentation?

What about color? Can this influence your audience's attention? The answer is definitely yes. There are multitudes of templates available for PowerPoint presentations and the generic template colors can be altered. As a presenter, peruse the templates and look for one that is appropriate for your audience/product. Consider these examples:

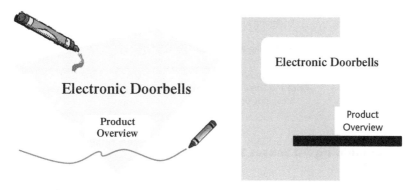

Figure 4.5   Slide Design Comparison

Both have the same content, but the one on the right is much more professional and appropriate for a product overview than the one with the crayon template. The audience's expectation of the presentation is automatically lowered when they see the crayons. Of course, if the presentation were introducing a new line of school supplies to a group of elementary school teachers, the crayon template would be acceptable, even preferable.

How much should I rely on slides during the presentation?

Another major drawback to using PowerPoint slides is when the presenter reads the slides to the audience. Sometimes this is definitely a temptation. Many presenters use the slides as a crutch and consequently find themselves reading to the audience. Avoid this at all costs. The audience members came to hear you and their interest is sparked when you are communicating and interacting with them and not just reading the slide content to them. Again, the slides should emphasize the main points of your presentation for the audience's benefit. You should know your subject well enough that you do not need the slides. A casual glance at a slide from time to time is fine. Constantly relying on them throughout the presentation is not recommended.

How can PowerPoint be used to keep my audience engaged?

Keeping the audience engaged and attentive can be tough, and with some audiences, the task becomes almost impossible. All audience inattentiveness cannot be placed on the presenter, but many times the presenter does play a huge role in creating this daydreaming atmosphere. Interesting slides that keep the audience involved can help to alleviate this problem. You, as a presenter, should try to keep the audience anticipating what will be shown next by displaying slide content in small sections. Examine the scenario shown below to promote a doorbell to the audience.

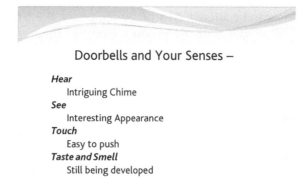

Figure 4.6   Combining All Senses Slides

This slide can be read in less than a minute and the audience already knows your sales pitch for the doorbell as it relates to the senses. So, they are now disengaged while listening to you explain this appeal in more detail. But, If you had kept them wondering how your doorbell and a particular sense were related, then their attention span would be heightened. Now consider the following examples:

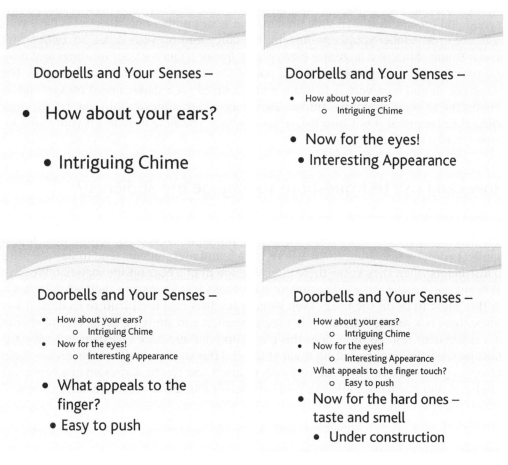

Figure 4.7   Engaging Audience Slides

Each slide gives the audience a view of the different senses and its related appeal. Note that the previous senses are repeated on each slide for reinforcement. By the time the taste and smell senses are the only ones missing, your audience is on the edge of their seats wondering what a doorbell can do for the nose and taste buds. As a presenter, you can pause between the slides and ask for audience input. What type of sound is charming to the ears? What type of color or shapes would a typical visitor like to see in your home's doorbell? Audience members are giving you suggestions and everyone is interested in how your doorbell is different. Hopefully, you have some sample doorbells to show to your audience as they are looking at the slides and thinking of a particular sense appeal. Then the final two senses are introduced. But, as the audience soon finds out, it is still up to their imagination. You have been able to capture their attention throughout the complete presentation and they will remember the three senses included.

Should I change the font on my slides?

This answer is debatable. We have all heard that variety is the spice of life and that change is good. But for a professional slide presentation your number one objective is have your audience to remember your content—not the fancy font on your slides. So, once again, keep it simple. Stick to a large size font—thirty-five or larger for your headings and titles and twenty-eight or larger type for your points. Use a simple easy-to-read font style. The font color should be a very light color and displayed on a dark-colored background. It is tempting to cram more lines into a slide by using a smaller size font, but refrain from doing this. Lengthen it out into two or more slides. The slide is useless if your audience cannot read it comfortably.

How can I use test questions to engage my audience?

As stated throughout this chapter, audience engagement and participation are important. You want audience members listening to your presentation and not letting their minds wander to other areas. Educational experts have found that students tend to stay attentive to instructors when they know there is an assessment or a quiz on the material. We have all heard the question that every student has voiced at least once in their school years— "Is this going to be on the test?" Even though teachers find it difficult to swallow many times, there is a strong correlation between listening and studying based on the chance of a subsequent test. So, how does this play into your audience's participation? For the most part, you will not be testing them at the end but you can scatter a few review slides into your presentation. These are very easy to insert and can be addressed in a very short timeframe and normally audiences find themselves trying to guess the correct answer.

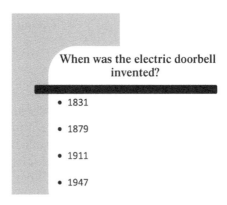

Figure 4.8   Quiz Question Slide

You could have actually informed the audience of this tidbit earlier or you might use it as a springboard into the doorbell discussion. Either way, your audience is put to the test to try to remember and/or guess when the doorbell came into existence. This slide gives them four options from which to choose. This is much more effective than just asking the question with no choices provided. You might have them discuss the choices with a partner or a group and come to a consensus or use it as an individual exercise. Then by simply clicking to the next slide, it appears to the audience that this slide has changed with the correct answer highlighted.

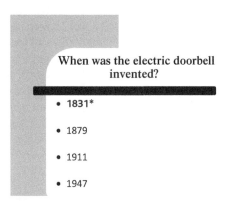

Figure 4.9   Quiz Answer Slide

Should my slide presentation have hyperlinks to Internet sites?

This is another debatable area. With the onslaught of the Internet, businesses and individuals are relying on it more and more. Information on millions of topics is literally at your fingertips by using the virtual world. It is very tempting for the presenter to include a hyperlink in the presentation that would link up to a website that lends itself nicely to the topic at hand. But, while you are presenting there is no need to have a network connection. This is an added distraction that can disrupt your presentation's flow. Do your homework and research the topic before your presentation. If you find a website that is of direct interest to your topic and will positively enhance your presentation, then place that content on your slides and include the link as a resource in handouts that you distribute after the talk. Refrain from clicking on a link to open a site during the talk.

Should I use slide transitions and animations?

PowerPoint is noted for its movement of information and graphics on the slide. These features might be helpful for a simple commercial or a presentation intended for young audiences. They should be used judiciously in a professional presentation. Audiences tire out quickly and are distracted with movement on the slide and the important text is often overlooked. However, the 'appear' animation effect is useful in some cases. This feature allows each point to appear after a certain amount of time (timing preset) or when you click the mouse. This is helpful when you do not wish for your audience to read ahead. Be very careful in preset timing since you run the risk of talking ahead or behind your points. Rapid clicking to catch up can be very distracting.

What comes after the slide show is prepared and before the presentation is given?

This question can be answered in one word—practice. Rehearse your presentation from start to finish until you know which slide is coming next and feel extremely comfortable with the sequence. Have a hard copy of your presentation in front of you during the show and use the speaker note section for reminders. Never be guilty of covering a topic and then finding a slide that addresses this issue five minutes later. Have your speech and your slide show in sync with one another. It should be new material for your audience, but certainly not for you. If at all possible, practice the slide show in the room in which you are presenting and use the equipment that you will be using in the actual presentation. Hardware and software can be tricky at times and often some tweaking must be done to make it function as it did on your equipment back at the office.

Finally, you need to always ask yourself what if the projector breaks and what if the laptop crashes. Do you have a Plan B in mind? Having paper copies handy and transparencies with an overhead projector has saved many presentations from being a lost cause when equipment failed. Be prepared, expect the worst and hope that you do not have to use your back-ups.

TIP: POWER POINT PRESENTATION SUMMARY

1. Hook your audience from the beginning.
2. Keep them engaged and waiting on the next slide.
3. Follow the 6x6 rule.
4. Use colors that contrast for easy reading.
5. Use fonts that are large enough to be seen in the room setting.
6. Use of sound and clip art should enhance and complement text, not overwhelm it.
7. Do your research and practice your presentation
8. Have a back-up plan (just in case)

How do I apply these communications techniques to actually running my organization?

Having come this far, you now have a communications arsenal at your disposal. It's time to put it to work on some tough organizational issues. Have you ever played the game "Hear What I Say?" Players sit in a circle and you begin by whispering a message to the person next to you. Your message is whispered from one person to the next, but by the time it gets back to you, it is dramatically altered. The final message can be rather comical in a game setting. However, organizational communication frequently works the same way and the results may not be amusing.

Managers must have good processes in place to ensure that everyone is sending and receiving messages that are consistent with the mission and vision of the organization.

Work efforts are fragmented and costly when employees do not have a consistent understanding of company goals, objectives and strategies.

Business is all about transactions between people. Successful managers understand and strive to build good linkages between their workers and the mission, goals and work of the organization. As stated at the beginning of this chapter, effective communication is an important tool used to develop and maintain essential linkages. Managers who understand the formal and informal culture of their organizations can more effectively guide the linkage process.

Lee Bolman and Terence Deal in their 2003 book *Reframing Organizations: Artistry, Choice and Leadership*, describe four different ways to view or frame organizations:

1. Structurally framed organizations focus on accomplishments of goals and objectives through formally organized divisions of labor and effective processes of coordination and control. They have written rules and policies, and clearly defined lines of authority.
2. Human resource framed organizations focus on people and the organization. They strive to hire people who are the best fit, emphasize employee value, and seek to serve employee needs. Managers of human resource framed organizations seek to understand employees and employee groups. Informal structures can be very influential in human resource framed organizations.
3. Politically framed organizations focus on internal competition for scarce resources. Internal conflict is inevitable. The success of these organizations relies on coalitions of individuals, jockeying for position, bargaining, and negotiating among stakeholders.
4. The symbolic frame involves the history, stories, symbols, ceremonies, rituals, heroes, and heroines of an organization. Members of symbolically framed companies have deeply rooted connections to their organizations.

Active listening will help you to better understand the multiple dimensions of your organizational culture. While the leaders of the organization set the tone for the formal organizational culture, there are a variety of other influences as well. Subgroups may have a profound effect on organizational culture.

Most organizations can be viewed through more than one cultural frame at any given time. Understanding the culture can help you to develop more effective strategies to communicate with and lead your employees. Recognizing the elements of your organizational culture helps you to develop more effective communications messages. It also helps you to select appropriate forms and channels of communication.

How can communication help my organization deal with change?

Change is inevitable. As a matter of fact, it is vital to the life of the organization. Successful organizations anticipate and respond to industry and marketplace changes. Organizations are comprised of individuals with a variety of abilities to respond to change. Spencer Johnson, author of *Who Moved My Cheese (2002)*, described two different types of people in organizations: those who seek change, and those who prefer familiarity. Most organizations are made up of both types of individuals making transitions through change especially challenging. Individuals who continually seek change may find dead ends for some of their ideas. While they can quickly adapt or readjust, the rest of the organization may resist even the most basic change.

The transitions of a changing organization can be invigorating or devastating, depending upon the communications skills of the managers and leaders. In *Managing Transitions: Making the Most of Change*, William Bridges (2004) describes three stages of organizational transitions. The phases include: 1) the ending or letting go of the old, 2) the neutral or in-between time, and 3) the new beginning.

During the first phase, people struggle with loss or letting go of what they once knew. Employees may be in various stages of grieving. Two-way communication is very important. Employees need information and they need a way to give constructive feedback. Managers should provide opportunities for people to grieve in productive ways. Consideration of what is being lost, recognition of the values of the organization and transparency about the changes are helpful. Individuals respond favorably to managerial characteristics such as compassion, strength, honesty, leadership, credibility and trustworthiness. Written formal communications and consistent key messages combined with interpersonal active listening are useful strategies.

William Bridges calls the second stage of this transition the neutral zone. It is the optimal period for reshaping new behaviors and strategies. The neutral zone is a time when managers should strive to help people see the new vision of the organization. During this phase, companies may lose valuable employees who fail to see or who disagree with the new direction of the company. Frequent and consistent communication about where the organization is headed is beneficial. In addition to formal communications, group forums and one-to-one communication strategies should be employed.

In the third phase, the organization takes on a new identity. A new beginning is the time to motivate the organization and generate new energy. Consistent messages in communication are important. Managers should continue to help employees see the vision and understand the direction of the company. Recognition and celebration of successes are important. Written communications such as mission, vision, and values statements, strategic plans, goals and objectives, and performance data are important tools. Remember, communicate well and communicate often. Reinforcing the new message and clearly communicating the new vision will help your organization to move forward.

Additional Resources

There are many associations and organizations providing resources for organizational communication including:

- The Association for Business Communication (ABC) is an international, interdisciplinary organization committed to advancing business communication research, education and practice.
- The International Communication Association is an academic association for scholars dedicated to the teaching and application of all aspects of human and mediated communication.

- Help with business writing, grammar, and visual and graphic aides include:
  - The Purdue Online Writing Lab website provides information about effective business writing.
  - *The AMA Handbook of Business Writing* published by the American Management Association is a comprehensive guide to style, grammar, punctuation, usage and formatting. The book includes sample business documents.
  - *The Elements of Style* written by William Strunk Jr. and E. B. White and published most recently by Allyn and Bacon is an easy-to-read guide to writing.

References

Bridges, W. (2004). *Transitions: Making Sense of Life's Changes*. 25th Anniversary Edition. Philadelphia, PA: DaCapo Press.

Bolman, L. and Deal, T. (2003). *Reframing Organizations: Artistry, Choice, and Leadership*. Third Edition. San Francisco, CA: John Wiley and Sons, Inc. Jossey-Bass Publishers.

Clampitt, P. (2000). *Communicating for Managerial Effectiveness*. Thousand Oaks, CA: Sage Publications.

Covey, S. (1989). *Seven Habits of Highly Effective People*. Fireside. New York, NY: Simon and Schuster.

Johnson, S. (2002). *Who Moved My Cheese?* New York, NY: G. P. Putnam's Sons.

5 *Strategy*

ERIC BOLLAND and JERRY WELLMAN

There is no absolute agreement on the definition of strategy. Some argue that a strategy is a plan of action for accomplishing a specific intent. This definition, rooted in the notion of planning, may well be derived from the military view of strategy, the art of combining and employing the means of war. The word strategy derives from the Greek "art of the general." Others view strategy as a vision about some end state or desired industry position, a definition that emphasizes the goal itself rather than the plan for accomplishing the goal.

Founders of strategic management have defined strategy in different terms but related concepts. H. Igor Ansoff (1965) calls it a common thread among the organization's activities, products and markets that defines the business now and what it will become in the future. Charles Hofer and Dan Schendel (1978) define strategy as the "fundamental pattern of present and planned resource deployments and environmental interactions that indicates how the organization will achieve its objectives."

Our purpose in this chapter is a practical one and starts with an exploration of what is strategy and then moves through the tools of strategic management. It is not necessary to have a definitive definition of strategy to accomplish this.

What cannot be denied is that strategy matters. Strategy is important because a powerful strategy leads to sustainable competitive advantage. Gary Hamel and C. K. Prahalad (1994) write about the importance of strategic intent. Firms with a clear strategic intent are more likely to be financially successful than less focused competitors. Having a suitable strategy clarifies an organization's purpose, aligns goals with efforts, improves efficiency and helps maintain a sense of direction during difficult times. It also provides a framework for prioritization and decision making.

Strategy choices have a direct impact on corporate performance. The Profit Impact of Market Strategies (PIMS) studies conducted by Robert Buzell and Bradley Gale (1987), which tracked the performance of several thousand business units, established that strategy is connected to profits. Other more contemporary research has solidified this connection.

This chapter offers you templates for developing and assessing the merits of specific strategies. Guidance is offered to answer questions such as: What should our strategy be? How should it be developed, implemented and changed? It starts with a look at the fundamental question of what should be the organization's strategy.

What should my strategy be?

Every business organization has a strategy. Even if it is not articulated, formally devised or evaluated. There is a strategy. Taken broadly, strategy is the path toward an organization's

Table 5.1   Strategy Choices

Strategy Choice	Description	When Used
Share Increasing	Increase business market share	Emerging industries, e.g. wind energy
Growth	Maintain position in a growing industry	Appropriate for new ventures in young industries e.g. iPhone applications
Profitability	Optimize profits, reduce costs, maximize sales	Appropriate for mature industries e.g. most retail stores
Market Concentration	Focus on underserved markets. Realign operations to fit new market conditions. Serve a niche market	When strategy reformulation is needed e.g. Starbucks
Turnaround	Reverse poor performance	Industry is in general decline with many companies struggling
Divestiture	Sell off profitable operations and liquidate the business	Industry is in decline with no growth, companies exiting e.g. landline telephone

goals. That path may involve an intensive examination of the external environment and internal operations which results in a formal strategy formulation process or it may be the passive acceptance of circumstances as they are with a goal of mere survival. Either way, or something in between, the organization that has a goal has a strategy.

If you are trying to establish a strategy, the question is what are your choices? The following guide describes several common generic or grand strategies and explains the circumstances of their use. This table shows the breadth of corporate level strategies that might be available.

The strategy choices just described are not the only generic strategies available. Michael Porter (1980) has described three generic strategies as well. These are very broad level strategies which take the competitive context into consideration and which are less defined by industry factors. Porter's three strategies are:

- Overall low cost leadership: This strategy emphasizes driving down costs, seeking cost reductions in operations and gaining efficiencies in operations. These actions produce lower product costs for customers. This strategy is very useful in a market crowded with competitors and when supplier costs can be controlled. The challenge with using this strategy is to maintain product quality while the costs of production are minimized. Wal-Mart is a good example of this strategy's use.
- Differentiation: This generic strategy aims at sufficiently differentiating the product or service in the eyes of the customers and the industry until it can be regarded as unique. The basis for differentiation can be brand, technology and innovation as well as service and support. This strategy works well in businesses that are not commodity providers. It works for companies that have more complex products where there is considerable value added along the way in the production process. The challenge for differentiators is to determine just how much to differentiate a product or service. Too much is unneeded and costly. Too little is not enough to win preference in

the marketplace. If you employ a differentiation strategy, you need to know your customers well and be able to deliver the right message effectively. Sony Electronics uses differentiation effectively.

- Focus: This generic strategy is marked by a concentration on a distinct segment of the market. When the segment is identified, it is served very well by those who are successful with this strategy. You could consider this to be a kind of 'customer is king' approach. There is a strong emphasis on customer relationship management and building customer loyalty. Focus strategies work well in market segments that have been passed up by others because they are too costly to serve, too remote geographically or simply not seen as being worthwhile. As an example of this strategy, McMaster-Carr focuses on the segment of the business market that needs industrial supplies quickly. Their specialty is immediate product delivery.

- These three additional strategy choices round out this section and demonstrate that even on a wide generic basis, there are many strategy choices available to you. Since different strategies are appropriate for different circumstances, all of these choices need to be examined as possible strategy choices.

How do we make sure our strategy is right for our circumstances?

Developing a strategy, no matter how satisfactory, by looking only internally is doing half the job. Your strategy has to fit the circumstances, or more appropriately, your external environment. This environment does not mean the natural environment, though that is an element of it. It means a fit with the larger environment in which the organization does business. An organization's environment means those aspects outside the structure that have an effect on the organization's performance, yet cannot be directly controlled by the organization.

To make sure the strategy is right for the environment, the organization needs to do an external analysis of environmental factors. In order to be comprehensive about the factors in the environment, use the broad based external analysis tool (Tool 5.1). This tool may seem conventional but it is revealing. The external analysis tool is comprised of a number of different perspectives that, taken together, offer an integrated picture of the organization's external environment.

The factors considered in the tool are:

1. Socio-Cultural
   This factor deals with social and cultural elements that may have an impact on operations. Social factors include consumer preferences and changes in those preferences. Cultural factors are the shared language, values, beliefs and norms that comprise an identified culture that differentiates it from other cultures. Subcultures exist within larger cultures that may have separate tastes and preferences. For example, subcultures abound within the larger Hispanic culture.
2. Political-Legal
   Political-Legal considers the impact of government, the political system and the legal system on an organization's operations.

3. Economic
    Economic factors are macro and microeconomic factors including supply and demand for the product. It does not deal with prices, since prices are often brief manifestations of market exchanges. Macroeconomic factors such as Gross Domestic Product (GDP) are important also. Economic policy is covered in the political-legal factor. Financial elements such as the cost of capital are included in this category.
4. Technology
    Broadly speaking, technology consists of the body of knowledge and tools with which we deal with the natural environment. Technology aims at making work and life easier for us as a species. Technology cannot be limited to just devices. It must also include human processes adopted for the same aims. High technology is often thought of in this context because it is rapidly transforming the way work is done but less glamorous technology also has an impact such as copper telephone wire carrying DSL.
5. Natural
    This factor deals with the natural world, the resources used that originate from the Earth and are returned to it. The disciplines of geology, oceanography, climatology, meteorology, among other fields, are devoted to the study of the natural world. Very often, issues such as recycling, pollution, conservation and reduction of the carbon footprint are associated with the natural factor.
6. Demographics
    Demographics include the many dimensions of human population: number, age distribution, gender, location, income, household size and family life cycle stage. Demographics are a slower changing element of the environment but they are predictable. Future population growth can be accurately estimated from upcoming age cohort fertility rates.
7. Global
    The global factor impacts all of the previously listed factors, but because globalism is now so pervasive, affecting all different sizes of companies wherever they are located, it merits its own heading. A progressively intertwined world economy including a sophisticated international financial system means financial transactions throughout the world have implications for local businesses. For example, the recession of 2007–09 was one with worldwide repercussions. Another global issue is the supply and composition of the labor force. The same applies for trade policies. Governments play major roles in the purchase of goods and services in the global market. The competition between Boeing and Airbus for commercial aircraft sales involved numerous governments trying to help their domestic firms. The big emerging markets in Asia and South America will reshape consumption everywhere.

These are the major external environmental factors. The following external analysis tool, will let you capture the essential elements of these varied but consequential factors in a single template.

Factor	Key Influencers	Trend	Importance	Actions
Socio-Cultural				
Political-Legal				
Economic				
Technological				
Natural				
Demographic				
Global				

Tool 5.1   External Analysis Tool

"Key influencers" are those factors that will have the most impact on your operations in each of the categories. Commonly, a five-year horizon is used. You can derive key influencers by doing an environmental scan. To do this, you simply run a Google search of the category and pick out prominent themes about the future. To make it manageable, you may have to limit your search geographically or make the topic much more specific to your business. A count of appearances of a topic is a way of filling the template. For example, you may find five articles on the need to design recycled coffee cups. Then you would place something like "Need to recycle coffee cups-5" in the natural category.
In the trend column, you can note whether the trend is positive, negative or neutral with respect to your organization. A positive trend might be increasing target market demand.

"Importance" is a summary point for both the trend and key influencer columns. It will enable you to identify the most consequential environmental factors, those that you will need to be most concerned with over the next five years. These can be rank ordered one to seven with one being the highest importance factor.

The last column, "Actions," contains instructions on what your organization needs to do about the category. This is an area where you alert yourselves to what may happen to your business as a result of the separate external factors.

The completed template itself then becomes a single source document for your external environment analysis. It ties together the most important information with your organization's possible responses.

How should we consider the interaction of external factors in determining strategy?

The factors assessed previously are only part of the external analysis. These factors and others are not totally independent and static. To cope with the dynamic nature of an organization's environment, Michael Porter devised the Five Forces Model (1980). It is very popular and is well accepted by strategic planners. This model can be used to evaluate competitive factors and supplier and buyer influences, more so than the external analysis tool even though it is more difficult to apply.

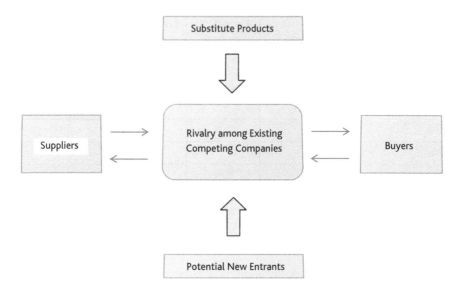

Figure 5.1   Five Forces Model

This model lets the user combine elements of competition (substitute products, new entrants and competitor rivalry) with the pushes and pulls from customers and suppliers. In the past, these were not recognized as forces. For example, industry analysis consisted of describing industries as fragmented or concentrated. The Porter model makes it much more dynamic and interactive.

You can put this model to work by dissecting each of the five forces and considering their impact on your business. The forces come together in the middle where competitors are seeking to gain an advantage over other competitors. Refer to chapter nine for more details on competition and the competitive environment.

In the central fray, actually more a melee, the existing firms will compete with single or multiple firms. There is more rivalry among companies when they are equal in size, when demand is slow, when price is used to win customers and when it costs a lot for a customer to switch from one provider to another. There are other competitive aspects as well but this identifies some of the key ones.

Considering the supplier element, the power of the suppliers affects the producers. If suppliers are few in number and they have access to raw materials that the producers cannot get themselves, they have considerable power in the model. They can be price setters, not price takers and can choose the provider firm with which to work. Suppliers are weak if they are many in number and the producer firms are few. This is the particular competitive advantage that Wal-Mart developed over its suppliers.

A similar thing happens with customers. When buyers order large quantities and consume most of the provider's output, they have real power over the provider companies. They can use their leverage and can specify terms of sales. These customers can be individuals or they can be businesses.

Another element of the model is the potential for new competitors to enter the market. A potential competitor may have a much more efficient way of producing something and the existing firms could have assets invested in more traditional production methods.

The existing firms will be driven to maximize asset utilization rather than innovation. That is a new entrant's advantage.

Lastly, there may be a shift in the entire market to substitute products. This is a quantum shift that affects all current competitors. It relegates existing technology, in the way products are produced or in the product itself, to a path of obsolescence. New technologies constantly feed this possibility. In consumer electronics, the effects of substitute products are felt constantly as new generations of communication devices replace older versions. The use of a new technology is an advantage for the new entrant if that new entrant can use the technology to create a substitute product.

You can use the Porter model at many different levels. At the most basic level, you would name and number the firms in the rivalry center. Then you would explore the outer elements. Suppliers would be named and counted. The same would be done for customers. You can make notations on the possibility of new entrants and substitute products. One of the strengths of this model is that you can build from this very basic level. You can use the tools from chapter nine on competition to evaluate the threat of new entrants and the extent of the rivalry among existing firms. Market shares of existing firms can be overlaid on the model to get a richer depiction of the competitors themselves.

On the supplier side, you can consider and plot their relative power over other suppliers and over your business. A similar approach can be taken with customers. Overall, the model can give you a good idea if the competitive dynamics are largely inside or outside the core circle of rivalry. The influence of customers and suppliers can be gauged to determine which of these might be the bigger driver of rivalry. The influence of new entrants and substitutes, or the combined effects of these (for example: all the substitute products originate from new entrants) can be assessed too. Lastly, the model can be used over time to see what year-to-year changes have happened.

How should we evaluate internal factors in developing strategy?

The previous question dealt largely with external factors in strategy choice. This section deals with internal considerations. What are our internal strengths? How valuable are our resources? The approach taken to this issue stems from the resource-based theory of the firm. Application of this theory will help answer the question about evaluating internal factors. The evaluation of internal factors is a keystone to completing the process of strategy making.

The way to do the internal analysis is to consider three main types of resources:

- Tangible assets that are real property, equipment, production and other facilities as well as financial resources.
- Intangible assets are resources, which cannot be measured readily but are nonetheless important. The knowledge held by the organization's employees, patents, trademarks or practices that can't be easily duplicated and the brand are resources that fall into this category.

- Organizational capabilities are the third and least tangible of all. They too are resources. The skills of the organization are a key factor. A skill may be the way a self-directed work team finds a way of making a better cell phone.

To do the internal analysis, you will need to sort your collective resources into these three categories and then determine the value of each. You will be mixing quantitative (mainly tangible resources) with qualitative resources (mainly intangible and organizational capabilities categories.) The qualitative and quantitative elements can be mixed using scoring. For example you can use a score between one and five for the aggregated tangible resources and similar scales for the other categories.

Is our company stronger or weaker than other firms?

For this, a comparison can be made between your company and industry level reported averages. This is easily done for the tangible resources using industry reports and stock analyses. Judgment may be needed in the other categories. That would consist of setting up an expert panel of individuals within your organization who could provide a clear point of view on the matter in addition to other strategies.

To help determine the value of your resources, you should make decisions about how much customers truly believe your product is necessary, how unique the product is, how easily it might be duplicated (consider substitute products), switching costs (their cost in switching to a new provider) and other screening factors you deem appropriate.

The preceding exercise will help you get a clearer picture of your internal strengths that is more than a one-dimensional guess about where you stand on internal resources. This can be helpful in developing your SWOT analysis, discussed in detail later in this chapter.

How do we determine if our operations are contributing to our higher-level strategic goals?

In elementary terms, an organization, including yours, takes inputs, makes transformations that presumably add value, and produces outputs in the form of finished products or completed services. This depiction is key to another internal analysis tool: the value chain analysis. In the following diagram, derived from Michael Porter, the staff functions (administrative) are separated from the line functions (mainly production) and the individual components are evaluated in terms of how much value they are adding.

The staff element adds value but its value is spread throughout all aspects of production. It is often less obvious where the staff element is figured into the value chain. On the line or production side, it is more evident where closer involvement in the production process occurs and that is shown in columns in the tool.

To make this work for you, staff functions can be translated into units of time and valued in accordance with the percentage of time associated with each item produced. The time can then be used to develop a labor cost per time calculation. As an example, one hour of human resource director time may be used for product A when that time is spread from the input to the exit point. For the line functions, the costs associated with

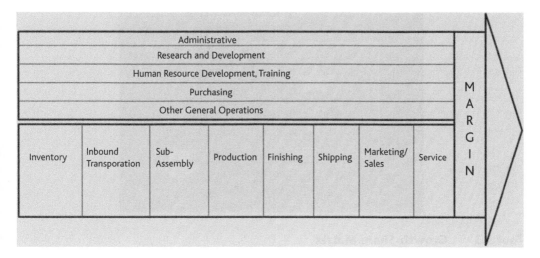

Tool 5.2   Value Chain

each of the functions (for example, operations) is calculated using a per unit or a per service basis.

At the very end of the value chain, at the output side, there may be a margin addition to both the staff and line elements. The margin can be and most often is a percentage increase over the aggregated costs. It is frequently used as a cushion to absorb unexpected costs.

The value chain analysis tool itself presents a holistic approach to the organization, something that strategy is supposed to do. It also identifies discrete points of value added to the organizational process. It can identify less efficient areas of the organization in addition to more efficient areas.

All the activities of the organization must be identified. It is also necessary to do the appropriate allocation of costs to these activities. Your organization will need to establish the cost of its labor for all jobs connected to the products or services provided. This can be done directly if your organization tracks such costs or it may be estimated using industry data sources. You will also need to customize the general value chain analysis tool to your specific operations.

If we have a lot of products or services, how can we best manage these?

For established companies that have a mix of products and services (perhaps even too many), an effective tool to use is the Growth-Share matrix that was developed by the Boston Consulting Group in 1968. The tool allows for the strategic management of the product mix.

This matrix is based on two important dimensions, industry attractiveness and relative market share position (also often plotted as relative strengths of the business. The matrix lets you find your product's place in this map. The idea is that not all products are equal in terms of the bottom-line. Some are contributing more to revenue and profitability

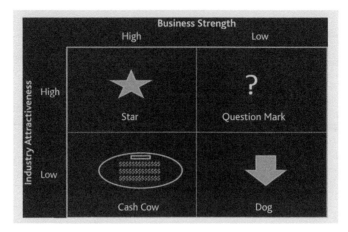

Tool 5.3   Growth-Share Matrix

while some are contributing less. With the Growth-Share Matrix, you can sort this out visually and strategically.

The industry attractiveness axis of the matrix is based on factors such as industry profitability, growth and size. The difference between high and low is often based on judgment. Choose a demarcation point in the middle of the range. If profitability is the sole criteria and the industry level profitability is 8%, then the demarcation point is 4%. Multiple criteria are most often used and when they are, the criteria are weighted and aggregated to determine the demarcation point. Separating high and low on either dimension cannot be done precisely but it should be estimated as closely as possible to make the tool useful. Industry forecasts, for example those done by trade publications and stock analyses, are a couple of sources for industry attractiveness data.

For business strength or relative market share, do an internal assessment of your organization. This can often be accomplished in an internal planning session of informed leaders. Some factors to consider would be product quality, relative market share, marketing effectiveness and customer relationships. This is done in a competitive context, so you rate yourself in comparison to major competitors. These competitors provide the range and you rate yourself on that range in similar fashion based on the industry attractiveness criteria. Honesty is the best policy in doing this so you should avoid the tendency to overstate internal strengths. Having objective outsiders review your internal analysis often helps.

You can now plot the positions of your own products in the product mix. In the question mark quadrant, the industry as a whole indicates growth opportunities but business strengths are low and may require cash to realize their potential. These products are on the edge. They can succeed or fail. They are very much question marks or may also be called problem children with possibilities. In the star quadrant, there is high industry attractiveness and your business has considerable strength regarding the product. This is the shift from a question mark to a successful sector.

The cash cow quadrant takes in products supported by high business strength but lower industry attractiveness. These products may be past their prime and later in the product life cycle and may be relegated to the animal kingdom of low industry attractiveness.

In the dog sector, where there is both low industry attractiveness and low business strength, reside candidates for termination. An honest use of this tool may produce many kennel kin.

When you plot the Growth-Share Matrix, you will likely want to seek balance in your mix of products. Essentially, the product life cycle of introduction-growth-maturity and decline can be superimposed on the matrix as a product moves from question mark to star to cash cow to dog.

The cash cow and star products can be used to fund question marks. The dog products can be terminated to shift resources to emerging products. If you find you have the great majority of products in a single quadrant, the risk is high of failing to have a diversified product mix. If the balance of your business is in a low growth industry, it is time to re-evaluate your industry strategy. The matrix helps clarify your competitive position while also highlighting where to shift resources. There are other matrices that have been built from this one including the GE model and the Hofer Life Cycle Matrix. These add sophistication to the simple matrix presented here.

Is our current strategy working?

Current strategy is working if it is resulting in progress toward goals or accomplishment of goals. This seems obvious but it can be explained in more detail by conducting a strategy evaluation.

Company strategies need to be constantly evaluated in light of new developments in the external environment. New competitors may be coming into the market. Some especially innovative technology might be poised to replace the way you are manufacturing products. Internal conditions may change too, requiring a new look at current strategy.

A well-established tool to use in evaluating strategy and, in fact, for establishing an initial strategy is the SWOT analysis. SWOT is an acronym for strengths, weaknesses, opportunities and threats. Strengths and weaknesses apply within organizations. Opportunities and threats occur outside organizations. Thus, the SWOT tool considers internal and external factors that create a simple yet revealing overview of the entire strategic situation. It is a qualitative tool that produces a picture of your strategic choices with respect to the larger environment. What you are aiming for is a good fit between the internal direction and external forces. A good fit means that the ship of your present strategy is making headway in the currents, tides and weather of the uncertain ocean.

To do a SWOT analysis, you will need to put together a small team of well-informed decision makers. Often, this occurs at strategic planning retreats. A neutral facilitator will ask the team to first list in short phrases, the current business strengths. Then they will do the same for the current weaknesses. The discussion will then shift to the outside and the question will be: what are outside opportunities and outside threats?

A strength, for the purposes of a SWOT analysis, is a specific advantage that you may have over competitors currently—something that you can control that is meaningful to customers. A weakness is the opposite, a deficiency in your present capabilities or resources with respect to competitors or something known to be a deficiency.

Looking outside, an opportunity is something happening in your market that is favorable but not currently exploited. A threat is something happening in your market that could impose a difficulty on current or anticipated strategic activities.

The next step in the analysis is to determine if the strengths exceed the weaknesses. This is best done by evaluating each of the strengths for factors like duration, distinctiveness and value. The weaknesses are evaluated as well. The comparison between strengths and weaknesses can also be done by a simple count and if the number of strengths is greater than the number of weakness, the organization is in a strong internal position.

The same kind of approach is taken with external opportunities and threats. As a last step, the results of the strengths and weaknesses assessment are compared to the opportunities and threats. If the internal side is strongly positive compared to the external side, you are prepared to respond to the environment. If not, you have identified the areas where work is needed.

Let's look at an example. You are operating a bicycle sales and repair shop in a city with a population of 200,000 with a trade area of one hundred square miles. There are five other such bicycle shops you consider to be competitors in the market.

Internal Strengths	External Opportunities
1. Positive cash flow and financial resources. 2. Respected sales and repair staff. 3. Effective management. 4. Very satisfied customers. 5. Broad bicycle line.	6. Expansion into other cities due to low cost of real estate. 7. Some competitors may be going out of business.
Internal Weaknesses	External Threats
1. High labor costs relative to competitors.	1. Entry of lower cost bikes from international competitors. 2. Five other established competitors.

Tool 5.4   SWOT Analysis

In this example, the strengths exceed the weaknesses and the external opportunities exceed the threats on the basis of counts. Internal positive factors surpass external factors so this shop is in a strong market position based on counting the elements in the grid. This simple example is one way of getting started with a SWOT analysis. It can be made more sophisticated by evaluating the strength of each element. For example, you could investigate how high the labor costs are relative to competitors. If you want to expand the simple SWOT, the criteria you use for doing so should be clear, manageable and few in number so that the tool will provide guidance, not confusion.

How do we formulate a strategy?

The answer to this question addresses the real nitty-gritty of strategy. There are many different models for strategy formulation and reformulation. In the practical and academic models, there are several critical characteristics that we will use as a guide. The first is that the strategy takes a look at internal and external factors, a theme repeated many times in this chapter. The second is that internal and external factors are reconciled. Third, there is a specific data and judgment based process used to shape a strategy. Current resources are identified and resources that are needed to meet strategic goals are stated. Gaps are identified and addressed between desired and actual conditions.

Those are the parts but how do they fit together? Some companies use formalized strategic planning processes while others are less formal. New firms and small firms tend to have far less formalized methods. Our advice is to use a process in which all functional areas of the organization have substantive input into the process. It should not be done solely at the top of the organization.

The process that follows identifies the steps, players and questions to be considered. These include:

1. Review of Current Strategy. Done by all managers. Often done in an executive strategic planning session. Have all levels of our strategy worked?
2. Environmental Analysis. Done by research analysts, consultants or executives. Most often done by staff or consultants. The outcome is the environmental analysis described earlier. What do we need to do in our environment?
3. Internal Analysis. Done by staff research analysts, functional area managers, consultants and executives. SWOT analysis can be used for this. What competitive advantages do we have?
4. Integration of External and Internal Analysis. Done at the executive level with functional level involvement. How do we leverage our internal strengths to best exploit opportunities in the external environment?
5. Resource Inventory. Considers all resources available or those that can be acquired. Done at the executive level with involvement of other management levels. What resources do we have or can we get to reach our organizational goals?
6. Gap Analysis. Done at the executive level. Is there a difference between what we want to achieve and what we can achieve and how can we close the gap if there is one?
7. Strategy Options. Done at the executive level with input from functional level managers using the strategy choice template described earlier. What should our core strategy be?
8. Strategy Decision. Done by executives. Product of the effort is strategy direction or redirection.
9. Implementation and Communication. Done by executives, managers, supervisors and staff. How can we achieve organizational commitment?

An important point about this process is that it needs to be done periodically, perhaps not as frequently as every year but certainly not as infrequently as every five years. New environmental factors must be evaluated and changing corporate level strengths and weaknesses must be taken into account.

Who should formulate strategy?

In the strategy making process described above, the principal players are identified in each of the stages. Strategy formulation should not be restricted to the upper levels of management. For small firms and flat structured organizations, this is a theoretical and moot point but organizations grow and the issue of who decides strategy occurs.

Strategy happens at every level of the organization, so if you have levels, even two levels, there is strategy happening. Generally, strategy can be divided into three organizational levels—corporate level strategy, business level strategy and functional level strategy. Corporate level strategies deal with operating multiple businesses that may be diversified. Business level strategies deal with the specific business line and functional level strategies deal with operations within the business itself.

Most often, the levels of interest and attention are the functional and business levels. If separate strategic planning occurred at these two levels, there would be the problem of overall strategy coordination. In short, strategies need to be coordinated across the organization with cooperation among the players at all levels. That means you should have functional level managers (e.g. production line supervisors, marketing managers and human resource managers) mutually agree on strategic goals and specify how they will contribute to those goals at their respective levels.

When should we change strategy?

As a general rule, strategy should change infrequently. An organization needs time to adjust to a specific strategy, time to acquire and develop the appropriate skills and time to be recognized for the differentiators it brings to the competitive arena. It may take years for you to learn whether your strategy choice has been successful.

So, when should strategy change? It should change when a current strategy is ineffective or may become ineffective. There are several events that may trigger strategy ineffectiveness. They are:

- Technology shifts—The Internet and Amazon in particular have had a profound impact on the strategies of booksellers and publishers. The introduction of e-readers has introduced yet another factor.
- Regulation changes —New aircraft or automobile safety requirements may affect the strategies of auto and aircraft manufacturers just as new food safety regulations may affect strategies of food processors and distributors.
- Scale shifts—Technology may be applied to enable manufacturers to make large volumes of product less expensively and more consistently than before. The introduction of robotics to the automobile factory is an example.
- Substitutions—Freon gas was a staple of air conditioners worldwide until environmental concerns about Freon damage to the atmosphere led to a substitute product that eliminated the use of Freon.
- New competitors—A thriving local hardware store may be undone by the arrival of a large national chain. A Home Depot may take away part of the high-end business while a WalMart may take away part of the low-end business.

These are only a few of the factors that may drive your business to rethink its strategy. This does not necessarily mean a total strategy revamp but it does underscore the idea that strategy choice needs to be continuously appraised in light of external environmental developments.

How do we take risk into account in devising and implementing strategy?

Risk is the possibility of loss. In managing strategy, there is always the possibility of loss since strategy deals with unknown future occurrences. If this possibility is always present, then strategy planning, if done correctly, must factor in business risk. A sound strategy is less about making decisions in the future to avoid risk and more about making present decisions endure into the future. So, a consideration of risk starts with strategy formulation. In your strategy formulation process, you will need to make assumptions about the future and these assumptions are part of your environmental analysis.

There are three main considerations: what can happen, what is the likelihood of it happening and what will be the consequences. For the first question, you can construct several scenarios of business loss that have some probability of happening. For these scenarios, you can calculate the probabilities of them happening. For the last question you can predict what that loss might be in both financial and non-financial terms. The computing of the probability of the loss can be based on your own past experience, the experience of the industry itself or other methods. It usually involves some form of executive judgment. You want the scenarios, when created, to come as close to reality as possible.

The explanation above takes a simple approach to risk for the purpose of making a point. It supposes that there are several separate scenarios. In reality, the scenarios are contingent on other events. For example, the risk of not making a sales goal may be related to a failure of the distribution system or the failure of an internal quality control process. In such cases, a decision tree will work for assessing risk outcomes.

A decision tree can be used in strategy development by plotting decisions and outcomes in a branching arrangement. For example, the decision at hand may be whether or not to purchase and implement a $100,000 customer management software program.

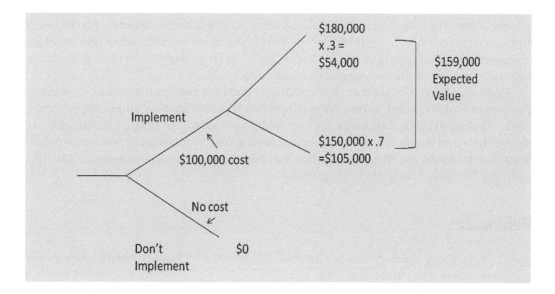

Tool 5.5   Decision Tree

The outcome may be that the system fails or succeeds and there is a 50% chance of either occurrence. If the system succeeds, there is a 30% chance it will produce $180,000 in additional income and a 70% chance it will produce $150,000 in income. Both the probabilities and the income projections are estimated before the decision tree is set up.

The other option is to not implement the program at all. If this happens, there would be no $100,000 investment and the probability of this option is 100% because there is just a single path with this option. This information can be shown on the decision tree on the preceding page.

On the implementation branch, the two possible income gains are multiplied by the estimated probability of occurrence and then they are added to produce an expected value of $159,000. Deducting the $100,000 cost produces an estimated gain of $59,000. On the "don't implement" branch there is no cost and no expected gain. The results from the two main branches are compared and the decision is made to implement the system since it produces an income gain.

This is just one tool for making strategy decisions under uncertainty. There are other tools and general approaches as well. The field of risk management has its own devices to deal with risk. In an ideal world, risk can be avoided, reduced or insured against. However in the practice of strategy, risk cannot be avoided nor can it be insured against in any practical way. That leaves the reduction of risk as the only viable option. Put in other terms, hedging is your best bet. This can take the form of not putting all your eggs in one basket. This may mean not using a single supplier or having a single customer who accounts for 90% or more of sales. For example, if these entities disconnect from the business and there are no contingency plans, then risk becomes a certainty. Risk management textbooks can help you flesh out these considerations.

Additional Resources

The primary organization devoted to strategic management is the Strategic Management Society (SMS). The SMS is a professional organization of academics, business practitioners and consultants who are involved in the development of research about the strategic management process along with the dissemination of knowledge in the field. It produces publications and conducts conferences around the world.

Company directories such as Hoovers Online and Dun and Bradstreet report on many companies and both sources provide different levels of information on individual firms. Trade associations and trade magazines are additional sources of strategy information at the industry and business level. Another excellent source of information on major public firms can be found on the US Securities and Exchange Commission website. The 10K company filings are particularly insightful.

References

Ansoff, H. I. (1965). *Corporate Strategy: An Analytical Approach to Business Policy for Growth and Expansion*. New York, NY: McGraw-Hill.

Buzzell, R. and Gale B. (1987). *The PIMS Principles: Linking Strategy to Performance*. New York, NY: Free Press.

Hamel, G. and Prahalad, C. K. (1994). *Competing for the Future*. Boston, MA: Harvard Business School Press.

Hofer, C. W. and Schendel, D. (1978). *Strategy Formulation: Analytical Concepts*. St. Paul, MN: West Publishing.

Porter, M. (1980). *Competitive Strategy*. New York, NY: The Free Press.

Prahalad, C. K. and Hamel, G. (1990). The Core Competence of the Corporation. *Harvard Business Review* (May–June).

6 *Developing Organizational Design and Culture*

FRANK FLETCHER

Organizations are planned social systems that create value by taking inputs from the environment and converting them into goods and/or services utilizing knowledge, skills and technology. Successful organizations have a clear mission, vision, structure, and culture as well as strategies, plans, goals, roles, and specialized activities. Once an appropriate corporate strategy, mission, and vision have been laid out (see Chapter five), developing an organizational structure is the next step in the journey toward organizational excellence.

This chapter will help you to understand exactly what organizational design is and how to choose or develop the best structure for your organization. It explains organizational structures and how they relate to many important areas including functions, policies and procedures, hierarchy and specialization. This chapter also examines the relationship between organizational design, strategy and organizational culture.

What is organizational design?

Organizational design is the process of assessing and selecting the structure and formal systems necessary to carry out strategy and achieve organizational goals. For competitive firms, organizational design is a constant search to find better ways of coordinating activities and motivating employees. Your design decisions require understanding both internal and external elements that include environmental factors, strategic choices, and technological factors. Although not a panacea, managerial research shows a direct link between organizational design and better financial performance, customer service, and employee satisfaction.

An effective organizational design facilitates the flow of information and decision making. See chapter two for more information on decision making. Effective design helps meet the needs and demands of various stakeholders including employees, customers, suppliers and regulatory agencies. The best designs will allow a fast and flexible response to ongoing changes in the environment. Organizational design helps define the authority and responsibility of departments and divisions as well as coordinating the activities of individuals and teams.

Ineffective organizational design can result in organizational failure. Poorly designed firms muddle through and have to deal with mix-ups, conflicts, duplication and wasted effort, delay and frustration. This adds costs to the bottom line and makes the organization less competitive.

Designing organizations requires decisions on these elements:

- Work specialization—the degree to which tasks are assigned to jobs.
- Departmentalization—the way jobs are grouped together.
- Chain of command—the division of authority and responsibility.
- Span of control—the decision on management levels and how many employees will report to specific managers.
- Centralization vs. decentralization—the extent to which decisions are made at the top of the organization.
- Formalization—the degree to which employee behaviors are guided by rules.

(Adapted from May, 2005)

An important step in the design development process is to determine decision making authority. Organizational decision making is either centralized or decentralized. Top managers make the decision in centralized organizations whereas lower level employees make decisions in decentralized organizations. Both strategies have pros and cons.

A centralized decision-making structure keeps the organization focused, but it can also result in manager involvement with day-to-day decisions causing them to lose sight of long term strategic issues. It may also lead to lower level managers and supervisors becoming risk averse and calling on up-level decision makers to make routine decisions creating inefficiency in the system. Decentralization offers flexibility and responsiveness but can make planning and coordinating more difficult.

How do organizational design and organizational structure differ?

Although often used interchangeably, organizational structure should not be confused with organizational design. Organization design is a process for integrating the people, information and technology of an organization, while organizational structure is how the firm is ordered. Organizational structure focuses on formal systems of task and reporting relationships that control, coordinate, and motivate employees to achieve organizational goals whereas organizational design is a process in which managers select and manage various components of organizational structure and culture.

So, what is organizational structure?

Garth Jones (2007) explains that the organizational structure is "the formal system of task and authority relationships that control how people coordinate their actions and use resources to achieve organizational goals." Structure involves functions, policies and procedures, hierarchy, standardization, and specialization. As organizations develop structure, they can move in one of two directions. Mechanistic structures have organizational members behave in predictable ways while organic structures promote flexibility and quick responses. A balance between mechanistic and organic structures is usually necessary depending largely on the organization's environment.

According to Jones, the organizational structure (often displayed in an organizational chart) emerges as the organization determines the division of labor (differentiation); how activities will be coordinated; who will make decisions; and how tightly the organization will control individual employee activities. Differentiation assigns individuals to specific roles.

Typically an organization can be broadly segmented into five functional areas:

- support—controlling the organization's relationship with its environment and stakeholders
- production—managing the organization's processes to create value
- maintenance—keeping operations going
- adaptation—adjusting to changes in the environment
- management—coordinating activities within and among departments.

Use these five broad categories to assess your organization's current strengths and identify weaknesses.

1. Support
• Planning takes into account technological, economic, social, and environmental aspects to ensure competiveness.
• The organization scans for and responds to important external trends that may impact the organization and its products and services.
How we're doing: Opportunities for improvement: Responsible party and timeframe:
2. Production
• The structure defines responsibility and is responsible for performance management. • Roles are clearly defined, but are flexible enough to adapt to change. • A procedure is outlined to monitor results. • Employees work together to provide good products and services. • Employees feel empowered by the problem-solving and decision-making processes.
How we're doing: Opportunities for improvement: Responsible party and timeframe:
3. Maintenance
• Employees feel there is adequate, ongoing communication about the organizational activities. • The organization has a staffing system. • Work-related accidents are rare. • Morale in the organization is generally good.

Tool 6.1   Current Assessment of Organizational Resources (continued overleaf)

- The organization effectively and efficiently manages the infrastructure, including building and equipment maintenance.
- Overall, the organization's level of technology is appropriate to carry out the organization's functions.
- Processes include adequate opportunities for review.
- Employees try to solve problems before they become big concerns.

How we're doing:
Opportunities for improvement:
Responsible party and timeframe:

4. Adaptation

- Research is undertaken to continuously improve product and services.
- Unit or divisional lines are crossed easily, especially when it means an improved product or service.
- Staff members can easily create important coordinating units.

How we're doing:
Opportunities for improvement:
Responsible party and timeframe:

5. Management

- Decision making is sufficiently decentralized to promote productivity and good morale.
- Employees have goals.
- Responsibilities for leadership and decisions are clear and understood.
- Leaders are concerned about getting significant tasks done.
- Leadership is prudent with both financial and human resources.
- The organization can forecast current and future demands for human resources.
- Leadership is flexible and ready to address challenges as they emerge.
- The organization has a clear strategy that is understood by all members of the organization – each unit has a written plan linked to the mission and strategy of the organization.
- Decisions are timely.
- Listening is valued.
- Strategy, processes, and all processes use data for decision making.
- Management structure both clarifies and supports the organization's direction.

How we're doing:
Opportunities for improvement:
Responsible party and timeframe:

Tool 6.1   Current Assessment of Organizational Resources (continued)

How do I group our employees?

employees can be grouped in a variety of ways. Grouping employees into subunits is horizontal differentiation while vertical differentiation creates organizational hierarchy and establishes reporting relationships that connect subunits. In a simple organization,

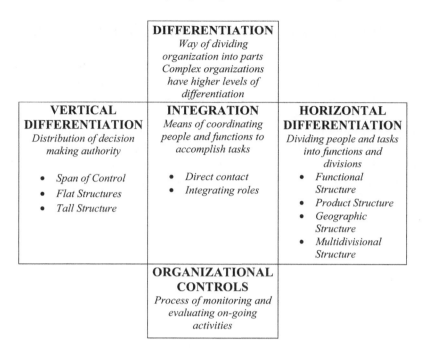

Figure 6.1   Organizational Design Terminology

the division of labor is minimal and there are fewer problems with coordination between subunits. However, as organizations grow and become more complex, a higher division of labor happens. The design challenge is determining the optimal horizontal and vertical differentiations to achieve organizational goals.

Is there a standard organizational structure?

There is no one specific organizational design that meets all needs. Organizational design models have evolved over time, reflecting technological advances, social norms, economic conditions, and political forces. During and after the industrial revolution, emerging businesses were largely traditionally structured. These organizations featured a strict division of labor, top-down decision-making, and extensive rules and procedures. This might describe the typical business pyramid that comes to mind when you think of organizational structure. Elements of these traditional bureaucracies exist in many of today's businesses.

These types of structures define levels of leadership, support specialization, and offer employees clear career paths. Depending on your generation, traditional structures may be familiar and comfortable with a clear chain of command. It's nice to know who does what and who reports to whom. However, communication within this structure can be slow and difficult. The organization may not be able to respond quickly to changes in the marketplace. Top down decision making may cause you to overlook good ideas. And finally, salaries for multiple layers of management increase an organization's overhead costs.

What are some common organizational design structures?

As a company's size and complexity grows and evolves, structure grows and evolves as well. In this sense, structure is closely tied to the organizational life cycle. Simple structures are very common in small start-up businesses. In the simple structure there are few departments and limited specialization. If you are the person in charge, everyone in the company might report directly to you in the first instance. And you may wear many hats. This structure allows for decisions to be made quickly, usually the owner-manager makes most of the decisions based on what is best for the whole organization. However, this structure is hard to maintain as the organization grows.

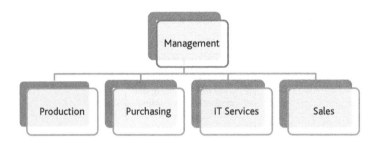

Figure 6.2   Sample Organizational Chart for a Simple Organization

As your start-up gets larger, a functional structure, which groups employees based upon specific jobs within the organization might emerge almost naturally. You might begin grouping employees based on their work such as production, marketing, or personnel. Functionally designed organizations have the advantage of being simple to understand with clear lines of command, specified tasks and responsibilities. They are a logical step from the first simple structure.

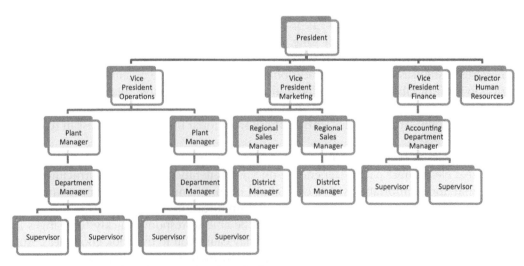

Figure 6.3   Functional Organizational Chart

The functional structure helps to maximize performance in specific areas by concentrating skilled workers together. This structure promotes the career development of specialists and allows for effective coaching and mentoring. On the downside, grouping units by function may cause a lack of broader organizational awareness. Functional units are also slower in responding to changes in the marketplace.

As your business continues to grow, divisional structures develop. A manager who focuses on a specific aspect of the business oversees each division:

- *Product structure*—A product structure organizes employees and work on the basis of products. If the company produces three different types of products, they will have three different divisions for these products.
- *Market Structure*—A market structure groups employees on the basis of the specific market. When a company has three different markets each is a separate division. For example, a company might sell its products retail, wholesale (Business to Business) and to the government.
- *Geographic structure*—A geographic structure has offices in different places. For example there could be a north, a south, a west, and an east zone.

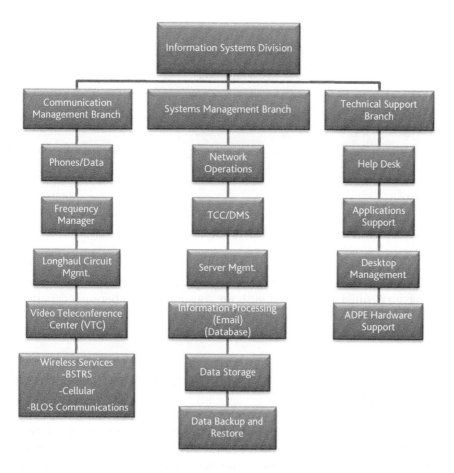

Figure 6.4   Divisional Organizational Chart

On the plus side, divisions allow a team to focus on a particular product or service or on the specifics of a particular region. This structure is very customer focused. A division's focus allows it to build a common culture and a deeper knowledge of the division's workings and target market. On the other hand, a divisional structure may cause competition among divisions diverting their attention from key corporate objectives. This structure also tends to create redundancies across support functions (for example, you could end up with personnel, accounting and distribution functions duplicating efforts and costs in three different divisions).

I have many different products in many markets. What's the best structure for me?

A multidivisional structure occurs when there are different products sold in a number of markets. A multidivisional structure consists of self-contained units that operate as their own separate entities. The division of labor caused by this structure will increase efficiency as well as accountability. In addition, it will provide opportunities for advancement and it can be more profitable as capital can be directed to areas with the highest income potential.

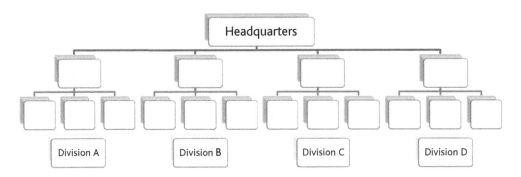

Figure 6.5   Multidivisional Organizational Chart

This kind of structure can challenge relationships. Although the division itself can be close and have a defined identity and purpose, communication between departments can be difficult. Conflict can exist because of competition and differences in values, systems, and expectations.

What kinds of designs offer more flexibility and better market responsiveness?

More contemporary forms of organizational structure include team structure, network structure, boundary-less structure, virtual structure and learning organizations. These organizational structures try to address the new external and internal complexity of the information age. These structures integrate theories of behavioral management, quantitative management, and systems thinking in ways that suit a particular organization at a particular time.

In designing the contemporary organization, the traditional pyramid structure is flattened to facilitate the flow of information to all parts of the organization and to reduce response time to external and internal demands. Unlike traditionally designed organizations, leaders of contemporary organizations stand at the bottom of the organization, supporting those who do the work. Employees are empowered and able to take actions and make decisions that are best for their part of the business.

Let's start with team structure. Team structures organize the entire organization into work groups or teams. The teams are organized both horizontally and vertically. In a team organization there is no hierarchy or chain of command. Teams and work groups figure out the most effective and efficient way to complete tasks. The focus is on the ends and not the means in this employee-empowered, results-oriented structure.

Teams have the power to be as innovative as they want. They are held accountable for their performance and this increases the urgency to perform well. Managers must be aware of how well team members work together. This often depends on the quality

Figure 6.6   Team Organizational Chart

of interpersonal relationships, group dynamics and their own team management abilities.

Team structures can have fairly permanent teams whose work is ongoing. Or teams may be organized along project lines, coming together to work on a particular project then moving on (similar to matrix structure as discussed below). One advantage to teams is that they break down functional barriers among departments. This creates more effective relationships for solving ongoing problems.

The team structure has many additional advantages. These include faster decision making and responsiveness to changing situations. In more even, more empowered organizations, employees are generally more motivated and administrative costs are lower. Some disadvantages include conflicting loyalties among the members, increased meeting time, and no clear chain of command. Team structures can be very effective when used in conjunction with traditional, bureaucratic structures combining flexibility and efficiency.

I've heard the term *matrix structure* before, how is that different from team structure?

The matrix structure provides the focus and efficiency of a divisional structure with functional specialization. One way to envision this structure is to imagine a traditional functional structure with an overlaid network of a team structure. In this structure a project manager brings a team together, selecting individuals from the functional areas to work temporarily on a team. Once the project is completed, the employees return to their original functional areas.

In this structure, an employee will effectively have two managers at any given time, their project team manager and their department or functional manager. Roles and authority are left vague by design. This causes minimal vertical control from the formal hierarchy but maximum horizontal control.

This structure improves strategic management and increases employee motivation. It facilitates cooperation and problem solving. Customers will be better served and the firm will perform better. The matrix structure also has disadvantages. Power struggles between

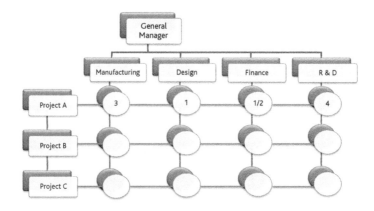

Figure 6.7   Matrix Organizational Chart

the functional area and project team can result from the two boss system. Workers in the matrix may also suffer confusion when taking orders from more than one boss. Team loyalties may cause a loss of focus on the overarching organizational goals. Successful use of matrix structures relies on excellent communication across the organization. See chapter four for more on organizational communications.

My organization has great technology. How can I use that to develop structure?

The boundary-less structure is an organizational structure developed by General Electric in the late 1980s and early 1990s. The structure is not defined by horizontal, vertical, or other boundaries. This structure is very flexible and uses talent wherever it is found. Managers eliminate boundaries using virtual, modular, or networked structures. Technology plays a major role in this structure as much of the work is done from a distance. This structure allows for collaboration among a broad range of individuals. Resources are applied to problems without regard to their physical location.

Expanding on the boundary-less concept and taking it one step further is the virtual organization. The virtual organization is a technology dependent strategy. The structure consists of a small core of permanent employees and work is outsourced as necessary. This structure maximizes flexibility because staff and operations can be reduced at any time quite easily. Costs are controllable as there is no significant investment in overhead. On the downside, it is harder to control supply quantity, quality and delivery due to a reliance on contractual workers. To be successful it is necessary to create and maintain a common task and group climate to focus on projects as well as on overall strategies.

What is a *learning organization*?

The term learning organization is credited to Peter Senge and it became popular after publication of his 1990 book, *The Fifth Discipline*, which follows earlier work by Chris Argyris, Donald Schon, and others. It has to do more with learning than with structure, but structure can either facilitate or hinder learning. Today's high value organizations derive success not from scale and volume but from discovery of new linkages between solutions and needs. They achieve competitive advantage through acts of innovation.

Creating knowledge within an organization requires personal commitment. To achieve this commitment, organizations must move away from hierarchical, management-driven organizational models to a stakeholder model of involvement. That means allowing everyone in the organization to have their say in shaping it, so they develop a sense of ownership. The task of today's management is to ensure everyone in the organization has the opportunity to buy into the vision. So learning organizations:

- Provide continuous learning opportunities.
- Use learning to reach their goals.
- Link individual performance with organizational performance.
- Foster inquiry and dialogue, making it safe for people to share openly and take risks.
- Embrace creative tension as a source of energy and renewal.

- Are continuously aware of and interact with their environment.

(Adapted from Kerka 1995)

To develop the learning environment, according to Peter Senge, organizations need to develop five disciplines:

1. *Systems Thinking*—the ability to see the big picture, and to distinguish patterns instead of conceptualizing change as an isolated event. Systems thinking needs the other four disciplines to enable a learning organization to transpire. There must be a paradigm shift—from being unconnected to interconnected to the whole, and from blaming our problems on something external, to a realization that how we operate and our actions, can create problems in themselves.
2. *Personal Mastery*—begins "by becoming committed to . . . lifelong learning," and is the spiritual cornerstone of a learning organization. Personal Mastery involves being more realistic, focusing on becoming the best person possible, and striving for a sense of commitment and excitement in our careers to facilitate realization of potential.
3. *Mental Models*—they must be managed because they do prevent new and powerful insights and organizational practices from becoming implemented. The process begins with self-reflection, unearthing deeply-held belief structures and generalizations, and understanding how they dramatically influence the way we operate in our own lives. Until there is realization and a focus on openness, real change can never be implemented.
4. *Building Shared Visions*—visions cannot be dictated because they begin with the personal visions of individual employees, who may not agree with the leader's vision. What is needed is a genuine vision that elicits commitment in good times and bad, and has the power to bind an organization together. As Peter Senge contends, "building shared vision fosters a commitment to the long term."
5. *Team Learning*—is important because currently, modern organizations operate on the basis of teamwork, which means that organizations cannot learn if team members do not come together and learn. It is a process of developing the ability to create desired results, to have a goal in mind and to work together to attain it.

What are some things that can go wrong when I implement my new structure?

Organizational structure, much like a human skeletal structure, determines what shape an organization takes. Effective organizational design facilitates communications, productivity and innovation. It creates an environment in which people can work together effectively. On the other hand, ineffective organizational design often leads to conflict (between individuals and/or units), delays in product delivery, quality problems, economic inefficiencies, poor customer service, and low employee morale. You know you have an organizational structure problem if you witness any of the following:

- employee role uncertainty
- poor workflow
- inefficient use of resources

- customer service problems
- a high level of friction and conflict.

Low productivity metrics can indicate an organizational design problem is causing inefficient resource utilization, poor vertical communication, and employee empowerment constraints. Employees may not have the proper environment to complete their work assignments efficiently. Another sign pointing to the organizational structure not being optimized occurs when some areas of the firm are routinely understaffed and must work overtime to meet workload requirements, while other areas are staying idle.

Organizational fragmentation or/and a lack of governance mechanisms can create dysfunctional units or departments that have a tendency to protect themselves by holding and maintaining data and other resources that are available centrally. This is referred to as the silo effect. Silos are characterized by a lack of cooperation and information sharing between areas. Sometimes silos will place their own goals ahead of organizational goals.

When designing my structure, how can I avoid creating silos?

In the design process ensure you avoid design flaws that might create silos in the organization. Organization silos happen when individual people, departments, or companies, conduct business without considering the consequences their actions have on the whole business. Silos usually happen in highly-vertical organizations, where the communication and collaboration across the organization is minimal.

What are some tools to help me integrate my employees across silos and subunits?

As we have been moving into designing organizations for the information age, organizational designers are integrating theories of behavioral management, quantitative management, and systems thinking. Organizations are now thought of more as systems,

	Seven useful integrating mechanisms
1	**Hierarchy of authority** which specifies reporting relationships
2	**Direct contact** requiring managers from different functions to meet to coordinate activities.
3	**Liaison role** requiring managers to coordinate with other subunits managers.
4	**Task force** creating a temporary cross functional committee
5	**Teams** requiring different functional managers to coordinate activities.
6	**Integrating roles** coordinating two or more functions or divisions
7	**Integrating departments** coordinating functions or divisions.

Tool 6.2   Integration Strategies

which are a collection of parts integrated to accomplish an overall goal. Structure determines behaviors that in turn determine events.

The sociotechnical system views organizations as an open system structure that integrates both the human and technical subsystems. It focuses more on work group interactions than individual performance. This approach suggests that organizations should structure task, authority, and reporting relationships around the work group. This includes delegating decisions on job assignments, training, inspection, rewards, and punishments to the group. Autonomous work groups and quality circles are popular examples of this perspective.

Strict command and control or bureaucratic organizational structures tend to create more fear and less risk-taking by employees because information sharing and decisions move vertically. Too much formality also slows information sharing and inhibits collaboration. Limiting protocol and the need to go through channels can help to eliminate silos. On the other hand, if the employees routinely bypass the standard chain of command it could also be a sign of poor organizational design. In an optimal business design, employees should feel their voices are heard through the standard management path. Poor structure may cause employees to feel the need to go directly over their manager to express concerns or recommendations.

Information is necessary for self-direction. Slow decision making limits opportunities and innovation. Decision making is best done at the level it impacts and not at multiple layers further up the organizational structure. Decision making processes should optimize innovation as well as linking authority with accountability. Organizational structures have to fit with environmental demands buffering uncertainties and environmental changes.

In addition to the Five Function Area Analysis, (Tool 6.1) what other assessment methods are available to help me understand my business?

Organizations are constantly addressing multiple and shifting factors. An organizational assessment done either internally or with outside consultants can help the firm, department, or unit to establish a baseline analysis. It can also help establish priorities for change by examining the environment, and the company's purpose, mission, strategy, structure, technology, systems, tasks, motivation, culture, leadership, capabilities, human relations and performance.

A number of assessments can assist a firm to better understand its organization. This section explores two of them: the 7S's Model, and the Six-Box Diagnostic Model.

McKINSEY'S 7 S's MODEL

Developed in the late 1970s by McKinsey Consulting the 7 S's Model examines seven key organizational factors. It can be used to identify organizational strengths and sources of competitive advantage, or to identify the reasons why an organization is not operating effectively.

Figure 6.8   McKinsey's 7 S's Model

Managers need to take into account all seven of the factors to be sure of successful implementation of a strategy since all the factors are interdependent.

The Seven S's are:

- Shared Values and Beliefs: A role of the vision statement is to impart to the organization (and to the external environment) what the organization stands for and what it believes in.
- Strategy: The strategy lays out how the organization will attain its vision and respond to the threats and opportunities. Capabilities are needed in marketing, distribution, product and service development, business requirements analysis, creation and management of alliances and partnerships.
- Systems, including Processes: Capabilities are required in information technology and information systems, sales and service, legal, actuarial.
- Staff: human resource and marketing management develop the skills and aptitude for building lifetime customer relationships. Needed are policies, standards and processes for recruitment, training and development, motivation and rewards.
- Style: This refers to the management style best suited for the organization. The challenge for management is to use appropriate styles for each situation without confusing staff.
- Structure: Organizations will find that changes to processes and style inevitably require changes to their structure (e.g. centralized, decentralized, network, matrix, process structures.)
- Skills: The degree to which necessary skills exist is the core of workforce planning and is often a major aspect in organizational diagnosis. If staff and managers are to acquire all the skills outlined above, then there needs to be an appropriate learning environment.

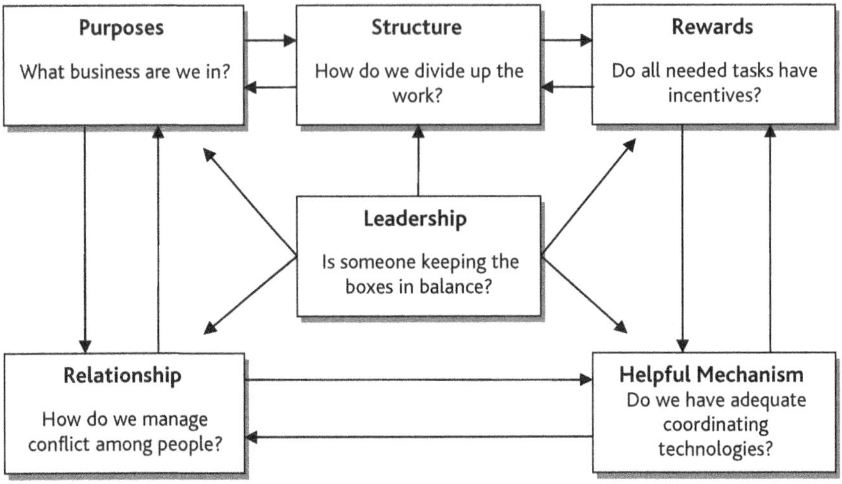

Figure 6.9 Six-Box Model

Using Organizational Development theory, Marvin Weisbord (2011) developed an organizational diagnosis that looks at six areas: purposes, structure, relationships, rewards, leadership and helpful mechanisms. It is a multi-step process that provides an understanding of key activities and variables including conflict. The first phase of assessment includes understanding the boundaries between the organization and its environment, input/output systems, satisfaction with outputs, and stakeholder issues.

In the next phase issues are identified through a series of questions:

PURPOSE:

1. What is the purpose of your organization?
2. Do you have a strategic plan?
3. What are your organizational values, vision, mission, goals?

STRUCTURE:

1. How is work organized?
2. What formal/informal systems exist for indentifying job expectations?
3. Does structure support the purpose?
4. How much does structure impact the relationships, communications, and processes?

REWARDS:

1. Do all needed tasks have incentives?
2. How are behaviors rewarded?
3. For what behaviors are they rewarded?
4. What incentives exist for helping people achieve goals?

HELPFUL MECHANISMS:

1. Are systems in place to keep the boxes in balance?
2. What communication processes exist?
3. What performance improvement measures exist?
4. What technology exists—how is it used?
5. How is coordination of processes managed?
6. What training/career development processes exist to help people achieve goals?

RELATIONSHIPS:

1. How is conflict managed?
2. Which technologies are used?
3. How would you characterize morale?

LEADERSHIP:

1. How well do the organization's leaders understand the impact of the other five boxes?
2. What is the leadership style of the organization (autocratic, democratic, task-focused, relationship-focused)?
3. Where do the leaders focus most of their attention and intention?
4. Do the leaders model the behavior they value from the work force?
5. Do the leaders have a clear vision of where they want to take the organization?

What role does strategy play in organizational design?

Strategy (covered in chapter five) answers two questions: what to do and how to do it. Strategy consists of actions a company takes to achieve its goals. It is vital that an organization's structure aligns with goals. Developing and implementing corporate strategy and assisting an organization to gain competitive advantage are essential tasks of organizational design. Bryan and Joyce (2007) state ". . . most corporate leaders overlook a golden opportunity to create a durable competitive advantage and generate high returns for less money and with less risk: making organizational design the heart of strategy."

Pateman (2011) proposes a four-step process to link strategy to organizational design:

1. determine the design framework;
2. design the organization;
3. develop the details;
4. implement the new design.

The first phase in this process is to understand the organization's strategic intent. According to Hamel and Prahalad (1989) ". . . strategic intent envisions a desired leadership position and establishes the criterion the organization will use to chart its progress." Once the strategic intent is established determine the capabilities required to achieve and maintain that desired future state.

Phase 1: Determine the design framework   • Understand the organization's strategic intent   • Determine the capabilities that are required   • Assess the current organizational capabilities   • Identify the gaps between what is needed and what exists   • Develop the design criteria for the organization
Phase 2: Design the work processes and practices   • How does the work get done?   • How does information flows?   • What are the required processes and capabilities?   • Who and what will be impacted (functions, departments, external/internal customers or business partners)?   • What behaviors will be impacting process outcomes?
Phase 3: Determine organizational structure   • Determine organization structure   • Assess the talent required   • Establish performance management requirements   • Integrate the parts, identify facilitators   • Identify inhibitors   • Establish metrics
Phase 4: Implement the design   • Implement   • Monitor   • Make adjustments as needed   • Evaluate success and failures

Tool 6.3   The Four Phases of Linking Strategy to Structure

What is organizational culture, how does it relate to organizational design and how is it developed and managed?

While you cannot see it, organizational culture is a social control mechanism that helps organizational members to understand events and processes. Organizational culture is the shared norms and values of individuals and groups within an organization. Elements of organizational culture may include: values (stated and unstated), expectations of people within the organization, customs, stories, myths about the organization's history and the common language used in the organization. Another important element is organizational climate. This represents the feelings evoked by the way members interact with each other, outsiders, and their environment.

According to Sorensen (2002), research shows that a strong corporate culture improves performance by facilitating consistent internal behavior. Behavioral consistency enhances a firm's performance and can assist by compensating for suboptimal strategies. This is important because even if a corporation has excellent strategies they still could fail if the strategies are not executed well.

MIT professor Edgar Schein (1997) defines organizational culture at three levels: 1) artifacts, 2) norms and values, and 3) underlying assumptions. Artifacts are apparent to everyone. They represent the most accessible elements of culture including facilities, furnishings, awards and recognition, uniform or dress and interaction of members both inside and outside of the organization.

The norms and values of any organization define its culture. Norms are the attitudes and actions of people in an organization. Norms provide a sense of shared values. Values can also create their own norms. Although norms and values cannot typically be observed, they are an embedded part of a company's slogans, mission statements and different operational creeds. Finally, underlying assumptions represent an unconscious level of culture. These underlying values have been assimilated and are taken for granted as an organizationally acceptable way of doing business.

The company's culture is continually reinforced via employee recruitment, assignments, and performance rewards. A stream of communications also reinforces culture. Everyone needs to be involved in the creation and reinforcement of a desired culture. All actions in the organization translate into cultural realities. The culture of an organization must reflect the philosophy that guides its policies towards its employees and customers. Organizational culture plays a significant role in determining structure.

Cultural hierarchies focus on efficiency and effectiveness through structure and control via a strict chain of command. Rules and regulations are guidelines by which authority, control, leadership and communication follow. Hierarchies respect position and power. Leaders will monitor employee performance closely to ensure that services and products are high quality and rules are being met. Organizational examples of this culture include government agencies and large multinational corporations.

This type of culture strives to provide its members a clear sense of focus regarding the organization's direction. It also tries to develop a deep sense of personal involvement in helping the organization reach its goals. There is also a belief that the most suited employees rise to the top and organizational success is the result of the most talented employees directing and training all the employees of the business.

Organizations with a market culture focus on the external environment and are results driven. All efforts go toward improving productivity, staying competitive, and meeting

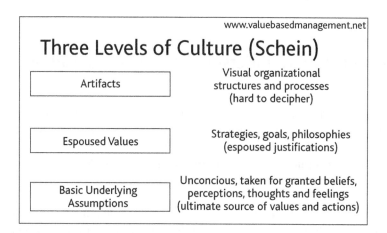

Figure 6.10 Schein's Three Levels of Culture

customer preferences. Transactions (exchanges of value) drive the organization toward its goals. However, these organizations do not just focus on marketing. All internal and external transactions are viewed in market terms. In an efficient market organization, value flows between the company and stakeholders with minimal cost and delay.

Leaders in market cultures are often hard-driving competitors who seek to deliver the goods. A typical leadership style in market culture organizations is that of GE's former CEO Jack Welch emphasizing superior performance and production. Employees in this culture are expected to produce results without too much coaching. Given the emphasis toward stability and control, market cultures have a current organizational chart that clearly outlines the authority, control, leadership, and communication flows within the organization.

Adhocracy cultures are the complete opposite of a traditional bureaucracy. They stress a great deal of independence and flexibility. Responding to a rapidly changing environment characterized by intensive competition and risk, adhocracy organizations focus on innovation and speedy reconfiguration. This culture is adaptable, flexible, and creative in responding to external opportunities.

An adhocracy will often use prototyping and experimenting rather than long-term projects and development. Adhocracies do not have many rules because they want to allow employees the freedom to be creative. Leaders tend to be visionary, innovative entrepreneurs taking calculated risks to make significant gains. Employee roles and duties are temporary and subject to change to meet the needs of current projects and clients. This form of organization is common among advertising agencies and other creativity-based companies.

In a clan culture the focus and orientation are on flexibility and discretion with less emphasis on structure and control. Coordination of activities occurs through shared values and beliefs versus an organizational chart, rules and regulations. In contrast to hierarchies, clans often have flat organizations and people and teams act more autonomously. Rules still exist and are communicated and inculcated socially. Shared strategies are the clan culture's keys to becoming an effective organization.

The clan organization draws on the involvement of all employees by building relationships with employees through development opportunities and empowerment. External stakeholders become partners of the firm. It is not uncommon for leaders to be viewed as mentors, or even parent figures, and fill a nurturing role.

How do I get started understanding my organization's culture?

Gathering survey data from your organization is a great way to understand culture as it provides insight into your employees' perceptions. Numerous surveys and frameworks exist that evaluate and assess organizational culture. The following are suggestions adapted from a list compiled by Scott, Mannion, and Davies (2003). These may serve as a guide and can provide useful insight into developing your own culture assessment:

- The *Competing Values Framework* (Cameron and Freeman 1991; Gerowitz et al. 1996; Gerowitz 1998), provides a model for evaluating corporate effectiveness. Key dimensions are staff climate, leadership style, bonding systems, and prioritization of goals. Assessment results in four different culture types, described as: clan, adhocracy, hierarchy, and market types. Each organization usually has more than one of these types.

- The *Organizational Culture Inventory* (Cooke and Lafferty 1987; Thomas et al. 1990; Seago 1997; Ingersoll et al. 2000) measures shared norms and expectations that guide thinking and behavior of group members, resulting in twelve thinking styles of individuals within a group. These include humanistic-helpful, affiliative, approval, conventional, dependent, avoidance, oppositional, power, competitive, competence/perfectionist, achievement and self-actualization. Analysis of these twelve styles results in three factors—people/security culture, satisfaction culture and task/security culture.

> **TIPS FOR FACILITATING CULTURE CHANGE:**
> - Define the new expectations.
> - Make the case for change.
> - Lead by example.
> - Develop new stories.
> - Educate and encourage the behavior you want.
> - Recognize and acknowledge the behavior you want.
> - Switch things around with new assignments and transfers.
> - Celebrate success.
> - Align reward systems to encourage the behaviors you want.

How do I better align my culture with my strategy and structure?

Changing an existing culture is a challenge because people don't like change. Changing a strong culture is even more difficult. Culture provides organizational stability and communicates why the organization behaves in certain ways. Once the culture is ingrained, for better or worse, changing it is time consuming, and challenging.

Based on your strategic plan, you should have an idea about the culture you are trying to build. An important strategy is not attacking the current culture head-on but finding ways to help everyone to do his job better. Finally, keep in mind that for large organizations making the change organization-wide may take five to ten years.

There are a number of change models, but the most notable is the three-step process developed by Kurt Lewin (1951) of unfreezing, changing, and refreezing. His model shows that change is a process and that people in organizations must be prepared for change before it can happen. Change can be daunting as people move away from the comfort of the way things are or have always have been to something unfamiliar.

Unfreezing is the first step in the process and it involves overcoming inertia to change existing mindsets. In the second stage the change occurs. Typically this is a period of confusion and transition during the move away from the old situation. The new state of things has not come into total focus. The third and final stage, refreezing, occurs as the changes are institutionalized. In this final stage it is important to take steps to make sure that people do not back away from the change that has been implemented.

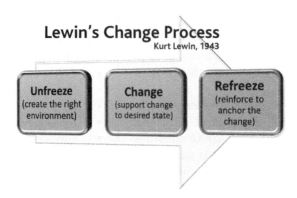

Figure 6.11 Lewin's Change Model

Additional Resources

For more information about organizational design or culture these sources can give you access to articles, etc: BNET, The Nonprofit Leadership of Tampa Bay, University of Southern California—Center for Effective Organizations, and the Harvard Business School Press.

OCAIonline (Organizational culture assessment instrument online) is a hassle-free tool for diagnosing organizational culture, developed by Professors Robert Quinn and Kim Cameron. Another resource for tools and assessments is MindTools.

References

Bryan, L. L., and Joyce, C. I. (2007). Better strategy through organizational design. *McKinsey Quarterly.* Retrieved from https://www.mckinseyquarterly.com/Better_strategy_through_organizational_design_1991.

Bryan, L. L. and Joyce, C. I. (2007). Better strategy through organizational design. *McKinsey Quarterly,* (2), 20–29. Retrieved from EBSCO*host.*

Hamel, G. and Prahalad, C. (1989). To revitalize corporate performance, we need a whole new model of strategy. Strategic intent. *Harvard Business Review,* 67(3), 63–76. Retrieved from EBSCO*host.*

Jones, G. R. (2007). *Organization Theory, Design, and Change* (5th ed.). Upper Saddle River, NJ: Pearson Prentice Hall.

Kerka, S. (1995). The learning organization: myths and realities. *Eric Clearinghouse,* http://www.cete.org/acve/docgen.asp?tbl=archive&ID=A028.

Lewin, K. (1951). *Field Theory in Social Science.* New York, NY: Harper & Row.

May, L. (2005). *Six Key Elements in Organizational Design.* Retrieved from http://www.emaytrix.com/mgmt307/section2.php.

Pateman, A. (2011). *Linking Strategy to Operations: Six Stages to Execution.* Penton Media, Inc. Retrieved from http://bpmmag.net/mag/linking_strategy_operations_1201/.

Schein, E. H. (1997). *Organizational Culture & Leadership.* Retrieved from http://www.tnellen.com/ted/tc/schein.html.

Scott, T., Mannion, R. and Davies, H. (2003). The Quantitative Measurement of Organizational Culture in Health Care: A Review of the Available Instruments. *Health Service Research*, 38(3), 923–45. Retrieved from http://www.ncbi.nlm.nih.gov/pmc/articles/PMC1360923/.

Senge, Peter. (1990). *The Fifth Discipline: the Art and Practice of the Learning Organization*. New York, NY: Doubleday.

Sorensen, J. B. (2002). The Strength of Corporate Culture and the Reliability of Firm Performance. *Administrative Science Quarterly*, 47(1), 70–91. Retrieved from EBSCOhost.

Weisbord, Marvin. (2011). *SIX-BOX MODEL*. MarvinWeisbord.com. Retrieved from http://www.marvinweisbord.com/index.php/six-box-model/.

7 *Human Resource Management*

SAL MIRZA and CORINNE FARNETI

The phrase human resource management (HRM) brings about a diverse array of thoughts, emotions and reactions. For many, these can be negative. What have I done wrong? What new policy will I have to adopt? What data do I need to provide? Or even, what now? The human resource department historically has been viewed by employees as nothing more than an administrative bureaucracy that contributes little to the organization's productivity. However, these impressions and the role of HRM have been shifting over the past several decades.

Changes in the business environment, such as the adoption of the innovative workplace, the increasing diversity of the labor force, work-life balance issues and globalization have resulted in a shift away from traditional human resource management. The focus has moved from employee advocacy to a strategic partner. HRM concerns and concepts are integrated into the strategic plan of the organization. HRM is now primarily concerned with developing human resource practices that enhance a firm's competitive advantage through its most valued asset, its people.

The human resources (HR) function can provide significant support and advice to management. The attraction, development, and retention of high caliber people are a source of competitive advantage for your business, and are the joint responsibility of HR and management. HRM is no longer just the responsibility of the human resource department. CEOs, directors, department heads, middle managers and line managers are also increasingly concerned with these tasks. Managers now have increased accountability for their direct reports in the areas of hiring, development, succession planning and performance management.

You as a manager will have to align your human resources through integration of decisions about your employees with decisions about specific organizational goals. This chapter offers HR professionals and organization managers processes, tools and resources to make informed HR decisions.

How do I discover my HR needs?

Human resource planning is an area that has become integrated into organizations' strategic business plans. Close collaboration between human resource professionals and management helps ensure that human resources are strategically aligned with current and future business requirements. Businesses and business plans need to evaluate and manage the resources required to reach organizational goals. These resources include the workforce.

Human resource planning can be thought of as the process of analyzing the workforce and determining the steps that must be taken to prepare for future human resource needs. Human resource planning involves identifying and developing plans addressing these four issues:

- Identification of the composition and content of the workforce that will be required to strategically position the organization toward its future goals.
- Identification of the gaps between the future human resource workforce needs and the existing organization human resource state.
- Development and implementation of succession, recruitment and training plans to close the gaps identified.
- Identification of external sources and partnerships that will enhance the company's internal human resource assets.

How can I assess and inventory my current employees?

Managers begin the HR planning process by reviewing the organization's current human assets, usually through a human resource inventory. This inventory is created from forms filled out by employees capturing information such as name, education, training, prior employment, languages spoken, special capabilities, and specialized skills. This data is collected and maintained in some kind of database. In other words, it is a bank of resume-like information that you keep on your own employees.

Companies such as PeopleMatch have developed sophisticated databases that maintain the aforementioned information in a very easy-to-use format. A manager would simply type in a desired quality and the database will pull up people who match the criteria assigned. PeopleMatch says, "We are particularly suited to giving *start-ups* the needed knowledge when *looking for capital* to fund growth. Knowing *who to hire, when to hire* and *how much it will really cost* as well as knowing *who not to hire* forms the foundation of the human capital component of the strategy plan for the business."

The next step in the process is to conduct a job analysis. A job analysis is often the most ignored aspect of the hiring process. Performed correctly, a job analysis focuses on the job and not on the person. The job analysis will lead to the development of the job description that aids in the hiring of quality employees. Job analysis information should be collected in the following areas:

- Duties and Tasks: task/duty frequency, duration, effort, skill required and complexity.
- Work Environment: work conditions and risks.
- Tools and Equipment: specific tools and equipment.
- Reporting Structure: supervision/management relationships.
- Job Requirements: knowledge, skills, and abilities.

Once a job analysis has been completed, the job description document can be drafted. Make sure to identify and prioritize the key requirements from the job description. What are the must-haves versus the good-to-haves?

Developing a job description is the next step. The job description document is important from the perspectives of you, the HR manager, and the employee. The job description is the document describing in precise detail the role and responsibilities of a job. It serves three vital functions:

1. It helps retention efforts by getting managers and employees on the same page in terms of duties and expectations.
2. The job description can then be used to advertise the vacant or newly-created position.
3. It helps ensure that your hiring process is non-discriminatory.

The creation of a job description is another critical step. An effective job description should:

- State the title of the position and its rank and status within the company hierarchy.
- Identify and list essential functions, tasks and expected outcomes.
- Specify job qualifications: Education, experience requirements, knowledge, skills, competencies, travel requirements, customer service skills, experience working on teams, etc.
- Describe physical demands of the position with a statement that reasonable accommodations will be made for disabled employees.
- Describe the typical environmental factors affecting the position (noise, high/low temperatures, outdoor work, etc.).
- List non-essential duties or responsibilities, clearly distinguished from essential functions. Non-essential duties may not be considered for hiring purposes under the Americans with Disabilities Act.

With the job analysis and description in place, the hiring process is more effective because potential job applicants are evaluated on a common set of measures. Since employees are hired based on clear, defined requirements and job expectations, the newly hired person should not be surprised after starting work. This aids in retention efforts down the road.

How do I determine my future HR needs?

A human resource supply and demand analysis focuses on future business plans and objectives with the purpose of forecasting future human resource needs. This forecast should take into consideration a broad range of business issues including, but not limited to, department diversification, new product lines, competitive forces, expansion/contraction in the market and forecasted workforce availability. Internal and external factors need to be considered in the demand analysis. Analyses of internal demand influences may focus on the following questions, among others:

- Do the current employees have the skill sets necessary to perform future work assignments? What retraining will be required? Your human capital database will be helpful here.
- Will current employees remain loyal to the organization? How will the organization culture and work environment change over time and how will this impact retention?

Analyses of external demand influences may include:

- How will the labor force change in the timelines considered? Is labor readily available with the skills and abilities needed by your evolving department?

You should also analyze the future human resource composition. This analysis may include questions such as:

- How many employees will be necessary to achieve business plan goals and objectives?
- What skills and competencies will be required for the new business?
- What is the composition of the available workforce population?
- What will the organization need to do to attract prospective employees?
- What will the organization need to do to attract and retain a diverse group of workers?

The gap analysis identifies disparities between the composition of the current and future human resource needs. The next step in this phase should be for you to work with senior management and the HR department to identify several possible future scenarios. Select the future that is most likely to occur, with contingency planning for alternative futures. When conducting this analysis, you should identify the additional number of employees with requisite skill sets that will be needed, as well as the employees who will no longer be needed due to limited skill sets.

It will be clear to you where you have gaps. The solution analysis focuses on how to address these gaps in current and future staffing needs through succession planning, recruiting, training and development, and outsourcing. This analysis answers the following questions:

- What are the future priorities of the department?
- How do these priorities link with the company's strategic plans?
- What possible solutions are out of bounds?
- What resources currently not in place will be needed for a possible solution?
- What would be the issues with acquiring the resources?
- What would be the issues with implementation and measurements of the results?
- What is the cost of the solution?

Based on the gap analysis results, you will develop a plan considering what are the major human resources priorities and what strategies will achieve the desired outcome. This is an ongoing process that should be carried out on a regular basis to keep the data current and to incorporate changes as needed. This phase allows you to modify and navigate your human resource needs based on internal and external changes.

What are some ideas for recruiting?

As you analyze your current status and examine your future needs, you may find shortages of human capital. It is your job, along with the HR department, to locate, identify, and attract capable candidates. Effective recruiting can make a big difference in the quality of your workforce. As Gary Dessler (2008) points out, if only two candidates apply for two openings, you may have no choice but to hire them. But, if there are twenty applicants, you can use techniques to screen out the best. You have several options in recruiting qualified candidates.

In today's world, online recruiting is the most efficient way to reach large numbers of diverse people. It is the first place where most people go to look for jobs. Some companies choose to place their own ads on sites like monster.com, careerbuilder.com, and theladders.com. Other managers choose to do keyword searches in online resume databases, in the belief that more qualified candidates are found in this manner. Listing openings on your company website brings in candidates specifically searching your company or industry. The downside is the massive numbers of potentially unscreened and unqualified candidates that will come your way.

Another way to find interested and more qualified candidates is to set up a booth or table at a job fair that is focused on your specific industry, especially if the positions you are filling are more than just entry-level. You should prepare brochures, newsletters, flyers, or any company information that you would not only like to give to potential employees, but to other companies within the industry as well. Do not miss this opportunity to gain further publicity for your company.

Employee referrals are probably the most important recruiting option. Oftentimes, cash awards and prizes are given to those employees who have made referrals that lead to a successful new hire. Below are a few incentives programs offered by various organizations:

- PricewaterhouseCoopers launched its referral incentive program in the mid-1990s. The accounting firm has since increased its referral incentives several times and claims that it hires one-third of new employees through referrals. The offerings included bonuses of several thousand dollars, depending on the level and complexity of the job filled. Employees who make referrals are also in the running to win prizes ranging from a mountain bike to a trip abroad.
- Computer hardware giant Intel Corporation uses a combination of monetary and nonmonetary incentives to get employees to refer others. In addition to a cash reward for referrals, the company also has offered a raffle for those employees who have made referrals. One year, the prize was a choice between a $1,000 travel voucher or a home-entertainment system. About 50% of the company's new hires come from referrals.
- During a referral drive, ReplayTV's work force went from 100 to 300 employees. The referring employee netted $2,000 within forty-five days of the new hire's start date and was also entered into a draw to drive a white Mercedes-Benz SLK convertible for two years.

In addition to referrals, campus recruiters can be involved. A campus recruiter has two main goals. The first is to attract good candidates and the second is to determine if the candidates are worthy enough to move along to the next step in the hiring process. It takes the right person to go and talk to (and hopefully inspire) a group of young adults to want to work for you. The HR representative or manager should have good communication skills, a sincere and informal attitude, and respect for the applicant as an individual. Also, building ties with a college's career center can help your organization establish a rapport that will be more likely to bring in more highly qualified candidates down the road.

Headhunters or recruiters are special employment agencies hired by employers to seek out top-management talent. Most of your company's jobs will not be filled in this manner. However, for executive and technical positions this may be a good option. Most recruiting firms use internet-linked computerized databases, gathering as many high quality candidates as possible. Many firms specialize in a particular field. These specialists will know the top performers in your field and may help you go after them.

Along that line, every manager should keep a most wanted list of people in the industry that you'd love to have work for you someday. If your sales force consistently loses business to the same sales rep at a competitor firm, you should go after that sales rep. If you consistently see the same people at industry meetings, develop a relationship with them and try to attract them to your company. You never know when someone might be interested in making a move. Make it known to top performers at other companies that you're interested.

When looking towards your current workforce to fill new positions, first publicize the position to your employees, usually through an email notification or bulletin boards. This can save you valuable time and money, especially if you have a qualifications inventory tool at your disposal (as discussed earlier in this chapter). Your inventory tool will help you find employees who have potential for further training or have the right background for the open position. By posting the position, you'll also know who's interested in moving up in the organization. And, it also serves as a good internal public relations move that strengthens retention efforts.

How do I select the best candidate?

An employee with the right skills will do a better job for you and the company. A good match between candidate skills and personality who also meets requirements and fits your corporate culture will help your retention efforts. Not to mention, the hiring process is costly so the fewer times you have to do it, the better. Selecting an employee is a challenging exercise in prediction.

As you sit at your desk with dozens of resumes scattered about, it is easy to become overwhelmed at the prospect of picking just the right person for the job. Luckily, there are several tools you can use to make your decision a lot easier.

Applications are often the first step in the prescreening process. Use them to quickly eliminate those applicants who do not meet your desired criteria. Go straight to your most important indicators for the position. Some positions may require previous experience, while others may emphasize education or potential. Once you've chosen the top applicants, it is time to learn more about each one. Applications are also a good way to make sure you are in compliance with legal hiring issues.

Written tests include tests of intelligence, ability, aptitude, and interest. They can be good indicators of how a prospect will perform at their job and reduce the likelihood of making the wrong hiring choice. There are some things to keep in mind when choosing and administering a test to a potential employee. First, you must determine if the test is both reliable and valid. To administer a test that is neither reliable nor valid would

Source	Advantages	Disadvantages
Internet/Online Recruiting	Reaches large number of people; can get immediate feedback; cost effective.	Generates many unqualified candidates; may not reach all demographics.
Job Fairs	Good publicity for the company; meet candidates in person; cost effective.	Need to make a quick judgment on a candidate based on short conversation.
Employee Referrals	Knowledge about the organization provided by current employee; can generate strong candidates because a good referral reflects on the recommender.	May not increase the diversity and mix of employees; if referral is rejected, employee may feel slighted.
Company Website	Wide distribution; can be targeted to specific groups; cost effective.	Generates many unqualified candidates.
College Recruiting	Large centralized body of candidates; offering of internships may lead to full-time jobs; meet candidates in person.	Can be expensive and time consuming; limited to entry-level positions.
Headhunters/ Executive Recruiters	Good knowledge of industry and requirements; produce high quality candidates.	Little commitment to organization; may misrepresent candidate's wants; can be expensive.
Print Ads	Good publicity for the company; can be targeted to specific groups.	Smaller viewing population than internet ads; generates many unqualified candidates.
Internal Sources	Candidate's strengths and weaknesses are known; employee is already committed to the company; less orientation required.	Employees who apply for jobs and don't get them may become discontented; may maintain the status quo when a new direction is needed.

Tool 7.1   Recruiting Methods Comparison

be a waste of time, money, and effort. Next, you must realize that the test takers have individual rights and that the tests must be relevant to the job that they are applying for. According to Dessler, these rights include:

- The confidentiality of test results.
- The right to informed consent regarding the use of the results.

- The right to expect that only people qualified to interpret the scores will have access to them.
- The right to expect the test is the same for one candidate as it is for another.

Another type of test is a performance-simulation test. These tests are made up of actual job behaviors. For example, to find out if a candidate would be a good fit as a computer programmer, have him/her write a small computer program. Or, if you need a public relations coordinator, give the candidate a hypothetical crisis to deal with and see how he/she does. There are two main types of performance-simulation tests: work sampling and assessment centers.

Work sampling is a type of job tryout where applicants demonstrate that they have the necessary skills and abilities by actually doing the required tasks. Usually this type of test is used for jobs where work is routine or standardized.

Assessment centers are used to evaluate managerial potential through activities such as mock interviews, problem solving exercises, group discussions, and decision making games. The simulation usually lasts two to three days during which ten to twelve candidates perform the mentioned exercises. The more realistic you can make the exercises, the better idea you will have of the candidates' abilities.

Interviews, along with application forms, are the most common method of getting to know job applicants. There are several types of interviews that can come in handy in different situations. Panel interviews and group interviews are increasingly replacing the one-on-one interview.

The panel interview is an interview conducted by a team of interviewers (usually two or three), who interview the candidate together and then combine their ratings into a final panel score. The panel format allows interviewers to ask follow-up questions that often elicit more meaningful responses.

In this variant of a panel interview, a group of applicants sit together in a room and are interviewed by the panel. Usually, the panel will pose a problem and then watch to see which candidate takes control in the formulation of an answer. Other roles within the group environment are monitored as well.

In a one-on-one interview, the employer meets with a candidate alone and asks a series of questions. In some cases, sequential one-on-one interviews are used to see if a candidate will be consistent with their answers or to allow different managers to have time with the candidate.

Once you have narrowed your choices somewhat, it is always wise to do a background check. There are two types of background checks: verifications of application data and reference checks. Both are inexpensive and straightforward ways to confirm what the applicant has reported. How deeply you search depends on the position you seek to fill. In all cases you should check employment history, education, identification, criminal records, social security numbers, and licensing verification (if applicable). While references can be a good tool, experts believe that the validity of these are not high, due to the fact that applicants usually only include individuals who will give them a glowing recommendation.

Depending on the position you are filling, a physical exam may be needed. Motor abilities such as finger dexterity, manual dexterity, and reaction times are often tested for those jobs needing these physical skills. Also, tests of strength and body coordination may be needed if, for example, you are hiring a warehouse worker who will be lifting

Tool	Strengths	Weaknesses
Application Forms	Easy and relatively cheap to administer; lots of biographical and background data can be collected. Helps cover legal requirements and disclosures.	Only a few items on the form prove to be a valid predictor of job performance.
Written Tests	Various spatial, mechanical, motor ability, and perceptual tests are valid predictors of lower-level jobs; Intelligence tests are good predictors for supervisory positions.	Some people are not good test takers and will not show their true potential.
Performance-Simulation Tests	Measure job performance directly; hard for an applicant to fake answers as compared to a written test.	Expensive to create and administer.
Interviews	Relatively cost effective; if well organized and common questioning is used, then a good predictor.	Interviewers must be aware of the legality of certain questions; subject to potential biases. Some people are not good interviewers.
Background Checks	Verifications of background data are valuable sources of information.	Reference checks may not work well as a selection tool.
Physical Exams	Has validity for jobs with certain physical requirements; useful for insurance purposes.	Must be sure that physical requirements are job related and don't discriminate.
Personality Tests	Get beyond the answers you would get out of an applicant in an interview or on an application; has proven to be effective predictor of job performance.	Can create legal problems; most difficult tests to evaluate and use; must find a relationship between measurable personality trait and success on the job for it to be useful.

Tool 7.2   Selection Method Comparison

and moving heavy boxes all day. While the jobs that require such tests are few and far between, many organizations give physical exams to be sure that new hires will not submit insurance claims for injuries or illnesses they had previous to their hire.

Personality tests measure basic aspects of an applicant's personality. These can be used in a variety of ways. A sales organization, for example, may find that a certain profile from a DISC® personality test or Myers-Briggs® (or similar) test works best in their organization based on results from existing top performers. They can then use the test to search for candidates with similar trait profiles.

Generally, companies will use a combination of several selection strategies.

Now that I've hired people, how do I introduce an employee into the organization?

Now that you've made your hire, you need to socialize the new employee to your organization. Socialization actually begins before the hire. Hopefully, in the interview process, you've given the employee an idea of the organization's culture and have set expectations through a realistic job preview (RJP). Some creative ideas for an RJP include creating a website or other media site showing a day in the life of an employee at your organization. Your company's written material and website also provide the start of this process.

There are two types of orientation. Work unit orientation, which familiarizes the employee with the goals of the unit, clarifies how their job contributes to those goals and includes an introduction to co-workers. The second type, organization orientation, informs the employee about the company's culture, goals, history, philosophy, procedures, and rules. Don't underestimate the importance of an orientation. Not only does it give the new employee insight to the organization's everyday procedures, it also should make the new person feel welcome and give them a chance to acclimatize. Make sure your employee knows who to ask if they have questions.

The format of an orientation can range from a short discussion to a week-long program. Orientation can be led by an HR specialist, a trainer or the manager. The leader should explain items such as working hours, benefits, and vacations. Some firms keep a new employee orientation checklist to maintain a record of if and when important information was reviewed. Also, it should be noted that the new employee should receive an employee handbook that includes all policies and rules of the organization.

The employee orientation should include a tour of the facility to help a new employee feel comfortable with their surroundings. A guided tour will allow other employees to see that they have a new teammate without a formal introduction. Also, a tour will often elicit questions from the new hire that wouldn't have come up otherwise. Take this opportunity to continue learning about your new employee.

The employee's orientation should include an overview of key human resource policies including:

- Pay Schedule: You should have a printed schedule of pay dates for your employees. Also, if the employee is paid on an hourly rate, outline the timesheet/timecard formatting and the procedure for turning it in if the system is not electronic.
- Benefits: Most full-time employees receive benefits. The following are required by Federal or most state law:
  - Social Security
  - Unemployment Insurance
  - Workers' Compensation
  - Leaves under Family Medical Leave Act
- Below are some benefits that employers may choose to offer:

- Disability, health, and life insurance
- Pensions
- Paid time off (vacations, holidays, sick, etc.)
- Employee assistance and counseling programs.

Employees should receive literature identifying and explaining the benefits your company offers. You need to be well versed in all of the details and options that an employee may have or you can refer the employee to a specialist for this information.

What are some recommended training methods?

Just because you've hired an employee with high potential doesn't guarantee that they will succeed. They need to know what you want them to do and how you want them to do it. Immediately after the orientation, employee training should begin. You have many training options from which to choose:

- On-the-job (OJT): employees learn their job by actually doing it. This is often done after an initial introduction to the task. Steps to help ensure OJT success:
  - *Step 1*: Prepare the learner
  - *Step 2*: Present the operation
  - *Step 3*: Do a test run
  - *Step 4*: Follow up
- Job rotation: employees work at different jobs in a particular area, getting exposure to a variety of tasks.
- Mentoring and coaching: employees work with an experienced worker who provides information, support, and encouragement.
- Experiential exercises: employees participate in role-playing, simulations, or other face-to-face types of training.
- Workbooks/manuals: employees refer strictly to their workbooks and manuals for information.
- Classroom lectures: employees attend formal training sessions designed to deliver specific information.
- Programmed learning: employees use a textbook, computer program, or internet to follow a step-by-step, self-learning method that consists of three parts:
  - presenting questions, facts, or problems to the learner;
  - allowing the person to respond;
  - providing feedback on the accuracy of answers.
- Computer-based training: employees participate in multimedia simulations to learn in an interactive manner.

How do I review and improve my employee's performance?

A performance management system is a necessary component for high performing organizations. Just having an idea of how your employees are doing isn't nearly enough to maximize your human capital. Before you can use one of the several available appraisal tools, you must first determine what to measure. Does the job require a certain number of car locks to be assembled in an hour? Or is the position a sales job, where the sales dollars brought to the company by the employee is what really matters? This is for you to decide, depending on your organization and the position being evaluated.

There are a variety of several appraisal tools with the most common shown in Tool 7.3:

Method	Advantages	Disadvantages
Written Essays	Widely used. Allows freedom of expression on the part of the candidate.	Reflects the writing skills of the candidate, subjective, time consuming. Difficult to compare and contrast.
Critical Incidents	Both positive and negative examples of work. Forces appraiser to evaluate subordinates on an ongoing basis.	Time-consuming. Lacks quantification for salary/promotional decisions.
Graphic Rating Scales	Provide quantitative data. Less time-consuming than others. Easy to use.	Do not provide depth of job behavior assessed; standards unclear. Subject to bias.
Behaviorally Anchored Rating Scales (BARS)	Focus on specific and measureable job behaviors. Provide clear and consistent feedback.	Time-consuming. Difficult to develop.
Multiperson comparisons	Compares employees with one another.	Hard to use with large numbers of employees; legal concerns.
Management by Objectives (MBO)	Focuses on end goals. Results oriented. Collaborative between employee and appraiser.	Time-consuming. May have unclear and unattainable objectives.
360-degree appraisals	Thorough. Team oriented. Reduced discrimination risk.	Time-consuming. Should not be used to determine pay, promotions, or terminations.

Tool 7.3   Appraisal Method Comparison

Your HR department may have a process or template already in place for performance appraisals. Once you've completed your appraisal, you and your subordinate should meet to review your findings and make plans to remedy deficiencies and reinforce strengths. There are four basic types of appraisal outcomes:

- Satisfactory—Promotable: You should encourage the employee to keep up the good work and discuss their career plans. If the person is promotable, you should develop a specific action plan for educational and professional development.
- Satisfactory—Not promotable: The object here is to maintain satisfaction. For whatever reason, the employee cannot move up in the company at this time. The best option is to find incentives important enough to the person to maintain the satisfactory performance in the current position.
- Unsatisfactory—Correctable: In this situation, you will want to set out an action plan for correcting the unsatisfactory performance. A Performance Improvement Plan is a way of doing this. It is a contract that both the employer and employee sign which outlines the improvements to be made by the employee over a given time period. A sample Performance Improvement Plan (adapted from HR.BLR.com) is shown in Tool 7.4.
- Unsatisfactory—Uncorrectable: Usually, an interview is not necessary in this case. You can either tolerate the person's poor performance for now or dismiss the person from your organization (terminations are discussed later in this chapter).

> **TIPS FOR CONDUCTING AN APPRAISAL INTERVIEW**
> 1. Talk in terms of objective work data.
> 2. Don't get excessively personal.
> 3. Encourage the employee to talk.
> 4. Don't tiptoe around the issues.

How do I motivate my employees?

To keep your employees satisfied and working to their best potential, you have to keep them motivated. Remember that your employees are motivated by different things and not everyone reacts the same way to incentives. Several psychologists have done research on motivation theories, which have resulted in the following suggestions:

- The best way to motivate someone is to provide feedback and challenge, which helps satisfy the person's higher-level needs for things such as accomplishment and recognition. In other words, this method addresses the employee's need for intrinsic motivation.
- Relying solely on extrinsic rewards (salary, bonuses, vacation days, etc.) can be risky. Extrinsic rewards can sometimes detract from the person's intrinsic motivation. Psychologists suggest that devising incentive pay for highly motivated employees may demean and detract from the desire they have to do the job out of a sense of responsibility.
- The reward must be of value to an employee. A manager should take individual employee preferences into account.
- The quantified benchmark of success, whatever it may be, must be viewed as attainable by the employee. A person will not be motivated to attain something that is out of their reach.

Employee Performance Improvement Plan

A. Employee's Major Strengths

1. _____
2. _____
3. _____

B. Areas for Improvement/Development

1. _____
2. _____
3. _____

C. Development Plans: Areas for Development

1. _____
2. _____
3. _____

D. Development Strategy: _____

_____

_____

E. Employee Comments on this Review: _____

_____

_____

F. Reviewer's Comments: _____

_____

_____

_____

G. Growth potential in present position and future growth potential for increased
responsibilities: _____

_____

_____

_____

Employee's Signature: _____   Date:_____

Reviewer's Signature: _____   Date:_____

Manager's Signature (if applicable): _____   Date:_____

Tool 7.4   Employee Performance Improvement Plan

Incentive Program	Description
Piecework Plans	Pay the worker for each unit he or she produces. Be careful to watch the quality of your products, as workers may be focused strictly on numbers rather than quality.
Merit Pay	A salary increase based on the employee's individual performance. Usually becomes part of the employee's base salary (not a bonus). Make sure not to throw around these raises carelessly. Established appraisal procedures will help avoid this.
Recognition-Based Awards	Includes "Employee of the Month" programs and less formal recognition such as praise, approval, or expressions of appreciation. Recognition may be given in private or in a public forum (on a website, newsletter, etc.).
Commission Plan	Incentive for salespeople: greatest incentive, as effort clearly produces reward. Watch for neglect of non-selling duties as these often get pushed aside in this program. May lead to quality issues and customer service problems.
Combination Plan	Incentive for salespeople where salary and commission are combined. Good for addressing quality and service issues.
Team Incentives	Tie rewards into the team's overall group performance. These incentives facilitate training, since each member has an interest in getting new members trained as fast as possible. Be aware of slackers, and perceived inequity between group members.
Profit-Sharing Plans	All or most employees receive a share of the firm's annual profits which helps develop buy-in to corporate goals.
Employee Stock Ownership Plan (ESOP)	A corporation contributes shares of its own stock to a trust which are later distributed to employees on retirement or separation from service.
Gainsharing Plans	Engages employees in a common effort to achieve productivity objectives and share the gains.
Annual Bonus	Designed to motivate short-term performance of managers and are usually tied to company profitability.
At-risk Variable Pay Plans	Plans that put some portion of the employee's weekly pay at risk, subject to the firm meeting its financial goals.
Stock Option	The right to purchase a stated number of shares of a company stock at today's price sometime in the future.

Tool 7.5   Incentive Programs

According to HR expert Gary Dessler, (also see Tool 7.5) a manager can follow these guidelines to make an incentive plan more effective:

1. Ask the question, "Are performance levels inadequate due to motivation?"
2. Link the incentive with your company's strategy.
3. Make sure the program is motivational.
4. Make the plan easy for employees to understand.
5. Set effective standards.
6. View the standard as a contract with employees.
7. Get employees' support for the plan.
8. Use good measurement systems.
9. Use a complete set of standards.
10. Make the incentive plan part of a comprehensive, commitment-oriented approach.

What should I consider when determining compensation?

There are several items you should consider when determining your employees' compensation. Each manager should closely evaluate the situation, make the best decisions possible, and don't be afraid to be flexible. Below are some of the factors you should consider when determining what to pay:

- *Size of Company*: How large is your company? Are there many people who do the same job? Or are there only a few key people who make the company run?
- *Employee's tenure and performance*: How long has the employee been with the company and how well is he or she performing the job? The longer an employee has been with you, the more you pay them...especially if they are doing a quality job.
- *Kind of Job Performed*: Does the job require high levels of skill? If so, the employee should be rewarded accordingly.
- *Kind of Business*: What industry is the job in? Different industries have different pay ranges.
- *Unionization*: Is the business unionized? Unions have legal protection and have the right to bargain collectively.
- *Labor or Capital Intensive*: Does the job require a great deal of manual labor? Or does technology, such as computers or machines, take care of the job?
- *Management Philosophy*: What is management's philosophy towards pay?
- *Geographical Location*: What is the cost of living in your area?
- *Company Profitability*: How profitable is your company? Profitability affects how much you can pay employees.
- *Industry Standards:* How much would my competitors pay for similar positions?

What are some ideas on developing compensation plans?

There are two main approaches to compensation: fixed and variable. Fixed pay (salaried) can be based on either job skills (competencies) or job title. Competency-based pay systems reward employees for the job skills and competencies demonstrated. This type of pay system can be broken down into two categories: skill-based pay and pay for knowledge. Skill-based pay tends to be used more for workers with manual labor jobs, while pay for knowledge plans reward employees for learning relevant knowledge.

Pros to using competency-based pay:
- When used with teambuilding and empowerment programs, it leads to higher quality, lower absenteeism, and fewer accidents.
- More successful in manufacturing organizations.

Cons to using competency-based pay:
- Implementation problems.
- Ignores the cost implications of paying employees for knowledge, skills, and behaviors even if they are not used.
- Not as successful in service organizations.

The second approach to compensation is variable pay. Variable pay, which includes merit pay and piecework plans, is a system that bases an individual's compensation on performance. As mentioned above, this type of pay system is often used to motivate employees to reach maximum output. Because of this, variable pay systems are popular. In 2005, a study by Hewitt Associates, LLC found that 78% of large US companies had some form of a variable pay plan.

Pros to using variable pay plans:
- Motivates employees.
- Promotes teamwork.
- Encourages creative problem solving.
- Supports an environment of continual learning, improvement, and innovation.

Cons to using variable pay plans:
- Expensive to administer correctly.
- May be difficult to calculate what outcomes you will reward (depending on the industry).
- Won't be as successful if goals are not achievable.
- May lead to quality and service issues.

What are some ways to restructure my workforce?

Every company eventually reaches a point where they have to change. Many times they have to reduce the number of employees in their workforce. Whether due to poor performance or a need for downsizing, it is never an easy or enjoyable task. There are a variety of ways you can reach your optimum workforce numbers.

1. Firing: Here are a few guidelines to making the termination interview as painless as possible.
   - Plan the interview carefully.
   - Get to the point. Avoid small talk.

- Describe the situation.
- Listen.
- Review all elements of the severance package (if applicable).
- Identify the next step. In other words, explain the process for leaving the premises, etc.

2. Downsizing and layoffs: Downsizing is the planned elimination of jobs in an organization. This happens when the firm is faced with declining market share, has grown too aggressively, or has been poorly managed. A layoff is a common way to eliminate (albeit temporarily) jobs within an organization. The term layoff generally refers to having selected employees take time off, with the expectation that they will come back to work. There are some rules of thumb to follow to artfully layoff an employee:

- Take responsibility.
- Cut deep and cut once. In other words, don't just layoff the absolute minimum number of people because you don't want to hurt feelings. This will lengthen your company's road to recovery. It is better to remove a group of employees up front and be able to hire them all back once the company gets back on its feet.
- Move fast. Once you make the first layoff it is only a matter of time before the entire organization knows and production drops.
- Clean house. A layoff is a good time to terminate marginal employees.
- Share the pain. When you are making layoffs it would be a good gesture to cut back on the extravagancies of your job. For example, take a smaller office or turn in the company car. Show your employees you are doing what you can as well.
- Show consistency. If you are making layoffs, then you obviously don't have a great deal of extra cash around to be throwing into large severance packages.
- Don't ask for pity.
- Provide support and offer counseling for those employees let go.
- Don't let people self-select. If you allow people to step up and quit or retire for the good of the company then you are apt to lose some of your best people. A layoff should be a proactive decision on the manager's part.
- Address legal issues. Review factors such as age, race, and gender before finalizing any dismissals.
- Address security concerns. With any layoffs, it may be wise to have security personnel in place in case there is a problem.
- Communicate with and motivate your remaining employees. They will need a morale boost.

3. Transfers: If your organization is large enough to have multiple departments, transferring employees may be an option in restructuring your workforce. A transfer is a move from one job to another, usually with no change in salary or grade. An employer may transfer an employee to vacate a position where he or she is no longer needed, to fill one where he or she is needed, or to find a better fit for the employee within the firm.

4. Reduced work weeks: Reduced work weeks refers to a temporary reduction in working hours by a group of employees during tough economic times as a way to prevent layoffs. Employees may work four days per week instead of five, for example.

5. Early retirement: Early retirement is often offered to employees as a way to help trim the workforce. These employees usually receive a financial incentive of a liberal

pension plus cash payments. While it is legal to use incentives to encourage employees to retire early, the employee's decision must be voluntary.

6. Job sharing: Job sharing allows for two or more people to share a single full-time position. For example, Employee A works from 8am until noon while Employee B works from 1pm to 5pm. While hours are cut in half, this allows for both workers to remain employed. This alternative may be more appealing to an employee than layoffs or termination and in fact may work well for employees struggling with work-life balance issues.

What do I ask in an exit interview?

Exit interviews should be conducted when an employee leaves the company for any reason. The purpose of the interview is to elicit information about the job and/or company in hopes of getting insights into what is right or wrong about the firm. Exit interview questions should include:

- How were you recruited?
- Why did you join the company?
- Was the job presented correctly and honestly?
- Were your expectations met?
- What was the workplace environment like?
- What was your supervisor's management style?
- What did you like most/least about the company?
- Were there any special problem areas?
- Why did you decide to leave and how was the departure handled? (if applicable).

What are some legal issues involved with human resource management?

Over the years, many laws have been passed to protect the rights of people in the workplace. You must be knowledgeable of and follow these laws. The following table lists and explains some of the major employment laws in the United States. For further information on legal issues and ramifications, please see chapter eighteen.

In executive orders issued by the Johnson Administration, affirmative action was required to ensure employment opportunity for those who may have suffered discrimination in the past. In today's world, white males no longer dominate the labor force, and women and minorities represent a large portion of labor force growth over the foreseeable future. Although diversity in the workplace is now more encouraged and valued than in the past, affirmative action is still a significant workplace issue today.

The key aims of affirmative action programs are to:

- Use numerical analysis to determine which (if any) target groups the firm is underutilizing relative to the relevant labor market.
- Eliminate barriers to equal employment.

Law/Regulation	Overview
Title VII of the 1964 Civil Rights Act	An employer cannot discriminate based on race, color, religion, sex, or national origin. This includes the hiring process and classification/status of employees once employed.
Equal Pay Act of 1963	An employer cannot discriminate in pay on the basis of sex when jobs involve equal work.
Age Discrimination in Employment Act of 1967 (ADEA)	Employers cannot discriminate against employees or applicants who are between forty and sixty-five years of age. Amendments have since eliminated the age cap of sixty-five.
The Americans with Disabilities Act (ADA)	Enacted in 1990, it prohibits employment discrimination against qualified disabled individuals. It also requires employers to make reasonable accommodations for disabled employees.
Pregnancy Discrimination Act of 1978	Prohibits using pregnancy, childbirth, or related medical conditions to discriminate in hiring, promotion, suspension, or discharge, or any term or condition of employment.

Established by Title VII, the Equal Employment Opportunity Commission (EEOC) administers and enforces the Civil Rights law in employment settings. The EEOC is empowered to investigate job discrimination complaints and sue on the employee's behalf.

All managers should have a working knowledge of the EEOC claim and enforcement process. The process consists of these steps:

- Charge is filed: The discrimination claim must be filed within 300 or 180 days (depending on state law) after the alleged incident took place. The filing must be in writing and under oath.
- Charge Acceptance: The EEOC accepts a charge and orally refers it to the state or local agency on behalf of the charging party.
- Serve Notice: After a charge is filed, the EEOC has ten days to serve notice on the employer.
- Investigation/Fact-Finding Conference: The EEOC has 120 days to investigate the charge and determine whether there is reasonable cause to believe it is true.
- Cause/No Cause: If no reasonable cause is found, the EEOC must dismiss the charge and must issue the charging party a Notice of Right to Sue. The person then has ninety days to file a suit.
- Conciliation: If cause is found by the EEOC, it has thirty days to work out a conciliation agreement between the employee and employer. If both parties accept the remedy, they sign and submit a conciliation agreement to the EEOC for approval. If the EEOC cannot obtain an acceptable conciliation agreement, it may sue the employer in federal district court.
- Notice to Sue: If the conciliation is not satisfactory, the EEOC may bring a civil suit in federal court.

What do I do if I'm involved in a discrimination complaint?

If a discrimination charge is brought against you, consult your HR department, manager and/or legal counsel. There are some key things to keep in mind when dealing with a discrimination charge. During the EEOC investigation you should:

- First, be sure that the EEOC has information demonstrating lack of merit of the charge in its file. You can do this by providing a detailed statement describing your company's defense. Also, limit the information supplied to only those issues raised in the charge itself. Lastly, get as much information as possible about the charging party's claim to ensure that you fully understand it and its implications.
- Meet with the employee who made the complaint to clarify all the relevant issues. Write down everything stated and request that the employee sign and date it.
- Be courteous with the EEOC investigators. It is their recommendations that are the determining factor in whether the EEOC finds cause.
- Submit documents as requested.
- Give the EEOC a *position statement*, outlining your own investigation and findings.
- During the fact-finding conference you should be aware that:
  - Only the EEOC investigator's notes are official and neither party can have access to them.
  - You may have an attorney present.
  - The conferences often occur before the employer is fully informed of the charges and facts of the case.
  - Parties may use witnesses' statements as admissions against the employer's interests. Be careful who you choose as a witness and what they say.
- During the EEOC determination and attempted conciliation you should keep in mind:
  - If there is a finding of cause, review it carefully and point out inaccuracies in writing to the EEOC.
  - Some experts recommend that you don't make a conciliation agreement. The EEOC views conciliation as a complete relief to the charging party. Even if the EEOC or charging party later files a suit, you can consider settling after receiving the complaint.

What are some things I need to know about sexual harassment?

Sexual harassment refers to harassment on the basis of sex when such conduct has the purpose or effect of interfering with a person's work performance or creating a hostile or intimidating work environment. Both Title VII and the EEOC assert that employers have a duty to maintain workplaces free of sexual harassment and intimidation. There are three main ways an employee can prove sexual harassment:

1. Quid Pro Quo: Occurs when employment decisions or expectations are based on employee submission to or rejection of sexual advances, requests for sexual favors, or other behavior of a sexual nature.

2. Hostile Environment Created by Supervisors: If a supervisor does or says things in a workplace that make the victim feel uncomfortable because of his or her sex the employee may have a right to sue the employer. It is not necessary to show a demand for an exchange of sex for a job benefit, the creation of an uncomfortable environment is sufficient under the law.
3. Hostile Environment Created by Co-Workers or Nonemployees: Actions of an employee's co-workers or even customers can cause the employer to be held responsible for sexual harassment. Remember, the creation of an "uncomfortable environment" is enough to deem sexual harassment present.

What can I do to minimize liability in sexual harassment claims?

- Take all complaints seriously.
- Inform the harasser directly that the conduct is unwelcome and must stop.
- Issue a strong policy statement condemning such behavior. The policy should contain a clear explanation of the prohibited conduct and a clearly defined complaint process that provides confidentiality.
- Inform all employees about the policy prohibiting sexual harassment and of their rights under the policy.
- Establish a management response system.
- Begin management training sessions to increase employee awareness of the issues.
- Discipline managers and employees involved in sexual harassment.
- Keep thorough records of complaints, investigations, and actions taken.
- Republish the sexual harassment policy periodically.

For a more in-depth analysis of legal information and ramifications, please refer to chapter eighteen.

Additional Resources

The US Department of Labor (www.dol.gov) is a great resource for diverse topics such as small business resources, discrimination, terminations, workers' compensation, among others.

Since 1948, the Society of Human Resource Management (SHRM) has been providing resources for managers across the globe. They are the largest of the associations dealing with human resource issues. Their website provides extensive information on a variety of related topics (www.shrm.org).

During the hiring process, as described above, personality and aptitude testing may be used to help identify the best fit between the candidate and the organization. Two sources of commonly used personality testing are HumanMetrics: Identify Your Type with Jung Typology™ Test and Personality Pathways: An informal Myers & Briggs Personality Test. More information on Myers-Briggs® can be found through the Myers & Briggs Foundation.

References

Banker, R. D., Lee, S. Y., Potter, G. and Srinivasan, D. (1996). Contextual analysis of performance impacts on outcome-based incentive compensation. *Academy of Management Journal*, 39(4), 920–48.

Barrick, M. R., Stewart, G. L. and Piotrowski, M. (2002). Personality and job performance: Test of the mediating effects of motivation among sales representatives. *Journal of Applied Psychology*, 87, 43–51.

Dessler, G. (2008). *Human Resource Management* (11th ed.). Upper Saddle River, NJ: Pearson Education, Inc.

Equal Employment Opportunity Commission. (2011). *Sexual Harassment.* Retrieved from http://www.eeoc.gov/laws/types/sexual_harassment.cfm.

Heathfield, S. M. (n. d.). *360 Degree Feedback: The Good, the Bad, and the Ugly.* Retrieved from http://humanresources.about.com/od/360feedback/a/360feedback.htm on March 7, 2011.

Henneman, R. and LeBlanc, P. (2003). Work evaluation addresses the shortcomings of both job evaluation and market pricing. *Compensation and Benefits Review*, 35(1), 7–11.

Hewitt Associates, LLC. (2005). *Hewitt study shows base pay increases flat for 2006 with variable pay plans picking up the slack.* Retrieved from http://benefitslink.com/pr/detail.php?id=39139.

HR World Editors (2008, March 11). *Employee Referral Bonus Jackpots: 15 Companies with Awesome New-hire Incentives.* Retrieved from http://www.hrworld.com/features/referral-bonus-jackpot-031108/.

Kawasaki, G. (2006, July 5*). The Art of the Layoff.* Retrieved from http://blog.guykawasaki.com/2006/07/the_art_of_the_.html#axzz1G9YAYblz.

PeopleMatch. (2010). Retrieved from http://www.peoplematch.com.

Robbins, S. P. and Coulter, M. (2008). *Management* (10th ed.). Upper Saddle River, NJ: Prentice Hall.

Swaggerty, K. (2009, March 6). *The Pros and Cons of Variable Pay: Is it Worth it?* Retrieved from http://www.resources.hrbrainbank.com/compensation/articles/pros-and-cons-variable-pay-it-worthwhile.html.

USLegal.com. (2011). *Hostile Workplace Environment Law & Legal Definition.* Retrieved from http://definitions.uslegal.com/h/hostile-workplace-environment/.

8 *Marketing and Promotion*

MARLA ASHE

The purpose of this chapter is to provide information and tools about comprehensive marketing planning, advertising, marketing communications and public relations for products and services. This chapter will initially discuss the definition and development of an Integrated Marketing Communication Plan (IMCP) and its four key elements. The creation of an IMCP ensures the delivery of a streamlined, cohesive message from the organization to the markets (consumer or business). Also, it builds relationships that hold all contributors to the IMCP accountable. The chapter will then address the remaining issues of advertising, marketing communications and public relations.

How can we best organize our marketing efforts?

An IMCP does exactly this. We'll start with a definition. According to Clow and Baack (2007), an Integrated Marketing Communication Plan is defined as "the coordination and integration of all marketing communication tools, avenues and sources within a company into a seamless program that maximizes the impact on consumers and other end users at a minimal cost." The overall objective is to create a one-message approach that eliminates confusion for the target markets.

In the past, an organization might create a marketing plan and present it separately to the advertising agency, public relations agency and promotional agency. The agencies then created their own interpretations of the target market, the message and the approach. This process produced several different messages aimed at different targets that caused confusion in the marketplace. This is why traditional marketing/promotional plans fell out of favor. The preference now is to create an IMCP. This avoids separate and sometimes conflicting strategies. The Association of National Advertisers reports that 74% of firms are using an integrated marketing communications approach to develop a marketing strategy and build brand equity.

What are the elements of an Integrated Marketing Communication Plan (IMCP)?

The IMCP approach consists of four building blocks described by Clow and Baack (2005) and depicted in Figure 8.1. The building blocks are dependent on each other for a holistic methodology that engages the target market's attention and creates a purchase mindset. The first building block is the foundation, the base of the plan. This section of the plan addresses corporate image and target market buying behavior. It also includes a promotion opportunity analysis.

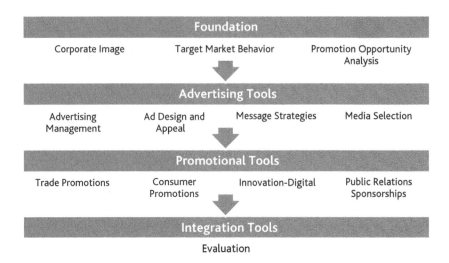

Figure 8.1   Integrated Marketing Communication Plan Building Blocks

The next building block consists of the advertising tools. This section focuses on all advertising concerns: ad agency management, design and appeal, message strategies and media selection. The third building block, trade promotions, covers all promotions: trade and consumer promotions, innovation-digital promotions, public relations and sponsorships. The fourth and final building block, integration tools, creates an evaluation plan for each element of the IMCP.

The foundation building block requires you to examine the organization's corporate image. The vision for the corporate image is established when the mission and vision statements are created. It is important to confirm that the products or services created or the existing ones are aligned with the organization's focus. Misalignment causes confusion in the marketplace. Next, assess whether the organization's perceived image is being projected and interpreted correctly by the target market. Here, you determine the uniqueness of the product and the basis for your product or service brand. In other words, you are evaluating your brand equity and your competitive advantage. Brand is a name for the product or service and brand equity is the added value given to the product or service by the consumer.

How do we determine the most effective marketing communications method?

The IMCP gives you a framework. Now you need an effective communications strategy. According to Clow and Baack, promotion opportunity analysis is the process marketers use to determine the target market's most effective communication vehicle for maximum reach. An analysis is conducted to determine the strengths, weaknesses, opportunities and threats that exist in an organization's marketing communications to the target audience. When this process is complete, establish measurable communication objectives. Figure 8.2 discusses communication objectives related to measurable marketing objectives.

Communication Objectives	Measurable Objectives
Develop Brand Awareness	Sales Volume Market Share
Increase Category Demand	Market Share
Change Customer Beliefs & Attitudes	New User Share
Repeat Purchases	Profit Sales Volume
Increase Market Share	Market Share
Increase Sales	Profit Return on Investment

Figure 8.2   Communication and Measurable Objectives

Method	Calculation	When to Use
The IMCP budget is determined by a percentage of total sales (past, current and forecasted sales).	The total sales dollars of carbonated soft drinks from May–September (key selling time) is $2,500,000. The IMCP will utilize 25% of the sales dollars during the May– September period or $625,000.	This approach should be used when the IMCP is going to be self-funded through product sales. This approach is geared toward an organization's departments (marketing, production, sales and finance) working together.
The IMCP budget has a predetermined dollar amount based on each item/unit sold.	For every carbonated soft drink sold for May–September, $0.25 will be set aside for the IMCP budget. Use past sales data: May, 700,000 units June, 800,000 units July, 1,000,000 units August, 1,000,000 units September, 900,000 units Totaling: 4,400,000 units × .25= $1,100,000 budget.	This approach should be used when past sales numbers were similar or less than the current sales forecast.
The IMCP budget is set based on the competitor's spending in the marketplace.	Currently all department store intimate apparel companies are spending $25 on product fulfillment.	Use this approach when you know exactly what the competitors are spending, based on market research or a formal agreement between manufacturers.
Determine the marketing objective and spend until the objective is met.	Marketing objective is to increase market share within the southwest region. Unlimited budget.	Use when an unlimited amount of financial resources are available.

Tool 8.1   Budgeting Approaches
Adapted from Boone and Kurtz, 2010.

What are the different ways we can develop a promotion and advertising budget?

The next step in a promotion opportunity analysis is the creation of a communication budget. This budget will be shared with all marketing communication partners (advertising agency, media buying agency, public relations and promotions agency). The optional ways of calculating the budget are shown in Tool 8.1.

Determination of the promotion strategy is next. It is defined as a well thought out, long-range plan to help achieve competitive advantage in order to earn a greater share of the profits available in the industry. Once the promotion strategy is determined, the challenge becomes execution. For example, if the strategy is to improve the corporate image, a public relations agency could be used to create an appropriate event or, the corporation could create an internal ambassador program for employees. To execute the good-will building program, a community-based organization is selected and the employees would do community service in different parts of the city. Coverage in the press and other visibility would help achieve the corporate goal of image improvement.

Business organizations require marketing departments to quantify promotional effectiveness. It is critical that organizations understand the effectiveness of the IMCP and the impact it has on the target market's decision to make an initial or incremental purchase. In order to evaluate IMCP effectiveness and viability, this information needs to be quantified. Therefore, developing the IMCP budget is vital.

There are several different budgeting approaches. A recommended option includes having a cross-function meeting with the sales and finance departments. This will help the marketing, sales and finance departments understand the budget allocation available to ensure the IMCP is successful. Use Tool 8.1 to help you choose a budget approach.

The next major section in the IMCP deals with an assessment of the organization's advertising strategy. The organization will begin to develop advertising goals, objectives, appeals, a creative brief and the budget. This will allow a marketing department to collaborate with an advertising agency successfully.

What is advertising management?

According to Clow and Baack, advertising management is the ability to create a systematic approach that will create one message from the organization's marketing department to the target market and to all internal or external partners. Effective advertising management results in a successful working relationship with internal and external agencies and develops an advertising strategy that becomes the format for all communication.

What kinds of advertising agencies are available?

Advertising agencies create and implement marketing programs. There are several different types of agencies. They fall into four main categories as shown in Figure 8.3.

Type of Agency	Primary responsibilities
Full-Service Agency	Provides service in four major areas: • Account Management- Assigns key employees to work as a liaison between the agency and organization. • Creative Services- Has the ability to develop different creative needs- ads, blogs, online and others. • Media Planning- Has the ability to strategically place the creative advertising time and space to achieve the marketing communication objective. • Media Buying- Has the ability to purchase airtime for clients to place their advertisement. • Account Planning- Has the ability to provide consumer insight concerning brand awareness and equity. Also includes the ability to conduct consumer research regarding the creative services on air, on radio or online.
Specialized Agency	Focuses on specialized functions- creative production, digital media buying or social networking advertising. Focuses on consumer targets, i.e. African-American and Hispanic advertising agencies.
Creative Boutique	Smaller agency with a small employee base, focused on assisting with a creative idea. For example, creating copy for print advertising. Execution is limited due to scarce resources.
Media-Buying Service	Purchases media for clients. For example, the service purchases the time slots in which an organization would like to run their TV, radio or digital ads.

Figure 8.3   Types of Advertising Agencies

Adapted from: Clow & Baack, 2007; Wells, Moriarty & Burnett, 2006

How do I select an advertising agency?

There are several factors an organization must consider in order to determine the contractual relationship with an advertising agency. Use the following tool to help you make the decision.

1. What type of agency do I want to work with?
2. What's the size of the agency?
3. What's my advertising budget?
4. What's the agency's experience in my industry?
5. What's the agency's reputation?
6. Does the agency represent my competitors (potential conflict of interest)?
7. Is the agency able to be my one-stop shop?
   • What are their media buying capabilities?
   • What are their public relations capabilities?
   • What is their creative production capability?
8. Does the agency work well with my organizational structure?
9. Are our organizational cultures compatible?

Tool 8.2   Agency Selection Questions

Once you've answered these questions you'll have greater insight into selecting an agency. For example, if your advertising budget is less than $500,000, consider using a specialized and/or creative boutique agency. If the budget is larger, a full-service agency might be able to do more for you. Price though, isn't the only determinant. A good match in terms of style and culture is also very important.

How do I work with an advertising agency?

The single most important element of a successful working relationship with an advertising agency is full disclosure in the creative/communications brief. According to Clow and Baack it should include the marketing problem, budget, advertising/communication objective, targeted consumer/market, brand position, brand uniqueness, sales goal and any agency restrictions or limitations. Please refer to Tool 8.3 for a sample creative/communications brief. The creative brief is developed jointly by the organization and all integrated marketing communication agencies (brand marketing and sales department, advertising, public relations, digital agency and social networking agencies). It is a living document that becomes the format for both the agency and the organization to ensure the objectives and goals are met. The major components are depicted in the following example.

Integrated Marketing Communication Plan

Creative Brief

Define the Marketing Problem:

Explain the Type of Promotional Budget and Why:

Advertising:

Promotions:

Ad Production:

      Digital:

      Other:

Project Objective:

Brand Positioning: Illustrate and Explain

Organization's Sales Goal: Quantify

Agency Requirements:

Tool 8.3   Sample Creative/Communications Brief

How do I define the marketing problem?

The marketing/advertising problem addresses the national, local and/or business-to-business dilemma that you are seeking to resolve. The problem is commonly linked to a business or sales objective that the organization must achieve internally. For example, one problem might be the need to increase national brand awareness within the target market. Another might be the need to increase sales with important retail partners (Walmart, Kroger or CVS) For example, in the southwest region of the United States, a solution to the problem would be to generate increased foot traffic into Walmart for the new product launch.

When identifying the marketing problem, be very specific and make certain the problem is clearly defined. Specification of a single problem will eliminate outcome confusion. Unsuccessful IMCPs are not due to execution failure, but are usually caused by the organization's inability to identify the real marketing problem. See chapters one and two for more on identifying and solving problems. A well-defined marketing problem creates a measurable objective that results in a successful integrated marketing communication plan.

What are some different advertising/communication objectives?

An advertising or communication objective is an actual measurable goal that can be determined after the IMCP has been developed and executed. For example, let's say the marketing problem is low sales in a new target market. The objective, increase sales by 20% in the specified market for example, must be stated. It aligns the goals of plan participants. The objective becomes the litmus test for every decision. Listed below are a few objective options and examples of when they should be used:

Objective	When to use	How it will be measured
Increase brand awareness within the target marketplace.	Have a new product or service. Have a new target market.	Target market focus group.
Help establish a brand image within the target marketplace.	Launch of new product or good/service with no prior connection to the target market.	The frequency with which the product was linked to a goal for the target.
Increase customer traffic.	Increase sales of the good/service to the target market. Increase incremental sales of a good/service to the target market.	Increased sales to the target market.
Increase retailer sales.	Increase a retailer's purchase of the product for the target market.	Retailer's sales data.

Tool 8.4   Communication Objectives

Source: Clow & Baack (2007); Wells, Moriarty & Burnett (2006).

Once the objective is determined, the target market, consumer or business-to-business must be addressed. Refer to chapter eleven for more on identifying customers and target markets. The creative brief must identify and clarify the target market. If the target market information is incorrect, it could result in a negative impact on the overall objective for the integrated marketing communication plan. For example, the objective is to increase awareness within the target market, which will result in increased sales. If the funding is directed to the wrong target, the objective will not be met.

What else needs to go into the creative brief?

The creative brief must identify all of the sales goals the organization wants to achieve. This allows all agencies to understand the procedure the organization will use to measure success. This section requires all IMCP participants to understand the restrictions or limitations the organization will implement. For example, all recorded agencies of the organization must work together on the plan. They know they cannot contract with other agencies within their network to accomplish the goal.

The creative brief is a working, living document that is subject to change. However, all active parties must be made aware of any changes. Once the organization's creative brief is completed, it is disseminated to all approved agencies. The document is discussed to ensure the agencies are informed and agreeable. This is the basis for the integrated marketing communication plan. As the old adage states, failing to plan is planning to fail. The purpose of the creative brief is to ensure a successful IMCP.

What are two main types of advertisements?

Advertising is a way of communicating your message to the world. It is the image or external face of your company, and an important piece of your overall marketing strategy. There are two basic types of advertising: product and institutional/corporate. Product advertising consists of impersonal selling of goods or service. Institutional/corporate advertising promotes a concept, idea, philosophy, or benevolence of an organization as noted by Boone and Kurtz (2010).

The proliferation of brands and products within an organization has caused an increase in the development of institutional/corporate ads. According to Kim, Haley, and Koo (2009), General Motors Corporation spent $100 million on corporate advertising in 2002, which was more than ten times their expenditures in 2000. In 2006, BP utilized institutional corporate advertising to help increase credibility, doubling its advertising spending to $150 million, although the Gulf Oil disaster certainly undermined this. There is a correlation between institutional/corporate ads and the developing of a positive impact on consumers' assessments of a company's product lines and brands, which causes increased purchasing consideration.

What kind of appeals can I use in my advertising?

There are several different types of advertising appeal options that can be used in an integrated communication marketing plan. Use Tool 8.5 to help determine which appeal strategy is best for you.

Advertising Appeal	How it is used in advertising	Purpose
Fear	Use consumers' fears to inspire purchase.	Fear appeal increases consumers' interest in the ad and is persuasive. The fear must be strong in order to attract consumer interest.
Humor	Used to reach the target consumer to help him/her remember the advertisement.	Humor has three advantages. It causes the consumer to watch, laugh and remember the product or organization.
Sex	Used to build brand awareness and gain attention.	Used in the decorative model in advertising, the goal is to embellish the product as a sexual or attractive stimulus.
Music	Helps gain attention and links emotions, memories and other experiences to a song.	Used to connect consumers to a product through the music—brand awareness. Equity and loyalty are developed when consumers have a connection with music.
Rationality	Used on products that require consumers to cognitively make decisions about a high involvement purchase, for example, a house or car.	It is used to develop or change consumers' attitudes.
Emotions	Used when a product or brand wants to connect to consumers' emotions: love, friendship, fear and security.	Helps develop brand loyalty by connecting consumers to emotions.
Scarcity	Used to create a sense of urgency for the consumers to purchase due to the limited availability of the product.	This appeal is used as a promotional tool, for example, sales promotion during key holidays.

Tool 8.5   Advertising Appeal Options

Adapted from Clow & Baack (2005); Clow & Baack (2007).

What are the advantages and disadvantages of media?

In developing a media strategy there are several determinants that must be addressed:

- the target market
- the theme of the message being developed for the target
- the limitations

For example, consider a national versus a regional integrated marketing campaign. Once the main objectives are determined, a medium or media are selected to accomplish the goal.

The three main types of advertising include word-of-mouth, traditional media and digital advertising. The most commonly used is word-of-mouth. The goal here is to get people talking about your product. To help get the word out, consider both traditional and digital strategies. Traditional media are no longer as effective because of a crowded field of competitors and new consumer preferences. These preferences have shifted toward digital advertising (social networking, Twitter, YouTube, blogging and pop-up ads). That said, traditional media is not completely dead and should be considered as part of your strategy.

There must be an effective blend of digital and traditional media options. Table 8.2 explains the advantages and disadvantages of traditional and digital media options and when to use them.

When assessing the use of different advertising options, there are two components to determine: message customization and feedback (Dolan 1999; Wosinska 2005). Figure 8.4 provides a view of the two components and their relationships to each advertising media.

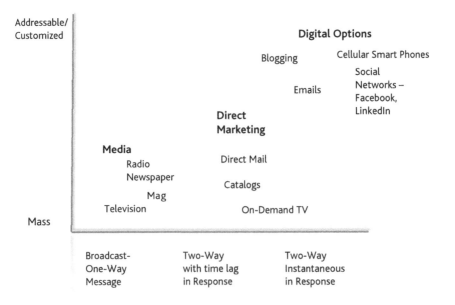

Figure 8.4 When to Use the Different Advertising Options

Adapted from Dolan (1999), Integrated Marketing Communications.

Table 8.2   Media Advantages and Disadvantages

Media	Advantages	Disadvantages	Recommendation
Television	Able to reach millions of viewers. Great visual stimulation with music and emotional appeal. Able to utilize in small to large areas—regional and national TV.	Very expensive. Limited to fifteen to thirty second spots to convey a message. Consumers increasingly do not watch commercials.	TV ads must be used very strategically. Many mass retailers (Walmart, Target and others) currently have TV in stores. This will ensure the target can be influenced at the point of decision, at the shelves.
Radio	Able to focus on a target market. Leverage the local DJ and radio personalities to influence the target—by word of mouth. Radio stations are able to provide added value services when ads are purchased. Appearance of radio personalities in the target market area.	Low attention from the target market. Internet and digital radio stations are causing a reduction in listeners to traditional stations. Regional focus.	To help create an on-air buzz word-of-mouth campaign in the marketplace use the DJ and radio personalities to do on-air banter about the product or services as if they used or currently use the product or service.
Outdoor Advertising	Visually appealing with new digital LCD billboards. Large size grabs attention. Many options to brand: park benches, bus stops, fences at sporting events and taxis among others.	Low attention from target due to clutter and limited visual exposure time. Costly for new digital LCD billboards. Easily missed, passive medium.	Use to gain attention for a product or brand. Consider a digital LCD billboard as an option. This lets movement and flashing lights get the drivers' attention. Digital LCD billboards can incorporate your digital media strategy.
Magazines	Can segment the market by focusing on target market—women's books, men's books, food fans and more. High color quality, the ads can "pop" in the book. Able to layer direct-response tactics—coupons, web promotions drive the reader to the product/brand website.	Expensive. Long development timeframe. Declining readership of hard copies. Consumers read magazines on the go.	Utilize if the purchase of an ad schedule in the hard copy magazine allows the organization added value, an additional ad in the digital version of the book and any other added value items the magazine can offer.

Table 8.2   (continued)

Newspaper	Regional. Room for a bigger ad with more copy space. Layer direct response tactics, coupons, website and promotional support for local businesses.	Decreasing readership. Newspapers are now offered online, increased competition with online ads. Low print quality for color ad.	Marketing funds are limited and regional. Create an ad in the local newspaper to help inform target about the product, brand or retail events sponsored by the company.
Direct Marketing Mail, Catalogs, Telemarketing, On-demand TV responses, Email Blasts and others	Able to target consumers based on addresses and zip codes. Able to develop a relationship with customers. Able to customize messages to the customers from the manufacturer	Direct mail can be expensive. Consumers may view items received as junk and never read them. Messages are often not received due to the clutter of advertising messages bombarding the customer.	Utilize direct marketing in conjunction with other advertising vehicles. Run an advertising campaign on regional (local) television, have the same message on local radios station in addition to sending out the advertising message to key zip codes by direct mail. By using direct marketing in an advertising campaign, you are able to reach the customers on several different touch points.
Digital Internet, Social Media and Outlets, Mobile/Cellular Phones Blogs	Able to send messages directly to customers in a just-in-time manner. Able to generate a buzz to help influence consumers. The modern-day word-of-mouth approach.	Must have a compelling advertising message that will connect with the consumers based on their values and beliefs. Traditional advertising messages do not always translate effectively in the digital world.	Use on target customer bases that incorporate digital technology as a part of their current lives. Top advertising trends for 2010 are aligning with smartphones and media platforms, utilizing social networking as a basis of generating a new sales channel for product awareness and more interactive online ads that mirror video games for the wow factor.

Keep these considerations in mind when planning your media strategy. While digital options are customizable and provide immediate feedback potential, they may not entirely suit your product or your message. In addition, your target market (the increasing pool of baby boomer retirees for example) may not be technologically savvy. In all likelihood, you will need a combination of different media to achieve your product visibility goals.

What are my promotion tool options?

The third level of the integrated marketing communication plan format consists of promotional tools, which include trade and consumer promotions, public relations and sponsorships. This section will discuss the following different tactical options regarding trade and consumer promotions:

Trade Promotion Option	Definition	Disadvantages	When to Use
Trade Allowances	Financial incentives to retailers to help ensure the products are placed on the shelves and sold.	Savings the retailers earn through trade allowances are not passed on to customers.	New product rollout. Need to move product in bulk. Need assistance in clearing out discontinued product lines.
Cooperative Advertising	Manufacturer pays for local, national and retail advertising for retailers to feature products sold in the retail outlets.	Clutter of different products being featured in the advertising.	When manufacturers are unable to pay for local, national and retail advertising and need to share the cost.
Trade Contest	To help retail outlets achieve sales goals a manufacturer will create a contest and reward the retail outlet, salesperson and agents.	With the changing gifting law, many retail outlets are unable to receive direct gifts from manufacturers.	If members of the channel network are not excited about selling products, develop programs that will allow them to win based on the sales of product.
Point-of-Purchase Advertising	Advertising on a permanent or temporary sales display in a retail outlet.	Not utilized as intended by the manufacturer. Displays are never put up or the retail outlets throw them away.	New product rollout. Limited shelf space. When a manufacturer needs additional shopping points within a retail outlet.

Tool 8.6   Trade Promotion Options

- The new approach to personal selling in the twenty-first century.
- How customer relationship management programs have revolutionized the consumer markets.
- Viewpoints regarding public relations and sponsorships for consumer and business markets.

Several trade promotion options are available to marketers. Tool 8.6 outlines the options and presents advantages and disadvantages of each. Tips are provided for when to use each option.

When the channel of distribution members' wants, needs and desires are understood, manufacturers and/or organizations can provide relevant goods and services. Trade promotions are potentially successful vehicles that enable the channel of distribution to focus on and sell your goods and services. The selection of trade promotions that can integrate with other crucial or essential promotions is indispensable for a successful IMCP.

What are consumer promotions?

Consumer promotions are designed to reach the end-users (the customers) of the products, goods or services. Consumer promotions, sometimes referred to as sales promotions, have two primary purposes, to encourage trial/usage of the goods or services and to increase awareness of the features and benefits of the goods or services. Ideally, this will create a strong brand loyalty that will place the goods or services on the consumer's preferred consideration list.

A successful IMCP must take into consideration the constantly changing competitive landscape that consciously and subconsciously influences consumer purchasing behavior. The design of a consumer promotion reflects a moving target, which means a marketer must develop a comprehensive and adaptable promotion that meets the needs, wants and desires of consumers. Due to the proliferation of brands and products, consumer promotions help to penetrate the noise that occurs in the marketplace.

Successful marketers have created a dual strategy with the channel of distribution members (trade) and end-users (consumers) when they work together. It is named the push-pull strategy. Manufacturers use the pushing motion with channels of distribution members. Products are introduced to the channel members who are enticed to carry the products in their storefronts. This approach may use the trade promotions just discussed. The pulling motion is used when manufacturers talk directly with the end-users and ask them to require their retail outlets to carry the products. This approach uses consumer promotions.

A marketer could use several consumer promotional options. They can be divided into two categories, traditional and innovative. Traditional promotional methods such as premiums, contest rebates and refunds, sampling, bonus packs and coupons have been used for several years. Innovative promotions utilize digital marketing, social networking, blogging, microblogging, Twitter, consumer generated videos, mobile and apps development.

How do I create a successful and innovative consumer promotion?

Innovative consumer promotions use both promotional and digital marketing. A marketer may not be familiar with this approach to marketing to consumers. If this is the case, create a relationship with a digital promotional agency that understands the evolution of the digital landscape. Refer to the beginning of the chapter to find out how to secure an agency. Ledward (2007) shares information on how to be successful with consumer promotions. He states:

> *There are a few rules for promotions, and the first is to use technology to engage consumers. Don't think of online as a one-off medium. Ensure your team is equipped with both promotional and digital specialists. Realize the idea in all formats, this is the model for the future. Don't allow the idea to be restricted by apparent limitations of any one channel (media). Everything is possible.*

Innovative consumer promotions require and respect limitations. A marketer must understand that the traditional go-to market strategy is not applicable to twenty-first century consumers. Larger organizations understand the need to have a relevant paradigm shift when engaging and interacting with consumers, the end users. In short, innovative consumer promotional strategy is moving like a tsunami through the marketplace. Now is the time to understand and use such strategies to remain relevant and active with targeted consumers.

What is the role of public relations?

There are many fallacies and misunderstandings regarding public relations. One misconception of public relations is that it attempts to make bad events and dishonest people look good. Another misconception is that public relations is only about garnering publicity. Commonly, we think of public relations as coming into play when there is a crisis. However, a deeper look at public relations will show that there is much more to the field.

The general term, public relations, includes various disciplines and responsibilities. It relates to both internal and external communications. It involves actual and prospective stakeholders. It involves the placement of communications in the media that is not directly paid for as a media buy. Public relations depends on relationships with news directors and editors to make it happen. It plays the role of message reinforcement. Often, marketers will plan and execute public relations strategies in conjunction with paid advertising campaigns.

How do I utilize public relations as a promotional tool?

When public relations tools are used in an IMCP, an organization is able to gain the competitive advantage in the marketplace. Public relations can be used to help build a corporate image within the larger community. It can also be used in crisis management situations.

During a crisis, public relations gets involved at three stages. These stages are: before the crisis, during the crisis and after the crisis. The 'before' stage is when an organization needs to create a two-way communication approach that allows the market to voice their concerns about the organization. In return, the organization can respond to the market creating a meaningful dialogue. Also, an organization needs to develop strategic alliances that can help create ongoing goodwill in the market. Accordingly, if an organization finds itself in crisis, the strategic alliances will become their advocates or their endorsers in the market. Additionally, an organization needs to create trust through disclosure, interaction and dialogue with their stakeholders. These mechanisms need to be in place before the crisis happens.

The second stage of using public relations as a crisis management tool occurs in the midst of the crisis. This is especially true when a crisis has become public and the market expects the organization to address the issue. You should establish a spokesperson for the organization, and get the organization's version of the story out first. This gives an organization the ability to define the story and begin the navigation process in the desired direction. Organizations are well advised to tell the truth during times of crisis. As our markets have become increasingly transparent, remember that news travels fast and facts usually become public.

The last stage occurs after the crisis, where the rebuilding of trust begins. In this stage, leaders in the organization need to remain in the public eye by being accessible and active in the community and the industry.

As formulated by Clow and Baack, the last section of an IMCP consists of integration tools, the final checkpoint to ensure all customers are being served effectively. This section requires a marketer to create a procedure to inspect and assess the measurements of a successful IMCP. The goal is to evaluate methods being used on the basis of whether they meet and achieve the overall objective of the IMCP. The evaluation is divided into two categories, message evaluation techniques and target market behavior evaluation.

What is message evaluation and how would I use it?

The purpose of message evaluation is to determine whether or not the advertising reached and affected the target audience within different developmental stages. This examination is conducted by experts and non-experts. Tool 8.7 outlines message evaluation methods and when to use them.

There are other testing options. The important thing to remember is to conduct a test that ensures you achieve the objective of the IMCP methods. Although the evaluation is discussed last within this chapter, it is highly recommended that you decide what evaluation method to use when developing each objective. This approach of keeping the end in mind allows you to create an IMCP method that is measurable and quantifiable.

Message Evaluation Method	When to Use It
Concept Testing—The advertising concept in storyboard format is shared with a focus group of customers. The goal is to get an initial reading/understanding of how the advertisement will be received by the target base.	Before the integrated marketing communication method copy is developed or produced. *Tip: This is an important test. If an organization has limited funds for advertising this step is necessary to ensure an irrelevant ad campaign is not developed.*
Copy testing—The copy of an ad or marketing collateral (flyers, banners and billboards) tests the main message. How was it received and understood by the target base?	In the final stages of development after the completed integrated marketing communication methods ad (traditional or innovative). *Tip: Many times marketers use industry terminology in ads. These terms may not have the same meaning to the customer market. This is a good test to ensure the actual meaning is being received.*
Recall Tests—This option asks customers to recall the ads they saw within a specific timeframe. They are asked if they can recall key information in the ad.	Use before an integrated marketing communication ad is launched in the market either local or national. *Tip: The purpose of this test is to make sure the key features, benefits and product name are retained in the minds of the customer. As a marketer you do not want to have the target like the ad but link it to the competitor.*
Recognition Test—Customers are given different ads and asked if they recognize them. If they say yes, they are asked to give more details in order to understand the impressions the ad made. The responses allow the marketers to gain more insight about attitudes and reactions of the target market.	Use after the integrated marketing communication methods have been launched in the local, national and international market. *Tip: This is a valuable test when the target market is new or differs in values and beliefs from existing markets. It is especially useful in high-context communication markets that are not as expressive or that use relationship building to establish trust.*
Persuasion Analysis—Assesses the marketing communication method to determine if it was persuasive enough to influence the target market's purchase behavior or attitudes.	Should be used immediately after the integrated marketing communication plan methods are launched/used. *Tip: This assessment is important to have a clear understanding of what the marketer wants the target customer to do. It must be measureable.*

Tool 8.7   Message Evaluation Methods

Adapted from Clow & Baack (2007).

What are target market behavior evaluations?

Target market behavior evaluations are the assessments of the behavior in the marketplace once the IMCP methods are implemented (Clow & Baack 2007). The purpose is to measure the effectiveness of the trade and consumer promotions, public relations and other methods.

There are three important measures:

- Sales rates
- Response rates
- The evaluation of public relations tactics.

The sales and response rate methods measure the impact of the IMCP methods on the organization's retail sales or outlets. Briefly, the sales rate is determined at the point of decision. The marketer needs to know whether or not the customers were impacted by the marketplace methods designed to influence their purchases of the targeted product, good or service. The use of internal sales data during a designated time period is vital in the measurement of this test. A marketer can use the data to determine the lift that the IMCP methods created in the marketplace. When using the sales rate measure it is important that a marketer can explain and identify the current external impacts on the marketplace. These external impacts may include price increases by the competitors (which could impact the sales data) or low product availability to retailers. Separating these factors from your analysis will give a true reading of the impact on sales. It would be nice to believe that every IMCP method has a direct correlation to increased sales, but that would be a naïve perspective for a marketer to assume.

When assessing innovative promotional ideas, the response rates are defined by assessing the length of time customers spend on a website and how that converts to sales. Due to the constantly changing digital landscape, the industry complains that the evaluation metrics are not capturing the actual impact on the marketplace. Based on the work of Bughin, Shenkan and Singer (2009), many organizations are developing their own innovative measuring metrics that assist them in allocating budgets for relevant, income-generated methods. Some current assessment metrics are:

- Clickthrough rates: Cost of an ad compared to the number of times the ad is shown.
- Conversion rate: The percentage of website visitors who make an actual purchase.
- Cost per click: The cost of the ad divided by the number of clicks.
- Website traffic counts: The total number of visitors to the site.
- Total online sales: Total revenue and profitability.
- Engagement: The amount of time the user spends on the site.
- Clicks to value percentage: Clicks that led to a visit to a value-creating (purchasing) page.
  Adapted from Boone and Kurtz

Developing effective online metrics with an innovative promotional agency ensures the organization's ability to optimize their online presence in the marketplace.

There are several options to assess the effectiveness of public relations activities. Namely, track the number of articles and news mentions, impressions, advertising value equivalent, sales, awareness and opinion research. Compare these to the IMCP objectives. Similar to innovative promotions, public relations activities can be difficult to assess and quantify.

A clipping service can be used to assess the total number of articles and news mentions. The goal is to count the total number of times an organization, product, service or brand is discussed in the news arena. Take that a step further to calculate the gross impression, how many times each mention is viewed by a consumer. The mathematical equation for gross impression is the total circulation of a newspaper, magazine or communication vehicle multiplied by the number of times the mention is in the publication.

For example, the *Lexington Herald-Leader* newspaper's daily circulation is 91,518. If an ad ran for ten days, the total gross impression would be 915,180. The public relations agency, working with an integrated marketing communication team, can collaborate with advertising agencies to create an advertising equivalent evaluation of public relation methods. This enables you to assess the contribution of your public relations methods in advertising value in order to help determine the return on the investment for each method.

You can also use sales to evaluate the success of a public relations strategy. However, as mentioned earlier you must always account for the external impact that could influence the marketplace. Another method that can be used to assess public relations involves awareness and opinion research within the target market. This research will help a marketer gain a greater understanding of the target market, while addressing whether or not the primary messages influence the target market at the point of decision.

The last measurement in your evaluation should compare the goals and objectives determined at the beginning of the development of the IMCP to actual results. Overall, the creation of an evaluation plan enables you to ensure the planned objectives are reached.

Additional Resources

The American Marketing Association is a leading organization that brings together marketing educators and practitioners. The Public Relations Society of America is a primary organization for public relations practitioners. You can use the Internet to find many other marketing organizations.

References

Boone, L. and Kurtz, D. (2010). *Contemporary Marketing* (14th ed.). Mason, OH: South-Western Cengage Learning.

Bughin, J., Shenkan, A. and Singer, M. (2009). How poor metrics undermine digital marketing. *McKinsey Quarterly*, (1), 106–07. Retrieved from EBSCOhost.

Clow, K. and Baack, D. (2005). *Concise Encyclopedia of Advertising*. New York: The Haworth Reference Press.

Clow, K. and Baack, D. (2007). *Integrated Advertising Promotion, and Marketing Communications* (3rd ed.). Upper Saddle River, NJ: Pearson Prentice Hall.

Dolan, R. (1999). *Integrated Marketing Communications*. Boston, MA: Harvard Business School Press.

Kim, S., Haley, E. and Koo, G. (2009). Comparison of the Paths from Consumer Involvement Types to Ad Responses between Corporate Advertising and Product Advertising. *Journal of Advertising*, 38(3), 67–80.

Kotler, P. and Keller, K. (2009). *Marketing Management* (13th ed.). Upper Saddle River, NJ: Pearson Education.

Ledward, C. (2007, December 6). E for excellence. *Marketing (00253650)*, 15. Retrieved from EBSCO*host*.

Wells, W., Moriarty, S. and Burnett, J. (2006*). Advertising Principles & Practices* (7th ed.). Upper Saddle River, NJ: Pearson Education.

Wosinska, M. (2005). *Marketing Promotions*. Boston, MA: Harvard Business School Publishing.

9 *Competitors and Competitive Intelligence*

ERIC BOLLAND

With the exception of a newly formed business with brand new products and legal monopolies, all businesses face competition. Organizations are not purely autonomous nor do they operate in a vacuum. As organizations deliver products and services, other business entities are watching and reacting. Markets and customers are always up for grabs and rivals can affect your business at any time. A whole Rube Goldberg series of events can happen at other organizations if your organization seeks new market territory or introduces new products.

The others in your industry may at first just note your move but, like the Goldberg device, it is more than likely a chain reaction of other things will happen. A competing marketing manager will decide if your action poses a threat. They may decide to offer a competing product as a countermove. Another action might be to attack not only your new product but your core strategy as well. The competition machine is in motion.

There may be many different reasons why you don't consider your competitor's moves as carefully as you should. You may not know who they are. You might think you can do nothing about competitors. You might also look at it on a return-on-time-invested basis and think it is not worth doing. Perhaps you feel that your returns will be better if you devote that time to taking care of your own customers.

All of these responses are understandable but they are also shortsighted. They dismiss real threats and leave you vulnerable to erosion of your own revenue generation process. If others are monitoring you, why shouldn't you monitor them? There is much to be gained. Discover the identity of your competitors. Monitor consumer preferences for products and you can be alert to changes in the market. Do something about your competitors. It is well worth the investment of resources to do so. This chapter is dedicated to answering your questions about competitors and to providing the tools to be a formidable competitor yourself.

How do I identify my competitors?

At one level, there is an easy answer to this. When your sales staff lost a sale to another company, who was that company? Did the sales staff ask the customer? Did you ask the sales staff? Instances like these are costly and sometimes burn the name of the winning competitor into our corporate memory. Often, we can list these quickly, but sometimes we can't. The customer doesn't necessarily volunteer the names of the competitor firms they are shopping. Train your sales staff to ask. Train yourself to ask your sales staff. Keep track. Chances are, the same names will come up again and again.

You also need to list the firms who were after your customers but the outcome was different, your company won. In both cases, you encountered competitors. Every time you had a selling opportunity, win or lose, you competed. So competition involves at least three parties: you, a competitor, and a customer. A result or consequence of that competition will be a win, a loss or something in between.

It is essential to look beyond single contests. If you look at these events as single instances, you are limiting your ability to develop a systematic way of dealing with competition. More than the individual encounters, which may make you feel triumphant or desperate, you should be looking at patterns in the actions of competitors. Why did you lose? Was it a result of product features, price or customer relationship? What was the consequence of the win or loss? What happened over time? Have your competitors been more intense or laid back in your recent encounters?

You can identify your competitors by asking your sales and marketing people to make a list of them. They can also identify who they think will be competitors in the future. You can identify competitors yourself by looking at a company directory such as Hoovers Online. If you look up your company online, the directory may list your competitors. You can then look them up and see if they list you as a competitor. If you are a small company, you almost certainly know who you are competing against. But you may not know who you will be competing against in the future. Frequent contacts with your customers and suppliers are sources that will often provide you with an answer to the question, "Who do I need to be concerned with today and in the future?"

One way of making sense of competitors is to summarize information about them on a competitor score sheet. As in Tool 9.1, list the name of the competitor, the number of times you were up against them and their (or your) success rate. You can also add a qualitative assessment of how consequential the encounters have been. Were they major (involving a significant gain or loss to you) or were they minor? A comment field in the table allows you to note your overall analysis of the competitor. Here's an example of a competitor score sheet.

Tool 9.1 provides a snapshot of activity but leaves something out. The missing ingredient is trend analysis. Peter Drucker, a prominent twentieth century business thinker, said that trends are very important considerations when looking at statistics and that is also true in the competitor analysis. The snapshot of information below can be easily put into a spreadsheet. Charts can be generated showing which competitors are becoming more current threats in their win percentages and which competitors are waning. The chart function in Microsoft Excel works well for this.

Competitor	# of encounters	% they won	How consequential?	Comment
Firm A	4	25%	Very	Secondary threat
Firm B	15	33.3%	Very	Primary threat
Firm C	2	0%	Not Very	Not a threat now

Tool 9.1   Competitor Encounter Tracking Device

While this scoring method works well with known direct competitors, it is much more difficult to identify more obscure, but nonetheless consequential competitors. In this case, you should use a checklist to identify sources of other possible competitors. These may be emerging competitors; who are not threats now but who could become so at a later time. This category could also include indirect competitors or competitors who sell substitute products. These competitors are easy to overlook but they still impact your market.

Finally, federal, state and local units of government may seek to provide your customer with products or services. An example of this could be with a city-owned utility which provides service to your customers if you are an investor-owned utility. You, a private utility, could be competing against a public utility. That is an example of competition coming in from left field. It may be unforeseen unless you at least mark it in the game roster. The main point of looking at the less obvious competitors is that they may become actual competitors. Considering these possibilities will help you be better prepared.

Competitor	Check Applicable Answer	
	Yes	No
Provider of Substitute products		
Emerging Competitors		
Governmental Units		

Tool 9.2   Competitor Analysis Tool

This kind of checklist can serve as a framework for your own particular set of realities. You may have other, more subtle competitors to add or subtract. Think creatively. You can also add a comment field if the answer is not clearly yes or no. Once you have the checklist, you can then use Tool 9.1, the Encounter tool, to dig further into competitor analysis.

The best competitor intelligence comes from within your organization. Unfortunately, information about competitors lives in isolated pockets or islands around the organization and it is not connected unless you build a competitive information system.

Most often, it is the sales unit that knows the most about competitors. They know how they are doing compared to the opposition. They also know what competitors are doing to win customers. A good start to identifying competitors, as mentioned earlier, is by interviewing front line sales people. The information you get may not be in depth but it is a start. You will be able to learn much more about competitor behaviors if you talk to your own sales staff.

Competitive intelligence professionals heavily involve these sales people in their information gathering process. If these intelligence practitioners are able to uncover competitor strategies, it is because they took the first step at looking internally for information. Facts provided by staff can be woven together into a pattern. Talk to enough sales personnel and you can discover what geographic areas are hot with respect to being a threat. You should be able to determine what competitors are promoting and where your product line might have weaknesses.

What do I do about competitors?

Now that you have a better sense of who you are competing with, you can begin to decide what to do about them. In deciding what to do about competitors, it is essential to ask which competitors. If you think you need to wipe out all competitors and dominate the market, you should first think about the problems inherent in doing so. Cornering the market leads to anti-trust scrutiny. And even if you enjoy a temporary monopoly, temporary is the operative word. Beyond that, it is a waste of time to worry about all competitors. If you are lucky enough to have established your business and it is prospering, many competitors with smaller market shares will simply compete against each other and only a few will survive to challenge you.

There are no hard and fast rules about which current competitors to watch carefully but you can set your own numerical range based on judgment. For small to medium sized companies five to ten competitors usually account for the great majority of an available market. For potential competitors, those less obvious, and those who may enter your market in the future, keeping track of two to four competitors is reasonable.

When compiling your list, first get competitors on your radar. Then, identify their direction and speed. Next, you can assess their strengths and weaknesses in comparison to yours and plan your actions accordingly. This is essentially a four-step process and you've completed steps one through three. When you get to this stage, you are ready to set up a competitive action program.

How do I set up a competitive action program?

A competitive action program is a systematic approach to responding to competition. As a program, there is a set of activities done by an individual or individuals who monitor and act on competitor initiatives. Done correctly, the program helps avoid surprises and provides continuous monitoring of a major outside influence on your success.

Companies usually start a program informally. Something will happen on the competitor front that will trigger a response from an executive. "We need to find out more about what is going on with them and I'd like you to get together a few people to see if we need to do anything," is the usual initial trumpet call. This is stage one. Someone is charged with the responsibility of doing preliminary research on a competitor. At this stage, it is helpful to get as much input as possible from the market interfacing staff. This certainly includes sales but other input can help too. Purchasing staff might be able to say if suppliers have information on competitor purchases. Customer service staff may be able to pass on information about what the customers tell them about the competitor.

From these bits and pieces, a picture of the competitor begins to emerge. That picture shows on your radar as an image with a vector and speed. This is the next stage. It is an analytical stage and it most likely will involve a team review of what the competitor is doing. If the threat is serious, then actions can be taken. Do we preemptively introduce a product or wait for the competitor to go first? Sometimes being the second mover, that is, entering the market after the competitor, can bring advantages. You can enter the same market with a superior product while avoiding some of the R&D and market introduction cost of production.

The reaction to a single competitive action scenario is the most common form of starting a competitor action program in small businesses. Even in larger businesses, this is frequently the prelude to a more formalized competitor action team. If you decide to further develop a team, there is a choice between an ad hoc team, or a formal team with a mission, charter, accountabilities and all the other manifestations that this will be an ongoing effort.

When is an ad hoc team needed and when is a formal team needed?

An ad hoc team is warranted if you are in a niche market and are following a focus strategy. That is to say, your product serves a relatively small market segment with specialized needs. See chapter five for more detail on strategy. If competitors are few in number and rarely pop up as a concern, an ad hoc team works. However, don't assume that just because your customers are satisfied, they will not leave if a better offer comes along. Before the Telecommunications Act of 1996, AT&T enjoyed a customer satisfaction rate of 96%. But when the Act enabled competitors to challenge AT&T, they lost customers by the droves.

If your business is in a growing or mature industry, a formal team may be justified. These stages of the industry lifecycle are generally teeming with competitors especially if the market is profitable. If there is considerable competitor intensity, then a formal team is needed. Competitor intensity is measured by how much of a fight there is to win customers. If there are numerous bids for the same business and if frequent rebids occur, this is a sign that competition is intense.

Who should be on the competitor team?

A formalized team should have representation from, at a minimum, sales, marketing and customer service. Other areas that may cause constraints on production such as legal, government relations and operations, may also need to be included. For instance, your sales force may be able to sell a product at a certain price by committing to a short delivery time. If your operations department can't deliver the product, your sales effort is in vain.

The competitor team should have a sponsor. The sponsor should have the resources to support the team and the ability to act on recommendations. The sponsor is presumably someone who can take action on the recommendations of the team. In competitive action teams, the sponsor is often a member of the team and may also be a member of senior management.

Meetings should be regularly scheduled but it is also important to have the capacity to act quickly since new circumstances may suddenly arise. Flexibility and response time are paramount to successful competitive response. A cagey competitor may hide their intrusion into your market or even bluff their intent so you have to react quickly once they reveal themselves. This aspect of the game is similar to a combination of war and poker and it should be no small surprise that many competitor intelligence professionals come from the military and the government.

Even for medium and large businesses, the competitive team should not have too many members. A team of five is recommended as a core group. As suggested in chapter two on Decision Making Problems and Pitfalls, a team should be built with complementary skills. One of those skills will be analytical and that member or members should be able to analyze and interpret numerical data. The team will also require someone who is good at synthesizing information. Often, these are different people.

Recall that data is not information until it has been processed. It is the information that is acted upon, not the data itself. The team needs to pour over the data, convert it to information (what are the trends? what are the dominant factors?), question one another concerning the information and arrive at a recommended action.

For competitor action team meetings, you might want to adopt the following agenda. This sample originates from several major companies that have competitive intelligence teams:

1. Attendance.
2. Review of Minutes from Previous Meetings.
3. Report from the Field of New Developments.
4. Discussion and Analysis of Competitors.
5. Recommendations for Action and Assignment of Responsibility.
6. New Reports.
7. Topics for Next Meeting.

This agenda gives you an opportunity to get everything covered in the competitive arena. Minutes should be taken as these meetings can be quite intense and minutes will help pinpoint what decisions were made and who took responsibility for each area.

How do I get information about competitors?

At the outset, it needs to be firmly stated that getting information about competitors should not be done by spying. Federal law provides that obtaining confidential information can be considered a felony. That certainly applies to material marked confidential. But it also covers material that is not marked as such but that the company does not want in the hands of outsiders.

Competitive intelligence gathering is not spying. It does not involve taking proprietary data and it is not pretending you are someone who you are not in order to get competitor information. Instead, competitive intelligence is using publicly available information to learn more about competitors. This may seem to be a huge limitation but there is so much public information available, especially with the rise of the Internet, that you can use your own powers of deduction to be a very effective Sherlock Holmes. Professionals in competitive intelligence pride themselves on and often astonish corporate executives with their ability to derive intent from competitors, all from public sourcing and their own dot connecting.

What are some of the public sources?

The Internet is the most accessible and comprehensive gateway to what you want to find out. An excellent starting point is the corporate website of the business that you want more information about. Companies, whether they directly sell online or not, usually have an array of information regarding product features on their website. This gives you the opportunity to learn in great detail about the competitor's products and how they compare to yours. You should also consider the website itself from a competitive standpoint. If you were a customer choosing between your company and the competitor, whose website impresses you most? Where does your own site fall short? See chapter nineteen for more ideas on website development.

As companies move to standardization of their sites, there are common areas where you can gain intelligence. The first section of interest is the "About Us" tab, which is sometimes labeled "The Company" or something similar. This is useful because it will frequently give you a history of the organization. This can reveal how the company developed and, by inference, how they plan to grow. Do they grow internally or through acquisition? That will provide clues for future direction.

The "In the News" section will give you their spin on recent accomplishments and perhaps their troubles (responses to lawsuits for example). You will quickly learn to separate fluff from core news. Executive hiring is found in this section. It may tell you about a new direction for the company if someone is brought in from the outside. An internal promotion may mean either business as usual or a shake-up if a Young Turk has been promoted. Google any new hire and you can discover something useful about your targeted competitor.

An extremely useful section of the company website is the area usually marked "Investor Relations." Here you will find the annual report that summarizes corporate performance. This is again, the company's perspective on what happened. There are packets of very useful information here. The financial information is helpful and chapter seventeen shows ways to use that data to learn about financial strengths and weaknesses. Check out what they are bragging about. Is it their core product or a sidelight product? If it is a sidelight, then the core product may be collapsing. Landline telephone companies often highlight DSL growth as their core landline business is fizzling. In other words, read critically and try to discover what is missing or what that space between the lines really means. Earnings statements can frequently be found here as well. This will tell you much about the company's capacity to compete. Again, chapter seventeen gives you guidance on analyzing financial statements.

The CEOs letter may also provide insight. There is a wide variation in the candor of these letters. Every once in a while you will find a CEO who deals openly with issues. If your competitor does, pay particular attention to what they plan to do about it. That may affect you. Along that line, if there are financial presentations and webcasts made to stakeholder groups, they are worth watching and you can learn much about where the company is going.

Finally, most websites have a "Careers" or "Job Opportunities" tab. Looking at the company's employment ads is a great way to get a sense of whether the company is growing or not. Are they hiring low-level workers (expanding capacity) or high-level management (developing new ideas)?

The United States Securities and Exchange Commission has a website where you can find a very important piece of corporate information. If a company is publicly traded and has a significant number of stockholders, it is required to file a 10K report. This report is filed with the SEC and it is a treasure trove of information. If you go to the SEC site, you can search for the 10K report by company name. In it you will find detailed information on the company's strategy, products, marketing, organizational structure and, very important issues of competition. Your own firm may end up on their list.

Aside from the corporate site, you can get a more objective review of what is happening by following the business media. The *Wall Street Journal* is a daily summary of business happenings. You can also get in-depth reporting on newsworthy aspects of what your competitors are doing in business magazines which include: *Businessweek, Forbes, Fortune, Fast Company, Industry Standard*, the *Economist* and *Savvy*. These have online options as well. Most major cities have publications dedicated to business news and they are often free and found in newsstands. They will often have a name such as *Business Lexington* (Kentucky). Some have staff reporters who have their fingers on the pulse of the local business community. They are often an outlet for media releases sent by local companies concerning business developments, expansions, etc.

In very competitive industries such as wireless communication, motor vehicles, computers, insurance, energy and others, the amount and nature of advertising will show what your competitor is doing. Companies like Mintel CompereMedia provide searchable databases with information about how much major national firms in particular industries are spending on advertising. The magazine *Advertising Age* provides similar information on the top one hundred US advertisers in an annual issue. Advertising expenditures as a percentage of total sales are a good indicator of just how serious a company is about winning market share from its competitors.

Every industry has its own trade journal. This is an industry specific publication and a rich source of information about the activities of leading businesses. You are probably already familiar with such journals in your industry but now you can look at them in a competitive light. Pay attention to the Employment Opportunities section to find out who's hiring. There is often a new products section as well, which will enable you to see what is coming down the pike. How companies are responding to issues of global competition, government regulation and the economy can provide hints of what they will do in the competitive arena.

A frequently overlooked source of information about competitors is the local paper where the company has its headquarters. Local reporters are very curious about the major businesses in their cities. They may be the first to report layoffs or hiring, even before the news hits the regional or national media. These reporters follow municipal governments and you can find out if your competitor has applied for permits, sought tax assistance or zoning changes and related information. Reporters may also share information that has not yet been covered in the press so you might even want to call them directly.

One year when I attended the National Restaurant Association Trade Show in Chicago, Illinois, there were large crowds at both the Coca-Cola booth and at the Pepsi-Cola booth. Each booth was mainly populated by the arch rivals' employees. Coke people were at the Pepsi booth and Pepsi people were at the Coke booth. The respective booth managers were nonplussed. They eventually understood that trade shows are snoop shows and have been for a long time. Companies will showcase new products at trade shows and you can see the future of competition there. At trade shows and at major conventions, there are networking opportunities in abundance. When the bars open, so do the mouths and you can hear quite a bit in a much more relaxed setting.

At conferences, don't overlook professional placement events. See who is recruiting and for what they are recruiting. Many conferences publish lists of companies that are recruiting. Who they are recruiting is a solid indication of what your competitor may be doing.

Conferences showcase who is doing the innovating. Companies that have been developing new technologies and products may proudly send their people to conferences. But they will stop short of saying they are developing a product for market introduction. That is something you will be able to infer if you are there.

The major Wall Street investment firms have staffs of analysts whose job it is to follow stocks and bonds and to make recommendations to investors about what to do with securities. Your company may subscribe to one or more of these analyst reports. These reports are not free. They are, however, quite insightful. They offer an outside view of what may be happening at a competing company.

To get to the very heart of some of the major strategy and performance issues your rival may be experiencing, an earnings conference call is an excellent source. These are sometimes called quarterly earnings calls. You can listen in for free. The competitor publishes the time, date and call-in number on the corporate website. Check this periodically (especially after the quarter or year-end). During the calls, analysts from outside investment firms will often ask critical questions of the chief executive, operating officer and financial officer. These calls can be very revealing and are also often entertaining.

The advent and now the maturation of Internet-based communications have opened new paths to competitive intelligence. In a sense, the Internet has provided a democratization of communication in which any voice can be heard as long as they have access to a computer and a connection.

Among the best sources for information about competitors are blogs. You can search for blogs on the company or companies you consider to be rivals. Here, unvarnished truths or deceitful accusations and everything in between are found. There are customer complaints about products or services. There are also compliments. You can determine if there are recurring and frequent themes in the blogs. Something to note here is that blogs are not entirely democratic. Blogs are owned by individuals who control access, so the information may be skewed.

Your competitor may use blogs to get their story out. Ford used the most popular blogs to get the word out on the Ford Fiesta. You could also set up your own blog and key it to your Facebook site. This will enable you to get information from your contacts about certain companies. The same can be done with LinkedIn.

Corporate gossip abounds in the blogosphere and as such, should be looked at, in Yeats' term, with a "cold eye". Consider the intent and credibility of the blogger when reviewing corporate gossip sites. Don't overlook Twitter as a way of getting your message out.

Hoovers Online is a corporate directory that provides basic profile information on companies at no charge. This was mentioned earlier in the chapter. More detailed information comes at a price but the basic information is very helpful and it lists the competitors of the company you are investigating. You will also find a brief description of the company and its products. Key corporate personnel are listed and sales information is presented. Using Hoover's is a sound first step and it is easy to use.

If you have a corporate library, a reference librarian is a skilled resource for finding information about companies. If you don't have a corporate library, public libraries may also have a reference librarian who can show you how to search databases for information on companies. If you have access to a college library, a librarian there may be able to do a search or help you do your own search.

In summary, you can look at internally generated information from the rival firm (websites, printed material, brochures, etc.). You can look externally for it from among people, publications, blogs and other social media. Once you get what appears to be a pattern or direction about their market moves, you should verify what you think that direction is by another source. That is standard practice in competitor intelligence and it prevents the mistake of acting too aggressively on information that ends up not being true.

How do I compile competitor information in a useful way?

If you do a diligent search of the above sources, you will produce a teeming pot of hot and tasty information. It now needs to be analyzed and reported in a meaningful way. The analysis and report should be focused on determining what information is important and what can you do about it.

One very useful way of putting your work in a high impact form is to create a competitor profile for each company. See Tool 9.3, Competition Profile Tool. That profile can reside in your Intranet for restricted or unrestricted use. If you put a profile up in electronic form, you should mark it confidential and make sure that associates of your company such as suppliers (who may also be doing business with your competitors) do not have free access to your hard work.

There are many variations of competitor profiles. The example that follows is a synthesis of the most appropriate features of profiles used by competitive action teams in major US companies.

The competitive threat level is derived from the SWOT analysis. The level is based on judgment of the competitive analysis and the competitive team. The business model contains information on how the firm conducts business. For example, do they self-fund or borrow? That is a component of the business model. The core strategy refers to their corporate level grand strategy. That may be growth, maturity, or retrenchment. There are many other variations of core corporate strategies found in business school texts on strategic management. The marketing and sales sections provide a picture of what and how products are provided. The Four Ps of Product, Place, Promotion, and Price are included here. The SWOT analysis, described in more detail in chapter five, is the most analytical aspect of the profile.

The profile is usually authored by one person and it needs to be owned by an individual or group. A regular schedule of updating is an essential element of the profile. It is rare that a profile can go beyond six months and still be considered useful.

The value of the profile is that it uses a consistent measure across many different competitors. It is comprehensive and highlights the most pertinent facts for possible action. The unit of analysis of the profile is at the company level. It could also be done

Name of Company	
Description	
Headquarters Location	
Key Personnel	
Level of Competitive Threat	☐ Very High ☐ High ☐ Moderate ☐ Slight ☐ Not a Current Threat
Business Model	
Core Strategy	
Marketing Summary	
Sales Summary	
Financial Performance	
Market Performance	
SWOT Analysis	
Recent News	

Tool 9.3   Competitor Profile Tool

at the business unit or product level if you are facing a well diversified company with a strong emphasis on product line management.

By focusing at the company level, the profile is conducive to bringing in other company level information. The company level, rather than the functional or strategic business unit level, is the choice for analysis for competitive intelligence professionals because market and product decision making happens at this level.

Competitive profile audiences are mainly sales and marketing staff and top level executives. Even in large businesses, executives need to know about major competitors. You should aim for conciseness in the profile so that most important points of the analysis stand out for the reader. After all, this is what they may act on or this is what they might be able to update.

The profiles themselves can be further summarized in tables that could simply show the firm, the threat level, and the result of the SWOT analysis. You can build in fields in the table for the display of your own firm's strategy against the opposing firms.

How do I use competitor information to compete effectively?

A very useful tool in determining how to compete effectively is the competition self appraisal based on Phillip Kotler and Kevin Keller's *Marketing Management* (2008) text. The tool puts you into one of four categories. Each of the categories is associated with a different marketing strategy. The first step is to identify where your company is now. You simply check where you believe you belong on the following:

Name	Description	Check If Name Applies
Leader	A few firms have most market share. They are price makers.	
Challenger	Many firms compete with small market shares. None are large enough to impact price.	
Follower	Most other firms are price takers who cannot impact the market.	
Niche	Serve small but cohesive markets that others bypass.	

Tool 9.4   Competition Self Appraisal

If you are a market leader, you want to defend your market share. You can act on your competitor intelligence and introduce a product before the challenger does. You can launch an assault directly against them (think Coke vs. Pepsi). You can move into new markets before the competitor can and you can simply wait out competitive actions. The market leader is mainly concerned with challengers, not followers or niche players.

In case you are a challenger, you can direct your marketing forces against the leader. One competitive advantage that challengers have is innovation. The challenger can build the better mousetrap while the leader tends to stifle innovation hoping instead to use present assets for maximum capacity. The challenger can also take on others in this same grouping, aiming to become the preeminent challenger. The challenger can look for vulnerable segments in the leader's domain and seek these customers.

For followers, imitation is not only a form of flattery, it is a form of practicality. The followers let the leaders incur the costs of creating a market and then offer a similar product. The product can frequently be offered at lower cost because the follower does not have to recoup investment costs. Followers attack other followers and build up customer bases. This area is marked by a less visible (because there is less media spending here) but very intense rivalry.

The last category is the niche player. They want to serve an unserved or poorly served market segment. The niche players are above the fray in many ways. The scale of their marketing operations is shallow but they fiercely defend their focus on select customers. In this way, they, at the other end of the spectrum, have a core marketing strategy the same as that of the leader, defense.

This depiction of the competitive assessment tool has a highly militaristic overtone but the consequences are not physically deadly. Campaigns are seldom all out war and strategies can be tested and retracted without total commitment. However, the terminology of the military is still a good representation of marketing movements in markets (battlefields), products and promotion (weapons). Just remember not to kill any customers (collateral damage) in the process.

The tool described has the strength of being a categorization device that can help you understand your own position. It also provides guidance for strategy. The categories are distinctive enough to provide the user with demarcations between one category and another. However, in diversified companies with many product lines, it may not apply. It should be used as a possible filter for the way you can better understand competition.

How do I determine what to do with competition as a whole, not just competitors?

Let's suppose you identify all your competitors, research them, write profiles and form a team to deal with them. Have you done the job? Competitors themselves are ships in the sea. It is essential to gauge the sea itself, its currents, tides and temperature before saying you have mastered sailing.

It is essential to deal with competition as a whole, not just competitors. That task involves looking at the competitive environment for your industry. The environment shapes much about what competitors can do, not just what they actually do.

The competitive environment is the boundary around you and your rivals. It consists of the elements of economics, political-legal factors, demographics, socio-cultural happenings, the natural environment and technology.

Practitioners of competitive intelligence wrap their arms and their brains around the external environment by using the tool of an environmental scan. As it implies, the environmental scan is a look at outside forces affecting competition in your industry.

The tool can be quite simple. In its simplest form, it can be conducted as content analysis. This is a method used by John Naisbitt in *Megatrends* (1988). In content analysis, you are looking for changes in the environment that will affect you and your rivals. It often takes shape by collecting media accounts of what is changing in the larger environment. Consider technology as one example. A person doing the content analysis would gather and report all the most pertinent articles and Internet accounts of what and how technology is affecting business. The information would be combined and scanned for significant trends.

Breaking out each element of the environment, the individual charged with this task could observe which environmental forces are positive for the company and which are negative. This is an outside look in and not an inside look out. The factors that make up the environment are too large to be affected by single companies or even groups of companies that make up an industry. You want to approach this by asking what is happening to you on the outside in the areas of economics, the natural environment, demographics, technology, political-legal events and socio-cultural trends.

Examples in economics are the cost of capital for your company and disposable income for your customers. In the natural environment, it may be the substitution of different forms of energy. In demographics, it is the number, concentration, location, gender, age and class of people among other factors. In technology, it is the development of tools to master the environment. In political-legal, it is the matter of taxation and regulation in part. For each of these areas, you should be able to identify other examples of environmental activities that will affect you.

These factors may seem to be hopelessly broad but to neglect looking at them, even in a nominal way (as a positive or negative for you), will prevent you from understanding your external environment. With an environmental scan, you will be able to detect and report on how turbulent your industry is. You should be able to discover your company's relative sensitivity or immunity from your environment. You can note which of the environmental factors affects you more and which affects you less. To put it another way, you will see how to go with the flow or swim against the tide.

Is there software to do competitive intelligence?

There is software for competitive intelligence but it is highly recommended that you launch your own program first, without a software program. If you do this, you will be able to see what you would want a program to do. Then you might start your search for software. It is important to understand how the program logic works as a decision tool if you want people to have confidence in it.

To find competitive intelligence software programs, you can Google the term. Definitely look before you leap. There are many programs but you need to be sure you are getting the right one for your needs, not a one-size-fits-all package. Different organizations have different competitive information needs.

Additional Resources

There are plenty of resources available for getting started in competitive intelligence. There are books, practitioners, organizations and software to help. There is also a professional field of competitive intelligence. There are competitive intelligence professionals and large organizations that have full-time intelligence teams. A director of one of these teams remarked recently that he was proud that he had built his team and prouder yet when the CEO of his company would go directly to one of his analysts to get an answer about some move by a competitor. "I knew that day we had established ourselves," he added. Those in the profession can help get fledgling competition teams going. You could contact them as possible resources. You may come across them at a conference of the Society of Competitive Intelligence Professionals (described next) or you could make contacts in organizations that have such units.

You may want to connect with the main organization that is dedicated to competitive intelligence. That is the Society of Competitive Intelligence Professionals or SCIP. It has a website, SCIP.org, where you can find out much more about its activities. SCIP holds an annual convention, publishes magazines and generally keeps members abreast of developments in the field of competitive intelligence. At the annual conference, there are sessions on how to do competitive intelligence. There are general sessions and workshops during the several day long conventions that meet in different North American cities.

SCIP is directed at providing education and networking opportunities for its members. The organization aims at the recognition of competitive intelligence as a profession and strives to establish professional practices in the field.

A major emphasis of SCIP is on ethical practices in competitive intelligence. Members adhere to a code of ethics that prohibits illegal spying on rival organizations, avoidance of misrepresenting oneself to competitors and a host of other actions aimed at keeping the practice on high moral and legal grounds. Their code of ethics is well worth reviewing.

There are local chapters of SCIP as well. Here members get together and hear guest speakers talking about topics relating to competitive intelligence.

References

Fuld, L. (1985). *Competitor Intelligence: How to Get It-How to Use It*. New York, NY: John Wiley & Sons.

Kahaner, L. (1996). *Competitive Intelligence: How to Gather, Analyze and Use Information to Move Your Business to the Top*. New York, NY: Simon & Schuster.

Kotler, P. and Keller K. (2008). *Making Management*. 13th Edition. Upper Saddler River, NJ: Prentice Hall.

Naisbitt, J. (1988). *Megatrends*. New York, NY: Grand Central Publishing.

Porter, M. (1980). *Competitive Strategy: Techniques for Analyzing Industries and Competitors*. New York, NY: The Free Press.

Prescott, J. and Miller, S. (ed.) and SCIP. (2001) *Proven Strategies in Competitive Intelligence: Lessons from the Trenches*. New York, NY: John Wiley & Sons.

Tyson, K. (2002) *The Complete Guide to Competitive Intelligence*. Chicago, IL: Leading Edge Publications.

10 *Pricing*

LAURA D'ANTONIO

Getting pricing right contributes mightily to business success or failure. But what does getting pricing right mean? The answer to that depends on what you are trying to accomplish with your pricing strategy. Pricing strategy, for purposes of this chapter, is defined as price planning as it relates to internal forces (cost and marketing objectives) and external forces (consumer demand, competition and market trends). Pricing also depends on where your product stands in terms of the product life cycle and where the particular product you are pricing stands in relationship to the basket of other products you sell. Price depends on company size, available resources, industry specifics and competition. Pricing strategy is part and parcel of marketing strategy. This chapter will explore these and other topics relating to pricing with the intent of providing practical tools and insights into this important topic.

What are we trying to accomplish with our pricing strategy?

Are you seeking to maximize total revenues? Are you seeking to gain market share? Are you trying to establish an upscale, exclusive brand name for your product? Or are you just trying to stay afloat?

Start figuring out your pricing strategy objectives by ranking your priorities:

Goal	Rank		
Maximize sales revenue			
Maximize unit sales			
Maximize profit (dollars)			
Maximize profit (margin)			
Gain market share			
Discourage competitive entry to the market			
Create quality or exclusive brand perception			
Encourage trial of new product			
Increase market knowledge			
Rank each item from the most important (9) to least important (1)			

Tool 10.1   Pricing Strategy Objectives

Understanding what you're trying to accomplish will help you garner a better idea of how to get there. All of these things can be accomplished through pricing. Prioritizing what you're trying to accomplish helps provide a focus and direction for resource allocation.

Now that you've got a sense of what you're trying to accomplish by using Tool 10.1, take a look at your existing strategy. "I don't have one," you say? Don't worry; you're not alone. Many fairly sophisticated executives running major businesses rely on seat-of-the-pants-pricing or the "find-out-what-my-competitors-are-charging-and-charge-less" (to steal business) or more (because my product is better) method. At one point in time, did you look at your cost structure, add a mark-up and run with it? That's OK. It's a great place to start and a necessary one. It's also a very common way of pricing.

Take a moment to complete this brief survey regarding your current pricing strategy. First, rate how you're doing in each area on a scale of one to five with one being poor and five being excellent. Then give each factor a high, medium or low relevance ranking:

Pricing Self Audit	H – High M – Medium L – Low	Poor				Excellent
Our pricing strategy	Relevance	1	2	3	4	5
Complements our overall marketing strategy						
Is coordinated across functional areas						
Is comprehensive						
Reflects the value our customers place in our product						
Assesses buyer sensitivity						
Considers competitive reaction						
Reflects buyers emotional response						
Accurately reflects fully loaded cost to produce						

Tool 10.2   Pricing Self Audit

So what is wrong with the strategy of figuring out cost per unit, adding a mark-up, then finding out what the competitors are doing and using that information to arrive at a price? Nothing's wrong with that. In fact, both of these are important considerations in determining price. The only problem is these methods fail to take into account the value of your product to your customer, an important consideration addressed in greater detail later in this chapter.

What does it cost to produce your product?

All products should have a calculated price range, as opposed to one specific and fixed price. This allows flexibility in price that is needed to accomplish different pricing goals (maximizing profit, gaining market share, undercutting the competition, etc.). The low end of the range should be closely tied to your break-even analysis (see following example). To determine the bottom of the pricing range, it's important to understand your cost structure. In the simplest case, where sales volume is fixed, determine the variable cost to produce the product, allocate some portion of fixed costs to each product and add the desired mark-up.

Using this approach the product's price is determined as follows:

price = (unit variable cost + unit allocation to fixed costs) X (1 + mark-up).

Consider this example:

Gizmo Guidance Systems has a contract to supply the Royal Air Force with advanced aircraft navigational equipment. Under the contract terms, the price of each navigational unit is determined as follows:

The variable cost of producing each unit (labor, components, electricity, etc.) is calculated. Gizmo's cost accountants then allocate some portion of the total fixed costs (salaries, insurance, R&D, building heat, debt service, maintenance, etc.) to each of the navigational units produced under the contract (in this case, the unit volume is known.) Together, these represent the full cost of producing each unit. For illustration, let's use these numbers:

Unit variable cost = $10,000
Unit allocation to fixed cost = $8,000
Mark-up = 15%
Unit price = ($10,000 + 8,000) x (1+.15) = $20,700

Example adapted from the Marketer's Toolkit, Harvard Business School Press.

Another approach to the cost plus calculation is to determine a desired profit margin. Then take your total cost and divide it by one minus the desired margin to determine the price. For example, the board of directors is expecting a 20% profit margin. Total cost per unit is $100. The formula would then be $100/.8=125. Your price is $125 per unit.

There are two things to watch out for when using a cost-plus model to determine price. First, it is very difficult to accurately calculate and allocate costs on a per unit basis, as seen later in Pricing Predicament #1. The fixed cost per unit is subject to change based on the experience curve, and people tend to underestimate costs. A few things that are typically overlooked include R&D costs and goodwill. Going back and checking actual costs versus estimated costs will help. And second, using this method alone can lead to many dollars being left on the table because it fails to take into account your product's value to the customer. Value to the customer will be discussed in greater detail later in this chapter. Finally, using a cost plus strategy only, runs the risk of pricing the product out of the market in the case of inefficient production techniques. That said, understanding cost is an important first step in developing an overall pricing strategy.

Once you have determined your costs and have determined a pricing starting point, a break-even analysis can help develop a sense of the relationship between cost and unit

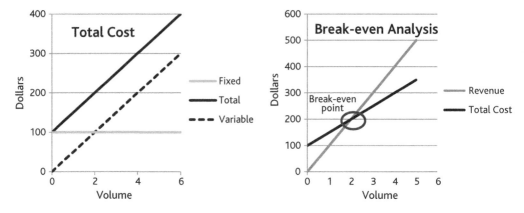

Figure 10.1 Break-Even and Total Cost

volume. In the simplest terms, the break-even point is the point where sales revenue exactly equals all costs incurred. More sales generate a profit. Fewer sales result in a loss. It may be helpful to graph a break-even analysis. To do this, plot sales volume on the horizontal axis and plot money on the vertical axis. A horizontal line represents fixed costs. Add an upward sloping line for variable costs to get a total cost. With total cost in place, add the revenue line starting at zero. When sales income equals total cost, the business is at break-even. See Figure 10.1 as an easy visual example.

Every business owner and manager should understand the business' break-even point. Ideally, a business will operate as far above break-even as possible for safety.

What do you need to know about your competitor's pricing?

The traditional pricing model includes two steps: determining your costs and adding a mark-up as previously described, then taking a look at what the competition is charging for the same or similar product (or service) and adjusting accordingly. Chapter nine considered the question of "who exactly is my competition?" Identifying the competition and doing market research on their products is an important step in developing a pricing strategy. There are many tools for identifying and analyzing the competition presented in chapter nine.

For purposes of pricing, identify the top three to six competitors in the industry. Here are some ideas on determining exactly who that might be at any time:

- Ask your sales force to track who they are losing business to.
- "Shop" your competitors.
- Buy your competitors' products and try them to see how they compare to yours.
- Browse your competitor's website.
- Read articles in the press for clues to competitor expansion plans and financial health.
- Note if your competitor is hiring by checking job listings.
- Order a Dun and Bradstreet report on your competitors.
- Track your competitor's stock price (if publicly traded).

- Keep files on the primary competitors in the industry and keep them updated.

Part of competitor analysis is to clearly define the industry. This may be more difficult than it sounds. Take Amazon.com, for example. Are they a bookseller (they certainly sell more than books) or are they an Internet company? Are they a fulfillment platform or a direct to consumer sales platform? Do they compete with Barnes and Noble or Walmart or both? Using the NAICS codes (North American Industry Classification System) can help narrow down your industry. For more information on NAICS codes, refer to these websites: http://www.census.gov/eos/www/naics/ or http://www.naics.com/search.htm.

Once you've identified your industry, take time to analyze it. How many companies compete in your industry? Is competitor intensity high? Is information regarding pricing and product freely available? Answers to these questions will impact your pricing strategy.

PRICING PREDICAMENT—#1

In the early 2000s, two entrepreneurial women came back from a trip to Europe with an idea to develop a business. Their product was new to the US market. It was a vehicle-sharing program. There were substitute products but no direct competitors. They spent many months estimating their costs and developing their pricing strategy based mainly on a cost plus approach. In addition to understanding their costs, they considered alternative products, and they looked at what the market would bear in terms of price points (points at which the customer will switch products.) Based on market testing, there seemed to be a psychological ceiling to what customers would pay for the product.

They launched the product concept and over the next eight years, the number of customers signed up for the product grew by from basically zero to over 400,000. They now serve thirteen cities and 150 college campuses in the US and Canada. 2009 revenues exceeded $130 million, a ten-fold increase from 2005.

They have grown rapidly through grass roots efforts and acquisition. They have successfully met or exceeded their growth plans each year. The only goal they have failed to meet is the goal of turning a profit.

In part, they suffered from many traditional start-up company problems. Many of their initial expense forecasts proved to be very low. Technology demands and logistics presented unforeseen difficulties. Low introductory pricing, used initially to woo new customers, proved difficult to increase.

This real life example is a cautionary tale of the importance of getting pricing right. It illustrates many common pricing pitfalls and highlights the difficulty of truly understanding and estimating costs. This company's pricing strategy was geared toward expanding its customer base and introducing its concept to the market. But ultimately, a company has to make money to survive.

Perhaps the most difficult competitor analysis to perform is for a new product, a first mover product, or a product with unique features. In these cases, not only is there the added challenge of having to educate the potential customer base, there are no direct competitors for comparison. Instead, substitute products come into play. What other products might a customer use in lieu of the new product? This makes comparing prices even more difficult.

If you're now deep into your competitive analysis, a visual (chart or graph) or a table might be helpful. Chart your competitor's products, rating them on important features and benefits, versus their pricing. Put your company and your product on this list to see how you compare both in terms of product features and price. Knowing your competition will help you become a pricing expert. In very competitive industries, pricing at par with the competition may be the best strategy.

How will my competitors react to my pricing decisions?

While on the subject of the competitor's product and their price, it's worth anticipating what competitor reaction will be to changes in potential pricing strategy. If the market is quite competitive, with a number of strong players aggressively competing for customers and if information is readily available, it is safe to assume that the competition will respond quickly to any new pricing strategies. Competitors may choose to match price. They may choose to undercut price or they may choose to wait out the lower price while maintaining their own price (assuming prices won't be able to remain that low for long). In the worst case scenario, if you drop your price, and your competitors respond by dropping their price, a price war may ensue.

Price wars are rarely a good thing for most companies. A price war will drain the industry of profitability. While in the short term, a price war may force industry shake-out, thereby lessening competition, it can force the remaining players to deplete their reserves. In addition, as will be talked about later in this chapter, consumers may become accustomed to lower prices and will be resistant to higher prices at a later date. A price war can permanently damage an industry. On the plus side, while avoiding a price war is important to retaining industry profitability, an industry that is only marginally profitable will discourage market entry by competitors.

How do pricing methods fit with Marketing Strategy?

Consider the following situation as it may apply to marketing strategy. Pricing strategy as it relates to marketing will depend on the goals as discussed in the first paragraph of this chapter. At this point, it is worth mentioning that pricing strategy and a greater marketing strategy are closely tied to product life cycle. In other words, a new product in the introduction phase will require a different pricing strategy than a product in the growth, maturity or decline phases.

During the introduction of a new product to the market, sellers seek to generate demand for their product. This may require considerable resources with heavy marketing support. One pricing strategy aimed at gaining market share is penetration pricing. With penetration pricing, the price of the product is set lower than the laws of supply and

PRICING PREDICAMENT #2—MARKETING

When you think of Apple, you think technology, quality, first-mover strategy and innovation. But maybe what you should think is pricing strategy. "Jobs is a master of using pricing decoys, bundling and obscurity to make you think his shiny aluminum toys are a good deal" Ben Kunz (2010) said in his *BusinessWeek* article, "Apple's Pricing Decoys." In the competitive high tech world, product popularity doesn't last and prices fall quickly as the second movers pile onto first mover successes. Apple has found ways to make these market dynamics work to their advantage.

Pricing decoys, as defined by Kunz, are products that the manufacturer doesn't really expect you to buy. They merely act as a reference to make other products look better. Consider the classic case of the realtor that shows you the $200,000 house that needs new siding, then shows you the $250,000 house that she really wants to sell you. The $250,000 house may or may not be a good deal. But it feels like a good deal compared to the $200,000 house that needs repair. Apple's tendency to price its products in series (adding features with added cost on top of a base model) serves the same function. If the top priced iPod sells for $399, and you can get one that's almost as good for $229, you think you're getting a good deal.

Decoy pricing has a close relative called reference pricing. Let's say a clothing store wants to charge $100 for a pair of slacks. Is that a lot? Or a little? If you have no reference point for that price, you don't know. But if the same clothing store prices the slacks at $200, then charges $100 (which is what it really wants to get) in a half price sale, the customer has a reference point, and suddenly $100 seems like a good deal.

As these examples show, pricing strategy is closely tied to marketing strategy. Pricing decoys, reference pricing and other related tactics are discussed in the next section.

demand would dictate with the aim of building market share. This strategy can help gain customers who might not otherwise try the product, and it encourages switching from competing products and substitutes. However, unit volume is gained potentially at the expense of profit margin.

Marketers adapting this strategy need to be confident that their cost estimates are accurate, or they may quickly find themselves losing money. In addition, this places great pressure on the production process with the risk that any problems in the supply chain (suppliers delaying shipment of inputs, etc.) will further erode already tight margins. Confidence in the production process is necessary if this strategy is going to work.

Often, this puts a new company starting out in a dilemma. On the one hand, gaining market share, product acceptance and recognition is the goal. On the other hand, production experience isn't there to support lower margins. Production experience or the Learning Curve Effect suggests that each time a task is repeated, efficiency increases. Another downside to a penetration strategy is buyer resistance to price increases and as mentioned, low margins. Low margins do have an advantage in that they discourage new entrants to the market. If penetration pricing seems appealing, your production and distribution plans must support this strategy.

Another popular choice for products in the introduction phase is skimming. Let's say Apple introduces a newer, faster, slicker mobile device that becomes a must-have for traveling sales people. Those initial buyers can be called lead users. They're the type of user that will buy the product regardless of what it costs. Some lead users may be reimbursed by a corporate expense account. They're not using their own funds for the purchase (see Tool 10.5 later in this chapter). Price is not an issue for lead users of a new first-mover type of product (think back to the days of the first cell phones, or PDAs). The product fills a need and this non-price-sensitive segment of the market is willing to pay for it.

The Harvard Business School's 2006 *Marketer's Toolkit* states that, "Once profits have been skimmed off the must-have segment of the market, the producer drops the price and skims the next tier of interested customers. And on it goes. Each price drop broadens the market for the new product." This is a typical pattern for high-tech products and works well as long as the company enjoys a temporary monopoly.

Meanwhile, the cost of production on the new product is hopefully dropping as the company gains production experience and ramps up capacity. This allows the company to maintain its margins even as the price drops. The risk is that a talented copycat company can jump in and undercut the first-mover with a similar product offered at a lower price. The so-called second mover can learn from the mistakes of the first-mover and exploit a lower cost structure (without the costs of R&D and educating the customer base). An additional risk is consumer anger if the market feels overly manipulated. Apple experienced this with the iPhone as the must-haves resented the 50% price drop that quickly followed their high priced purchases.

Another pricing strategy favored by high tech companies is decoy pricing, as illustrated by the Apple example in Pricing Predicament #2. Although high tech companies use this strategy regularly, they aren't the only ones to practice decoy pricing. This practice happens all around you. Here's a real life example. My husband and I recently went on vacation. We booked a hotel room on the Internet for $159 a night. When we arrived at the hotel, we were presented with a number of room options. We could take the standard room we had booked for $159, we could upgrade for $20 to a newer room in the renovated section of the hotel with breakfast included or we could book a deluxe view room in the newly renovated section of the hotel for $249. It seemed only natural that we should take the $20 upgrade to be in the new wing and that we would congratulate ourselves on the good deal we got while we enjoyed our free breakfast. The decoy in this example is the $249 room. In comparison to that price, our $20 upgrade seemed like a bargain.

Decoy pricing has elements in common with good-better-best pricing. A good-better-best scenario might work as follows. A customer walks into Home Depot wanting to buy some paint. There's the Home Depot brand for $12.99 per gallon, Beher for $16.99 per gallon and the Ralph Lauren designer paint for $20.99 per gallon. According to most studies published on this topic, over 60% of buyers will buy the mid-priced item. The psychology seems pretty clear— the cheap paint is probably too cheap and won't do a quality job, and the designer paint probably isn't worth the money you pay just to get the Ralph Lauren name. So the mid-priced paint is the compromise position. As the seller, it's important to make certain that the mid-priced product has the best margin and is the one you build your business around.

How can you use segmentation to better understand and manage relationship profitability?

The good-better-best strategy ties into the concept of customer segmentation. Customer segmentation means grouping customers into clusters based on similarities in behavior. Traditionally, segmentation strategies grouped customers according to demographics, attributes, and buying behavior. A more contemporary view of segmentation called value-based segmentation groups customers in terms of revenue and profitability. Analyzing the company's customer base in terms of profitability can help establish a pricing strategy that retains profitable customers and lets go of those that aren't profitable (after attempting to make them profitable). Some commercial banks use this strategy. See Chapter 11 for more details.

Commercial loan officers review detailed monthly analyses of their customers ranked by overall relationship profitability. These rankings include relationship profitability based on loans, deposit accounts, cash management services, etc. These reports help the loan officer determine how to allocate their time profitably (either in servicing their most profitable accounts, improving profitability on moderately profitable accounts, or culling unprofitable accounts). This type of overall profitability reporting also helps the loan officer when pricing new product requests or when competing with other banks for customer retention. The institution can then use customer profitability to incent loan officers to focus on more profitable relationships. A standardized, quantifiable way of measuring customer relationship profitability is a must for every business. The results are often surprising.

Decoy pricing, good-better-best strategies, and customer segmentation can lead to complexity challenges. The arrival of the Internet has decreased the cost of offering flexible pricing and has enhanced the sellers' ability to price discriminate. But there are trade-offs. Customers can be bewildered and frustrated by an overwhelming array of pricing options. Complex tier structures can mystify and turn off a potential customer. These kinds of strategies also require a level of sophistication on the part of your sales force. In theory, your sales force needs to be armed with the knowledge of what they should sell to best maximize firm profitability, not just to maximize their commission. Organizational pricing integration across business functions is addressed later in this chapter.

Back to the paint example, if the Beher paint will do the job for $4 less per gallon, why would a buyer ever purchase Ralph Lauren paint? The answer lies, in part, in the consumer belief that you get what you pay for. Consumers believe that the moderately priced product has acceptable quality, while the higher-priced product has a level of excellence and exclusivity not found in lesser-priced products. Pricing is closely linked to brand image and prestige pricing. It can be a viable strategy for product positioning. This explains why customers are willing to pay more for seemingly imperceptible product differences.

The law of supply and demand suggests that as price falls, demand increases. But, with prestige pricing, just the opposite occurs. Prestige pricing supports a differentiation strategy (see chapter five for a discussion of a discussion of strategy) and must be supported with strong packaging and marketing support. The risk, when adopting a prestige pricing strategy, is that competitors can relatively easily undercut your pricing by offering a copycat product with only slightly different features at a lower cost.

Loss-leader pricing, aka "bait and hook" pricing, can be an effective pricing strategy as well. If you own a printer or use a cell phone, you're already familiar with this strategy. In it, the manufacturer of the cell phone or printer prices the basic product at a very low price point making it appear to be a low cost option. In order to make the product work, you have to buy the high cost, high margin ink or get locked into a two-year contract. For these companies, the profit is in the ancillary product, not in the product itself.

The risk of course is that competitors will begin making generic replacement parts (ink toner refill kits, for example) either cutting into profits or forcing the original manufacturer to cut the price to maintain market share. Some protection against the incursion of generics is warning consumers that use of generic replacement parts will void warranties. Additionally, printer manufacturers like HP have sued refill kit makers and have attempted to put expiration chips in their cartridges in an effort to fight back.

Another spin on loss leader strategy uses a reduced price on a staple item to help increase store traffic. The idea here is that once inside the store, customers will purchase other higher margin products. Best Buy for example, offers great deals on TV's, while it may sell HDMI cables at a 400% mark-up.

Should you use price promotions?

Price promotions are special short term deals that can be used to introduce a new product or service to the market, entice users of another brand to switch brands, or to clear out excess inventory. Price promotions can take the form of rebates, coupons and sales. Promotional pricing can be an effective short term strategy. However, there are often unintended consequences. Consumers can become so accustomed to promotional pricing that they may become reluctant to purchase at the full price. They may, instead, delay purchases until the price is discounted. Promotions also encourage brand switching which may lead to a lack of customer loyalty. In the long run, price promotions may be better for the buyer than for the seller.

Pricing plans communicate a message to the marketplace about the company and its personality. They reflect other attributes (approachability, affordability, friendliness, exclusivity, etc.) that need to be aligned with the rest of the marketing plan. The pricing strategies discussed above and other common marketing strategies are summarized in Tool 10.3.

What are some customer considerations and are they at odds with organizational pricing goals?

The customer's goal: acquire the most desirable features at the lowest possible price. The producer's goal: maximize profits by minimizing costs of providing features, products, and services that offer greater overall value than the competition. Finding the price point that satisfies both goals is the objective of the successful business owner or manager.

As previously indicated, customers can be a fickle lot waiting for promotions and discounts before making a purchase. They can also be a contrary lot, defying the laws of supply and demand (prestige pricing). Consumer behavior is a complex subject, one only touched on lightly here. The first question to ask of consumers is "how much are they

Strategy	What it is	When to use it	Things to watch out for
Skimming	Reaping high profits from lead users then resetting price at lower levels.	Use for start-up companies – especially high tech offerings. Allows time for production ramp-up.	Invites competition who undercut your price and copy-catting.
Penetration Pricing	Setting initial price lower than supply/demand dictates.	Use for start-up companies –creates broad based demand and generates unit volume.	Difficult to raise prices later. Locks company into low margin business.
Experience Curve	Prices gradually decline as cost of production drops.	Maintains cost advantage over later entering competitors. Use for first to market companies that are good at production.	Low cost business requires constant production improvements.
Prestige Pricing	Creates perception of quality or exclusivity through high price.	Use to capture a small but free spending market segment. Tied into marketing/packaging.	Invites low cost rivals.
Loss Leader or Combination pricing	Combines low priced product with high priced complementary product.	Works with consumable product parts.	Risks under pricing by generic replacement parts.
Promotions	Special, short-term deals(rebates, sales, coupons, etc).	Use to reduce excess inventory, introduce new product, steal competitor's business, retain customers (defensive strategy).	Encourages brand switching. Customers wait for sales.
Good-Better-Best (segmented)	Expand product line to include variations on the product.	When raising prices isn't possible. Mature markets.	Customers trading down.

Tool 10.3   Pricing Strategy Comparison

willing to pay?" The second question may well be "what price point will force consumers to trade down to lower priced/lower quality products (e.g. going from Beher paint to the Home Depot brand)?"

The cost-plus strategy is an internal strategy. Perhaps it is useful to reverse the process. Instead of having an internal process that flows out to the market, let market forces drive price. How can you determine what price consumers are willing to pay for your product? There are many tools for answering this question. These span the range from simply interviewing the sales force and customers to sophisticated market simulations and conjoint analysis.

Conjoint analysis assumes that buyers value products based on the sum of their parts. For example, the value a golfer places on a golf ball depends on the distance the ball travels, how long it will last, how much it costs, and the perception of quality inherent in the brand name. Knowing how buyers value separate components and how to translate that knowledge into improved profitability is an important piece of developing a pricing strategy. Ric Johnson, founder of the Sawtooth Software Company, explains:

> "Conjoint (trade-off) analysis has become one of the most widely-used quantitative methods in Marketing Research. It is used to measure the perceived values of specific product features, to learn how demand for a particular product or service is related to price, and to forecast what the likely acceptance of a product would be if brought to market (n.d.)"

Rather than directly asking survey respondents what they prefer in a product, or what attributes they find most important, conjoint analysis employs the more realistic context of respondents evaluating potential product profiles. Each profile includes multiple conjoined product features (hence, conjoint analysis), such as brand, speed, memory, price and weight. This may be used for laptop computers, for example.

Conjoint analysis is best used when price is one of multiple product features being evaluated and examined. This would be the case when trying to determine consumer preferences for an entirely new product, for example. If product features are already set, and price is the only flexible variable, then conjoint analysis isn't needed. Conjoint analysis can help achieve specific goals using price, to optimize market share and/or achieving a profit.

Let's assume your company isn't in a position to hire a consultant or spend money on software for a sophisticated analysis. Maybe you're not comfortable interpreting the data anyway. What else can you do to understand your customer's price sensitivity better? One of the best things you can do is ask your customers about their buying habits. Regardless of how you do it, careful, recurring market research can provide valuable insight into pricing decisions.

Does your price reflect economic value?

It's a common misconception that the price of something reflects its value. Economic value, in its simplest form, is the amount consumers are willing to give up to get something. In a market economy, dollars (or other currency) are the universally accepted measure of how much someone is willing to give up for something. Economic value measures consumer preferences. It indicates what consumers are willing to pay for something, as opposed to what that item costs.

It may come as a surprise to sellers that consumers might be willing to pay more to obtain their product than the actual price. In order to capture these extra revenues (and extra profits), an Economic Valuation Estimate (EVE) or True Economic Value (TEV) should be performed on all products and services. Tom Nagle and John Hogan explore the EVE concept in their book, *The Strategy and Tactics of Pricing*. Robert Dolan (1995), formerly of the Harvard Business School, developed the TEV idea. Both strategies follow a similar plan for estimating value.

The process for calculating either EVE or TEV is basically the same and follows these steps as explained by Dr. Larry Robinson and Ralph Zuponcic in their pricing blog:

- **Step 1—Identify the cost of the competitive product or process that the customer views as the best alternative to determine the product's reference value.**

- **Step 2—Identify all factors that differentiate your product from the competitive product or process**. For example:
  Superior (inferior) performance.
  Better (poorer) reliability.
  Additional (reduced) features.
  Lower (higher) maintenance costs.
  Higher (lower) startup costs.
  Faster (slower) service.
  Longer (shorter) useful life.
  Lower (higher) total cost of ownership (TCO).

- **Step 3—Determine the value to the customer of these differentiating factors.** Sources of value may be subjective (such as greater pleasure in consuming the product) or objective (such as cost savings, profit gains). The positive and negative values associated with the product's differentiating attributes are the differentiation value.

- **Step 4—Sum the reference value and the differentiation value to determine the total economic value.** TEV is the value someone would pay when they are fully informed and economically rational when making the purchase decision. The company may also be able to add in a "reputation premium" based on brand equity and a "switching cost premium" if the cost of changing suppliers is a consideration of the buyer.

Tool 10.4   Economic Valuation Estimate

The formula will end up looking something like this:

$$TEV = \text{Cost of the best alternative} + \text{(or minus) Value of Performance Differential} + \text{Premiums}$$

When considering a product's TEV, bear in mind that value depends on the needs and preferences of the individual. Determining consumer preferences and how the market values your product may require some effort, but it's an exercise worth doing.

At this point in pricing strategy development, the bottom end of the price range has been established (using cost plus analysis), as has the top of the range using the EVE or TEV model. The competition has been analyzed with comparative products and features graphed. A price has been set. It's time to test the market and get real feedback.

Be aware that pricing isn't static. Market conditions, input costs, and the product life cycle are all subject to change. Macroeconomic forces, including changes in interest rates, inflation, and unemployment all have an impact on price.

When should pricing change?

Pricing inertia is a common pricing problem. When prices are low, they tend to stay low. When prices are high, they tend to stay high. While on the one hand, continually changing price can cause confusion and frustration in your market, many firms get stuck in their pricing rut and never change their price. In a cost plus environment, at the very least, pricing should change when underlying costs change. This seems obvious, but it is surprisingly difficult to do.

If your prices need to change due to an alteration in your cost structure but you're concerned about losing customers, consider using the Customer Price Sensitivity Survey (see Tool 10.5) to better understand your customers' buying habits and your risk. For example, if the decision maker for the buying decision isn't using his own money for the purchase, he may be less sensitive to increasing price. If switching costs (changing to another supplier) are high, then the customer again is less likely to leave when prices increase. On the flip side, if the buyer can easily compare price and performance of alternatives, volume may be negatively affected by a price increase.

Pricing decisions are impacted by economic trends. Consider times of economic recession. The following dilemma is now common among sellers. Input costs are rising, yet consumers are in an unprecedented bargain-hunting mode. Raising prices simply may not be realistic in the current economic climate. Instead, sellers might look at other strategies to keep profits in line with plan. Go back to good-better-best pricing discussed above. Maybe in this market, appealing to the bargain buyer is a good idea. Retailers hope that customers can trade down while maintaining brand loyalty and sales. They can be encouraged to trade back up later.

Product bundling can also be a good strategy when it's difficult to raise prices. A recent advertisement from a local electronics retailer provides an example. The product circular advertised a 3D starter kit that included a free 3D Blu-ray disc player, free 3D glasses, and a few 3D movies, all with the purchase of a 3D TV.

Changes in cost can lead to price changes both upward and downward. If input prices increase, revisiting costs is important. However, as a firm moves along the production experience curve, costs should decrease. This allows for more pricing flexibility.

While the company's internal environment is changing based on input costs and process improvements the external environment is changing too. The product's life cycle will also trigger pricing changes. Scheduling regular pricing reviews will help keep the price-value relationship in line. Keeping an eye on what the competition is doing is important here too. When the market share leaders raise their prices, it may present an opportunity.

Price stickiness is the resistance of price to change. Producers tend to think that price changes have to be significant. This depends largely on unit volume of course, but study after study has shown that a minor increase in price can lead to a significant gain in the bottom line. M. V. Marn and R. L. Rosiello (2009) report in "Managing Price, Gaining Profits", that for the 2,463 companies in the Compustat aggregate, a 1% increase in price yields improvement to the bottom line of 11.1% on average. So while raising the price on a $100 item to $110 may trigger a rebellion, what about raising the price to $101? Collecting only an extra dollar on every sale can generate substantial bottom line premiums.

Unless you are a single product/single distribution channel company, you not only have to be aware of competition in the market, you also have to consider competition from within. In the down market, you decide to go with a good-better-best strategy. So you develop a cheaper version of your product. However, you run the risk that your new product will cannibalize your existing product line so don't expect sales to be the aggregate of the new and the old.

Customer Economics:
- Will the decision maker pay for the product using his/her own funds?
- Is the cost of this item substantial as a % of the total project or purchase?
- Is the buyer the end user?
- Does a higher price signal higher quality in this market?

Customer Purchase Barriers:
- Is delivery timing important?
- Is it costly for the buyer to shop around?
- Can the buyer easily compare price and performance of alternatives?
- Are switching costs high?

Competition:
- How does this product differ from the competition?
- Is the company's reputation a factor?
- What other intangibles impact buyer behavior?

Adapted from the *Harvard Business Review*, Manager's Toolkit, Sept–Oct 1995.

Tool 10.5   Customer Price Sensitivity Survey

As an alternative to creating different product versions, different price levels depending on the delivery channel may be an idea. For example, since marketing products on the Internet does not require the overhead of a retail location, products are generally priced lower. Multichannel pricing can create internal competition as well as confusion/frustration on the part of the customer. If the new product is part of a portfolio of products, in addition to deciding price on the new product, it's important to develop a pricing strategy for the existing products.

The market's tough, so what else can you do to maintain profitability if you can't increase price?

One potential strategy would be to add features to your product that don't cost much. This can make the product more attractive and competitive without adding cost. It can help justify increasing your price. Other alternatives include repackaging the product to give it a new look, which can also help justify a price increase. Discounting the product might be a reasonable defensive strategy to help hold on to market share. Offering warranties is another alternative to lowering price.

How can you be innovative about pricing?

When thinking of pricing, most sellers think of a standard transaction where the buyer pays cash (in some form) for a purchase. When faced with shrinking margins and a tightening market, one consideration would be to offer payment options while maintaining price.

PRICING PREDICAMENT #3—SERVICE BUSINESS

The equine dentist visited my farm yesterday; I'll call him Bob. While he was floating my horses' teeth (the technical term for filing off the sharp edges), we got to talking about what he was doing with his life these days. Bob is from Louisiana and most of his family still lives there. A family friend recently started a thoroughbred breeding operation in Louisiana. Bob has been splitting his time between Louisiana and Kentucky and plans on spending most of his winters there.

While he was there, he decided to drum up some equine dentistry business. He charges $55 per horse to hand-float teeth in Kentucky. He decided to charge $65 in Louisiana for the same job. I asked him "why the price increase?" He responded that most of his Kentucky clients were well established, and had been paying that price for many years. He didn't want to disrupt his local clientele by raising his prices. Since he was new to Louisiana, he felt he could start with a new, higher price.

I asked him how his new book of business was developing. He admitted that it wasn't going that well. After much discussion, it came out that in the Louisiana marketplace he was targeting, there was one other equine dentist who floated by hand. He charges $85 per float. There are a number of veterinarians and other specialist who "power float" (using power tools) and they charge $125–$150.

From Bob's perspective, he was raising his price from historical levels, so he felt like he was charging a lot. From the new market's perspective, since he was so "low-priced" that customers were suspicious that he didn't know what he was doing, or didn't do as good a job as the higher priced competitors.

Bob's case illustrates not only the challenges faced by service providers but also the market perception of the price/quality relationship.

Some of these could include: financing, renting, leasing, or the Netflix model of paying a monthly fee for unlimited access.

Most of what has been discussed thus far has focused on sale of a product. With service businesses comprising approximately 70% of the US GDP, pricing considerations for service businesses deserve attention. Service businesses face unique pricing challenges. The traditional cost plus starting point isn't really relevant. Sure, there are costs associated with the service business—overhead transportation, etc.—but the real challenge is determining what the service provider's time costs. The service business can fall back on the competitor method, but does that really reflect the value brought to the table?

How can you communicate pricing strategy within the company and get organizational buy-in?

Good communication, as discusses in chapter four, is an important part of implementing pricing strategy. Often, the price you set isn't the price you get! If your sales people have pricing flexibility, there is a tendency to give away price whether or not it's necessary. Sales people often like to give away price. The company goal is to maximize profit. The sales force's goal is to maximize sales. Salespeople are hired to sell the product based on their ability to understand customer needs and to match product to those needs. All too frequently they sell on price.

Salesperson compensation needs to be tied to profitability not just sales. If salespeople are compensated solely on volume, and they can negotiate price, holding the line on a higher price isn't in their best interest. Many salespeople think they need to lead with price. They are convinced that the company should always meet or beat the competitors' pricing. Salespeople forget that they do know how to sell through price objections. Holding the line on price, or even better, getting that extra 1% on price may require revamping the compensation plan and conducting additional sales training.

Managing price doesn't mean just doing one thing right. Instead, it means managing a myriad of diverse issues. Pricing is a cross-functional activity. It requires input from planning, finance, production and sales. Each of these areas contributes. According to the HBS Manager's Toolkit "Marketing contributes the pricing strategy; sales provides specific customer input; production sets supply boundaries; and finance establishes the requirements for the entire company's monetary health." Without strong coordination and good data, implementation of the pricing strategy becomes the downfall of even the best-researched plan. When implementing a pricing strategy company-wide, bear in mind three salient points—know the pricing objective, communicate it so that all participants understand the pricing objective, and make sure that participants are incented to work toward meeting that objective.

Where should you start?

Every business should have a well documented, well thought out pricing strategy. Following these steps should help get you on your way:

- Assemble a pricing team. Make sure the major functional areas (planning, finance, sales and production) are all represented.
- Start by articulating your pricing goals. Are you looking to maximize profit? Increase market share? Introduce a new product to the market? Get agreement among the members of the team.
- Understand your industry. Know your customers and your competitors. Understand your industry's structure and its profitability.
- Schedule regular pricing reviews. Make sure that pricing keeps up with changes in input costs, changes in product life cycle and changes within the industry.

Additional Resources

The Professional Pricing Society offers workshops, conferences and online courses for strategic pricing strategy methodology. They offer a Pricing Experts Directory and many other resources. Websites abound with assistance and software for EVE/TEV analysis and Conjoint Analysis.

Pricing books to include in any pricing library: *Competing on Value*, Hanan and Karp, *Power Pricing: How Managing Price Transforms the Bottom Line*, and the classic *Strategy and Tactics of Pricing* by Nagle and Holden.

References

Baker, W. M. (2010, October). Do You Have a Long-term Pricing Strategy? Retrieved 10 30, 2010, from *McKinsey Quarterly*: http://www.mckinseyquarterly.com/article_print.aspx?L2=16& L3=19&ar=2682.

Dolan, R. (1995). How Do You Know When the Price is Right? *Harvard Business Review*, 4–11.

Eyink, C. (2008). Getting Pricing Right. *McKinsey Quarterly*, 1–3.

Gimpel, L. (2006, Winter). Pricing: The Magic Number. Retrieved 10 30, 2010, from *Businessweek*: http://www.businessweek.com/print/magazine/content/06_52/b4015452.htm?chan=gl.

Huyler, B. (2010, October 18). Gaining Competitive Advantage with Price Segmentation. Retrieved 10 30, 2010, from IndustryWeek.com: http://www.industryweek.com/printarticle.aspx?ArticleID =23009&sectionID=11.

Johnson, Ric. (n.d.) What is Conjoint Analysis? Sawtooth Software.com. Retrieved 04 20 2011, from http://www.sawtoothsoftware.com/solutions/conjoint_analysis_software.

Kunz, B. (2010, September). Apple's Pricing Decoys. Retrieved 10 25, 2010, from *Bloomberg Business Week*: http://businessweek.com/technology/content/sep2010/tc2010091_060916.htm

Marketer's Toolkit: The 10 Strategies You Need to Succeed Chapter 9, (2005), Chapter 9: Pricing It Right: Strategies, Applications and Pitfalls. Boston, MA: Harvard Business School Press.

Marn, M., Rosiello, R. (2009). Managing Price, Gaining Profit. Boston, MA: *Harvard Business Review*.

Marn, M. C. (2003, 8). Pricing New Products. Retrieved 10 30, 2010, from *McKinsey Quarterly*: http:// www.mckinseyquarterly.com/article_print.aspx?l2=16&l3=19&ar=1329.

Matanovich, T. C. (2010, 9). Profitable Pricing in Professional Services. *The Journal of Professional Pricing*, 30–34.

Mohamed, R. (2010, 3 2). A New Pricing Plan to Lure Dormant Customers. Retrieved 10 30, 2010, from *Bloomberg Business Week*: http://www.businessweek.com/print/smallbiz/content/mar2010/sb2010032_742820.html.

Passeqitz, G. (1995). Small Business Series – Pricing. Retrieved 10 25, 2010, from Ohio State University: http://ohioline.osu.edu/cd-fact/1326.html.

Robinson, L. and Zuponic R. (n.d.) Pricing Points. Retrieved 4 20 2011, from http://www.pricingpoints.blogspot.com/2008/05/pricing_strategy_strategy_development_and.html.

Smart Answers. (2006, 11 6). The Secrets to Price Setting. Retrieved 10 30, 2010, from *Bloomberg Businessweek*: http://www.businessweek.com/print/smallbiz/content/nov2006/sb20061106_303504.htm.

Wreden, N. (2002, 4 15). How to Think About Pricing Strategies in the Downturn. Retrieved October 25, 2010, from *Harvard Business Review*: http://hbswk.hbs.edu/archive/2884.html.

11 *Identifying and Serving Customers*

MARLA ASHE

Knowing and understanding customers and their needs is paramount to business success. According to Gerald Zaltman (2003), "Approximately 80 percent of all new products or services fail within the first six months". Failure to understand target market demand is extremely costly for organizations. Successful businesses should first seek to understand customer demands and needs.

This chapter will explore different target markets and the factors that influence them. We will look at using marketing research to understand and identify target markets and to forecast demand. Since customers have several product options to satisfy their needs, wants and desires, this chapter will provide an in-depth examination of the customer buying process in both the consumer and business-to-business markets. Finally, this chapter will discuss a process for the development and cultivation of ongoing relationships with target markets.

Who are consumer and business markets today?

Before this question can be answered, we must ask, "What determines a consumer?" For 80% of the business world, lack of understanding of this underlying question is the reason for failure. There are numerous key elements within an organization's structure that are guidelines for all decisions regarding target market development and new products/services. These include the organization's mission, visions and goals both on their physical and symbolic manifestation for stakeholders to view and in actual practice within the organization.

The company's mission, vision and values are the litmus tests for understanding the values the organizations would like to identify within the target market. According to Zaltman, understanding consumers' values allows "an organization the ability to foresee and adjust to the consumers' feedback towards products and services." The answer, then, to the implied question—what determines a consumer for an organization?—are the shared values and beliefs that govern both parties. Therefore, before an organization can determine the target consumer/business market, it must look inward to understand its own values. Once the organization's values are determined, it can begin to understand the changing perspective of the consumer and business markets today.

How do I approach the consumer market?

Three core behavioral categories influence consumer behavior. They are cultural, social and familial. Let's first look at the influence of culture on consumer behavior. Cultural influences are defined as shared values and beliefs that are passed to each generation. Cultural influences are not merely the understanding of a consumer's religion and ethnicity, but also the understanding of different groups of individuals that share an expressed and implied value or belief. For example, there is a new global cultural trend of fashionistas. As defined in the Oxford English Dictionary, a fashionista is a person who dresses very fashionably. The term originated in 1993 and has the connotation of a person who is interested in being fashionable, but who is not interested in paying a lot of money for fashionable clothing and accoutrements.

The fashionista culture shares the values of fashion and saving money—high quality fashion items for a low cost. To capture this market, TJ Maxx and Marshalls have created marketing strategies leveraging the shared core values of their organizations (fashion at low prices) and this target market. On their corporate websites, TJ Maxx is described as "an ever-fresh selection of great apparel and home fashions at great values across the US." Marshalls is described as "offering great, off-prices value on apparel and home fashions throughout the US."

TJ Maxx and Marshalls are subsidiaries of TJX Companies, Inc. whose vision statement says, "Our vision of TJX is as a global, off-price, value company. We remain focused on driving profitable sales through sharp execution of the fundamentals of our off-price business model." This is an example of how an organization matched its core values with a consumer culture that shares those same values.

What are reference groups and why are they important?

In 1948, social psychologist Solomon Asch described social influences of group membership on consumer purchasing behavior, known as the Asch Phenomenon. The desire to conform to group norms creates pressure on group members and influences consumer behavior. Due to increased awareness of social causes such as sexual orientation, environmental sustainability issues, racism, and corporate corruption, many social groups encourage their members to make purchasing decisions to support or be aligned with their causes. The purchases from the members represent status in the group. This is an example of the power of a reference group. When a reference group is understood and successfully marketed to, organizations are assured that consumers will use their products and services.

Keller and Berry stated in their 2003 book *The Influentials*, "One American in ten tells the other nine how to vote, where to eat and what to buy; they are the influentials." However, that has changed with the growing age of social networking. Social networking is a new medium that has replaced opinion leaders/influentials or that has at least provided them a new way of communicating. Arnold Brown (2008) stated consumers are not waiting for the expert to tell them where to go and what to do. He states that, "Consumers feel free to share their experiences, perspectives and opinions on any subject via blogging, to the whole world. The power of word of mouth from a peer has demonstrated the strength of social influences in consumer behavior."

Online forums provide an outlet for consumers to share their perspectives and therefore influence the market. Leveraging online forums should be part of your marketing strategy. For example, InnoCentive was founded in 2001 to help organizations leverage innovation. They built the first global web online forum. This enabled organizations to use over 200,000 scientists, engineers, professionals, and entrepreneurs to create innovative solutions for complex business problems. They specialize in crowd sourcing of new ideas and validate direct consumer feedback. This format allows organizations to use the consumer market to create business solutions, generate new product ideas and receive general consumer feedback.

In 2010, Toyota Motor Corporation (TMC) participated in massive auto recalls resulting in significant negative publicity. The company understood the power of social influences and the need for consumers to share their perspectives on issues that impact their purchasing behavior. TMC and InnoCentive created a campaign called "Ideas for Good—Our Technologies Your Ideas—Let's make the world a better place." The purpose was to utilize consumer generated sustainable solutions to leverage automotive technologies in other industries for TMC. According to *New York Times* columnist Stuart Elliott (2010), "The campaign invites consumers to come up with new ways to use five existing TMC technologies." This is an example of how an organization created a two-way dialogue platform for consumers to discuss the social influences that could and would affect their behavior in the marketplace.

The third consumer influence is family. In today's society, families throughout the world have many different arrangements and structures. Understanding of the family influence perspective gives an organization an in-depth, unconscious insight into consumer values that influence their purchasing behavior. Understanding these influences on a consumer provides deeper understanding and appreciation for the target market.

What are consumer market segmentations and how do I use them in my business?

Your organization must identify a specific group of consumers who are able and willing to purchase the goods and services you offer. Target marketing subdivides (segments) a large population into smaller categories with similar characteristics. Each organization has a large pool of potential consumers in the United States and globally. According to the 2010 US Census, there are 311 million people in the United States and 6.9 billion people in the world. A common marketing fallacy is that an organization has a product that everyone could use, and that your marketing goal is to reach and talk to everyone. Even with an unlimited marketing budget, that's an impossible undertaking. However, if an organization with a limited marketing budget wants to maximize its impact through the strategic use of the marketing funds, there are several strategies it can use.

The first task is to determine how to narrow the United States and the world into smaller manageable clusters. Here are some segment parameters that need to be defined first:

- The segment must be a measurable size.
- The segment must have the ability to purchase the goods and services and the organization should have the ability to access and measure the purchasing authority.

- The segment should be accessible to the market.
- The segment must have profit potential for the organization.
- The segment should match an organization's marketing ability.

After defining these parameters, the market can be segmented. There are many ways to divide the market in order to identify the target market. Four of those will be addressed: geographic, psychographic, behavioral and product usage segmentations.

GEOGRAPHIC SEGMENTATION

Geographic segmentation means separating the target market based on location. For example, an organization might offer products in specific regions of the United States— Southern Region, Northern Region, Western Region, and North Eastern Region—or in identified key markets/cities such as Los Angeles, Chicago, Dallas, Atlanta, and New York. Concentrating marketing resources geographically will help to increase awareness of products and services in those markets. There are tools a marketer can use to determine systematically the geographical segmentation. Two of the tools are Core Based Statistical Area (CBSA) segmentation, and Metropolitan Statistical Area (MSA) data. Both segmentation tools are easily accessible through the United States Census website (http://www.census.gov).

PSYCHOGRAPHIC SEGMENTATION

As stated by Louis Boone and David Kurtz (2010), "Psychographic segmentation is dividing consumers into homogeneous groups based on lifestyles, attitudes, values and beliefs." This is the most commonly used approach to help you understand the complex levels of a target consumer. The process allows marketers to explore several dimensions that comprise the essence of the target market. Your organization can use several options to acquire an in-depth understanding of the target consumer based on budget and problem complexity. These include:

- Working with a consumer/marketing research agency that can create a customized research experiment that is targeted towards the organization's specific products or goods and services.
- Utilizing existing consumer segmentation secondary research created for mass use by different organizations and industries. For example, VALS™ Framework originally developed by SRI International (a nonprofit research organization in Menlo Park, California), is now owned and operated by Strategic Business Insight (SBI).
- Requiring the organization to conduct its own consumer research in a small segment of the population.

The mostly commonly used secondary research for consumer psychographic segmentation is VALS™. It divides the US adult population into eight categories:

1. *Innovators*—Successful, "take charge" people with high self-esteem. They have the tendency to purchase items that are upscale and utilize niche products and services.

2. *Thinkers*—Mature, comfortable people who seek information when making a decision. They purchase items based on functionality and value.
3. *Believers*—Traditional people who respect rules and authority. They purchase familiar items and established brands.
4. *Achievers*—Goal oriented individuals focused on family and/or career. They prefer brands/products that have been used by family, friends, and peers.
5. *Strivers*—Fun at heart individuals, who have limited discretionary income. They prefer aspirational purchases that reflect a wealthy lifestyle.
6. *Experiencers*—Unconventional and impulsive people who spend a high percentage of their income on fashion, socializing, and entertainment.
7. *Makers*—Self-sufficient and practical people who prefer value basic products.
8. *Survivors*—This group has limited resources and their primary concerns are safety and security.

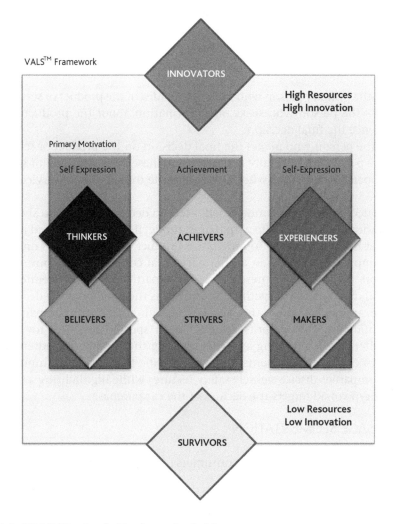

Figure 11.1 VALS Strategic Business Insights

Source: Strategic Business Insights (SBI)

In addition to the eight categories, the VALS™ framework includes consumer resource dimensions: income, education, self-confidence, health, the eagerness to buy, and energy levels. Finally, another dimension is a person's primary motivations, that is, the ideas, morals and principles by which one lives including ideals, achievement, and self-expression. Knowing what motivates a consumer and understanding their resources provides insight into their purchasing choices. Figure 11.1, the VALS™ Network, provides a pictorial perspective of a consumer's psychographic approach to decision making.

The Claritas Corporation offers another method of segmentation. Using geodemographic segmentation, the company splits the United States into distinct segments.

BEHAVIORAL SEGMENTATION

According to Kotler and Keller (2009), "Behavioral segmentation divides consumers into categories based on their knowledge, attitude, usage and responses to a product or service." Each consumer displays a decision making preference. The decision role helps identify the purchasers of the product and their power to influence the use of the products or services. As commonly described in most marketing textbooks, there are five roles:

- Initiator—the primary person who initiates the idea of the product or service purchase.
- Influencer—the person who seeks out information about the product or service to help influence the final decision.
- Decider—the person who makes the final decision on the product or service.
- Buyer—the person who actually makes the purchase of the product or service.
- User—the person or persons who use or consume the product or service.

When the decision roles are understood, you can decide on who you should focus on and who you should communicate with. For example, if you are interested in influencing the person that initiates the idea to purchase a product or service, focus on the initiator. A real-life example of this is when a pharmaceutical company asks consumers to "talk to their doctors about . . ." a prescription for a particular pharmaceutical drug. The pharmaceutical marketers are targeting the patient as the *initiator* in the decision process.

Another example is during the holiday season, many toy companies focus on children to influence their parents to purchase a specific toy. The toy commercials focus on children using, enjoying and experiencing the product. Children are targeted as *influencers* to ensure their parents purchase specific toys. As an example of a similar strategy, car companies discuss vehicle safety features while highlighting a teen driver or children. This type of ad targets the decider of the car purchase.

PRODUCT USAGE SEGMENTATION

Product usage segmentation separates consumers into differing types of usage relationship groupings based on:

1. Benefits people seek when purchasing the products or services
2. Usage rates
3. Brand loyalty

In 1968, Russell Haley came up with the idea of the benefits category test stating that "Establishing benefits category tests gives a realistic understanding of the target market's values and needs." An example provided by Arnold Brown, indicates that there are several benefit groups of college students:

1. Socialites
2. Conservatives
3. Sports enthusiasts

Understanding how each category uses and benefits from the product is crucial to understanding how to effectively market to them.

Determining usage rates means dividing the market based on how often they use the product or service. For example, there would be a heavy, moderate, and light user segment. This segment strategy is used frequently when discussing media usage of consumers. The Pareto Principle, which states that 80% of the volume of products are purchased by 20% of the population also applies here. This is just a rule of thumb. However, the main point is that heavy users make up a relatively small percentage of the target market. You can use this principle to help determine the consumer market in order to develop a relevant strategic marketing communication plan.

As stated by Kotler and Keller (2009), "Brand loyalty segmenting is based on the actual purchasing behavior of the target consumer." According to them, there are four brand loyalty categories:

1. *Hard-core*: loyal consumers who purchase the same brand all the time.
2. *Split loyal*: consumers who purchase multiple brands of a product.
3. *Shifting loyal:* consumers who are willing to try and shift usage of different brands of the same product.
4. *Switcher:* consumers who switch brands and are not loyal to any brand.

There are many approaches to segmenting the consumer market. You could select one or more segmenting methods by layering them. This allows you to develop a comprehensive methodical target market consumer and ensures you are "fishing where the fish are," as the old adage goes. Consumers are multidimensional which requires companies to understand as many dimensions as possible. The ability to use the different segmenting approaches enables a company to cultivate and understand consumer segments beyond age and gender.

What is the business-to-business market (B2B)?

According to Kotler and Keller, "Business markets are the organizations that acquire goods and services used in the production of other products or services that are sold, rented or supplied to others." You may wonder how the business market differs from the consumer market. The business market end users are other businesses or organizations, whereas the consumer market end users are people.

For example, in the automotive industry, Toyota Motor Corporation (TMC) represents the business market for its suppliers. Organizations or small businesses that sell goods or services, such as paint, parts or tools to be used on the assembly line, aid and assist in the development of a TMC vehicle. This constitutes the business-to-business market. Another example is when a small business owner goes to an office supply store or warehouse to purchase cleaning supplies and/or business supplies. The store where the purchases are made provides products to the B2B market. Organizations can sell to both the business and consumer markets providing you know the identity of the end user and target them appropriately.

What comprises the B2B market?

There are four unique components of B2B markets:

1. Geographic market concentration;
2. Size and number of buyers;
3. Purchasing decision procedure;
4. Buyer-seller relationships.

The B2B market components can be used to narrow the B2B market for your organization. Narrowing the B2B market by geography for instance, can facilitate the development of a target market.

As a marketer, you will need to decide where you want to do business. Once the region or division is selected, narrow the business market by the size and number of buyers of the organization's goods and/or services. There is plenty of available statistical data to assist in this process. The United States Census provides in-depth data on several different business industries—construction, government, foreign trade, manufacturing, mining, retail, service and wholesalers. This is located at http://www.census.gov/econ/overview/index.html.

The United States Census also provides statistics on all different types of businesses. It is located at http://www.census.gov/econ/susb/. This data will help you to understand how many actual businesses could be targeted in the region or division. This website also provides industry data using the North American Industry Classification (also noted in chapter twelve) System (NAICS). NAICS is federal standardization coding for the purpose of collecting, analyzing, and publishing data relevant to United State businesses. The statistical data/ information is free— http://www.census.gov/eos/www/naics/. This is a great tool to understand the buying potential in different industries in the United States.

What does my business need to know about international industry coding systems?

If you are interested in developing a target business market globally, there are several global industry coding systems that measure feasibility, international compatibility and economic activities. These include International Standard Industries Classification and North American Industry Code for Canada. Other sources to help inform you about market size potential are trade and business publications and financial reporting organizations such as Dun & Bradstreet.

Once a business market, geographical market and industry buyer potential size are determined, you then need to understand the purchasing decision process for each organization/business. Understanding this process will enable you to identify all the primary decision makers. This is important because the B2B purchasing process is potentially very formal, complex and time consuming. The steps in the B2B buying process are described later in this chapter.

The last component in the B2B market explains the unique relationship between buyer and seller. The B2B market buyer and seller relationship is complex and must be developed over time. The United States government is the world's largest procurer of goods and services. According to Rogers (2010), it takes, on average, two years to secure a government contract because businesses do not understand the buying process and complex relationship between the United States government and its suppliers.

What are the recommended criteria for segmenting business markets?

Five key criteria, created and developed by Shapiro and Bonoma in 1984, must be addressed in order to effectively segment the business market. They named the criteria the Nested Approach, which helps marketers start at the broadest category and end with the most specific and relevant information needed to isolate the target market.

Demographics criteria contain basic information about the industry, company size and the geographic location the organization serves:

- *Operating variables* address the stability of the organization's finances. Its brand and product awareness to the organization's target, and lastly, the strengths and weaknesses of its customer base.
- *Purchasing Approach* criteria are the ones many organizations fail to understand. These criteria address the purchasing hierarchies that exist within the targeted organization/ business market and focus on purchasing functions within the organization and the

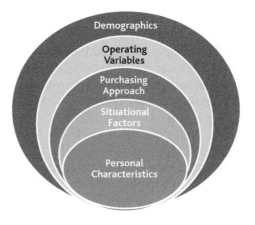

Figure 11.2 Nested Approach

decision making power structure. They discuss the buyer and seller relationship and the organization's purchasing policies and criteria for new vendors.

- *Situational Factors* criteria begin to separate individual companies and allow the marketer to understand the actual need for goods and services. They address the urgency of meeting and fulfilling an order. Using these criteria, the marketer will understand how his goods and services will be used in the organization and what order size might be anticipated.
- *Buyer's Personal Characteristics* deal with understanding the buyer's motivation, risk management approaches and loyalty factors to existing vendors and new vendors.

When properly applied and understood, the criteria enable a marketer to fine-tune their B2B market targeting to ensure they provide goods and services that are needed or required by the different businesses. This systematic approach is very beneficial in creating a guidebook that ensures you are reaching the B2B targets that are relevant to your business. In short, this approach will create a win-win for all parties.

What are some of the benefits of marketing research?

We have explored the different approaches to understand the B2B markets. Now we will explain the different steps for marketing research and how they can help you understand the target consumer market more clearly. First, let's define marketing research. According to Boone and Kurtz (2010), it is "the process of collecting and using information for marketing decision making." The marketer uses marketing research to find out if there is a need and/or desire for products/services. It is one of the most valuable research tools a marketer needs in order to create or produce relevant products and services. Marketing research also helps to improve the quality of decision making within the organization. It allows a marketer to remain connected to the ever-changing marketplace and consumers' needs, wants and desires. Marketing research ensures an organization's sustainability.

Who does marketing research?

Depending on the organization's size and the marketing research budget, marketing research can be done in one of several ways. An organization can use a full service marketing research agency. Alternatively, it can purchase syndicated data about consumers or work with an organization's in-house marketing research department. If a marketer has a limited or non-existent marketing research budget, you can start with free research documents from full service marketing research agencies called white papers.

A local college is also a good source to use to help conduct free or low-cost marketing research for the organization/business. For example, at Midway College in Midway, Kentucky, the business department has a business club—SIFE—Students in Free Enterprise. The students use the information they learn in the classroom to solve local business owners' issues or deal with their concerns. Organizations and clubs such as SIFE may help your business with marketing research. You may consult the business department at your local college for opportunities of this kind. Any one of these options enables a marketer to acquire relevant consumer information that will help the organization/business meet or exceed its target's wants and desires.

How do I locate a marketing research firm?

A great source to help locate a marketing research firm is the American Marketing Association (AMA) Marketing Resource Directory. The AMA is a professional association made up of individuals who teach, practice, and create marketing strategies worldwide. It has created a comprehensive online directory of different marketing resources/services. The directory provides a detailed company profile, website address, email, and phone number for a variety of marketing research firms.

What are the steps in the marketing research process?

The marketing research process is a systematic approach to solving a marketing problem. The process has some overlap with other problem solving models found earlier in this book. There are six primary steps in conducting marketing research. They are:

1. Define the problem (see chapters one and two for more on defining problems). Be sure you are not describing the symptom of a problem. The problem must be clearly defined in order to have an effective marketing research process.

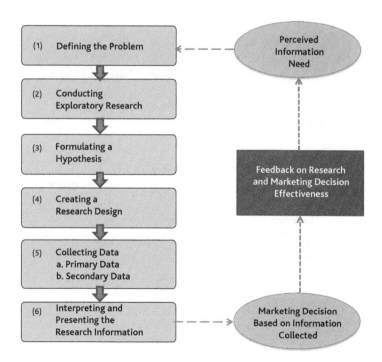

Figure 11.3 The Marketing Research Process as Depicted by Boone and Kurtz (2010)

2. Conduct exploratory research. That is the process of collecting information that explains the cause of the problem.
3. Create a possible hypothesis. This should speculate why the problem exists within the organization.
4. Develop a research design by using either observation, controlled experiment, or survey research to test the hypothesis and find the solution to the marketing problem. Figure 11.3 provides an example of the research process.
5. Collect all pertinent data. Secondary data consists of information that is published about the general marketing research problem/topic. Examples of secondary data are local and state government agency reports, information from business, industry and trade publications. Primary data is collected for the specific market from the original sources. All data falls into two categories: qualitative or quantitative. Quantitative data is expressed in numbers, figures, percentage and/or charts. Qualitative data consists of answers and statements gathered from surveys, questionnaires, and focus groups.
6. Interpret and present the research findings.

As a follow up to the depiction of the marketing research process, it will also help to review the different kinds of research. This is shown in Figure 11.4.

The marketing research process is a scientific approach used to resolve a business problem or discover solutions. Therefore, marketing research can be used to understand both consumer markets and B2B markets. Gerald Zaltman (1975) stated, "The object of market research is to collect and analyze data concerning the interface between the

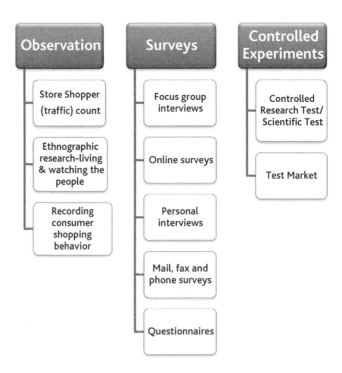

Figure 11.4 Primary Research with Examples

firm and its market, thereby enabling the marketing decision maker to maximize the effectiveness of decisions relating to product, price, promotion and distribution."

How can I better understand buying processes for consumer and B2B markets?

After the marketing research process is completed, you need to understand the buying processes for consumers and B2B markets to help ensure your goods and services are selected at the point of purchase. By definition, the consumer buying process is the process which consumers make conscious and unconscious purchasing decisions for goods and services. Earlier in this chapter, we discussed that consumer buying decisions are influenced by culture, social and family pressure. As a marketer, you may not be able to directly impact the interpersonal factors. However, knowing the core values and beliefs of the target audience provides a deeper perspective and encourages companies to create products and services that are more relevant to the target consumer's values and beliefs. An understanding of the target consumer's self-desires, awareness and concepts create a link that helps persuade the consumer at the point of decision.

Conducting in-depth consumer marketing research helps to reveal the consumer markets' self-desires and interpersonal factors. The consumer decision process consists of six steps as identified by Blackwell, Miniard and Engel (2005).

1. The consumer must be aware of a problem or a void that has impacted him/her.
2. The consumer will begin consciously and unconsciously to search for information to address the problem or void.
3. The consumer will evaluate the alternatives to resolve the problem or fill the void. This step enables the consumer to begin to develop evaluative criteria that will be used to narrow options.
4. The consumer decides on an option and purchases the goods or services.
5. The consumer will conduct a post purchase assessment. The consumer determines if the option he/she selected addressed the problem and provided a sense of satisfaction.
6. The consumer will provide feedback on the option that resolved the initial problem or void being addressed. At this point, the consumer becomes an influencer on his/her culture, family and social groups. In addition, if the decision satisfied the consumer's needs, wants and desires, that helps to create a positive self-concept he/she has internalized.

In this example, an individual wants to lose a hundred pounds in order to purchase fashionable clothes. The individual's decisions are added to the consumer decision process.

The consumer decision process can happen in a short or long period of time depending on the level of purchase involvement. A higher level of purchase involvement is for big-ticket items, such as cars and houses, whereas a lower level purchase involvement is for items such as groceries, gas for the car and others. The level of involvement determines the time duration spent in each decision process step.

Rust, Zeithaml & Lemon writing in their 2000 book state that "Understanding the reasons why consumers selected goods and services to address problems or voids in their

Figure 11.5 Example of the Consumer Decision Process

lives creates an opportunity for marketers to provide a reliable solution that will fulfill the consumer's internal desires, resulting in brand and product selections leading to brand equity and loyalty."

How is the B2B buying process different from consumer buying?

The buying process for B2B is different. Instead of focusing on influencing factors that affect a personal decision process, B2B focuses on organizational factors that can influence the procurement process. Applying the Nesting Approach outlined earlier in the chapter gives you an understanding of the types of businesses that should be the initial target market(s). In the B2B procurement process, the buying center must be identified prior to establishing any contact with the organization.

The buying center is the central division of all procurement activities within an organization. Each buying center has key players who directly impact the final decision of the purchasing process. Understanding the roles and responsibilities of buying center employees enables a business to ensure it provides goods and services that are meeting the current and future needs of the targeted organization. There are typically six important roles and responsibilities, shown in the following table.

Knowing the buying-center players will help you understand why the timeframes for the B2B buying process are potentially lengthy.

Buying Center Roles	Responsibilities
1. Initiators	This is a group of employees that posts the Request for Proposals (RFPs). They also field all initial contact with future vendors. They are the first point of contact within the Buying Center. They work closely with the different departments within the organization to ensure their needs are being met with efficient and precise RFPs.
2. Influencers	This group of employees reviews the RFPs against the specifications needed for the contract. This group often includes an expert/technical person. They provide the decision makers the list of approved candidates/vendors.
3. Deciders	They make the final decision on which vendors are approved as organizational vendors.
4. Approvers	They notify potential vendors of the awarding of the organizational contract.
5. End-User/Buyers	This person/department uses approved vendors' goods and services. The vendor works until this group completes the contract.
6. Gatekeepers	This department guarantees that all approved vendors remain active and approved. In addition, it ensures that all potential vendors submit inquiries and organization packets to them. It is responsible for disseminating potential vendors' information to proper departments/channels. It guards access to the organization from outside vendors.

How do I build a long-term relationship with target consumers and business markets?

The simple answer is to continue to meet their needs. However, this is often easier said than done. In order to continually meet the target's needs, you must be in constant communication to ensure understanding of changing demands. There are several recommendations to assist with this effort. First, establish an Internet-based mechanism to solicit and collect customer satisfaction feedback and important contact information. Second, once it is determined that the goods and services meet a targeted need, create a strategy that will generate repeat purchases. This will help you categorize the customer's usage frequency.

How do I improve customer retention?

When a strategy is created that focuses on repeat purchases and frequent use, the essentials of a customer retention program are born. The information gained from the customer retention program enables you to understand and use the characteristics of the different levels of users. Also, it integrates central concepts within the marketing mix, namely: product, price, promotions, and placement/distribution. This ensures that goods and services are relevant to the ever-changing marketplace. Finally, create a customized communication for each customer that discusses their mission and values, current and new product needs, and how the organization can help the customer reach their goals, wants and desires. These recommendations are relevant to organizations that focus on consumer markets and business markets.

What is customer lifetime value (CLV) and how can I use it?

CLV, according to Kotler and Keller (2009), at the point of purchase is "the net present value of the stream of future profits expected over the customer's lifetime purchases." It is a mathematic formula to determine the future profits from the customer. As the old adage goes, work smart not hard. Many websites, including the Harvard Business School, have created interactive programs to help marketing managers assign a dollar value to the targeted consumer. This and other websites provide an in-depth explanation of the CLV concept, sample problems, a glossary, and the CLV tool that deals with the following statistics:

- Average amount spent per purchase
- Average number of purchases per year
- Direct marketing cost per customer per year
- Average gross margin
- Average customer retention rate
- Annual discount rate

In the Harvard Business School model, after inputting the data from these statistics, the online tool will provide you with the average contribution, before mailing, cost per customer per year. This information will be useful in determining the diminishing rate of return on a customer and in ranking customers based on profitability. Finally, the website will generate the results in either of two formats, a grid or a chart. Overall, the website is extremely useful in determining the profitable amount of marketing dollars that should be allocated to a specific target market. Remember the goal of the CLV is to know if the target market that has been selected is the right or profitable target. This customer data can also help direct your sales force's effort and energies to those customers who are most profitable. The link below will allow you to download the CLV calculation tool. http://hbswk.hbs.edu/archive/1436.html.

Additional Resources

US Census government website is an excellent resource for consumer and marketing research. The US Census website contains in-depth research on US consumers' demographic and regional information: http://www.census.gov/geo/www/. This will allow a marketer with limited resources access to secondary research. In addition, a marketer should align with business professional organizations such as the American Marketing Association:. http://www.marketingpower.com/ResourceLibrary/Pages/default.aspx.

The organization provides free research and white papers, which are position papers on varying subjects that can be used to support or enhance your marketing strategies. Finally, cultivate a working relationship with a local college or university business department. Business faculty members should have practical marketing experiences that they are able to apply to marketing strategies and tactics for a local business.

References

Ahmad, R. (2003). Benefit segmentation: a potentially useful technique of segmenting and targeting older consumers. *International Journal of Market Research, 45*, 373–88. Retrieved from EBSCO*host*.

Asch, A. (1948). The doctrine of suggestion, prestige, and imitation in social psychology. *Psychological Review*, 55(5), 250–76.

Blackwell, R., Miniard, P. and Engel, J. (2005). *Consumer Behavior* (10th edition). Boston, MA: South-Western College Publishing.

Boone, L. and Kurtz, D. (2010). *Contemporary Marketing* (14th ed.). Mason, OH: South-Western Cengage Learning.

Brown, A. (2008). The consumer is the medium. *The Futurist, 42*(1), 29–32. Retrieved November 21, 2010, from EBSCO*host*.

Elliot, S. (2010, November 8). Toyota turns to consumers for 'Ideas'. *New York Times*, Retrieved November 21, 2010, from http://mediacoder.blogs.nytimes.com/2010/11/08/toyota-turns-to-consumers-for-ideas/.

Greenbook: Market Research and Focus Group Companies Directory. (n.d.). Retrieved from http://www.greenbook.org/AboutUs.cfm.

Haley, R. (1968). Benefit segmentation: A decision-oriented research tool. *Journal of Marketing 32*, 30–35.

Keller, E. and Berry J. (2003). *The Influentials*. New York, NY: The Free Press.

Kotler, P. and Keller, K. (2009). *Marketing Management* (13th ed.). Upper Saddle River, NJ: Pearson Education.

Rogers, J. (2010). Winning government contracts: Five things you need to know [Electronic Version]. *Entrepreneur*. Retrieved December 28, 2010, from http://www.entrepreneur.com/article/printthis/217779.html.

Rust, R., Zeithaml, V. and Lemon, K. (2000). *Driving Customer Equity: How Customer Lifetime Value is Reshaping Corporate Strategy*. New York, NY: The Free Press.

Schultz, D. (2009, November 11). Pareto Pared. *Marketing News*, 43(18), 24.

Shapiro, B. and Bonoma, T. (1984). How to segment industrial market. *Harvard Business Review, 62*(3), 104–10.

Strategic Business Insights. Retrieved at www.strategicbusinessinsights.com/VALS.

TJX. (2010). TJX company information and profile. Retrieved November 21, 2010, from:http://www.company-statements-slogans.info/list-of-companies-t/tjx.htm.

US Census Bureau. (2010). *Census Regions and Division of the United States*. Retrieved from http://www.usastudyguide.com/regionaldifference.htm.

Zaltman, G. (2003). *How Customers Think: Essential Insight into the Mind of the Market*. Boston, MA: Harvard Business School Press.

Zaltman, G. and Burger, P. (1975). *Market Research: Fundamentals and Dynamics*. Hinsdale, IL: The Dryden Press.

12 *Operations Management*

RIK BERRY

The day-to-day activities of business, even in the smallest of firms, are complex, with multiple activities occurring concurrently, sequentially or both. The interaction of activities is often critical to successfully executing the overall business strategy. Each functional area plays a part. Marketing identifies and targets sales opportunities while sales closes the deal. Production creates the goods or service. Human resources finds and develops personnel. Finance provides the funds and accounting keeps track of financial activities. None of these functional areas operates independently. The customer purchases the goods or service to satisfy needs. Operations provides the goods or services to satisfy those needs.

The vast majority of organizations in the US are classified as service organizations. Therefore, while operations may move physical goods, often these goods are a small part of the overall package. This applies to all sizes of organizations and at all stages of the product/service and firm life cycles. Planning and executing are critical to success. While it may be that management wants to control all aspects of the business, it is usually one or maybe a few critical operations that really matter. These primary processes need significant management attention for successful execution of the firm as a whole. These are the points that require performance measures and are leveraging points in the management information system used to manage operations. Operations management is at the core of business and suggestions for focused operations management are the main topics of this chapter.

How does operations management fit into the business?

If marketing and sales are the external focus of a company, operations are where the internal emphasis lies. Astute managers know that no part of a company stands on its own. Effective integration of the many roles and responsibilities in a company is a key indicator of excellent management. There are many components of a company:

- Finance (see Chapter sixteen): which provides the capital resources needed for innovation and ongoing operations.
- Human resources (see Chapter seventeen): which provides qualified individuals with education and training to keep those individuals at appropriate levels of knowledge and skill.
- Accounting (see Chapter fifteen): which keeps track of activities and ensures enough cash is on hand to meet short, medium and long-term obligations.

Operations is the area that ties other areas of the organization to the company's objectives. Operations management is a balancing act involving a firm's ability to meet market demand while staying within budget and managing costs. While most companies strive to develop adequate capacity to meet demand, firms with limited ability to meet market demand may enjoy greater profitability than those with excess capacity. Efficiency is rarely the correct objective of operations. Instead, effectiveness is a more appropriate measure of company profitability. Management of operations is often one of the most complex undertakings in a company, but this need not be so. Effective operations management recognizes and acts to take profitable advantage of system limitations.

Isn't operations management more of an issue for manufacturing than service organizations?

It has been said that there are only a very few means of creating wealth. Traditionally these have been through extraction (mining and logging), agriculture (fishing and farming) and manufacturing. Contemporary theorists recognize that creativity is a source of wealth creation (advertising and entertainment) as well. All other activities are simply transfers of wealth among the economic players. Depending on how the numbers are reported, manufacturing in the UK is roughly 8% of GDP. In the US, manufacturing now accounts for between 3% and 12% of all jobs, so most managers are not working in manufacturing settings.

Despite the downturn in US manufacturing numbers, both manufacturing and service continue to play important roles in the economy. Manufacturing has learned some hard lessons from the service sector where resources expire frequently—the redeye flight with the unfilled seats or at midnight for example. The airline industry now fills those seats or changes their flight schedules to avoid low travel periods. Manufacturing learned to likewise develop methods for maximizing capacity utilization. The service sector has also learned a great deal from manufacturing such as quality control in accounting audits and specialization in hospitals to name a few. While the various business systems may involve different resources and have different goals, they each function as systems and need to be managed as such. Much of the discussion in this chapter will relate to manufacturing, but much can be applied to service businesses as well.

What do I need to know about business systems and change?

Companies are systems. At the same time they are part of larger systems including the local economic system, the global trade system, the transportation system, etc. Human resources, purchasing and operations are subsystems of company systems. Each system and subsystem has a single constraint that is either internal or external to that specific system. Internal constraints may be physical or, as noted theorists Goldratt and Deming both indicate, in approximately 90% of all cases, they are policy constraints. In other words, the constraint is the way someone, probably management, says things are to be done. Sometimes it is just the complacency of a rigid, perhaps bureaucratic system that keeps things the way they are, "that's how we've always done it."

In the dynamic times of the early twenty-first century, few organizations can afford to be rigid. Most must welcome, even seek out change to remain viable in the hypercompetitive globalized rapidly changing world. Even staid local, state and national governmental agencies must change with the times as technological, human resource and other environmental factors demand better and better ways to do things. Because systems are generally quite complex and often very large, it is important to find the single most important part, the weak link of the system and focus on making it strategically the best it can be. With a shareholder induced short-term focus on the bottom line, this becomes a significant source of conflict. This distracts management from things that matter for the long-term viability of the firm and shifts focus to things that really need little to no direct attention.

How do I identify the system limiting factors in my operations?

Businesses have the potential to experience great longevity. Houshi, an inn in Japan, has been in continuous operation for nearly 1,300 years. Stiftskeller St. Peter, a restaurant in Austria, has been serving customers for over 1,200 years. However, to live a very long life, a business needs to adapt to its ever-changing environment while maintaining a sense of purpose. Japanese companies sometimes take what Westerners consider to be a very long view of business, with twenty, fifty or even hundred year goals. While short-term plans are often very detailed and quite achievable, long-term goals such as a hundred year goal must be broad to be reasonable.

The opposite is true of strategic constraints, the overall limiting factor of any system. A strategic constraint is the choice of the organization and is very long-term in nature, but it is also very precisely identified and maintained. It remains the focus of the organization for many years, providing consistency to operations, marketing and/or other functional areas as it remains the chosen limiting factor for the organization. As the chosen limiting factor, the activity becomes the central focus of all subsystems of the organization: management information systems, human resources, operations, marketing, etc.

There are mathematical means of identifying a system limiting factor, but often it can be found intuitively. Ask yourself where the work is always stacking up? Consider this example. In a life insurance company, if you're verifying and settling death claims, paperwork is both the bane and reason for your existence. One particular life insurance company had a slower than average claim settlement process which averaged thirty-five days. Competitors were able to sell against this point during meetings with potential clients. This long claim settlement process resulted in a competitive weakness for the company.

As with an estimated 90–95% of all companies, this company actually had excess internal capacity. By reviewing its claims process for value adding and non-value adding components, this company was able to take actions that provided great improvement in its market disadvantage, slow claims processing, with minimal commitment of additional resources. The end result was a leaner approach with higher quality of operations and significantly improved market standing.

In our example, the various departments needing to sign off on each death claim were located remotely from each other. A first step was to, where possible, relocate the departments involved in claims processing to contiguous areas. This allowed for greater interpersonal interaction in resolving issues in the claims process and exploited the system's existing capacity. More effective use of resources reduced the operating expenses of the company while helping sales overcome the market objection of slow claims processing.

It is important to effectively utilize the existing resources in a company. Activities need to coordinated by subordinating them to the limiting resource. In the case of the insurance company, a number of signatures were required because "that is how we've always done it." Work and work flows had changed over the years, obviating the need for the signatures, yet they had persisted. These non-value adding steps were identified and eliminated by use of a process map. A process map is a graphical depiction, similar to a flow chart, of an organization's activities. Each detailed activity is designated as value adding or non-value adding by the use of different shapes or symbols. In a well-developed process map, it becomes very obvious from this picture of work flows where unneeded activities should be eliminated. An internet search will produce many examples of process maps and guidance on how to prepare your own.

In the analysis, the company learned that mail had been picked up and moved once daily between the seven work centers required to sign off on each death claim. This alone added substantial time to claims processing. As part of the solution, new mail clerks were subsequently hired and mail was moved from desk to desk every hour, taking nearly seven of the thirty-five days out of the claims process. The existing system was exploited to take advantage of professional staff capabilities by supporting them with faster movement of their work through the system at minimal costs. Batch sizes were reduced from an eight-hour batch to a one-hour batch. Streamlining paperwork electronically is a primary goal for workflow improvement. Electronic medical records and enterprise resource planning programs, for example, facilitate faster flow of digital data. Improvements in quality and timeliness, two characteristics discussed later in more detail, are important to nearly all customers. Improvements to each of these customer-centric qualities are enabled by this overall improvement process.

Very few businesses operate in a monopolistic environment. Competitors rise to the occasion, attempting to garner industry profits for themselves. No company can remain competitive while resting on its past accomplishments. While improvements in simple activities might provide competitive advantage in the short term, long-term competitive advantage comes from strategically improving processes. Inertia, allowing the status quo to remain, is debilitating, even fatal. Preparing for the next competitive threat before it arises is an appropriate use of resources. It is particularly effective when improvements are more complex and therefore more difficult to duplicate. Being two steps, not just one, ahead

---

TIPS FOR SYSTEM FOCUS—

An acronym that helps maintain the system focus is **IESEI**:

Identify the limiting factor of the system.

Exploit the limiting factor with regard to the system's objectives.

Subordinate all system activities to the system constraint.

Elevate the capacity of the limiting factor.

Inertia—competitive advantage is temporary and you must fix what is not yet broken to stay ahead.

of competitors allows a company to be proactive and less reactionary in setting its own direction rather than having actions dictated to it.

Taking a systems approach to developing and maintaining competitive advantage can be accomplished by taking the five steps: I, E, S, E, I (Identify, Exploit, Subordinate, Elevate, and overcoming Inertia). It might even be so obvious that some of the sequential steps can be eliminated and the improvement made. There is a cautionary note here. A consultant pointed out to a subsidiary company's management that production was not that company's strategic constraint, but that the market itself was the constraint. Management failed to take notice and did not prepare for the coming idleness of resources. With low resource efficiencies resulting from great improvements in the production end of the system, the corporate performance management system keyed in on the subsidiary. It was eventually closed because it had not developed sufficient markets for its highly effective operations. This scenario has, unfortunately, been carried out many times. Develop the market. It is likely the organization's true limiting factor.

How can operations management maximize profits?

The old axiom of buy low and sell high is true, however, there is much more to the story. Buying low for many organizations refers to focusing on cost cutting. In their 1994 work, *Reengineering Performance Measurement*, Archie Lockamy and James Cox describe three stages to the buy low process. The first stage should be to take a long-term view of what the organization wants to achieve and to set plans for achieving that overall objective within the limitations of its strategic constraint. The second stage is to determine the interim objectives that are needed to get to the long-term goal on the journey. Finally, after the goals are set and plans are put in place to reach them, the cost of getting there should be considered. In theory, organizations should stage their planning. The reality of the short-term profit focus often reverses the process.

The first stage to maximizing profitability is to clear the way for future sales. Align the overall system and its subsystems with the goal of making more money now and in the future. This future component is critical in that it causes actions that would not otherwise be taken. In this case, the future is *not* the next quarter or year, but is the long term, perhaps as much as fifty to a hundred years. Toyota's long-term goal is not to be the number one auto maker in the world, but to be the primary personal transportation source in the world. Cars as we know them will someday be replaced by newer technologies. Toyota is actively searching its horizons to determine what those might be.

Aligning current actions with this long-term future pushes the organization towards appropriate markets and resources and encourages the organization to strategically plan accordingly. It is rare that anyone driving would do so without some type of destination in mind. Once that destination is chosen, the appropriate path, be it the scenic route or the interstate, can be determined. A map comes in handy in choosing the most effective route to take given the parameters of the trip—leisure, speed, or effective use of resources (time, money, human abilities, roadways, etc.).

Focusing on current sales is the second stage of maximizing profitability. Align what is possible today with where the organization wants to go in the future. This provides the framework for actions for the next quarter, one year and five years. Decades ago, Toyota recognized that energy prices were rising and that unstable oil markets and resources would change the face of personal transportation. This recognition led to the development of the Prius, the world's most successful hybrid automobile, with current annual sales of more than 800,000 units worldwide. The company is now licensing its hybrid technology to late-comers to the market, further increasing company revenue. Continued development of current leading edge technology keeps a company in a position of market leadership and profitability.

In tough economic times, many companies resort to focusing on cost cutting in current operations. While this may make some sense, making effective use of resources means getting the most profitable use out of them. If cost cutting becomes the primary focus of an organization, it may lose sight of its market. The financial problems that Toyota experienced and its recall of millions of vehicles provides an example of having a primary short-term focus on cost cutting with only a secondary regard for future profits. Cost cutting today still needs to align with achievement of current and long-term organizational goals. Reducing costs is not the goal of a company, increasing profits is.

How can I connect customer satisfaction with operations management?

Any organization's planning needs to have short- and long-term components. A continued focus on profitability by satisfying customer needs drives activities that lead to long-term profitability. A number of authors have selected numerous criteria for customer satisfaction, achievement of which moves the organization towards profitability. The following discussion is adapted from Schonberger's Six Customer Requirements:

1. An appropriate level of *quality*
2. The *flexibility* to meet different customer requirements
3. An appropriate *service level* for each class of customer
4. Acceptable levels of *variation* in the product/service bundle
5. Adequate *lead times* to meet customer expectations
6. Minimal *lifetime costs* of the product or service to the customer.

It is the bundle of these characteristics on which customers judge the company and its products and services. Research indicates that it is many times more expensive to get a new customer than it is to keep an existing customer. Meeting customer requirements can significantly improve retention of customers.

How much quality is enough?

Quality is in the eye of the beholder. With physical products, measurement of attributes can be done physically and checked against standards that become customer expectations. With services, this comparison of what is delivered by the organization to what is expected by the customer is more difficult and complex. In advanced economies, it is nearly impossible to separate the service from the product so that even measuring physical products provides only part of the story of customer expectations. The Seven Tools of Quality, as catalogued by the American Society for Quality, are basic building

1. Check Sheets: A check sheet is a prepared form for collecting and analyzing data.
2. Control Charts: These are graphs used to study process changes over time.
3. Process Flow Charts: PFCs are useful for mapping and understanding your processes.
4. Histograms/Pareto Charts: These two different types of graphs show frequency distributions.
5. Cause-effect diagrams: Also known as a fishbone chart, this is useful for identifying possible causes and for sorting ideas.
6. Scatter diagrams: Help identify relationships by graphing pairs of numerical data.
7. Stratification diagrams: Used to identify patterns in the data.

Tool 12.1   Seven Tools of Quality Selection Guide

blocks for quality programs across the economy. Use this tool to determine which of these building blocks is best for your quality improvement plan.

How do we meet differing customer expectations?

Flexibility is the ability to meet differing customer expectations for similar products. The auto industry is a prime example of this. Customers can purchase from over a million variations of some manufacturer's vehicles, and that is of just a single model. This creates unneeded complexity in the production system. Some car manufacturers have greatly simplified this by bundling options. Remember the ES and LS models of the Hondas you see on the road? They are good examples of the bundled feature strategy. Flexibility is the ability to meet exacting customer specifications for a product: color, weight, length, reliability, etc. and can lead to customer loyalty.

In service organizations, meeting the various needs of customers oftentimes requires employees involved in the service encounter to have broad capabilities. Cross training in various tasks and allowing significant access to broad types of information helps employees be flexible in meeting the changing needs of customers. When a customer calls a company for resolution of an issue, the image of the company is enhanced when the customer is not shuffled among employees to meet the customer's needs. Again, performance measures for individuals at each level of the organization need to capture the requirement for flexibility.

The service level is the attention given to the customer's detailed requirements, some of which may be unknown to the customer. When a bank teller automatically provides a customer the account balance after a transaction, this may provide information to the customer leading to greater satisfaction with the service and increased customer loyalty. The service level sets the tone of the customer experience. At Neiman Marcus repeat customers are greeted by name. "Good afternoon, Dr Berry. I hope you are enjoying your shoes [a recent purchase]. How may I help you today?" This is substantially different from the Walmart's greeters "Welcome to Walmart."

Ergonomics are part of the service level and are integral to the product/service being offered. Providing the service ergonomically enhances the customer experience. Performance measures that guide individual employee conduct at all levels must be developed to move the customer experience to the desired level of service. The appropriate service level varies by organization and customer. This offers the company an opportunity to set the customer expectations so that differentiating standards are set and delivered by the company and provide competitive advantage.

What is process variation and why is it important?

Variation is any difference from the expected and it is the enemy of management. Variation differs from flexibility, which is the ability to meet customer requirements. Variation is relatively easy to measure in manufacturing by measuring physical attributes like milliliters, centimeters or even levels on the light spectrum. In services, variation is harder to measure because there is often an intangible component to the delivered product. When differences between service providers are small, variation is subject to intuitive judgment by the customer.

Because each customer has a different background against which he or she evaluates intangibles, the expected level of achievement is less certain. Greater variation is likely in the subjective evaluation of the service by the customer even in situations where the service provided to each customer is virtually the same. The Seven Tools of Quality discussed earlier can be used to evaluate variation. The best tools for evaluating variation are control charts that use statistical process control (SPC).

An SPC chart (pictured in chapter fourteen) helps the user confirm that the process being measured is under control statistically speaking. SPC evaluates outcomes. Outcomes can't be managed. The inputs that created those outcomes, the components of processes and their relationship to one another, are what you need to manage. Processes are the series of activities that make the good or service and the interaction of these activities determines the outcomes.

Variation measurement and control is critical at the limiting work center and all work centers in the production flow downstream. It is less so at work centers upstream of the limiting work center. This helps management focus attention on fewer activities by giving priority to one or a few. Once they've been determined, the timing and quality levels can then be specified to other centers. Activities can be designed that allow production at only the levels of output where standards are maintained. System variation is minimized and acceptable output maximized.

What are lead time considerations in operations management?

The time it takes from when something is ordered to the time it is delivered is lead time. The ability to minimize lead time comes from rapid production of goods and services and minimal distance for delivery of those goods and services. Physical goods (clothing, cars, etc.) need to be produced near the end consumer to minimize lead time while some services (bank teller, medical operations, etc.) must involve the customer and be co-located with the customer. Other processes can take advantage of technology and be provided remotely (radiology readings, investment purchases and sales, etc.) Off shoring and outsourcing also need to be considered when managing your lead time.

Off shoring (sending production to lower cost areas overseas) takes advantage of favorable wage rates in other countries, especially in the developing world. However, lead times and shipping costs may increase substantially, reducing or even eliminating the advantages sought. When looking systemically, the costs of long lead times and potential supply chain disruptions may exceed savings. Unless these costs are quantified, decisions can be inadvertently made with negative profit impact.

Outsourcing (relocating your customer service center to Bangalore as the most well-known example) differs from off shoring because it is a service that is outsourced. This may yield cost advantages but both customer service and output management may suffer unless information systems are seamless. More discussion of this topic can be found in T. Friedman's (2005) book, *The World is Flat*.

Are you ready to outsource?
The cost savings of outsourcing are tempting, but before you write that contract, here are some questions you should ask yourself:

- What am I looking to accomplish with this strategy?
- Do I have a firm understanding of my current operations?
- Do I understand my process strengths and weaknesses?
- What will the impact of outsourcing be on my employees?
- What will my customers think of my outsourcing decision?

The following tips will help ensure the best possible outsourcing experience:

1. Establish an outsourcing team responsible for managing the project. Use project management techniques to arrive at the decision.
2. Engage an executive sponsor to champion the decision.
3. Consider engaging an outsourcing expert or consultant to aid in the process.
4. Understand your management style and your organization's culture. Choose an outsourcing partner who matches your style.
5. Establish channels of communication. Be very clear on when and how communication will occur.
6. Establish performance benchmarks and expectations. Your contract should include financial penalties for failure to meet performance goals.
7. Decide on what to outsource. Functions may be outsourced partially or completely. Remember to outsource the process, not control of the process.
8. Use sources such as the Outsourcing Center, Yankee or Giga to help research the process.
9. Seek legal counsel with outsourcing expertise to help develop the contract.

Note to users—while this tool was developed for outsourcing, it applies to off shoring as well.

Tool 12.2   Outsourcing Readiness Guide

What do we need to know about operations capabilities?

Resource availability affects an organization's ability to meet customer requirements. Most managers can never have too many resources. However, sub-optimal use of resources stemming from an effort to try to get the most out of each individual resource is common. When individual efficiencies of people or machines become a key measure, a shift away from maximizing organizational profitability has occurred.

The use of resources needs to be considered as each resource's contribution to the whole, not its local efficiency. Minimizing waste at each step is always a good idea but should not be the sole guiding philosophy. A technique used to achieve this objective is to determine the resource's ability to produce the quality of goods or services desired. Process capability is an appropriate tool in this situation.

Process capability compares the output of an in-control process to the established specification limits by using capability indices. The comparison is made by forming the ratio of the spread between the process specifications (the specification "width") to the spread of the process values, as measured by the desired number of process standard deviation units (the process "width").

In human systems, the number of process standard deviations may be as little as one, capturing about two thirds of activities as being in control. In automated systems (computer controlled) with little human interaction, the number of process standard deviations can perhaps reach greater than six (very high control). The process capability ratio (c_p) calculation is:

$$Cp = \frac{\text{Upper Specification Limit—Lower Specification Limit}}{6s}$$

S is the standard deviation of the sample. The upper and lower specification limits are specified by your customer. By completing the calculations, the result will be a ratio and if this ratio is one or greater, the process is capable of producing products within the desired specifications. A ratio of less than one indicates that the process is not capable of good production. It is also possible to have the process produce results between the limits, but for the process not to be centered as shown below.

In this case, either the limits should be changed to reflect reality or issues causing the off-center condition should be determined and addressed to bring the process back

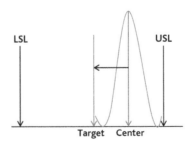

Figure 12.1 Target Versus Center Variance Results

to a centered state. This is not a standalone calculation. The calculation of the process capability index, c_{pk}, should be undertaken.

$$c_{pk} = \text{The lower of} \quad \frac{\text{Upper Specification Limit} - x}{3s} \quad \text{or} \quad \frac{\text{Lower Specification Limit} - x}{3s}$$

This determines how centered the data is in the specification limits and the higher the number the more centered the data, with a reading above one indicating that the data is within the two limits. You can use results from this type of calculation to determine how close or far you are from your target.

How is price linked to operations management?

Pricing is covered in chapter ten of this book. This section will focus on the relationship between price and operations management. Overall, the market sets prices, not the firm. Prices asked by the firm are merely confirmed by the market. With this in mind, pricing is an important component of management. Setting sales prices incorrectly reduces available profits.

As outlined in chapter ten, traditionally price calculations cover costs and a profit margin. Determining cost is often the challenge. If many costs (salaries of workers/managers, insurance, rents, etc.) are not calculated on a piece rate, these fixed costs will be incurred whether or not additional units are sold. Because these costs are incurred during each period within a narrow range, they should be considered period costs of operations and not included in calculation of the cost of goods and services, but in the cost of doing business overall.

By considering all but raw materials and purchased parts as period costs, a stronger picture of profitability emerges. Using the best case product mix and armed with this information, marketing and sales can be geared to maximizing organizational profits. If the ideal product mix cannot be created internally, then the decision whether or not to buy products from others and sell under the company's name can also be made with maximum profits predicted ahead of time. Caution needs to be observed here; some companies have eliminated products that were complementary products or were less profitable products and were faced with a market impact for their more profitable products. Due diligence must be exercised in decisions as to whether or not to add or eliminate products from the lineup. Considerations other than finance may dictate the ultimate choice in product mix decisions.

How can I match production flow with demand?

Once the product mix has been determined, getting the products out the door in a timely manner is crucial. See chapter thirteen for more on product distribution. As in the production process, the delivery process will also have variations. Allowing for variation should not imply that schedulers are given carte blanche to plan on deliveries when they want. The promised due dates provided by the sales force must be met. Meeting these due dates requires coordination so that sales does not promise more product than the company has capacity to deliver. Once a due date is set, managing the system is important to optimize flow of products through the system. In a life insurance company, this may be death claims. For a hospital, this is patients. For a manufacturer, this is goods to be sold. The use of goods will be used to provide an example, but the following concepts apply widely to most organizations.

How do we manage production flow?

There are five primary uses of time in a single work center system:

1. *Setup* takes place when the work center is being made ready to do the next batch of work setup and is important for work centers that are not dedicated to a particular type of work.
2. *Queue time* occurs when the setup is complete, but an item is waiting to be worked on.
3. *Run time* is when the item is being worked on at the work center.
4. *Wait time* is when work on the items has been completed but the rest of the batch has yet to be completed at this work center.
5. *Transportation time* is when the batch is being moved from one work center to another.

The sum of these times across all items and all work centers is the length of time it takes to fully process a batch. Each of the five uses of time is subject to variation. Because variation is a natural occurrence, it should be anticipated and planned for. Normal variation is the result of differences in time commonly found in operations. Here's an example. On the route you take to work, you normally hit five of the seven lights red and have to stop. One day all seven are red when you hit them. This is called common cause variation. On the flip side, special cause variation refers to things that should not be expected to occur like an accident en route.

Because common cause variation is normal to every system, it should be allowed for in the course of operations. Special cause variation is not allowed for. No one knows if or when it will occur. Because variation is the enemy of management, finding ways to reduce it should be the focus of everyone's attention. People are risk averse, so they naturally want to allow for Murphy. The tendency for anything that can go wrong will go wrong. This must not be accommodated. Doing so adds unneeded time to operations, reducing the competitiveness of the organization.

In project management (see chapter fourteen), this is a particularly onerous problem dealt with through education of the project managers. Flow should be matched with demand, not production capacities, and optimum profitability is achievable. This is a critical competitive point. Work is not done to keep high efficiencies at each work center for the sake of efficiency. Effectiveness is what organizations should strive for. Efficiency is needed only in a few instances as excess physical capacity exists in nearly all organizations. As stated earlier, it is policies, almost always set by management, that are the source of internal constraints.

Most systems have more than a single operation and when this is so, the traditional approach is to try to drive waste (excess capacity) out of the system by balancing the production line. Work processes at Toyota for example, are designed so that take time (or cycle time), is set to the same amount of time across all work centers. When one work center varies from the standard, this can cause a ripple effect. When more than one work center varies from the standard, the plant is in trouble.

In a balanced system, if an allowance is made for common cause variation, there will be too much time available at work centers that do not experience much variation. There may not be enough time to complete work properly at work centers that do experience significant variation in the work time needed to complete assigned tasks. Minimizing the unneeded time and maximizing needed time is not accomplished through changes in capacity but through a simple technique of buffering only at specific places in the process.

How can our operations keep pace with the market?

You can keep pace with market demands by employing Drum-Buffer-Rope (DBR). With a marching band, the drumbeat is the signal to all of the musicians, majorettes and baton twirlers as to the speed at which to proceed. The same holds true in a production system, with the market setting the pace. Once this pace (the drum) is determined, it is necessary to allow for common cause variation. This is necessary at only a limited number of work centers. If the production capacity of the system is greater than market demand, then the market limits the system and finished goods are warehoused to provide a buffer against variation in demand from the market.

If the internal system can only meet part of what the market demands, there is an internal constraint. A buffer needs to be established immediately upstream from the constraint. In rare circumstances, the system limit can be caused by vendors unable to meet demand (i.e., the scarcity of rare earth minerals in 2011). A buffer of items is used to accommodate the common cause variation. The size of the buffer depends on the degree and frequency of variation in the flow of products.

The buffer itself should be divided into three zones: "next in line" (red zone), "soon" (white zone), and "in a while" (blue zone). The absence of items in the red zone can cause delays in production or unexpected setups. Some 90 to 100% of items in the red zone need to be physically present in the buffer when work begins to prevent a loss of throughput and the resulting loss of profit. Because there is more time to make up for variation in the system upstream from the constraint, somewhere in the range of 50 to 80% of items in the white zone need to be present until these become red zone items.

Blue zone items have even more time available to make up for variation in the system and need only be 25 to 50% present when red zone items are being produced. These are early percentages. As management identifies and resolves sources of system variation, the percentages can go higher as variation is less of a problem.

The third component, the rope, ties the release of resources from the constraint to the gating operation, allowing items to be released into the production system in time to get the work into the constraint buffer to fill it to the appropriate level. This is similar to a Just-in-Time (JIT) system with a major exception. In JIT systems, kanbans, standard quantities of work in process such as an egg carton carrying twelve eggs, are placed between every work center. In the aforementioned system, the only place where work in process is stored is in specific buffers.

How is Total Quality Management (TQM) connected to Operations Management?

A systematic approach to managing operations is summarized in Deming's fourteen points, which help link TQM to operations management. Deming's fourteen points are a basis for quality transformation of an organization. Adoption and action on the fourteen points are a signal that management intends to stay in business and aims to protect investors and jobs. Such a system formed the basis for lessons for top management in Japan beginning in 1950 and continuing through today (W. Edwards Deming Institute, 2011). The fourteen points are:

1. Create constancy of purpose toward improvement of product and service, with the aim to become competitive and to stay in business, and to provide jobs.
2. Adopt the new philosophy. We are in a new economic age. Western management must awaken to the challenge, must learn their responsibilities, and take on leadership for change.
3. Cease dependence on inspection to achieve quality. Eliminate the need for inspection on a mass basis by building quality into the product in the first place.
4. End the practice of awarding business on the basis of price tag. Instead, minimize total cost. Move toward a single supplier for any one item, on a long-term relationship of loyalty and trust.
5. Improve constantly and forever the system of production and service, to improve quality and productivity, and thus constantly decrease costs.
6. Institute training on the job.
7. Institute leadership. The aim of supervision should be to help people and machines and gadgets to do a better job. Supervision of management is in need of overhaul, as well as supervision of production workers.
8. Drive out fear, so that everyone may work effectively for the company.
9. Break down barriers between departments. People in research, design, sales, and production must work as a team, to foresee problems of production and in use that may be encountered with the product or service.
10. Eliminate slogans, exhortations, and targets for the work force asking for zero defects and new levels of productivity. Such exhortations only create adversarial relationships, as the bulk of the causes of low quality and low productivity belong to the system and thus lie beyond the power of the work force.
11. Eliminate work standards (quotas) on the factory floor. Substitute leadership. Eliminate management by objective. Eliminate management by numbers, numerical goals. Substitute leadership.
12. Remove barriers that rob the hourly worker of his right to pride of workmanship. The responsibility of supervisors must be changed from sheer numbers to quality. Remove barriers that rob people in management and in engineering of their right to pride of workmanship. This means abolishment of the annual or merit rating and of management by objective.
13. Institute a vigorous program of education and self-improvement.
14. Put everybody in the company to work to accomplish the transformation. The transformation is everybody's job.

Deming emphasized a systems approach to operations management and his fourteen points capture this direction. He emphasized that since it is management that controls resources, it is management's responsibility to use those resources to develop a system that can achieve the desired results. System objectives direct actions not local optimization of resources.

Operations are core to all organizations. Basic economic activity centers on agriculture, extraction and manufacturing, but advanced economies have significant service sectors. Management of operations at the various levels of economic development share key components: (1) relationships with other parts of the organization, suppliers and markets, (2) quality standards, and (3) strategic goal alignment. Communication is critical in developing and maintaining relationships inside and outside the organization. Appropriate quality standards for the market need to be determined and consistently achieved. The activities of conducting operations should be aligned with the strategic goals of the organization. Tools that help achieve these goals are discussed in more detail in various parts of this book.

Additional Resources

There are many sources of information on operations management and only a few are mentioned here:

- The Goldratt Institute in the UK provides information and assistance with identifying and managing system constraints in ongoing operations and unique projects.
- The British Quality Foundation provides education on quality improvement, sustainability and other issues important in operations.
- An investigation of the logic behind constraint management can be found in Dettmer's book *Goldratt's Theory of Constraints*.
- *Managing Operations* is a very thorough book on the subject authored by Cox, Blackstone, and Schlier.

The American Society for Quality, administrator of the prestigious Malcolm Baldridge award, provides training and certification. This long established professional organization holds conferences and events in support of the Quality movement.

References

American Society for Quality. (2010, Dec 23). *Seven Tools of Quality*. Retrieved Dec. 31, 2010, from American Society for Quality: http://asq.org/learn-about-quality/seven-basic-quality-tools/overview/overview.html.

Friedman, T. (2005). *The World is Flat: A Brief History of the 21st Century*. New York, NY: Farrar, Straus & Giroux.

Goldratt, E. M. (1982). *The Goal*. Great Barrington, MA: The North River Press Publishing Corp.

Kleiner, A. (2002). What Are the Measures That Matter? *Strategy and Business*. First Quarter, 2002.

Lockamy, A., and Cox, J. (1994). *Reengineering Performance Measurement*. Boston, MA: Irwin Publishers.

Schonberger, R., Knod, E. (1994). *Operations Management: Continuous Improvement*, 5th edition. New York, NY: Richard D. Irwin, Inc.

W. Edwards Deming Institute (2011), retrieved January 5, 2011 from http://deming.org.

13 *Distribution and Supply*

ERIC BOLLAND

Let's start with the basics. A business, whether service or manufacturing, is an entity that takes inputs and transforms them into outputs. Once they've been transformed, the product or service needs to get into the hands of the customer. This process needs to be seamless. Seamless processes result in greater efficiency and effectiveness. Greater efficiency and effectiveness result in higher profitability.

Inputs are on the supply side of the business or the upstream side. Outputs are on the distribution, or downstream side of the business. Both of these subjects will be explored in this chapter. Combined, distribution and supply can be labeled *supply chain management.* This term encompasses the entire transformation stream from vendors to distributors. Without this chain, the producer is in isolation, an island by itself.

When well managed, supply chain management is just the opposite; a vibrant and engaged continuation of the flow through the producing firm to ultimate customers. Factors like the geographic location of your suppliers, inventory and transportation are all crucial to the success of the supply chain. The merging of supply and distribution functions is a more modern view of the realities of businesses today. This seamless process is supply chain management sometimes referred to as value chain management, a concept popularized by Michael Porter in the 1980s. Porter's view emphasized the value that was added at each step in the process.

The issue of supply chain management goes beyond just establishing the network and flow. Not only must the supply chain exist, it must also be coordinated. Bottlenecks may result in accumulated inventory with associated carrying costs. They may also result in delivery slowdowns potentially leading to customer service problems. Timely delivery of a quality product can be a selling advantage. Supply chain interruptions can leave you vulnerable to competitive poaching. An uncoordinated system is an inefficient system and it doesn't take much to get the instrument of supply chain management out of tune, like lute players who spend half their life tuning a lute and the other half playing an untuned lute. Hence, the inclusion of the term management is appropriate whenever we encounter distribution and supply issues in this chapter. Suppliers and distributors link the business with players in the external environment. How well these connections work and how well the flow goes from supply through the producer to the customer, determines organizational success.

What is distribution?

An organization is a value-creating and value-adding entity. Distribution is the means by which the organization's products or services get into the hands of consumers. The organization's offerings are made available to customers at the right place, at the right time, and in the right number. Distribution is much more complicated than turning on a pipeline. Too much flow and it is a fire hose. Too little and it is a trickle that leaves customers thirsty.

David Blanchard (2007) calls supply chain management the "sequence of events and processes that take a product from dirt to dirt." Less colorful, but more in line with the Supply Chain Council definition, supply chain management is to "plan, source, make, deliver and return." This definition is appropriate for this chapter, which looks at the full circle aspect of supply and distribution.

Though manufacturing processes are most frequently used as examples in supply chain discussions, distribution applies to more than just physical goods. Services are distributed too. An airline distributes a transportation service and a barber shop distributes haircuts. While services are distributed and many of the same issues apply, there are important differences as well. Services are supplied and consumed at the same time. Services cannot be inventoried while products may be stored and used at other times. Products can sit on a shelf.

There is crossover between pure product and pure service distribution though. To provide a plumbing service, the plumber needs tools. A restaurant needs both food and servers. Most services require some level of physical goods as part of their input group. While crossovers exist, this chapter deals with the physical aspects of supply chain management.

Distribution faces a wide range of issues, but there is a subset of issues that recurs persistently and those will be our focus. The major issues of distribution can be put together in a series of questions. These are the who, what, when, where and how of distribution.

Who should do our distribution?

The main question here is should we distribute our products and services ourselves or should we do it through others? This is the fundamental question because all the other "who" questions follow from it. A company may choose to handle its own distribution as part of its marketing function. Controlling both of these activities may be a very good strategic decision and may make sense if quick delivery is part of your competitive advantage. The company may be able to distribute its products for a lower cost or they may simply be more effective than an outsider.

Another matter to consider in making this determination is how much power you have as the producer in comparison to the power of the distributor. Chapter five introduced this consideration in the Porter Five Forces Model. Having the power in the distribution process means determining who calls the shots and who can get the distribution deal done in their favor. A way of looking at distributor power is provided in the classic article, *Distributor Portfolio Analysis* by Peter Dickson (1983) in which he presents a graphic distributor power tool which is still quite applicable.

Since getting the product to the customer (distribution) is paramount to company success, the question of doing it yourself or contracting it out comes down to who can do it better. Related to that is the question of who could do a more cost-effective job. Distribution should be direct if:

- You have frequent contact with customers
- Customers are demanding
- Only you know your products due to product complexity.

A simple tool in determining if you should do your own distribution or not is the following distribution preparedness checklist:

Question	YES	NO
Are there outside distributors available?		
Are outside distributors willing to distribute for us?		
Does a cost analysis (both on separate transactions and in total) for distribution favor outside distribution?		
Can an outside distributor more effectively get our products to consumers? (consider timeliness, volume, reliability, reputation).		
Will an outside distributor partner with us in optimizing distribution?		
Will an outside distributor compete with us in any way?		
Are we realistic about what we expect from an outside distributor?		

Tool 13.1   Distribution Preparedness Checklist

Answering questions on the checklist is clear-cut but the process itself requires you to do some soul searching. These are not simple yes or no answers. The answers, whether yes or no, should be conclusions based on analysis, not just immediate reactions. Don't just jump into it without having the right people on your distribution taskforce who will honestly evaluate these questions. The tool works best if you thoughtfully and conscientiously spend time with each question.

There is no magic scoring system in which a certain number of yes answers versus a certain number of no answers will absolutely guide you one way or another. Answering all questions candidly will likely be very informative for you. Distributors may not even be available if you are in a newly formed business. It might be presumptuous to do the checklist without finding out first if you can even get a distributor. If you can't find a major carrier, seek out small, independent distributors in your market. These are generally small operations (often a single person) who may distribute products for various producers for a fee.

What should be distributed?

It might seem that you would want everything out the door and on the way to customers as quickly as possible, but this is a facile and flawed response. Customers don't know what they want in many instances. Flexibility needs to be built into your distribution system to prepare for demand ebb and flow. A way of doing this is through distribution capacity flexibility. At times, you might need to run below your distribution system's peak capacity to take care of sudden and significant new demand. Starting out at full capacity doesn't let you make adjustments for greater demand.

Capacity contingency needs to be built into what you are doing. Just how much of a flexibility factor is needed can be shaped based on historic performance and indicators of future customer demand. There are many software programs available to do this. You may want to take pen to paper yourself first to develop a better idea of what software capabilities are really needed. Before you invest in a program, it's always good to make sure you know what you want it to do.

Controlling the amount of product that is distributed is an important strategic decision. At times, it may be beneficial to put through most of what you produce. At other times you may decide to strategically put through nothing at all. The cornerstone base unit of information should come from the customer and may be closely tied to your marketing objectives. An example of the relationship between distribution and marketing involves the direct distribution decision. Direct distribution happens when the customer beats a path to your door to buy.

Until the 1980s, Coors Brewing Company in Golden, Colorado had no national distribution system making it something of a Western novelty beer. You had to drive to their Colorado plant or visit local distributors to buy beer. Many East Coast visitors would pick up a case of Coors to take home with them. This created a mystique about the beer that was lost when they developed a national distribution system. If there is high demand and no alternative provider, direct distribution is clearly a choice that helps you avoid distribution costs and that can, as in the Coors example, be used to develop a sense of exclusivity about the product.

At the other distribution extreme, putting everything in the channel is more like a pure process operation. An electric utility company comes to mind as an example of an extreme case. Everything is throughput and value is added by the channels. These include the major transmission lines and the local electric distribution entities.

The issue of customization plays into the distribution question as well. Are you delivering a complete product? Or, are you delivering a partially complete product with some customizable details? It may be worth doing some customization at the end point, much in the same way that vehicles are sold. This is another link between your marketing and your distribution strategies. Customization plays on the consumer psychology of wanting something designed just for them without paying the higher price of total customization. For you as the producing firm, customization and product accessories afford opportunities for additional customer touch points. This concept is at the very heart of customer relationship management. To address the question of customization, the product offering needs to be deconstructed to determine if there are marketing or other advantages to be had by creating several separate transactions with customers. In a similar vein, add-on services can be retained by you and then offered to customers at a later date. Warranties are an example. In this sense, a product is not entirely delivered if the producer takes it back for repairs and upgrades.

When should we distribute?

The important factor of time now becomes part of the distribution discussion. Distribution timing can be an issue on many fronts. Purely seasonally based products, like selling Christmas trees before Christmas and steers when they have grown to market weight are two very obvious seasonally based distributions, but there are more subtle aspects of time considerations in distribution. There are all kinds of software-based programs that can be used to predict when a market will be ready to pay the most for what you have to offer. Capitalizing on these market peaks helps boost profitability.

Maximizing profit is of course what you want to do. You want to do it on the basis of exclusive, even privileged information and not on the basis of what the market already knows. So how do you obtain this kind of information? There are software programs that do the job of predicting optimal distribution dates. These programs have quite variable predictive success and you should be cautious about prediction claims. Foolproof modeling has not yet been developed. Some of the barriers to accurate predictions are game playing by competitors. They may act as though they are ready to deliver product but then pull back at the last minute with the hope that they have triggered you to rush to market. This in turn drives down prices. Then, when supply is down they will enter the market and enjoy a higher price.

Some seasonable distribution is totally predictable, but other seasonality may be unpredictable. If you have something that is seasonable such as clothing, the orders have to be made well in advance. Distribution of products and services for scheduled events, like football or rock concerts, locks the distribution to a known timeline. If you know event schedules, you can then work with your distributors to prime the channel before the goods are ready. The channels can be readied by reserving capacity at a certain time in advance. This way distribution capacity is scheduled even though you can't yet say exactly what the mix of goods will be. You can also go back to past seasonal distribution events and tweak the quantities according to the historical information. Additionally, seasonality effects may be predicted by asking your high volume customers what their needs are.

In a purely economic sense, you want to distribute product when supply is low and demand is high, but neither condition may be detectable. Predictable high demand, while seeming like a good thing, will certainly draw in more competitors which reduces economic gains by reducing industry profitability. There is considerable gamesmanship in distribution timing because there is much to gain or lose.

How should we distribute our products?

This question is perhaps the most thorny when entering the bramble thicket known as distribution. As such, it is appropriate to consider a series of related questions all bearing on the topic of distribution methodology:

IS A SINGLE PATH OR ARE MULTIPLE PATHS BETTER FOR DISTRIBUTION?

The channel is your route to your customer, in other words, your path. In the distribution discipline, paths are called channels. They are the routes to your final customer, that network of people, programs, policies and practices that delivers the goods. The answer to the single versus multiple channel question involves thinking about what choices you may realistically have. If you are a new business start-up, you may not have a choice. You may have a challenge getting any distributors let alone multiple distributors in multiple channels. In fact, if your firm has not yet established a track record, you will most likely have to build a distribution system from scratch. This would start by finding an agent who can work a single channel for you until you establish a market presence.

In considering the single verses multichannel option, it would seemingly be obvious that multichannel is the best option because there are more ways to get to customers. But what if you only have a handful of customers? What if you are predominantly a business-to-business operation? In either of these cases, single channels are preferable.

Multiple channels are parallel paths to the consumer. Your products are getting to customers in different venues. Consider toothpaste for example. It is sold in grocery stores, airports, drug stores, through catalogs and over the Internet. This means simultaneous delivery points. Multiple channels work better if you want to have intensive distribution to a wide range of customers. If your product is an appropriate consumer good, this may be the way to go.

When considering the volume of product you want to move, conduct an analysis of your circumstances. Pay particular attention to your industry's stage of evolution. How many customers do you have and what is their bargaining power? How much control do your competitors have over distributors? These questions are all part of this analysis.

HOW DO WE CONSIDER IF MIDDLEMEN SHOULD BE PART OF THE DISTRIBUTION SYSTEM?

A very common marketing strategy is to offer a lower price by eliminating the middleman. That sounds fine unless you are the middleman. Middlemen add consumer touch points in the delivery of goods to consumers. They also add transaction costs. Nonetheless, middlemen abound in the distribution system. If there are that many of them, there must be a reason. Middlemen might have a strong relationship with a customer or with the retail store that sells to the customer. Middlemen might have credibility with the final customer or retailer that you do not yet have.

They might even have geographic access to customers that you don't have. This is especially true in remote markets. Middlemen might even personally control access to the market. An example of this could be a middleman who owns the only form of transportation, say an island ferry. There are many ways that a middleman can be valuable in the distribution process. It could even be that the middleman is a link between other middlemen in a complex, multi-agent distribution arrangement. Before jumping to the conclusion that eliminating the middleman is a good thing, consider the value these individuals or firms may offer.

WHAT ARE WAYS TO CONTROL THE INTENSITY OF DISTRIBUTION?

The intensity of distribution is your choice. Marketers have categorized three different methods as follows:

1. Intensive distribution is conducted by using all available channels to the customer. This means you want your product in every available outlet: in retail stores, on the Internet, and directly from your factory or warehouse. This is appropriate if you have something to sell for which there is considerable demand.
2. Selective distribution occurs if you don't want (or cannot afford) intensive distribution. This could be because of production capacity constraints or resource limitations as well as costs. Selective distribution helps keep costs low while building demand because the products sold are controlled in number. Luxury items often follow this method.
3. Exclusive distribution happens when you, as a producer, choose to use just one channel in a select area.

SHOULD DISTRIBUTION SYSTEMS BE MANAGED?

Answering this is not setting up a straw man question just to be beaten down for the sake of mental exercise alone. Answering it reveals the management and control issues that are at stake. These are fundamental to creating and maintaining effective distribution systems.

Consider what happens when a traditional distribution system is used. The members of the distribution chain operate independently. They don't cooperate with one another. The passing of the product from one member of the chain to another is transaction based. The exchange is based on agreement on price and nothing else. If you use the traditional approach, the locus of control transfers from you and to profit seeking entities along the way to the final customer.

An antidote for the purely independent method is to look into the establishment of a vertical marketing system (VMS). Most fundamentally, this is when all the channel members focus on the customer, an all-for-all orientation that solves many of the problems of traditional distribution. The channel only works if the customer is the focus. A house of cards can collapse if customer orientation is lost, in distribution, and everywhere else.

To make a VMS work, it is essential to honestly assess and respond to customer demands in the whole process. The distribution players will have to give and take. As part of this, concessions need to be made for the good of the order. If you decide to do this as an exercise, you'll likely need an outside facilitator. You'll need the engaged participation of all the channel members. It will be hard work but the benefits will include greater sustainability, reduced channel member conflict and better customer service. When a VMS is designed and agreed to, it should be formalized on the basis of channel member responsibility, shared information and issue resolution.

Having addressed major distribution issues, it is time to circle around to the other side of your operations, the supply side. Suppliers are the input conduit to your business system. Unless you are a vertically integrated company (which most are not), you are dealing with suppliers that are not a part of your company. Firms have become increasingly dependent on suppliers as they seek to right-size their operations and pare down costs. That doesn't leave much margin for error. This section considers supplier questions likely to be of concern.

Supply chain management is the concept that links both supply and distribution. Considering the entire process stream from procurement of raw materials to placing the product in the hands of the consumer, the supply aspect of the business has to do with both upstream and downstream management.

Upstream management involves the sequence of raw material sourcing followed by the logistics of getting material to the producer and finally into inventory. Supply chain management is not logistics. Logistics is the handling, storing and transportation of products and material. Logistics deals with the physical aspects of moving goods. Consequently, supply chain management is more broad an activity than logistics. That said however, logistics are a critical component of supply-side management. Different parties handle logistics in different ways. Third party logistics firms are playing an increasingly significant role in logistics. These are specialist companies like Penske Logistics that, for a price, eliminate logistics responsibilities from producer firms.

What do I need to consider in working with suppliers?

The first thing to consider is the structure of your industry. Different supplier relationships occur in different industries. The set of businesses that include you, your competitors, and non-competing businesses populate an industry. The North American Industrial Classification System (touched on in chapters ten and eleven) gets down to highly refined definitions of industry groups. It is well worth exploring this system. Most businesses in an industry use the same distribution and supply practices.

Once you have classified yourself and defined your industry, it is useful to look at the dynamics of supplier relationships. From Michael Porter (1980), suppliers co-exist with industry groups and they influence the rivalry among competitors. What you want to see in your industry is a situation where suppliers are abundant in number and competitive with one another. This is an indication that they are in a weakened bargaining position compared to you. You also want to discover that your supply chain is stable and reliable. To confirm this, look for a relatively small percentage of suppliers moving in and out of the market. Still, you don't want to have suppliers in such a stable, self-protected condition that they control most of the supplier connections to you and other producers.

Another favorable situation in your industry is if you have multiple sources for your material enabling you to easily switch between suppliers. Low switching costs will keep suppliers seeking your business on their toes. Still another positive industry structure characteristic is if there are substitute goods available so that you could bypass all present suppliers. For example, a bronze sculptor may be able to switch her art medium to an entirely different resin molding process instead of limiting herself to traditional bronze casting. The new substitute process has then bypassed the suppliers of bronze castings.

You also need to evaluate the industry structure of your suppliers or potential suppliers. If there are a large number of suppliers, then the level of competition will be high, given a constant demand. If the material you need for production is a commodity and the commodity is easily available, then suppliers are in a weaker negotiating position with producer firms (similar to the low switching cost advantage).

Producers can blunt the development of too much supplier power by creating supplier dependency on the producer. Geographical proximity is one of those strategies. Automobile manufacturers now like to keep their suppliers close to them to reduce transportation costs but, in more subtle ways, this increases the costs to the supplier of leaving the area and increases their dependency on a specific producer.

How do I find suppliers?

Suppliers like to find you, although this doesn't alleviate the need for you to also find them. It helps to be visible. Let them know that you're out there. A simple internet search will provide names of potential suppliers. Suppliers can also be can be found in industrial catalogs such as the Electronic Products' Buyers' Guide and the Thomas Register. Trade magazines are another useful source.

How do I find the right suppliers?

There are many suppliers out there, but only a few will really fit the bill. Finding the right supplier means searching for a business partner who is a match in terms of product, price

---

1. What, in precise terms are my supply needs? The more you know what you are asking for, the easier it will be to get the right fit with a supplier. Knowing the quality, quantity and timing of your input needs will get your supplier discussions off on the right foot.
2. What can I find out about how a supplier runs their business? Some due diligence is in order. You want to know not only if the prospective supplier can provide you with materials or subcomponents, you also want to know about their business practices. A Dun and Bradstreet report can tell you about their financial health. So will interviews with businesses that have worked with the candidate supplier before.
3. Are our business practices compatible? In many ways, as stated previously, you are looking for a partner, someone who shares your vision, someone with whom you know you can work. This has both a business and a cultural aspect to it. Interviews with supplier employees and a site visit can provide you with insight into the subject's business practices. Don't forget to check out their website if you haven't already. It can tell you a lot about how a company does business.

Tool 13.2   Supplier Selection Questionnaire

and culture. For this question, a selection tool is offered. The tool is qualitative in nature. This tool is a series of questions to ask of yourself and your potential supplier. This tool can be used to evaluate single suppliers and can be used to compare multiple suppliers by simply adding a scoring scale for each question and then calculating a total score for the separate suppliers.

Once I establish a supplier relationship, how should I manage it?

If you were asked how to effectively manage your own areas of responsibility within your company, you would very likely be able to provide a long list of techniques and strategies. If you were asked how you manage your suppliers, most likely your list would be much shorter or nonexistent. That's not uncommon since many managers just assume things are going well and suppliers don't need to be closely managed. When managing suppliers make use of the general principles of effective management. With respect to suppliers, your management objectives should deal with:

Planning Issues—Meet periodically with your critical suppliers to share your respective visions of what the future holds. Regularly might mean only yearly. The joint planning of input acquisition will head off pitfalls.

Organizing Issues—Again, in coordination with key suppliers, you should work out issues about organization. Who will do what and when? You need to jointly coordinate and schedule supply tasks. An internet search will produce software programs to accomplish this. Organizing issues have to do with production scheduling, inventory management and demand forecasting.

Leading Issues—There needs to be an identification of accountability of who is responsible for the work. Especially important are hand-over points. At hand-over points, the supplier delivers what is supposed to show up and you as the producer pick it up and move it on. These crucial transfer points are common problem areas.

Control Issues—Control is concerned with monitoring a process, comparing outcomes to standards, and analyzing the variance to determine how the supply process is working. The important thing in the control process with suppliers is to be able to depict the process as a whole and not have supplier tasks separate from producer tasks. Control requires good IT data and reports (chapter nineteen) to determine what needs to be fixed. Again, this is a matter of joint supplier and producer planning at the outset. You want to agree to the action type, frequency and responsibility that emerge from the data. The reports can address measures that have been communicated and agreed on up-front like throughput time, quantity produced, quality measures etc. However it is done, things will go more smoothly by having a supplier control process.

The preceding discussion focused on the *issues* to be managed with suppliers. Actual management can take many forms. One strategy might be to develop a formal contract between supplier and producer. Another might be a less formalized relationship but one that still accomplishes overall supplier management objectives. An important note to this is that the supply process is not a single function. It is made up of sourcing, procurement, and conversion of supplies to finished products and has many moving parts to keep track of.

There is also a financial aspect to supply. Generally spelled out in the supplier contract, the financial aspect of supply deals with payments. The terms of payment by the producer to the supplier are established in this area. There are also terms for rework by the supplier if necessary, delivery parameters and so forth.

Perhaps the most visible aspect of supply is inventory. That is where raw materials, subcomponents, and the like are stored. You can see and touch inventory. There is both a science and an art to managing it. Inventory decisions have to do with the quantity, location, and quality of inventory. Quality assurance practices emphasize just-in-time goals in inventory and production processes. These cost minimization and availability optimization methods are part of production and operations management issues in your organization.

The primary role of a supplier is to provide the materials you need to produce your product. Looking at suppliers in an enlarged role, as your business partners, there are many more things they can help with that may not be immediately apparent. Suppliers can help provide information about your competitors. Suppliers can alert you to new advances in the materials they supply thereby becoming a leading agent in industry developments. You can also help one another out in emergencies of all kinds. You want to build and maintain trust and also codify it. When you negotiate agreements with suppliers, you should discuss the management aspects of the relationship. How often do you want to communicate? What do you want to communicate with one another? Provide such mechanisms and you'll no longer think of suppliers as mere providers of inputs.

What do we need to know about transportation?

Transportation is an essential aspect of both supply and distribution. The elements that need to be addressed in considering transportation concerns start with what form of transportation to use. A single transporter or multiple transporters can be used. The issue is an important one because for commodity-like supplies (sand, soil, cement, water, and the like), it is the transportation cost that makes up the bulk of the expense. For example, the transportation cost for sand and gravel is generally 55% of the total. Even for subcomponents, in a global economy, goods are transported all around the world and transportation costs are very significant. In the following table, the major transportation methods are described with comments on their advantages and disadvantages.

The table shows the advantages and disadvantages of the methods. Is any alternative best? The answer can be traced back to your customers. In so doing, you should develop a transportation strategy as part of your supply chain management process. That strategy needs to incorporate criteria like frequency, routes (for time considerations) and costs.

A consideration in transportation is the quality of the infrastructure that is available and the level of government support of that infrastructure. Additionally, governments at many different levels regulate transportation, even in so-called deregulated industries like

Table 13.1 Transportation Comparisons

Method	Advantages/Disadvantages
Air	Fast delivery, many providers, frequent availability, dependable, high cost.
Overland trucking	Moderately fast, many providers, frequent availability, ability to handle variety of goods, dependable, increasingly high cost.
Rail	Frequent availability, ability to handle many goods, dependable, some geographic restrictions, moderately low cost.
Ships and boats	Very low cost, ability to handle a variety of goods, geographic restrictions.
Pipelines	Low cost, suitable for liquid goods, dependable, geographic restrictions.

trucking and airlines. The way to evaluate government regulations is to look at them in an overall sense and then drill down to the specifics of the mode of transportation you are considering. Certainly, this is a matter to discuss with your suppliers.

Early in this chapter, we explored the topic of logistics. Supply chain logistics bear further investigation. The logistics aspect of supply chain management has revealed itself as being very consequential. In the aftermath of the April, 2011 Japanese earthquake, Toyota's largest North American plant in Georgetown, Kentucky and others were shut down due to a shortage of parts from Japan. While only 15% of the parts for these cars come from Japan, they are crucial to production.

The North American shutdowns affected 25,000 American workers. This story illustrates not only how tied together global supply chains are, it also demonstrates that a cataclysmic event happening half a globe away can stop production at local plants. Production managers should examine the vulnerabilities of supply chains that are far away. The impetus for faraway sourcing originated from a desire to reduce sourcing costs but it has increased system vulnerabilities as well.

What are major inventory considerations?

Transportation moves goods. Goods that are not in motion are in inventory. Inventory is what is in the system that has not been delivered to the final customer. Inventory may be a solid, a liquid or a gas. Inventory exists on both sides of the supply chain. It may exist in warehouses before it gets to your production facility or it may be in another warehouse, having left your facility on its way to the customer.

There are managerial tradeoffs as far as inventory is concerned. Because there are costs in keeping inventory, expressed in financial parlance as inventory carrying costs, you want to keep these costs down by minimizing inventory levels. However, your customers may want your products very quickly. If you have kept your inventory level and inventory carrying costs low, it is going to take you awhile to get your product stream flowing again. Your customers might not tolerate the delay. That is the tradeoff. Calculation of the inventory carrying costs in comparison to the value of customer order fulfillment needs to be done on a continuous basis. Balancing these needs is a major issue in inventory management.

Another major issue in inventory management is the matter of creating useful information about the inventory system itself. There is a clear need for data on how the inventory system is performing. The set of metrics that should be used includes turnover ratios at each stopping point, carrying costs at each inventory location, effectiveness of damage reduction processes, losses and other factors. Evaluation of these measures allows the detection of problem areas. These metrics allow you to assess the overall performance of the inventory system.

The information systems used in inventory control must serve the whole operation, not just parts of it. You don't want separate databases in each warehouse for example. Yet that has a tendency to happen if each location is separately managed. For performance data to be collected and effectively analyzed, system consistency and communication is essential.

Your customer information systems might also have room for improvement if you are not now collecting and interpreting detailed buyer-behavior data. Customer satisfaction surveys may show high levels of satisfaction with your methods of delivering product, but this alone does not provide an accurate indication of customer behavior. Your customer may rate you very highly simply because there is no other available provider. If one comes along, they may abandon you in a heartbeat for lower cost.

Predicting customer loyalty has more to do with understanding what the customer values and how to meet those demands. Inventory systems can help you anticipate buyer behavior. Measure the result of inventory control processes, the speed of delivery, the reliability of delivery, the minimization of damage and the like. That is meaningful measurement. Discovering potential behaviors, not just measuring satisfaction rates, is what should be aimed for. A behavioral question you could ask takes the following form. Does the speed of delivery we provide mean you would recommend us to others? Compare the answer to the actual speed you are delivering to get a more accurate prediction.

How can I understand my own supply chain management system?

Because of the complexity of most channels from suppliers to customers, a very useful tool is a diagram of how the whole process looks. A diagram is worth a thousand words in this case. The Supply Chain Management Mapping Tool, Tool 13.3, takes only a few steps to create and it is truly a map of a critical process.

It starts with you or your firm in the center of the diagram as the producer. From that you depict your supply system to the left and the distribution system to the right. You may end up with a simple and direct line from your supplier to you and an equally simple and direct line from you to your customers. Chances are it is more complex than this, and that's the main point of doing a diagram.

The next step is to show the number of basic or raw material suppliers. Then ask yourself if the path is direct from the supplier to you or if there are other value-added points in between. Do the raw materials get put together in subassemblies? If so, who does this? Are there agents who don't deal with suppliers but are part of the buying system? They need to be added in too. The same kind of approach is taken at the distribution end as well. The distribution points are shown along the way. The diagram ends when the product is in the hands of the retailers.

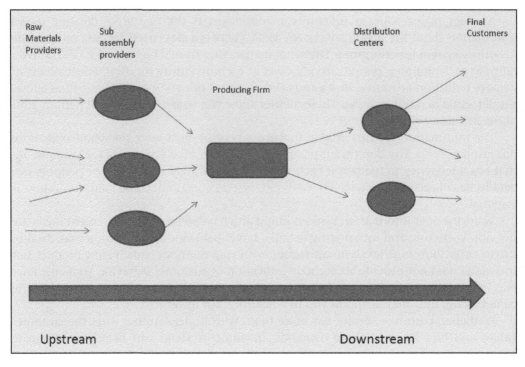

Tool 13.3   The Supply Chain Management Mapping Tool

Draw conclusions about the level of complexity of the diagram you have created. Identify where you can streamline or simplify. Once the diagram is done, you can apply cost accounting principles to determine where and how much value is being added to your products at every step of the process.

If you do cost accounting of the process, you should expect to see the greatest value added to be in your own operations. If it is found on either the supply side or the distribution side, there is a power imbalance that could be a problem for you, especially if both the suppliers and distributors are adding more value than you are.

After you have completed the diagram, you should take a look at two different dimensions. One is how long the chain is and the second is how wide it is. On the horizontal dimension, you want to ensure that the length of the chain from raw materials to final user is not excessively long. Length implies time delays and coordination issues.

On the vertical dimension, you want to make sure that there are not too many unneeded paths to the end user. Intensive distribution gets to as many end users as possible but there may be too much of a good thing. Are the channels too numerous? It is inefficient and contradicts the whole purpose of supply chain management if your customers are getting bombarded by many undifferentiated distributors. Still another thing to look for in your diagram is the number of intermediaries on both sides of the chain. Do you need them all? Are they all adding value? You can use the diagram to highlight areas where you might want to look closer at value-added points in the process.

What levels of our organization should be involved in planning supply chain management?

The management of the supply chain is inherently complex and requires involvement at all different levels of your organization. At the top level, where strategy is implemented, directional goals for supply chain management are the domain. Organizational direction is the concern. Ask yourself if your company really does have a supply chain strategy. At the top level, the answer should be more than, "we follow industry practices." That is not taking the bull by the horns. It is drifting without thinking. As strategic management experts advise, start by looking at current and future customer needs. Then establish what you need to do with your supply chain to fulfill these needs.

At the tactical level, inhabited by mid-management and supervisors, there are other issues. Here, you want to emphasize coordinating operations. If the marketing department head is getting people to make more sales but the production people are oriented to driving down production costs, the production people might not even want to have sales increase if it means more cost to them.

At the functional unit level, the point where the line workers handle the product, the rubber really meets the road and specific issues about problems are detected. Enabling problem resolution at the factory floor level is important. Even if this cannot be done, the reporting of problems is a necessity.

Is there a way in which supply chain management can be coordinated throughout our business operations?

It can be helpful to recognize that supply chain management is something of a freight train through your company. It can be fast. It can deliver supplies from afar and send them to customers even farther away. It is not just physical goods but transactions too that are on the train (mail, bills, and the like). All this indicates that a high level of coordination is needed.

A way of achieving the needed coordination is through Enterprise Resource Planning (ERP). ERP integrates management information throughout the entire system and all the relevant work units and departments. It ties together the finance area with manufacturing, marketing, and sales. Each of these functions shares data and reports. Additionally, parts of the ERP mechanism are available to channel members and customers. The idea is to have a way of automating the entire process using a single software application. Usually accomplished with a shared database, the ERP system must be understood as a software-based method of planning and coordinating supply chain management.

There are, of course, many different providers of ERP software. That leads to the matter of how you might arrange to evaluate possible providers. If you want to see what ERP could do for your supply chain management, you will want to go through a vendor review process. Some vendors are listed at the end of this chapter. You should first establish your requirements. What are the interoperability requirements between and among the business units? Does the system need to operate in real time or not? What are the absolute essentials of the system? What about connectivity to existing systems? What about connectivity between companies? These are just a few of the many questions you may want to address.

Vendors will be happy to demonstrate their program to you but you want to make sure you are guiding the presentation so that all your questions are answered. You'll work closely with vendors at this stage by gathering requested data. The more you can specify in your request for proposal, the clearer you will be to your vendors.

As a final note, effective supplier and distribution management are intrinsic to the success of any major enterprise. Taken together, they constitute supply chain management. Decisions about supply chain management use tools found in many chapters of this book. In closing, supply chain management has now assumed a greater role in most businesses and it is well worth your involvement in this practice.

Additional Resources

The Institute for Supply Management is an organization that serves the profession of supply managers. They publish a journal, the *Journal of Supply Chain Management*, and hold professional conferences. The organization also offers a certification, the Certified Professional in Supply Management.

Another professional organization is the Council of Supply Chain Management Professionals. It strives to provide leadership in occupations that involve logistics and the management of supply chains.

There are many providers of software for supply chain management. For inventory management, QuickBooks Inventory Management is one such software package. Supply chain management software is also provided by big companies such as Oracle, SAP and Microsoft.

Consultants abound in this field. CAPS Research is one firm and Softeon is another. Major universities offer degrees in supply chain management and there are certification programs offered as well.

References

Blanchard, D. (2007). *Supply Chain Management Best Practices*. New York, NY: John Wiley & Sons.
Dickson, P. (1983). Distributor Portfolio Analysis and the Channel Dependence Matrix: New Techniques for Understanding and Managing the Channel. *Journal of Marketing*, 47. 35–44.
Friedman, T. (2005). *The World is Flat*. New York: Farrar, Straus & Giroux.
Porter, M. (1980). *Competitive Strategies*. New York, NY: Fire Press.

14 *Project and Process Management*

JERRY WELLMAN

Successful projects and stable processes are essential elements of overall organizational success. Leaders must ensure that their organizations select worthy projects, provide resources to enable those projects to succeed and monitor the performance of those projects. They must also ensure that their organizations understand their processes, maintain process stability and continually improve process performance. Yet, too often projects cost more than planned and take much longer to complete. Sometimes they completely fail to accomplish their goals wasting precious time and resources.

Processes are also vulnerable to erratic performance. Too often they unpredictably yield poor quality outputs that increase costs and cause customer service issues. This chapter offers managers a pair of templates for understanding and monitoring project and process activities. When implemented, these templates will improve the likelihood of success.

How are projects and processes different?

Organizations perform work that generally involves either projects or processes. A project team may design a new product or reconfigure the production line. A project team may select, deploy and test a new software system. Processes, on the other hand, are a continual presence in the organization. Products are manufactured by recurring processes. The order fulfillment process accepts customer orders and ensures they are delivered from the end of the production line to the customer. The equipment calibration process ensures quality control. Projects and processes are an essential part of any organization.

Projects and processes share several important characteristics. First, as stated above, both activities involve performing work. Second, people are actively engaged in both activities. Third, both project and process work activity must be planned, executed and controlled in order to accomplish the desired outcomes. Fourth, both projects and processes must be accomplished with limited resources including people, time, money, facilities or equipment. Fifth, processes and projects may occur at any level of the organization from individual employee to department or corporation.

These similarities lead to some commonality in management and oversight. The classical functions of management (planning, organizing, staffing, controlling and directing) certainly apply to projects and processes. However, there are critical differences between projects and processes. These differences influence how work is planned, how it is accomplished, how it is monitored and how it is managed.

Projects and processes are fundamentally different in several ways. A project is a one-time activity. A project has a defined beginning and end. For example, a project team may be tasked to install and test a new stamping machine in a foundry. The project begins with a decision to buy the new machine and ends when the new machine in use on the production line.

A process, on the other hand, is a recurring activity. For example, the process for assembling fifty inch flat screen television sets may yield a hundred sets a day. The process cycle itself has a beginning and an end. The cycle starts with the gathering of the parts and ends with an assembled set ready to be shipped. Unlike a project, the process is repeated over and over again. A project team strives to accomplish a one-time task while a process team strives to accomplish a task many times with an identical result. This difference means that managers should monitor and assess projects differently than they do processes.

Another difference between projects and processes is the nature of learning. Process activity improves as the organization iteratively learns how to accomplish the same activity over and over again (the experience curve). The process team seeks to understand how to make the process more consistent, faster and less expensive. On the other hand, projects attempt to accomplish unique work activity. This activity does not generally get repeated. Project learning is focused on discovery of new relevant knowledge for one-time use.

Consider a project team working to design a new product. The team uses customer survey data to understand what potential customers value and how they rank product attributes. Prototype designs are built and tested to discover fundamental design problems. Qualification units are built and tested to discover material or structure problems. First-run production units are built to discover design flaws that may make production costs too high. Much of what is learned in the development phase is only relevant to the one-time project activity.

On the other hand, consider a process team working to paint automobiles on an assembly line. The team uses statistical process data to confirm that the paint is being applied precisely as intended. They also continually search for process improvements that will make the painting more consistent, faster, less expensive or higher quality. Their learning is applied to a process that is performed thousands perhaps even millions of times. What process teams seek to learn is different from project teams. Further, the organization may benefit again and again from what process teams learn while it may benefit only once from what project teams learn.

Staffing requirements and activity are also different between processes and projects. Project teams assemble for the duration of the project and then disband while process teams remain in place for long periods of time. Thus team building, role definition and day-to-day tasks differ greatly. The project team member roles must be defined uniquely for each new project and must adapt as the project team makes new discoveries and adjusts to them. A process team may redefine roles only when a major process change occurs.

Project performance is measured differently than process performance. Typical project performance metrics include assessments of cost versus plan, schedule versus plan and actual work accomplished versus plan. Project metrics may also include progress milestone completions such as product design verification, design document release, qualification testing and first article build. Typical process metrics include process stability, yield, quality, cost and cycle-time. Managers must ensure that appropriate metrics are in place, monitored and responded to.

Projects may include process activities within them. For example, a project may establish a process for identifying, validating and sharing changes to their initial plan. New learning may lead to potential changes to the work plan. Those potential changes must be understood and approved before they can be implemented. Individuals cannot make changes without coordination with others who may be impacted by them. Approved changes must then be communicated to the whole team. Project teams usually adopt a configuration change control process to deal with the many changes that will occur.

Process activities may overlap with project activity. For example, the process team in an auto assembly plant may have learned that dipping assemblies in an acid bath before they are painted helps the paint adhere and significantly reduces the number of chassis that must be repainted. The process team may put together a project team to design, build, install and test a new acid bath system.

The differences between projects and processes are significant, so significant that they mandate different management and control approaches. This chapter offers managers two guides, one for assessing project performance and another for assessing process performance.

How can a project be planned and monitored?

Successful project performance is built on a foundation of nine fundamental activities. The project manager is responsible for ensuring these nine activities are accomplished on a particular project. Organizational leaders are responsible for ensuring that the organization facilitates rather than impedes these activities.

Tool 14.1, Guide to Project Management, summarizes the most important features of the nine activities. It also provides a list of questions managers may ask about individual project performance and about the overall performance of projects across the organization. The answers to these questions should help managers understand where improvement is needed.

What is vision management and why is it important?

A shared vision is perhaps the foundation of foundations for a successful project. Disparate visions will without a doubt condemn a project to failure. Disparate visions cause misunderstandings and disagreements about priorities, which in turn lead to confusion and conflict about resource allocation. Disparate visions also ensure that at least some, if not all, of the stakeholders who care about the project will be dissatisfied with its outcome. On the other hand, a shared vision that is clearly documented, communicated and maintained gives the project team a good start toward success because at least then everyone knows what is to be accomplished. Stakeholders are also more likely to make resource and priority decisions that will enable project success rather than make decisions that conflict with one another and impede success.

Creating project vision involves many parties including the project team members, the executive and functional leaders of the organization, certain subcontractors and

VISION MANAGEMENT	
Key Features:	**Critical Questions for Project Reviews:**
• Customer, internal senior management and project team have a shared vision of what the project will accomplish. • The shared vision is clearly documented in an approved mission and goals charter statement. • The document includes statements of what is NOT included within the project scope, as well as what is included. • Deliverable work product and results are mutually agreed and described.	• Has the project charter statement been completed and approved by all stakeholders? Do all stakeholders understand and embrace the project charter statement? • Do all stakeholders understand what is to be delivered when it is to be delivered and what requirements must be met? • What is the project team's strategy for validating, adjusting, communicating and maintaining consensus around the project vision?
PROJECT PLAN MANAGEMENT	
Key Features:	**Critical Questions for Project Reviews:**
• Project vision is translated into a project management plan that breaks the work into specific tasks, resources and responsibilities. • Project management plan describes how all the major elements of the project will be approached.	• Has the project plan been developed? • Have functional leaders approved the plan? • Are there any planned deviations from standing policy or normal procedure? Have the deviations been approved by the appropriate parties? • What events will trigger a review of the plan?
SCOPE MANAGEMENT	
Key Features:	**Critical Questions for Project Reviews:**
• Development of a Work Breakdown Structure (WBS) provides a systematic method for scope planning. • The WBS decomposes work for planning, scheduling and estimating. • Statement of Work is based on WBS. • Product (deliverable)-oriented WBS format provides focus. • WBS facilitates earned value measurement techniques. • WBS forms the basis for cost accumulation and reporting architectures.	• Is the WBS product (deliverable)-oriented? • Is the WBS decomposed to the level where planning, scheduling and estimating can easily be accomplished? • Does single-point accountability (Cost Account Managers) exist on the lowest WBS levels? • Does the WBS structure align with the cost account accumulation and reporting structures? • Has a Statement of Work (SOW) been developed for the program work scope? • Does SOW provide sufficient detail to clearly define the deliverable item(s)?

Tool 14.1   Guide to Project Management

COST/RESOURCE MANAGEMENT	
Key Features:	Critical Questions for Project Reviews:
• WBS is used as foundation for development of resource needs. • Provides accurate estimate of labor, materials, hardware, etc. • Defines activity duration. • Information rolls up to define project budget and schedule. • Historical data, models or three-point estimating to be used as basis for cost and schedule	• How were resource requirements for the program developed? (Historical data, three-point estimate, other) • Are resources aligned with the WBS activities? • Are the resource needs available/ attainable? • What other projects are competing for these resources? • Are required facilities, capital equipment, tooling, material, etc. available to support the activities? • Is management reserve sufficient? • Have risk mitigation actions been funded/resourced?
SCHEDULE MANAGEMENT	
Key Features:	Critical Questions for Project Reviews:
• Schedule has been built based on WBS. • Schedule integrates horizontally and vertically. • Schedule controlled through Change Management. • Schedule includes milestones, NPI or IPDS Phase Gates, critical path and contract deliverables. (See page 25). • Schedule risk analysis is considered. • Schedule includes critical path analysis.	• Does the master schedule show evidence of integration? • Is schedule structure consistent with WBS? • Is a critical path identified? Is there any slack in the critical path? How much? • Has a schedule risk analysis been performed? • What is the probability that the program will be completed by the target date and budget? • What critical outside decisions/ deliverables have significant impact on schedule? • How are those activities going to • be monitored? • Is the schedule under change control?

Tool 14.1   (continued)

SUBCONTRACT MANAGEMENT	
Key Features:	Critical Questions for Project Reviews:
• A Subcontract Management Plan documents objective, strategy, responsibilities, schedules, resources and risks. • Defines activities required to manage subcontracts. • Facilitates early supplier involvement. • Required for work at sister business units within the company.	• Does a subcontract management plan exist? • Who is responsible for the execution of the plan? • Does the responsible person directly report to the project leadership team? • How will the team assure the plan is executed? • Are the subcontractor milestones integrated into the master schedule? • Does the plan enable early supplier involvement? • Have processes and metrics been established to monitor the performance of the subcontractor?
PERFORMANCE MANAGEMENT	
Key Features:	Critical Questions for Project Reviews:
• Based on WBS, integrated schedule and budget. • Provides objective technique for potential problem identification, progress, status and projections. • Provides an objective trigger for corrective action planning. • Employs objective measurement techniques. • Based on specific milestones.	• Are adequate milestones defined to provide accuracy within the earned value measurements? • What is the project schedule and budget status? • If the project is behind schedule or over budget, what get-well strategies have been implemented? • How will an under-budget condition be corrected to satisfy cash flow goals? • How much is the project going to cost at completion? • When will it be completed?
RISK and OPPORTUNITY (R/O) MANAGEMENT	
Key Features:	Critical Questions for Project Reviews:
• R/O is directly tied to cost, schedule and technical performance. • Includes process to identify, analyze and respond to events affecting • project outcome. • R/O Management integrates directly with the Project Management Plan. • R/O Management engages the entire team.	• Has an R/O Management Plan been developed? • Has a project level R/O baseline been developed? • Have R/O activities been accounted for in the schedule and budget? • Is the R/O management plan fully integrated into the project management plan? • Has the project team been trained in R/O management? • Do action plans exist for the top R/Os? Are the action plans being executed? What is their status?

Change Management	
Key Features:	Critical Questions for Project Reviews:
• Develop a structured approach to identifying, adjudicating and implementing changes to vision, goals and deliverables. • Keep stakeholders aligned. • Keep internal project team aligned. • Assure work activity is consistent with changing but mutually agreed vision, goals and deliverables.	• Does the team have a plan for identifying potential and actual changes? • How does the team intend to evaluate potential and actual changes? • How does the team intend to keep stakeholders aligned with change? • How will changes be implemented and communicated within the project team?

Tool 14.1   (continued)

perhaps customers for whom the product may be intended. Indeed, it may not be easy to initially align all these parties around a shared vision. For example, there may be disagreement about what product features will be most important to potential customers. Later, as the project progresses organizational executives may believe it is important to keep the project within budget, even if that means sacrificing some product capability while customers may believe it is more important to finish the project on time with all the promised capability.

The most important stakeholder is the customer (who may be internal or external). This stakeholder will in the end determine if the project has met its objectives. For example, a firm may win a contract to build a warehouse for another firm. That firm, or perhaps select individuals in that firm, is the external customer. On the other hand, a firm may decide to build a warehouse to support expansion into another geographic area. The customers in that situation are internal. Whether external or internal, the customer must have a clear vision of what the project is trying to accomplish.

Multiple customers introduce additional complexity. For example, let's assume a firm started a project to design a new software system for tracking university alumni and their financial contributions. The marketing team presold the software to three different universities. Although their needs are similar, each university has asked for specific capabilities to make the software compatible with their existing systems. These differences were not clearly understood by the marketing team and were not communicated to the project team. As a result, each customer and the project team itself have a different vision of project success.

Senior management is another vital stakeholder. Internal management may share an external customer's vision but they also have their own addendum to the vision. If the project is for an external customer then internal management certainly expects the project to be a financial success, something external customers may not particularly care about. Internal management may also have a vision that the project results will be applicable to other customers or may meet internal needs in addition to satisfying external customer expectations.

Senior management is not a monolith. Individuals on the leadership team may have different visions of project success. These visions may not be stated openly and that may be in conflict with the vision of other members of the leadership team. Marketing managers may envision a very capable product that sells for a low cost. Engineering managers may envision product features that are technically superior to the current model. The Chief Financial Officer may envision a project that is completed on time and within budget. As a result, this stakeholder group is often evaluating project success against disparate, even opposing, visions of success. The different visions may cause leadership to give the project team contradictory or confusing messages. The unstated differences may also encourage conflict and delay regarding resource allocation and prioritization that may affect project success or failure. In short, a fuzzy or conflicting project vision among senior management increases the likelihood of project failure.

The project team also has a vision of project success. They may view success as a project that ends quickly so they can return to their normal work routine. They may believe the project cost goals are entirely unrealistic and so have tacitly decided that they will attempt to meet the technical goals without regard for cost. Or the project team members may have several individual visions of project success, conflicting versions that increase the likelihood of project failure.

Let's assume for a minute that the customer, senior management and the project team all have a shared vision of project success. That shared vision must be clearly documented in an approved project mission and goals charter statement. First, the act of documenting, reviewing and approving the statement is a way to verify that all stakeholders share the agreed upon common vision. Second, people come and go. As time passes, some individuals who were not party to the original understandings may replace the original stakeholders. The project mission and goals statement helps encourage consistency over time. Third, the power and influence of individuals changes over time. Individuals who failed to get their way in the past may later have more influence and be in a position to reinterpret the project vision. Again, the documented vision provides stability and a basis for dealing with change. Fourth, visions sometimes must change: customer needs shift, technical learning occurs or competitive forces emerge. The mission and goals statement provides a baseline from which to understand the extent and impact of a changed vision. It enables all stakeholders to move to a new consensus.

The project mission and goals charter statement documents what is NOT included within the project scope, as well as what is included. For example, the statement may indicate that the new warehouse construction project includes the structure and basic utilities but excludes any security or access control systems. These exclusions help further define the project limits and deliverables.

How can a project plan be developed and managed?

The shared project vision must be translated into a specific plan of action that can bring the vision to reality. The project plan translates the vision into a budget, staffing plan, list of physical resources, schedule, technical requirements, testing and verification plan, risks and opportunities, subcontractor management plan, etc.

The plan serves many purposes. The act of developing the plan helps the project team to think more deeply about the challenges before them and in so doing develop more feasible approaches to overcoming those challenges. The plan also breaks the project into discrete task elements, assigns individual responsibilities, identifies the necessary task inputs and outputs, etc. This activity also discloses any deviations from organizational policy or procedure that must be discussed and approved. The plan lets the organization know what the team needs and when they need it. These needs can then be communicated to the functional areas for planning purposes.

Plans change. As discussed earlier, visions change and in turn the project plan should be revised to reflect the new vision. Plans also change for other reasons. Project teams may discover that the original plan is no longer feasible. Reasons may include:

- A critical supplier has gone out of business.
- The design was flawed and must be modified.
- A decline in sales has forced a project budget cut.
- An engineer has discovered it is possible to reuse some existing designs, saving significant money and time.

Any significant change in vision or plan should trigger a thorough review, and perhaps a revision, of the project plan. Some organizations ask project teams to schedule a project plan review after every major project milestone:

- After the initial design review;
- After the prototype functional testing;
- After environmental testing;
- Before production begins.

Strong project planning includes an approach to reviewing and revising the plan as the project moves forward.

Social and political forces often foil disciplined planning at the beginning of a project. External customers may have taken longer than planned to get a contract signed. Once it is signed, they often press the project team to make up for the delays. Internal customers and senior management may have delayed authorizing the project but once it is authorized they too press the project team to make up for lost time. Project team members are often anxious to get started on the new work and are frustrated when they must spend time working out the planning details. However, studies have shown time and again that poorly planned projects are much more prone to failure. Senior management must ensure that projects are well planned before they commence.

How can I manage the scope of a project?

Scope management is a critical element of the overall project plan. This activity helps the team understand more accurately just what work activity is to be done, how long each task will take, what specific resources will be required and who is responsible for each discrete element of work. A Work Breakdown Structure (WBS), such as the one shown in Figure 14.1 below, is a technique for depicting the discrete work activities.

A WBS that is focused on deliverables helps the project team focus. The examples in Figure 14.1 depict a project phase oriented WBS based on the major time-sequenced activities and a product- oriented WBS based on the basic elements of the product to be developed. WBS structures based on product elements are typically preferred because

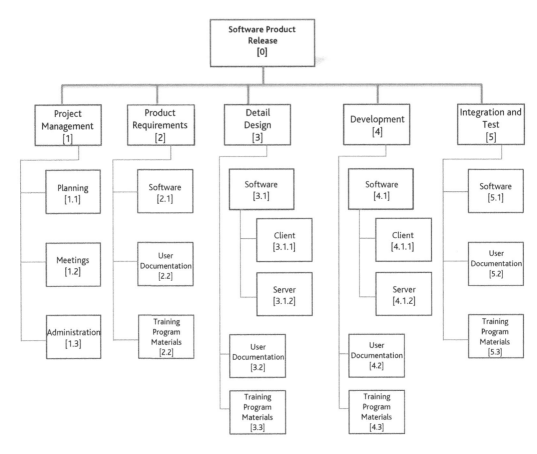

Figure 14.1 Work Breakdown Structure

they allow for the collection of work performance data that can be used for future project cost estimates. Each of the WBS boxes represents a specific work activity. An individual, typically the Cost Account Manager (CAM), is responsible for accomplishing that specific work activity within the mutually agreed budget and schedule.

Each team should also develop a Statement of Work (SOW) consistent with the WBS elements. This SOW is a narrative description of the work that the project team plans to do in accomplishing the project vision, mission and goals. It also itemizes specific deliverables. Each work package has its own task description, budget, schedule, list of deliverables, etc. and is managed by a Cost Account Manager (CAM).

These two tools, the WBS and the SOW, enable a project team to manage their work scope. The WBS establishes an organizational structure for breaking down the work activity into pieces for which individuals can be held responsible. The SOW clearly describes each of the work pieces and the deliverable work product for each piece.

How do I decide what resources are needed?

The WBS is the foundation from which the team determines resource need and timing. Each block within the WBS is a discrete package of work activity for which the CAM has planned the cost, schedule, staffing and other resources. This estimate, once it is integrated with the rest of the work packages, becomes part of the overall cost and resource plan for the project.

Cost and resource estimates must allow for uncertainty. No estimation methodology can foresee all possible, or even all reasonable, outcomes. Projects are, by their very nature, an iterative learning experience. Teams learn that the chosen materials will not work for their specific application, or that the component does not perform exactly as specified, or that the subcontractor cannot deliver what they promised, or that a major storm destroyed the suppliers' factory. Cost and resource estimates should include flexibility to shift funds and a reserve to handle surprises. Project teams should identify reasonable risks they may encounter and include in their estimate the potential cost. Teams should also set aside a percentage (5% to 20%) of their budget so they have the flexibility to fund modest changes to the plan.

Cost and resource problems typically threaten project success in one of two ways. Either project teams fail to anticipate and ask for the budget and resources they need or the host organization fails to provide the promised funding and resources. The former happens when project teams fail to build effective plans or when they encounter unexpected surprises. The latter happens when leaders refute the project requests, when overall organizational resources are insufficient to meet all the organizational commitments or when surprises on one project force an unexpected conflict for limited resources.

How do I manage the project schedule?

Successful projects nearly always begin with a coherent integrated baseline schedule. That schedule is the yardstick against which progress is measured. It is maintained and adapted as the project progresses.

The WBS is the foundation for the schedule. The top-level schedule is broken down into progressively more discrete elements that align with the WBS elements. As a result each cost account has its own corresponding schedule element and that element is interconnected with the schedules for the interrelated cost accounts. Thus, the schedule elements are integrated both horizontally (cost account to cost account) and vertically (cost accounts to WBS elements to higher level WBS elements).

The schedules must include all significant project milestones including project deliverables, product design reviews, major test and verification events, key process approval points, production releases and so on. Many organizations use formal product development processes such as NPI and IPDS to foster disciplined design activities. NPI and IPDS phase gates and process milestones should also be included in the schedules.

Schedules do not need to be fully detailed for the full duration of the project. Brief projects expected to reach completion within a few months may be detail planned but larger and more complex projects do not benefit from attempts to detail plan them in the out years. It is instead more practical to use a rolling wave approach in which a rigorous detailed plan is developed for the upcoming several months. The rest of the project may be planned at a less detailed level. Every few months the detail plan is extended another six to nine months and the top-level out-period plan is reviewed and modified to reflect new learning. This rolling wave avoids the problem of continually planning out-year activity in great detail only to revise it over and over again as requirements change; designs are modified, funding changes, etc. Instead, the teams can plan into the future only as far as their knowledge allows.

Schedules should be constraint driven and include a critical path analysis. Constraint schedules consider the interdependencies among various tasks. Generic, low cost and standard parts may be ordered before new product designs are completed but unique and high cost parts cannot be ordered until the design is final. The procurement of some parts may be constrained by the completion and approval of the design activity.

Project teams need to do enough schedule analysis to find these constraints and build plans to cope with them. The critical path is determined by the shortest constraints driven path from the start to the finish of the project. It may be that some work can be accomplished in parallel but other activities are constrained by the necessary completion of preceding tasks. This shortest possible chain of interdependent events is the critical path.

Schedules, like budgets, need to include allowances for things going wrong. Suppliers sometimes deliver late. Designs sometimes need to be revised. Schedules may also benefit from good occurrences such as early completion of a task, work being less complex than assumed, etc. Schedules should include consideration of such uncertainty. It is good practice to include problem resolution time at selected points in schedules. For example, a team may believe there is a 30% probability that a new chassis assembly will fail environmental testing because the chassis is to be made with materials not previously tested for this particular use. The cost account budget should include a dollar reserve to deal with an environmental test failure. The schedule should also include a reserve to allow time to deal with the failure.

Recall that the baseline schedule is the yardstick against which progress and work performance is measured. Therefore, schedules must reflect the work that is actually being accomplished, not the work that was planned before things changed. Highly effective projects establish a discipline for identifying potential and actual cost, technical and schedule changes. They also have a discipline for reviewing, approving and communicating those changes to the team as well as integrating them into the cost, technical and schedule baseline plans.

How do I manage subcontractors?

Subcontracted work requires at least as much and quite often far more management attention than does work done within the organization. Typically, several subcontractors compete for a single job on the basis of price, quality and risk management. This competitive effort requires a great deal of management oversight. Once the bids are in, a specific statement of work and requirements package must be developed and negotiated with the winning subcontractor.

Subcontractors often have different work processes, documentation requirements, monitoring systems, etc. These differences may make it difficult to understand quickly and accurately just how the subcontracted work is progressing and just what to do if things go awry. Negotiating changes with subcontractors is often complex and risky. And communications are often more difficult because of differing organizational cultures, vernaculars, practices and processes and because of physical separation from the core project team.

Managers should recognize that work between different business units within a firm may be as challenging to manage as external subcontracting work. Many of the challenges mentioned above often also apply to two business units within the same organization. Sadly, many organizations tend to neglect planning, negotiating, communicating and monitoring activities when dealing with a sister business unit. Such neglect increases the likelihood of problems.

Project teams should develop a detailed Subcontract Management Plan (SMP) addressing how they will work with subcontractors and with intra-organizational business units. In general, it should include at least the following:

- A description of the overall objective of the subcontracted work activity;
- The procurement strategy (how the subcontractor will be selected);
- The execution strategy (reuse of existing designs, etc.);
- The overall schedule and the specific dates of important delivery items;
- The resources to be provided to the subcontractor;
- How the subcontractor will be monitored;
- The approach to risk management.

When and how do I measure project performance?

Is progress being made? Is the team on schedule? Are the expenditures accomplishing the planned results? Are the technical requirements being met? How has the current plan changed from the baseline plan and does the current plan reflect the work actually being done? In short, how is the project doing? The answers to such questions are made possible when teams establish performance monitoring disciplines at the beginning of the project. Team members must know how the project leaders will measure their performance and project leaders must know how senior leaders will measure their overall project performance.

Three tools are typically used to monitor project performance:

- A WBS/SOW and its associated cost accounts, was described earlier in this chapter.
- An integrated schedule, was also previously discussed.
- An aggregated cost account, budgets along with any reserves, the overall project budget baseline against which project expenditures are monitored.

These tools are tied together by an EVMS (Earned Value Management System). An EVMS is an accounting system that allows teams to determine their actual cost of work performed versus the planned cost of work performed and the actual time taken to perform that work versus the planned time to perform that work. Many organizations avoid using an EVMS because they mistakenly believe it is an overly formal tool that is very expensive to deploy and operate. However, the fundamental intent of EVMS can be accomplished using simple tools if the project team has two elements available to them. First, they must have, and use, a cost and schedule plan for the project and the work actually being done. Second, they must be able to frequently track their actual costs incurred and their actual schedule accomplishments versus that plan. Everything else is a matter of simple mathematics.

Project performance is very effectively monitored using an EVMS and the three tools/ disciplines on which it is founded. However, an EVMS system alone is insufficient for several reasons:

- EVMS monitors budget and schedule versus plan but by itself offers little insight into technical accomplishments. For example, a team may be underspending and ahead of schedule but the work being accomplished will not yield a design that meets the specifications.
- EVMS tools are historical in nature. They forecast future performance based solely on past performance. For example, a shortage of staff in the past is assumed to be a problem that persists into the future even if the team is currently fully staffed. Likewise, a team may be ahead of schedule and under budget because it has benefited from a senior experienced engineering team. The EVMS system will project those efficiencies into the future even if several members of that engineering team have recently been reassigned. In short, EVMS is a good tool for monitoring what has been accomplished versus plan but is an inadequate tool for forecasting what will be accomplished.

Savvy managers use periodic project reviews as a forum for discussing both past performance and forecasted future performance. These managers require project managers and their senior team members to report on past performance using the EVMS. They also require project managers to explain how future performance may differ from past performance and what factors are driving, or might drive, that difference.

Effective leaders ask their project teams to provide a set of performance management metrics and an associated reporting plan as part of the initial project management plan. The parties can negotiate a set of metrics tailored to the needs of each project.

How can risks be managed and opportunities maximized?

"The essence of risk management lies in maximizing the areas where we have some control over the outcome while minimizing the areas where we have absolutely no control over the outcome and the linkage between effect and cause is hidden from us", says Peter Bernstein (1996). Bernstein, in his book, *Against the Gods: The Remarkable Story of Risk*, explains that good risk and opportunity (R/O) management is as much about mindset and worldview as it is about probabilities and analyses. Successful project teams believe they can have an impact on their likelihood of success. They envision what may happen and take actions to increase or reduce the likelihood of occurrence.

The project R/O Plan, a subset of the overall Project Management Plan, documents the overall project risk condition and outlines how the team will manage and communicate the R/O status and actions throughout the project life cycle. The R/O Plan describes how the team will periodically review changes in the cost, schedule and technical baseline to assess corresponding changes in R/O predictions. The plan also describes how the project team will integrate its R/O outlook and actions into the overall project baseline and estimate at completion.

R/O management involves a three-step process:

1. Teams must identify R/Os for their project.
2. They must assess the magnitude and probability of those R/Os occurring.
3. They must take actions that will influence the magnitude and probability of the R/Os.

Without action to influence the future there is no R/O management, only forecasting and reporting.

Knowledgeable managers use the project review sessions as an opportunity to discuss project risks and opportunities with the project leaders. They strive to create an open dialogue in which the team can share their hopes and anxieties about the project. More importantly, they work to help the team identify specific actions that can influence the likelihood or impact of those future events.

How do I handle changes?

Change happens. Project management is, by its very nature, about change management. Suppliers have problems. Components don't work exactly as expected. New designs flaws must be discovered and corrected. A documentation error causes the wrong parts to be ordered. Resources become available later than planned. An engineer develops a less complex than anticipated design solution. Technological changes enable the new design to be accomplished on fewer circuit cards than planned.

Effective project teams know they must deal with change and so they develop and use a structured approach to identifying changes, assessing their impact and adapting project plans to accommodate them. They also have effective communications methods to ensure all interested and affected parties are aware of the changes (see chapter four for more tips on organizational communication).

Let's get back to process management. How is process performance planned and monitored?

Recall that processes are fundamentally different than projects. Processes accomplish the same objective over and over again while projects accomplish a new objective one time.

Successful process performance is built on a foundation of six fundamental activities that are summarized in Tool 14.2. The process managers are responsible for ensuring these six activities are continually accomplished for their process or processes. Organizational leaders are responsible for making sure the organization facilitates rather than impedes these activities. Leaders are also responsible for ensuring each process team understands and accomplishes these activities. Tool 14.2 also provides a list of questions managers may ask to determine where improvement may be needed.

CONFIGURATION MANAGEMENT	
Key Features:	Critical Questions for Process Reviews:
• Process configuration is documented and agreed. • Document includes statements of what the process does NOT do.	• Is the process configuration clearly understood and mutually agreed? • Do process suppliers and process customers understand the relevant aspects of the process? • Is the process configuration stable?
CHANGE MANAGEMENT	
Key Features:	Critical Questions for Process Reviews:
• Structured approach to managing organizational change expectations. • Process changes are planned and tested before implementation. • Process configuration changes are documented and communicated.	• Has the process undergone recent changes? • Have changes resulted in any unexpected outcomes? • Are any process changes being contemplated? • Has the future state after the change been defined? • Have the pending changes been tested? • Have the suppliers and customers been informed of the pending changes? Do they have concerns? • What contingency plans are in place should the change cause unexpected problems? • Have metrics been defined to measure the success of the change? • Is a control plan deployed to sustain the change?
INTERFACE MANAGEMENT	
Key Features:	Critical Questions for Process Reviews:
• All process inputs/outputs are understood, acceptable performance limits defined and documented. • All input providers and output benefactors agree to the definitions and performance limits. • Process owners, input providers and output benefactors have mutually agreed on input and output metrics.	• Have there been any unplanned/ unanticipated input changes? • How have changes impacted the process performance? • Have there been any unplanned/ unanticipated output changes? • How have changes impacted users/ customers? • Are input/output metrics within agreed control limits?

Tool 14.2   Guide to Process Management

PERFORMANCE MANAGEMENT	Critical Questions for Process Reviews:
Key Features: • Input, output and in-process metrics agreed. • Metric data gathered and analyzed on established frequency. • Analyses drive actions. • Metrics confirm process activity is under control.	• Have metrics been established for all key input, output and in-process parameters? • Is statistical process control (SPC) being used to monitor and control the current process? • Are metric results and trends within desired limits? • What metrics are, or are trending, out of desired limits? • What actions are being taken to understand undesirable performance?
BALANCED PERFORMANCE MANAGEMENT	Critical Questions for Process Reviews:
Key Features: • Process performance is a balance of cost, cycle-time, delivery and quality goals. • Meeting cost and cycle-time performance satisfies process owner needs. • On-time delivery of expected quality outputs satisfies customer/user needs.	• Is the process meeting overall cost goals? If not what is being done to reduce costs? • Is the process meeting cycle-time goals? If not what is being done to improve cycle-times? • Is the process meeting on-time delivery commitments? If not what is being done to improve this? • Is the process meeting output quality commitments? If not what is being done to improve this? • What are the historical and projected cost, cycle-time, quality and delivery trends?
IMPROVEMENT MANAGEMENT	Critical Questions for Process Reviews:
Key Features: • Process owners seek ways to provide cost, cycle-time, delivery and quality improvements that will result in aggregate benefit. • Seek to provide overall system benefit rather than independently optimize each process.	• What improvements are being considered? • Are lean techniques being used to find and implement process improvements? • What constituents would be impacted? Which would benefit? Which would be harmed? • What is the potential cost of making the change? • What are the risks of making the change? • Are all affected parties engaged in the decision and implementation process? • Does the change enable early supplier involvement?

Tool 14.2   Guide to Process Management (continued)

How do I more clearly define the process?

Processes are defined by their boundaries. The boundary definitions clarify what is considered within the process and what is outside the process. The boundary definitions outline what are considered process inputs and outputs. The boundary definitions influence whether the process is simple or complex and they define the areas over which the process managers have accountability, responsibility and control.

Processes are also defined by their internal sequence of components and their interrelationships. The sequences and interrelationships influence the process structure, complexity and stability.

A process configuration document, like the one shown in Figure 14.2, captures these important boundaries, internal components and interrelationships. The act of creating the document encourages organization members to identify and resolve different opinions and understandings about the process configurations. The document also provides a reference point for new employees. Finally, the document provides a baseline for recognizing and dealing with process changes over time.

The components of a process include:

- **Inputs:** Inputs are man, method, material, machine, measurements and mother nature. These are referred to as the 6M's.

  - **Manpower**
    - candidates
    - trainers
  - **Method**
    - class lecture
    - activities
  - **Material**
    - flip charts
    - markers
    - notebook

  - **Machine**
    - computer
    - electronic viewing system
  - **Measurements**
    - attendance
    - # of people caught sleeping
  - **Mother Nature**
    - temperature
    - humidity

- **Transformation:** Series of activities or tasks that change (transform) the inputs.
- **Outputs:** Goods, services or consequences.

Figure 14.2 Process Components

How can I facilitate process changes?

Processes change for several reasons. The process management team may make changes in an effort to reduce output variability or to move closer to the specified performance. The team may make changes in an effort to reduce resource needs or cycle time, making the process more efficient. The team may make adjustments to accommodate changes in process inputs. For example, a supplier may have made a material change that will now affect how the material can be used in the process.

These types of process changes are generally reactionary in nature. That is, the changes are made because something has happened to or within the process, forcing the team to respond. In these reactive situations, the team's response may not be as rigorously evaluated and tested as it otherwise would be. Process managers should be responsible for managing responses carefully and organizational leaders should hold them accountable.

Sometimes, process change occurs without the team's knowledge. Equipment drifts out of calibration. Suppliers make changes to materials without informing customers. New operators misunderstand some part of their training and perform tasks incorrectly. The process metrics and operator vigilance are the first lines of defense for detecting such changes.

How do I manage process boundaries and interfaces?

Process boundaries were discussed above. Transactions across those boundaries are the process inputs and outputs. Each transaction, whether input or output, should be clearly understood by both the provider and the receiver. Performance limits should be defined and mutually agreed on by all parties. Metrics should be in place to guaranty inputs and outputs meet performance expectations.

Sometimes process inputs and outputs go undetected or unacknowledged. For example, the process for the packaging of crystal glassware for shipment generates waste packaging materials. Those waste materials are gathered and sorted by a recycling team. Someone discovers that the waste materials from the glassware packing process can be ground up and used as filler material for packaging other dishware. Later, the crystal packaging team finds and begins using a less expensive packaging material that saves them a few cents per package. The material looks quite similar but it turns out the new material contains chemicals that leach into the stoneware dishes leaving a discoloration. The process change and resulting problem was only discovered after several hundred customers returned their stoneware.

The interface between the two processes was created inadvertently. The provider did not know the interface existed and so did not inform the receiver of a change. The receiver did not recognize the process input as one that needed to be controlled and thus the change went unrecognized. One process, glassware packaging, got "fixed" while another process, dishware packaging, got "fixed-up" if you will. Process managers should be passionate about understanding all the interfaces to and from their processes.

What kind of process performance management is needed?

The process manager should have an established routine for reviewing and communicating performance metrics. The internal process team should periodically review all the metrics to ensure they understand and control process performance. The suppliers and the contributing process managers should review metrics to ensure they are providing the agreed inputs. The process customers should review metrics to guaranty they are receiving the agreed process outputs. The senior leadership team should be briefed periodically on process performance to ensure the process is under control and that all segments are interacting efficiently.

Statistical Process Control (SPC) is the process counterpart to the EVMS system. It is an established methodology for continually monitoring the performance of all process inputs and outputs. Each input or output metric is assigned a target performance level and an acceptable performance range, its upper and lower control limits. The actual performance data is monitored to assure it is within the acceptable range and to identify trends suggesting it may be drifting toward the upper or lower limits. See Figure 14.3, SPC Chart.

SPC is a sophisticated and effective methodology for controlling processes. SPC, like EVMS, is often misunderstood and underappreciated by process managers and by organizational leaders because it is imagined to be cumbersome and expensive. However, the fundamental SPC principles can be deployed with relatively little effort. See the additional resources section of this chapter for more on SPC.

How does the balanced scorecard help monitor processes?

For any process control system to be effective, companies need to develop a visually simple and succinct report card or control chart. Process managers must use a balanced approach to the various process performance standards. They should maintain a complement of process metrics addressing at least four chosen areas. Our example in Figure 14.4, is built upon the notion that the objective of any process team is to increase quality and delivery and to decrease process time and cost.

In the example, quality and delivery are always defined in such a way that improvement is recorded as an increase in the measure (up arrow). Conversely, continuous improvement in process time and cost is shown as a decrease in the measure (down arrow). The performance criteria should always be shown together when reviewing the performance of the process. Priorities can be made explicit by simply emphasizing one criterion more than the others when evaluating actions.

The process balanced scorecard (Figure 14.4) should be reviewed regularly by the process team and monitored by senior management to guaranty everyone understands

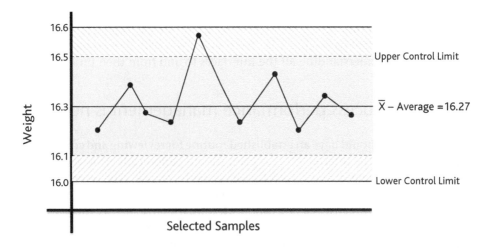

Figure 14.3 SPC Chart

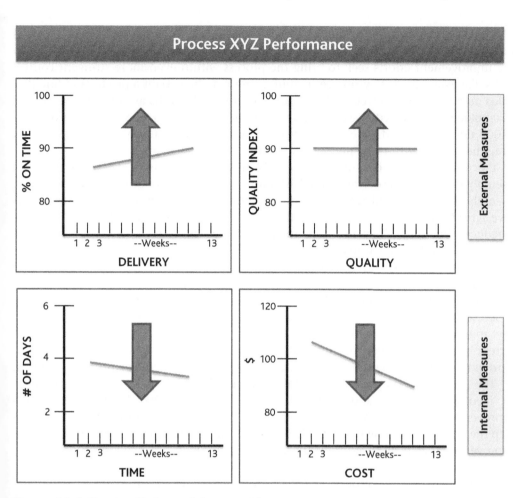

Figure 14.4 Process Balanced Scorecard

the relative importance of, and the performance in each area. The process balanced scorecard also fosters healthy discussions about the merits and risks of proposed process changes. Advocates for change must explain how they will ensure the proposed change will affect each area, not just the area targeted for improvement.

Note that process teams should not limit themselves to only one metric in each of the four dimensions of the balanced process scorecard. For example, a process for painting automobiles may have several quality metrics including yield at final inspection, color match, amount of overspray, etc.

What does "improvement" mean in project and process management?

You might initially think that efficiency/effectiveness management and process control management are very much alike. And it is correct that there is overlap. However, process managers and organizational leaders should be sensitive to the differences.

Processes may be improved in an effort to make them more stable. The SPC metrics may indicate the process regularly operates within the mutually agreed control limits. The improvement efforts seek to bring the process within even more stringent control limits. For example, a television set manufacturer may have built a production line that yields on average one defective TV set out of every 20,000 units assembled. The process stakeholders have agreed to explore ways to improve the defect rate to one out of every 30,000 units assembled. The process team may investigate improvements that would bring the process within the new control limits.

Processes may also be improved to make them less expensive. The current TV set assembly line includes several manual assembly steps that could be modified for robotic assembly techniques and robots are less expensive than assemblers. The stakeholders have agreed to explore process changes that would incorporate more automation in order to reduce labor costs. They also hope the automation will result in fewer process errors and yield fewer defective units.

Processes may be improved to reduce cycle-time. The current assembly line yields 400 sets in a ten-hour work period or about one set every one and a half minutes. Marketing has forecast higher sales volume for the latest TV set and says production must increase to 600 sets per ten-hour shift in order to satisfy the forecasted demand. Production may elect to build a second assembly line or they may elect to shorten the cycle-time on the current line to one set every minute. A process team has been assigned to explore ways to shorten the process cycle-time without hurting other process performance requirements.

The process managers should have an established approach and techniques for identifying, testing and deploying process improvements. "Lean" is a process improvement methodology often associated with SPC. SPC techniques help process teams keep the process operating stably while lean techniques help process teams make process improvements such as shortening the process cycle time and reducing the resources required.

Leaders must oversee process managers and their process teams to ensure individual process improvements are well managed. Leaders must also guaranty that disciplines and procedures are in place to identify inter-process improvement opportunities and hazards.

Additional Resources

Such books as *The AMA Handbook of Project Management* by Dinsmore and Cabanis-Brewin, *Microsoft Project 2007 Bible* by Marmel and *Q&As for the PMBOK Guide* by Anbari will help answer questions regarding project management. In addition, the Project Management Institute is a membership organization that promotes the project management field and offers certifications. Their website is a great starting point.

Two excellent sources for understanding SPC in detail are the *Statistical Quality Control Handbook* originally published by Western Electric in 1958 and the *Quality Control Handbook* by J. M. Juran (1979). More recent Six Sigma literature such as *The Six Sigma Handbook* by Pyzdek (2009) also addresses SPC.

One source of lean knowledge is *Lean Six Sigma* by George (2002). Another classic source is *The Goal* by Goldratt (1986), a novel that explains fundamental principles of manufacturing process improvement.

References

Ambari, Frank T. (2010). *Q & As for the PMBOK Guide* (3rd edition). Newtown Square, Pennsylvania: Project Management Institute.

Bernstein, P. (1996). *Against the Gods: The Remarkable Story of Risk*. New York, NY: John Wiley & Sons, Inc.

Dinsmore, P. C. and Cabanis-Brewin, J. (2006). *The AMA Handbook of Project Management*. New York, NY: American Management Association.

George, Michael L. (2002). *Lean Six Sigma*. New York, NY: McGraw-Hill.

Goldratt, E. (1986). *The Goal, a Process of Ongoing Improvement*. Croton-on-Hudson, NY: North River Press, Inc.

Juran, J. M. (1979). *Quality Control Handbook*. New York, NY: McGraw-Hill Book Company.

Marmel, Elaine (2007). *Microsoft Project 2007 Bible*. New York, NY: John Wiley & Sons, Inc.

Pyzdek, Thomas and Keller, Paul. A. (2009). *The Six Sigma Handbook* (3rd edition). New York, NY: McGraw-Hill.

Western Electric Company Inc. (1958). *Statistical Quality Control Handbook*. Western Electric Co., Inc. Barton, PA: The Mack Printing Company.

15 *Accounting*

LAURA BARTHEL

Henry Ford, an engineer and inventor, who started developing race cars in the 1800s, then went on to begin the first mass production of gasoline engine vehicles. Though Ford did not invent the Model T in its entirety, he has been credited with starting the company now well known as Ford Motor Company.

Ford had an idea for a gas engine vehicle with interchangeable parts that could be mass produced and sold to the middle class with the help of other inventors such as C. Harold Wills. Idea in hand, Ford needed additional funding to purchase land and to develop a manufacturing facility.

Ford had to make decisions about how to obtain the funding for his new business as well as how to finance the growth of the business. Ford's financial decisions were recorded and reported using accounting. Accounting records and reports the financial decisions of a business. This chapter will help you answer the following questions about your business:

1. How does accounting record financial decisions?
2. How does accounting report financial decisions?
3. What do my everyday decisions mean for the financial health of my company?

The goal is not to turn you into an accountant, but to form a link between management decisions and their impact on the bottom line.

What standards govern accounting?

Ford had an idea and was able to develop that idea into a business that ultimately grew into one of the nation's largest auto makers. The accounting process recorded the transactions that started the business as well as the transactions required to operate the business.

The accounting process is both standardized and required. Businesses across the world recognize standard recording and reporting based on governing standards. In the United States, the standards are called Generally Accepted Accounting Principles (GAAP). The most widely used standard worldwide is called the International Financial Reporting Standards (IFRS). Both sets of standards were developed to protect users of financial information from bias or misrepresentation of financial transactions and information.

Both sets of standards govern how transactions should be recorded and reported. GAAP is sanctioned by the Securities Exchange Commission and governed by the Financial Accounting Standards Board (FASB). IFRS is governed by the International Accounting Standards Board (IASB). The two governing bodies are in the process of converging GAAP and IFRS. According to exposure drafts and related comments from the convergence efforts of IASB and FASB the conceptual framework or basis for the standards are not theoretically different, but technical and specific recording and reporting differences exist. Updates and the status of the convergence process can be found on websites of large accounting firms such as PricewaterhouseCoopers and the website of the Financial Accounting Standards Board.

The standards outline the accounting process by answering the following questions:

1. How does accounting record the origination of a business?
2. How are operations of a business recorded?

When I start my business what do I need to know about accounting?

Like Henry Ford, many individuals have an idea for starting a business. Entrepreneurs require resources to move from idea stage to an actual business. Generating resources is the first financial decision faced by individuals wanting to start a business. Accounting records begin during the initial steps of starting a business, so as a manager you will know where your business starts and how it continues.

The entrepreneur can provide the resources needed to start a business. Like Ford and other inventors, by the time the business is ready to start production the entrepreneur has depleted their personal resources and must seek outside funding. Initial resources to start a company can be generated from outside sources by either borrowing or exchanging ownership in the company for funding.

The entrepreneur can borrow funds from banks, venture capital companies, or other individuals in exchange for a promise of repayment and the payment of periodic interest at a specific rate. These banks, companies, or individuals who lend the entrepreneur funding are called creditors. Creditors lend in the hope of earning money by charging interest on the amount loaned. Therefore creditors' earnings are not based on the success of the company, but guaranteed interest.

Companies or individuals who provide resources to start a business in hopes of reaping the benefits of future earnings from the business and do not expect repayment are called owners. In exchange for the resources they provide, they receive claim of ownership in the company and a portion of the income earned by the company. Owners can also be called stockholders or investors. Entrepreneurs who invest in their businesses are considered owners, because they are investing their resources in exchange for ownership and they share in the earnings of the company. Owners and creditors are called stakeholders, because they provide resources and accept the risk of possible business failure and loss of the amount invested or expectation of return.

Accounting is the process by which the financial decision to receive resources from the entrepreneur, creditors or additional owners, is recorded. When the business founder is given the resources to begin a business, the transactions are considered economic transactions.

The resources provided to the business by creditors and owners are called assets. Assets are economic resources that provide a future benefit to the business. Examples of assets include cash, buildings, items for resale (inventory), supplies and land, among others.

The accounting process records what assets were received and how the assets were received. For example, an entrepreneur started a business with $60,000 in resources. $10,000 was received from creditors and $50,000 from owners. The $10,000 from creditors is borrowed and the business has an obligation to repay it. Until the amount is repaid, the creditor has a claim on the assets equal to the amount to be repaid. The financial decision to borrow is recorded as the creditor's claim to the assets, called a liability. The $50,000 represents the amount invested by the owners and equals the owners' claim to the assets after the creditors have been repaid. The owners' claim to the assets is called owners' equity.

The accounting standards identify this sequence of financial information as the accounting equation.

Assets	=	Liabilities	+	Owners Equity

Our example would look like:

Assets	=	Liabilities	+	Owners Equity
$60,000		$10,000		$50,000

The accounting equation provides valuable insight into the financial decisions of the company. For example, the scenario recorded above indicates that the company made a financial decision to borrow $10,000. The accounting equation establishes the method of recording not only initial business formation transactions but all financial transactions relating to operations of a business.

How do I keep track of business operations?

Once an idea becomes a business, the owners begin making financial decisions and take steps to begin operations using the assets that were provided to form the business. To begin operations, owners will answer questions such as business location, facility ownership or rental, how many supplies or how much inventory is needed. These questions all require a financial decision.

For example, the decision to rent or own requires generation of funds from existing cash assets, bank loans or additional investors. In our sample scenario the business started with $60,000 in cash. If the desired building cost $100,000 then the owners could choose from one of the following options. The impact on the accounting equation for each transaction is represented below each of the transactions. Each transaction is independent.

Transaction 1: Purchase the building using the $60,000 the business has from its original loan, plus owners' equity, plus the owner invests an additional $40,000.

Assets	=	Liabilities	+	Owners' Equity
$60,000		$10,000		$50,000
($60,000)				+$40,000
+$100,000				
$100,000	=			$100,000

Transaction 2: Purchase the building by acquiring a loan for the cost of the building.

Assets	=	Liabilities	+	Owners' Equity
$60,000		$10,000		$50,000
+$100,000		$100,000		
$160,000	=		$160,000	

Transaction 3: Attract an additional owner to contribute the building as their provided resource in exchange for ownership in the business.

Assets	=	Liabilities	+	Owners' Equity
$60,000		$10,000		$50,000
+$100,000				$100,000
$160,000	=		$160,000	

As shown in transaction 1, the asset was acquired by using an asset and increasing the owners' claim. Transaction 2 increased liabilities and assets by acquiring a loan, and transaction 3 increased owners' equity and assets. The key is that the accounting equation should always balance. The transactions indicated three ways to obtain assets, first with using other assets, second by increasing liabilities or third by issuing additional ownership interests.

The primary purpose of operating a for-profit business is to generate income. Income is the excess of revenue over cost. Accounting standards define revenue as resources earned through the provision of a service or product. Costs are termed expenses and should be recorded as a reduction to revenue in the period incurred if not related to the sales of a product. Alternately, they can be recorded in the period the product is sold if the costs relate to the production of the product. This principle is called the matching principle from the FASB conceptual framework and seeks to match expenses with revenue. There's more on the matching principle in the income statement section of this chapter.

Revenues and expenses are not assets, liabilities or owners' equity. However, since the owners have a claim to the assets plus a claim to the income of the company then revenues directly increase the owners' claim and expenses directly decrease the owners' claim. Therefore, owners' equity is increased by the amount of income earned by the company. This is the fourth type of transaction that increases assets. For example, if a company had income the first year of operations of $50,000 then the accounting equation would be impacted as follows:

Transaction 4: Income increases assets and owners' equity.

Assets	=	Liabilities	+	Owners' Equity
$100,000		$10,000		$90,000
+$50,000				+$50,000
$150,000	=		$150,000	

In transaction 4, when the company sells inventory, the business receives another resource. The resource received by the business for the sale of a product is either cash or a promise for payment called a receivable. For companies selling products, the reduction of the inventory cost when it is sold becomes an expense and decreases the owners' claim. The revenue from the sale increases the owners' claim. A service business uses assets such as cash for wages of employees providing the service or for supplies needed to provide the service, as opposed to inventory. For example, a business selling shoes has purchased $1,000 of shoes with a promise to pay at a later date. This creates an account payable. The following month the business sells the shoes for $1,500 in exchange for payment at a later date (receivable). The transaction would be recorded as followed:

Transaction Description	=	Assets	+	Liabilities	Owners' Equity
Formation		$100,000		$10,000	$90,000
Purchase of Inventory on Account		+$1,000		+$1,000	
Sale of Inventory on Account		+$1,500			+1,500
Expense of Inventory		($1,000)			-($1,000)
		$101,500	=		$101,500

The accounting equation is used to record the financial decisions of the business and to provide information regarding financial decisions. The reporting process summarizes the financial decisions into comparable and formal reports, provided to decision makers inside and outside the business.

How do financial decisions get updated?

Whether they are owners, creditors or managers of a company, stakeholders want and need to know how the company is doing financially. According to the FASB and IASB, when businesses report financial information to users outside the business, they must follow GAAP or IFRS. These standards were developed for the purpose of providing relevant and reliable information useful for external decision makers such as investors and creditors.

GAAP identifies four standard reports of financial information called financial statements that provide information regarding the financial decisions of the business:

1. Balance Sheet (also referred to as the Statement of Position).
2. Statement of Income (also referred to as the Statement of Operations or Profit & Loss).
3. Statement of Changes in Owner's Equity.
4. Statement of Cash Flow.

In addition to the financial statements, the standards require notes to the financial statements, providing users with additional information not clearly presented on the financial statement. The notes to the financial statements provide information about amounts and methods of valuation reported, and relevant plans of the business that are useful to the user of the financial information. Much can be learned by reading the notes to financial statements.

What does the balance sheet tell us?

The balance sheet presents the balance of assets, liabilities, and owners' equity on a specific date. It is a formal representation of the accounting equation, and reports the financial position of the company. The balance sheet also reports how the company received its assets by either, receiving credit through a liability, by giving rights to the company in exchange for ownership equity or by earning income and increasing the equity claim of the owners.

The balance sheet can be presented as a simple listing of the assets, liabilities and owners' equity as shown in Figure 15.1. The simple listing of the accounts included in the accounting equation has been discouraged from use by the FASB. The IASB and IFRS require classification of assets and liabilities into categories of current and non-current discussed in greater detail below. The classification into current and non-current provides users of financial statements more information about the financial decisions that have already occurred or are likely to occur. A balance sheet with classifications of current and non-current is called a Classified Balance Sheet. The sample balance sheet of Ford Motor Company is not classified, but has been annotated to note the possible classification of current assets based on the statement information alone and not considering information about the line items in the notes to the financial statements.

Assets are ordered based on liquidity, which is how fast the asset can be converted to cash. A current asset converts to cash or is used within an operating cycle or within one year. Assets that can be used up within a year or the operating cycle include prepaid expenses in which the expense has already been paid and the company is waiting on the benefit. For example, prepaid rent for the next month is an example of a current asset because at the end of the month the prepaid expense will have been used and the benefit of that asset has expired because use of that property has already taken place. Examples of current assets include but are not limited to:

- Cash and Cash Equivalents—Cash or holdings that can be exchanged for cash within three months or less.
- Accounts Receivable—Amounts due from customers for services or products provided, less any reasonable estimation of loss due to uncollectible amounts.
- Inventory—Materials or goods to be sold to customers. The amount is based on valuation and flow of inventory cost assumptions reported in the notes to the financial statements.
- Supplies—Office or manufacturing supplies to assist with operations or production but not included in the product for sale.
- Prepaid Expenses—Expenses already paid for by the company in order to receive future benefit (service) without the required use of cash in the period the benefit is received.

Non-Current assets, also called plant assets, are resources that cannot be converted to cash or that do not expire within either one year or the operating cycle. Non-current assets include:

- Property Plant and Equipment—Long-lived assets that are used in the normal operations of the business are reported at historical cost less accumulated depreciation.

FORD MOTOR COMPANY AND SUBSIDIARIES CONSOLIDATED BALANCE SHEET As of December 31, 2009 and 2008 (in millions)		December 31, 2009	December 31, 2008
ASSETS			
Cash and cash equivalents		$ 21,441 $	22,049
Marketable securities (Note 6)		21,387	17,411
Finance receivables, net (Note 7)		76,996	93,484
Other receivables, net	Current Assets	7,587	5,674
Net investment in operating leases (Note 8)		17,270	25,250
Inventories (Note 10)		5,450	6,988
Equity in net assets of affiliated companies (Note 11)		1,550	1,599
Net property (Note 14)		24,778	24,143
Deferred income taxes		3,440	3,108
Goodwill and other net intangible assets (Note 16)		209	246
Assets of held-for-sale operations (Note 24)		7,923	8,612
Other assets		6,819	9,734
Total assets		$ 194,850 $	218,298
LIABILITIES			
Payables		$ 14,594 $	13,145
Accrued liabilities and deferred revenue (Note 17)	Current Liabilities*	46,599	59,526
Debt (Note 19)		132,441	152,577
Deferred income taxes		2,375	2,035
Liabilities of held-for-sale operations (Note 24)		5,356	5,542
Total liabilities		201,365	232,825
EQUITY			
Capital stock (Note 25)			
Common Stock, par value $0.01 per share (3,266 million shares issued of 6 billion authorized)		33	23
Class B Stock, par value $0.01 per share (71 million shares issued of 530 million authorized)		1	1
Capital in excess of par value of stock		16,786	10,875
Accumulated other comprehensive income/(loss)		(10,864)	(10,124)
Treasury stock		(177)	(181)
Retained earnings/(Accumulated deficit)		(13,599)	(16,316)
Total equity/(deficit) attributable to Ford Motor Company		(7,820)	(15,722)
Equity/(Deficit) attributable to noncontrolling interests		1,305	1,195
Total equity/(deficit)		(6,515)	(14,527)
Total liabilities and equity		$ 194,850 $	218,298

Adapted from Ford Motor Company SEC 10K for YE 2009
*Current liabilities may not be all inclusive because the balance sheet is not classified. More information was provided in the notes to the financial statement in the 10K filing.

Figure 15.1 Ford Motor Company Balance Sheet

 – Accumulated Depreciation—Amount of the historical cost that has been systematically used through normal operations of the business. For example, Company A purchased equipment for $1 million in 2010. If the equipment was expected to be used in the production process for ten years, then the cost of the equipment would not be expensed entirely in the first year but divided over the ten years of use ($1,000,000 / 10 = $100,000 depreciation expense each year of use). The depreciation is accumulated and decreases the historical cost value reported on the balance sheet. Note: Land is never depreciated.

- Intangibles—Resources that lack physical substance. Examples include patents, goodwill, copyrights, trademarks and customer lists. The valuation of intangibles is amortized (like depreciation) if the intangible has an identifiable life of expected benefit. Intangibles with indefinite-life are reviewed for decreases in value, called impairment.
- Other Assets—Assets that do not fit into other identified asset categories. Other assets may include long-term receivables or long-term prepaid expenses.

Liabilities are also classified as current and non-current on a classified balance sheet to provide users with a better understanding of when liabilities are to be repaid. The category of current liabilities identifies the liabilities that will require the use of current assets or require creation of an additional liability within the operating cycle or one year. Examples of current liabilities include:

- accounts payable
- salary payable
- interest payable
- current portion of long-term debt
- unearned revenue

By far the most important non-current liability is long-term debt. This would include any payments for loans longer than one year, mortgages payable, etc. Less common non-current liabilities include:

- capital lease obligations
- bonds payable
- pension liability
- deferred tax liability

A great place to look for an explanation of these items is in the notes to financial statements.

Owners' equity is not classified as either current or non-current because it neither comes due for repayment nor converts to cash. The accounts and reporting of owners' equity vary based on organization of company ownership and regulations of state corporation laws. For corporations, owners' equity typically includes three sections:

- Capital Stock—Stated value of shares issued.
- Additional Paid-In Capital—Amount paid in addition to the stated value.
- Retained Earnings —Earnings of the company yet to be distributed to the owners or used to finance business expansion. Retained earnings increase the owners' claims.

The claims of owners are expected to earn a return from the income of the company and be distributed to owners as dividends.

Companies with organizational structures other than corporations (such as partnerships—see chapter eighteen for a discussion of business legal structures) typically do not include an additional paid-in capital account, and capital stock, but merely list the capital contributed by the owners and retained earnings.

The key for companies preparing balance sheets and determining the measurement of reported value is to first check for any specific reporting requirements related to value measurement (specifically Statement of Financial Accounting Standard [SFAS] No. 157). Second, report relevant information about financial decisions that have potential impact on a user's decision about investing in or lending to the company by disclosing the method of measurement. Third, report reliable information that is verifiable and neutral (SFAS No. 2).

Do I have to show my assets at their historical cost or can I use fair market value?

GAAP standards include a set of conceptual rules that serve as the basis for all GAAP. Included in those rules is a standard on the Recognition and Measurement in the Financial Statements SFAC No. 5. This sets the general rule that financial information is measured at historical cost and not market value. Exceptions to the general rule include trading and available-for-sale securities that are measured at current market value instead of cost. Assets or liabilities that are permitted or required to be measured at fair value (current value) according to SFAS No. 157 require a footnote disclosure (yet another reason to pay attention to those notes). Assets or liabilities that may be measured at fair value include financial instruments or impaired assets. Fair value measurement is an area of continued convergence efforts between the IASB and FASB.

Balance sheet classification of debt and equity securities requires special reporting depending on the intent of the company and design of the security. If the security is bought for the purpose of short-term purchase and sale to generate earnings, then it is classified as a current asset called a trading security. If the security is purchased without intent to sell but the company is willing to sell it then the security is considered debt and equity and is generally classified as non-current. If the security allows for on demand cash available for operations then the security would be reported as a current asset. The third classification of securities is Held-to-Maturity. Held-to-Maturity securities are debt only securities and are classified as non-current assets and are typically bonds. Additional information on reporting rules for debt and equity securities can be found in reference to SFAS No. 115 on the FASB website.

What does the statement of income report?

The income statement presents the results of operations for a period of time. The income statement reports revenue. Revenue is received or to be received from customers for the products being sold or services being provided. The basic formula of the income statement is shown below:

Net Income	=	Revenue	−	Expenses

Deducted from the revenue are expenses such as:

- Cost of materials to make or sell the products sold during the period.

- Amount of building and equipment cost used to produce the products sold.
- Interest accrued for the loan during the period.
- Cost of supplies used during the period.
- Cost of overhead such as utilities and maintenance used to make the products sold and run the office.
- Cost of paying employees during the period.
- Amount of income taxes related to the current period income.

Net income is the amount earned by the company after all expenses are covered. Net income is the amount attributable to owners' equity, which increases the owners' claim and is recorded in retained earnings. The income statement is often prepared in one easy step of revenue minus expenses. The following income statement of Ford Motor Company reports the net income in a single-step format (see Figure 15.2).

Like the classification of current and non-current assets and liabilities for the balance sheet, the income statement can also be divided into sections to provide additional useful information. Divided income statements are called multiple-step income statements (See Figure 15.3). A multiple step income statement reports the following sections or line items:

- **Net Sales**—The amount earned less any returns or allowance for doubtful collection of receivables. For service companies this amount would be service revenue.
- **Gross Profit**—The amount earned after covering the essential costs of making a product. Gross Profit is the amount earned before any operating, selling, general and administrative costs associated with running the business.
- **Operating Income**—Income earned from central operations of the company. To calculate operating income operating expenses such as selling (e.g. advertising, sales commissions), general and administrative (e.g. utilities, office supplies, etc.) expenses are deducted from gross profit. Any income or expense incurred for investments or operations outside the normal operations of the business are excluded from this figure.
- **Other Income, Gains and (Loss)**—Income and losses from non-operating transactions. Transactions that are from discontinued operations, investments, interest, etc. are added after the income from operations has been calculated.
- **Income from Discontinued Operations**—Income or loss during a period from a business segment that is dissolved or sold, or the sale of a held-for-sale security should be reported separately as income or loss from discontinued operations.
- **Extraordinary Income**—Income and/or losses from transactions and events that are both unusual and infrequent are considered extraordinary and are required to be reported separately.
- **Other (Loss)**—Losses or expenses from discontinued operations, investments, interest, etc. are deducted after the income from operations has been calculated.
- **Net Income**—Income earned during the year or period. Excess of earnings over expenses.
- **Net Loss**—Deficit of earnings below the incurred expenses.
- **Basic Earnings Per Share (EPS)**—This is the amount of income each outstanding share of common stock has earned. Companies usually break out EPS by income

FORD MOTOR COMPANY AND SUBSIDIARIES
CONSOLIDATED STATEMENT OF OPERATIONS
For the Years Ended December 31, 2009, 2008 and 2007
(in millions, except per share amounts)

	2009	2008	2007
Sales and revenues			
Automotive sales	$105,893 $	129 , 165 $	154,379
Financial Services revenues	12,415	15,949	16,193
Total sales and revenues	118,308	145,114	170,572
Costs and expenses			
Automotive cost of sales	100,016	127,102	142,587
Selling, administrative and other expenses	13,258	21,430	21,169
Goodwill impairment	—	—	2,400
Interest expense	6,828	9,805	11,038
Financial Services provision for credit and insurance losses	1,030	1,874	668
Total costs and expenses	121,132	160,211	177,862
Automotive interest income and other non-operating income/(expense), net (Note 20)	5,288	(726)	1,161
Financial Services other income/(loss), net (Note 20)	552	1,149	1,869
Equity in net income/(loss) of affiliated companies	10	176	403
Income/(Loss) before income taxes	3,026	(14,498)	(3,857)
Provision for/(Benefit from) income taxes (Note 23)	69	63	(1,333)
Income/(Loss) from continuing operations	2,957	(14,561)	(2,524)
Income/(Loss) from discontinued operations (Note 24)	5	9	41
Net income/(loss)	2,962	(14,552)	(2,483)
Less: Income/(Loss) attributable to noncontrolling interests	245	214	312
Net income/(loss) attributable to Ford Motor Company	$ 2,717	$ (14,766) $	(2,795)
NET INCOME/(LOSS) ATTRIBUTABLE TO FORD MOTOR COMPANY			
Income/(Loss) from continuing operations	$ 2,712	$ (14,775) $	(2,836)
Income/(Loss) from discontinued operations (Note 24)	5	9	41
Net income/(loss)	$ 2,717	$ (14,766) $	(2,795)
Average number of shares of Common and Class B Stock outstanding	2,992	2,273	1,979
AMOUNTS PER SHARE ATTRIBUTABLE TO FORD MOTOR COMPANY COMMON AND CLASS B STOCK (Note 25)			
Basic income/(loss)			
Income/(Loss) from continuing operations	$ 0.91	$ (6 . 50) $	(1 . 43)
Income/(Loss) from discontinued operations	—	—	0.02
Net income/(loss)	$ 0.91	$ (6 . 50) $	(1 . 41)
Diluted income/(loss)			
Income/(Loss) from continuing operations	$ 0.86	$ (6 . 50) $	(1 . 43)
Income/(Loss) from discontinued operations	—	—	0.02
Net income/(loss)	$ 0.86	$ (6 . 50) $	(1 . 41)

Figure 15.2 Ford Motor Company Income Statement

Adapted from Ford Motor Company SEC 10K for YE 2009

component (operating income, discontinued income and net income) if a multiple-step income statement is reported. EPS can be calculated as shown:

$$\text{Earnings per Share} = \frac{\text{Net Income} - \text{Preferred dividends}}{\text{Average number of common shares outstanding}}$$

- **Diluted Earnings Per Share**—This is calculated to determine the earnings as if the convertible preferred stock was converted to common shares thus increasing the amount of common shares outstanding and spreading the income over more shares. The diluted EPS is always less than the basic EPS.

Example Company Statement of Income For Year Ended December 31, 2010 (in millions except EPS calculations)		
Net Sales		$ 2,000
Less: Cost of Goods Sold		575
Gross Profit		1,425
Operating expenses		
Selling	200	
General and Administrative	225	
Less: Total Operating Expenses		425
Operating Income		1,000
Other Income (Expenses)		200
Net Income (Loss)		1,200
Earnings Per Share of Common Stock (200 million shares)		$6.00
Diluted Earnings Per Share (100 million convertible preferred)		$4.00

Figure 15.3 Example of Multiple-Step Statement of Income

When does income appear on the income statement?

According to the Statements of Financial Accounting Concepts No. 5 Recognition and Measurement in the Financial Statements, revenue can only be reported when it is earned and either realized or realizable. A company has earned the revenue when a contract is substantially completed and/or the goods have been transferred or services have been rendered. "Realized" indicates that the money or consideration has been received.

"Realizable" is when a contract to pay has been made and the company has a legal claim to the cash or consideration. This concept is designed to protect the users of financial statements from interpreting income that maybe overstated due to uncompleted sales or promised sales. For example, if an oil company forms an agreement on 31 December to ship 100 million gallons of oil to Shell gasoline stations across a region during January of the next year, the company cannot report the income in the year of the agreement. The income cannot be reported until the gasoline has been delivered.

Similarly, when do expenses appear on the income statement?

Also according to SFAC No. 5, the matching principle protects users of financial statements from understatements of expenses and thus overstatement of income. The matching principle states that expenses necessary and related to reported income are required to be reported in the same period the revenue is earned. For example, if a company is in the business of selling custom t-shirts and the company purchases the shirts in one year and sells the shirts the following year the cost of the shirts should be expensed in the second year instead of the first year.

Expenses that expire or are not directly related to the production of products or providing of services should be expensed when incurred. Expenses for the general operations or administration of the business should be expensed in the period they are incurred or expire. For example, utilities, rent and office supplies are expensed in the period of use. Depreciation is the systematic expensing of the purchase of large plant assets and equipment that are necessary for the production of products or provision of services.

These two concepts result in unrealized revenue (earned and realizable), unearned revenue (realized but unearned), unrecognized expenses (incurred but not expensed) or unused expenses (paid but not used). A third accounting concept from SFAC No. 5 defines this waiting process of recording revenues and expenses as accrual accounting. The opposite of accrual accounting is the cash method. Under the cash method revenue and expenses would be recorded when cash is received.

What can I learn from the Statement of Changes in Owner's Equity Report?

Owners' claims to business assets are impacted by changes in ownership, earnings, and losses of the company and distributions of earnings. The Statement of Changes in Owner's Equity reports how the company moved from the beginning balance of Owner's Equity to the ending balance of Owner's Equity reported on the balance sheet. Earnings are presented on the Statement of Changes in Owner's Equity as comprehensive income, which is the income obtained from sources other than owners.

The Statement of Changes reports valuable information to owners and potential owners about their investment. The statement also reports to potential investors the type of business (partnership, corporation, etc.), classes of ownership and investments in subsidiaries. The Statement of Changes in Owner's Equity begins by reporting the beginning balance reported on the previous period balance sheet and the changes that occurred during the reporting period for each component of stockholder's equity including:

- **Capital Stock**—The owners' investment and claim is represented in a capital account. Depending on the type of business organization the name of this account may change. For example, for corporations with multiple classes of stock, the statement would include a capital account for each class of stock.

- **Additional-Paid-In-Capital**—Some capital stock is assigned a stated or par value. The Additional-Paid-In-Capital account represents the amount contributed for each share over the par value.
- **Retained Earnings**—Owners of the company are unlike creditors because they have a claim to the company's earnings. The company records income and expenses in the Retained Earnings account at the end of the period. Retained Earnings acts as a reservoir for earnings. Earnings are maintained in this account until distributed to owners.
  - Net Income—Retained Earnings is increased by the amount of income reported on the Statement of Income or decreased if a loss is reported.
  - Dividends—Owners can receive portions of the earnings via the distribution of dividends. Dividends are typically distributed as cash or additional stock. The amount of the dividend is deducted from the Retained Earnings account.
    - Stock Dividends—If stock dividends are issued then the amount of the dividend decreases retained earnings and increases the capital stock account and additional-paid-in-capital (if applicable). This event merely changes the location of the claim from being undistributed in Retained Earnings to being distributed to the owner. Thus this event does not change total stockholder's equity.
    - Cash Dividends—A cash dividend, on the other hand, is returning a portion of the owner's claim thus decreasing the claim of the owner by decreasing retained earnings, so the stockholder's equity account is decreased by a cash dividend.
  - Prior Period Adjustment—Retained earnings can also be changed by a prior period error. If an error was found in a previous reporting year that impacted the amount of income or loss reported then the retained earnings account is adjusted to reflect the correct amount. If the income from a previous year was overstated then retained earnings would be decreased or if the income was understated then retained earnings would be increased.
- **Other Comprehensive Income**—In addition to the income reported and recorded in retained earnings, some income is not reported on the statement of income because it does not meet the requirements of income of being either realized or realizable or alternately, earned. For example, if a company owns or has a majority interest in a foreign company, the impact of translation of the foreign currency for reporting purposes could result in an unrealized gain or loss. This amount is reflected in other comprehensive income but is not part of the net income reported on the income statement.

There are four possible sources of non-owner events or transactions that make up other comprehensive income and are directly related to stockholder's equity adjustments. These sources include: (1) foreign currency items, (2) pension changes in funded status, (3) effective portion of cash flow hedges and (4) unrealized gains and losses. According to GAAP, other comprehensive income can be reported either on the statement of income, on the statement of comprehensive income or as part of the Statement of Changes in Owner's Equity. These adjustments reflect an unrealized impact on the owner's claim to the assets.

- **Treasury Stock**—Businesses may wish to purchase their own shares of stock currently outstanding. The stock is usually purchased to offer in stock plans of employees and executives, as an investment option or as a strategic decision. The purchased shares are called treasury stock. Treasury stock does not change the amount of stock outstanding because ownership of the shares just switches from a stockholder to the company. Treasury stock does not hold the same ownership rights as preferred or common stock. A portion of retained earnings equal to the cost of the treasury stock is restricted from being used in the calculation of dividends. This rule may vary depending on state of incorporation. Owner's equity is decreased by the cost of the purchase of treasury stock.

- **Equity Attributable to Non-Controlling Interest**—Consolidated statements include the earnings, assets, liabilities and equity of investments in which the company owns more than 50%. If a company does not own the entire investment then the company is required to show the portion of earnings, assets, liabilities and equity that is attributable to the portion of the investment that is not owned by the reporting parent company. This amount is reported as part of equity on the balance sheet and the Statement of Changes in Owner's Equity. For more information on reporting for Non-Controlling Interest search the FASB and IASB websites for the most current standard.

The Statement of Changes in Owner's Equity can be vertically or horizontally formatted (ee Figure 15.4). In Figure 15.4, a section of Ford Motor Company's Statement of Changes in Equity is presented in a horizontal format. The horizontal format presents

(in millions)	Capital Stock	Capital in Excess of Par Value of Stock	Retained Earnings/(Accumulated Deficit)	Accumulated Other Comprehensive Income/(Loss)	Other	Total	Equity/(Deficit) Attributable to Non-controlling Interests	Total Equity/(Deficit)
YEAR ENDED DECEMBER 31, 2009								
Balance at beginning of year	$ 24	$10,875	$ (16,316)	$ (10,124)	$(181)	$(15,722)	$ 1,195	$ (14,527)
Comprehensive income/(loss)								
Net income/(loss)	—	—	2,717	—	—	2,717	245	2,962
Foreign currency translation (net of $ 0 of tax)	—	—	—	2,236	—	2,236	38	2,274
Net gain/(loss) on derivative instruments (net of $64 of tax)	—	—	—	(127)	—	(127)	—	(127)
Employee benefit related (net of $131 of tax benefit)	—	—	—	(2,851)	—	(2,851)	(1)	(2,852)
Net holding gain/(loss) (net of $ 0 of tax)	—	—	—	2	—	2	(3)	(1)
Comprehensive income/(loss)					[	1,977	279	2,256
Common Stock issued for debt conversion, employee benefit plans, and other	10	5,911	—	—	—	5,921	—	5,921
ESOP loan , treasury stock, and other	—	—	—	—	4	4	3	7
Cash dividends	—	—	—	—	—	—	(172)	(172)
Balance at end of year	$ 34	$16,786	$ (13,599)	$ (10,864)	$(177)	$ (7,820)	$ 1,305	$ (6,515)

Figure 15.4 Ford Motor Company Statement of Changes in Owner's Equity

Adapted from 2009 portion of Ford Motor Company SEC 10K Statement of Equity for YE 2009

the components of owner's equity horizontally across the top of the statement and then lists vertically the change of each component to the beginning balance. For example, at the beginning of 2009 Ford Motor Company's Retained Earnings had a negative balance of $16,316 million. During the year Ford Motor Company earned Net Income of $2,717 million, thus changing the balance of Retained Earnings to negative $13,599 million that is reported as the year end balance.

What does the Cash Flow Statement tell me?

The Cash Flow Statement provides investors and owners a recap of the sources and uses of cash and cash equivalents during the reporting period. GAAP requires a reconciliation of net income to the cash from operations. There are two methods of presentation that are allowed by GAAP, the direct method and the indirect method. The difference between the methods is the presentation of the reconciliation of net income and cash from operations. The indirect method presents cash from operations via reconciliation of cash sources and uses from net income to arrive at the cash from operations. The direct method lists sources and uses only to calculate cash from operations. The reconciliation of net income to cash from operations is presented on a separate statement.

Both methods of presenting the cash flow statement divide the sources and uses of cash flow into the following three sections:

1. **Cash Flow From Operations**—Typically, this is the first section of the cash flow statement and is the primary difference between the direct and indirect methods. Both methods will result in the same balance of cash flow from operations as shown in Figure 15.5.

Direct Method		Indirect Method	
Cash Received from Customers	$ 2,000	Net Income	$ 900
Cash Paid to Suppliers	1,000	Depreciation and Amortization	100
Interest Received	150	Increase in Accounts Receivable	(150)
Income Taxes Paid	100	Decrease in Inventory	250
		Increase in Prepaid Expenses	(50)
Cash from Operations	$1,050	Cash from Operations	$1,050

Figure 15.5. Example Direct vs. Indirect Method Cash Flow from Operations Example

2. **Cash Flows From Investing Activities**—Companies often engage in activities other than the central operations of the business that generate sources or uses of cash. For example, utilizing a bank savings account for excess cash can be a source of interest income or a service fee expense. Other examples of investing activities include purchase or sale of investment securities, acquisition or disposition of long-term assets or property or funding provided to other entities. The sources and uses of cash from investing activities are listed similar to the direct method shown in Figure 15.5.

3. **Cash Flows From Financing Activities**—Companies obtain assets by receiving resources from owners or investors. Often, transactions with owners are sources of cash such as issuing stock. Paying dividends to owners is a use of cash. Transactions with investors include the paying of interest on loans, receipt of loan principal or repayment of loan principal.

The statements of cash flow and included items are presented below from Ford Motor Company SEC 10K filing for the year ended 2009 (Figure 15.6).

The financial statements are prepared from information recorded regarding economic transactions. Accounting provides users and stakeholders with relevant unbiased information useful in decision making. In addition to the income statement itself, the most important items that help understand the operations of the business can be summarized as follows:

- The statement of retained earnings reports to the owners the change in their investment.
- The Cash Flow statement reports the changes in cash, as well as the causes of the changes based on financial decisions regarding operations, investing and financing.

Use financial statements for decision making such as "should we finance the equipment needed for our new product line with liabilities or open the company up for additional ownership opportunities?" The financial statements are also a tool for creditors and owners to evaluate the company. If a manager is seeking additional funding it is important to understand how performance and purchasing decisions impact the financial statements and how external stakeholders will evaluate the company. Additional information about these questions and the use of the financial statements as a means of organizational performance measures is covered in chapter seventeen—Organizational Performance.

Additional Resources

For additional information about accounting and the required reporting standards, helpful resources include the websites of the Financial Accounting Standards Board or large Certified Public Accounting Firms such as PricewaterhouseCoopers, Deloitte & Touche, and Ernst & Young. These websites and organizations also provide regular updates on the United States accounting regulation convergence with the international accounting standards.

References

Business Essential. (2009). London, UK: A&C Black Publishing.

Financial Accounting Standards Board. (2008). *Statement of Financial Accounting Concept* (No. 5).

Horngren, C., Harrison, W., and Oliver, M. (2009). *Financial & Managerial Accounting*. Upper Saddle River, NJ: Prentice Hall.

PricewaterhouseCoopers. (2010). IFRS and US GAAP Similarities and Differences.

Securities and Exchange Commission, (2010). *Ford Motor Company 2009 10K.*

US GAAP & IFRS Convergence Overview. (2/9/2011). Retrieved from http://www.pwc.com/us/en/ issues/ifrs-reporting/ifrs-gaap-convergence.jhtml.

FORD MOTOR COMPANY AND SUBSIDIARIES			
CONSOLIDATED STATEMENT OF CASH FLOWS			
For the Years Ended December 31, 2009, 2008 and 2007			
(in millions)			
	2009	2008	2007
Cash flows from OPERATING activities of continuing operations			
Net cash (used in)/provided by operating activities (Note 27)	$ 16,042	$ (179)	$ 17,074
Cash flows from INVESTING activities of continuing operations			
Capital expenditures (Note 28)	(4,561)	(6,696)	(6,022)
Acquisitions of retail and other finance receivables and operating leases	(26,392)	(44,562)	(55,681)
Collections of retail and other finance receivables and operating leases	39,884	42,061	45,498
Purchases of securities	(78,789)	(64,754)	(11,423)
Sales and maturities of securities	74,933	62,046	18,660
Settlements of derivatives	478	2,533	861
Proceeds from sales of retail and other finance receivables and operating leases	911	—	708
Proceeds from sale of businesses	382	6,854	1,236
Cash paid for acquisitions	—	(13)	—
Transfer of cash balances upon disposition of discontinued/held-for-sale operations	—	(928)	(83)
Other	(377)	316	(211)
Net cash (used in)/provided by investing activities	6,469	(3,143)	(6,457)
Cash flows from FINANCING activities of continuing operations			
Sales of Common Stock	2,450	756	250
Purchases of Common Stock	—	—	(31)
Changes in short-term debt	(5,935)	(5,120)	919
Proceeds from issuance of other debt	45,990	42,163	33,113
Principal payments on other debt	(61,894)	(46,299)	(39,431)
Payments on notes/transfer of cash equivalents to the UAW Voluntary Employee Benefit Association ("VEBA") Trust (Note 18)	(2,574)	—	—
Other	(996)	(604)	(88)
Net cash (used in)/provided by financing activities	(22,959)	(9,104)	(5,268)
Effect of exchange rate changes on cash	470	(808)	1,014
Cumulative correction of Financial Services prior-period error (Note 1)	(630)	—	—
Net increase/(decrease) in cash and cash equivalents from continuing operations	(608)	(13,234)	6,363
Cash flows from discontinued operations			
Cash flows from operating activities of discontinued operations	—	—	26
Cash flows from investing activities of discontinued operations	—	—	—
Cash flows from financing activities of discontinued operations	—	—	—
Net increase/(decrease) in cash and cash equivalents _from Balance Sheet_	$ (608)	$ (13,234)	$ 6,389
Cash and cash equivalents at January 1	$ 22,049	$ 35,283	$ 28,896
Cash and cash equivalents of discontinued/held-for-sale operations at January 1	—	—	(2)
Net increase/(decrease) in cash and cash equivalents	(608)	(13,234)	6,389
Less: Cash and cash equivalents of discontinued/held- for-sale operations at December 31	—	—	—
Cash and cash equivalents at December 31	$ 21,441	$ 22,049	$ 35,283

from Balance Sheet

Figure 15.6 Ford Motor Company Cash Flow Statement

Adapted from 2009 portion of Ford Motor Company SEC 10K Statement of Equity for YE 2009

16 *Finance, Budgeting and Cash Flow*

RIK BERRY and LAURA D'ANTONIO

Finance and budgeting are at the heart of any business organization. Understanding the language and the concepts of finance and budgeting helps you master what many regard as the critical function of business. Without such understanding and application, the heart of a business is unknown. In Joseph Conrad's terms, it is a heart of darkness. With understanding, the enterprise can be directed to profit making and other organizational goals in a more comprehensive way. This chapter will give you a basic understanding of finance and budgeting so that you will be ready to sit and participate at the corporate decision making table with greater understanding.

As a prelude to a detailed look at finance and budgeting, an overview of financial management is appropriate. As a starting point, the traditional goal of the business organization is to maximize shareholder value. Issues of social responsibility have changed this view somewhat. However, we'll use this premise as a starting point. The value to the shareholder is expressed by the market price of the company. Shareholders are those who have a financial stake in the organization. They own equity in the company or they hold company debt. Here, the shareholders are understood to be more narrowly defined than the broader and more contemporary group of stakeholders. Stakeholders are not just investors but other parties such as community members, customers, employees, and government leaders.

It may seem that financial management is complex and difficult to master. At its heart, it is directed toward three decisions as described by James Van Horne (1986) as being the investment decision, the financing decision, and the dividend decision. The investment decision concerns the allocation of capital with the expectation of future benefits. As Van Horne states, uncertainty about future gains exists because risk is involved. Risks need to be evaluated in terms of their potential returns. The pattern of investments taken together determines the total assets held by the company. The investment decision applies to both starting new investments, exiting existing investments, and any combinations of the two. Companies invest on a continuous basis for the most part as new investment opportunities present themselves. Companies also need to distribute invested capital into assorted baskets to mitigate risk.

The financing decision involves determining the best financing mix or capital structure for your operations. There are different ways this can be done. The goal is to select a financing strategy that leads to the maximizing of market share price for your business. The last major decision is the dividend decision. It concerns the percentage of earnings paid to stockholders in dividends and other benefits. The dividend decision deals with how much your business wants to retain and how much it wants give back to investors. This chapter will focus primarily on the first two functions.

All of these decisions have interactive effects. They are not independent. New capital investment requires financing decisions and has an effect on the level of dividends paid, as Van Horne notes. As a whole, financial management involves working on solutions for all three questions. For most financial managers their task is to make the best possible choices from among these interrelated and sometimes conflicting decisions.

What do financial managers do?

The people who help answer the questions described above are financial managers. In short, financial managers span the range of finance related activities: planning, obtaining and using funds in ways that maximize the value of the firm. They may write financial reports and they may strategize about financial goals. Knowing what financial managers do should help you see the importance and the variety of their roles. You may know this role as chief financial officer, controller, or treasurer. Generally speaking, the chief financial officer runs financial operations. The controller does accounting, auditing, and budgeting operations. They work with outside accountants to prepare financial statements including the balance sheet, income statements, and cash flow reports. See chapter fifteen for more on accounting. Controllers also prepare other reports as needed. Treasurers often play a more formal role. They direct the budget and supervise other finance functions.

At the front line of finances are the cash managers who make sure there is sufficient cash flow to run the day-to-day business. They gather funds that are owed to the company (accounts receivable for example) and pay those who provide supplies and services to the business (accounts and notes payable). In smaller companies, many of these functions are combined while in larger firms they have separate titles. Financial managers as a whole interact with others outside the organization. They are likely to work with financial institutions, such as commercial banks and other lenders, to arrange loans. They may also work with government regulators to file reports and otherwise comply with regulations. The world of financial management is much larger than the company itself.

What are the issues that financial managers must deal with?

In addition to the decisions that must be made in financial management, another framework element that helps define this function is the range of issues that must be dealt with by managers. These issues are described in the *Encyclopedia of Management* (2011). They are "the acquisition of capital for start up and growth, the management of working capital and cash flow and the construction and implementation of a capital budgeting process." While the decisions required of financial management have already been introduced, these are the functions of financial management that you have encountered or will encounter as a manager. By reviewing these, you will be able to see your business through the eyes of those who are immersed in the financial operations of your organization. Also, you will benefit from the financial framework concept that is being used in this chapter.

The first step into the arena of financial management happens at the birth of the business. Quite simply put, owners must get the funds they need to start the business. At first, the business is a newly hatched bird with a beak agape for nourishment. Expenses are immediately encountered and, until the fledging takes off on its own the owners have to do the feeding. Newly formed companies can use funds provided directly by owners, venture capitalists, banks and grants from public and private sources. The technical details of creating your first balance sheet are discussed in chapter fifteen. Financing start-ups is a special field within financial management. This endeavor demonstrates the crucial role of financial management at the very genesis of the business. It is a role that continues as long as the business operates. Financial management then, is an enduring and permanent part of business.

Founders of new businesses will often mix their sources of start-up funds. More and more, new businesses are started with the savings of the owners and personal debt including cash advances on credit cards or home equity loans. The next most common source of start-up funds is loans from family members or friends. That is supplemented by the two main devices for raising capital, the same two that are available for established companies. These are the debt and equity markets. The management of debt and equity are intrinsic to all business organizations. Financial managers live in the world of debt and equity management. All managers need to visit it from time to time.

The equity side raises funds through the sale of part of the business, most often in the form of shares. A note for entrepreneurs here is that it is important not to give up too much equity in order to raise cash. Entrepreneurs who relinquish too much initial equity early often end up in a bind later when they still need more cash to run the start-up. They go back to the investors and may have to sell off even more of their equity. They risk losing their majority ownership in the company they created. The net result can be that they become staff in their own venture. The equity investors may be entitled to dividends as described earlier. They also get a voice in the running of the company; so don't give away too much. There is more on the legal aspects of corporate ownership in chapter eighteen.

The other major way of raising funds is through debt. The company raises funds by borrowing money, which it repays based on a schedule of repayment. Financial institutions such as banks and other lending institutions loan the funds for the most part but loans can come from individuals too. With a start-up company this is often the case. Financial management issues involving debt include the amount borrowed, the duration of the loan, and the interest rate. Although lenders are not owners per se, they usually secure their loans with the company's assets. They therefore have a claim prior to the owners in the event of liquidation of the firm. Bank loans can range in duration from a thirty-day bridge loan and annually renewable lines of credit to long-term notes and mortgages. An analysis of the pros and cons of debt versus equity financing is presented in the next chapter of this book.

Still another broad financial management issue is how to best treat assets and liabilities. There is more on this in chapter fifteen. It is worth repeating here because some of the conceptual foundations are from the perspective of financial management, not exclusively from accounting. How assets are handled is a primary consideration. The most obvious manifestation of a business asset is cash. It is the way in which day-to-day financial obligations are taken care of. It is totally liquid so it is available instantly for payments. Financial managers want to keep a certain amount of cash in reserve, so it is available if needed. They also want to avoid having too much cash on hand because cash in and of itself is not necessarily an earning asset. The intricacies and importance of cash management are detailed later in this chapter.

Another important asset is in the form of accounts receivable. This is money that is due to the corporation but that has not yet been received. Physical inventory is another asset. Inventory may be raw materials, work in process, or completed product. Products may be stored in a warehouse or they may be en route to the customer. Wherever it is located, it can be considered an asset. Increasingly, companies are carrying far less inventory and are practicing just-in-time inventory management techniques in an attempt to manage costs.

The management of assets is part of the realm of financial management. So too is budgeting. Budgeting of financial resources enables organizations to purchase productive assets and to pay for marketing programs. The budgeting process ensures that there is adequate cash on hand for timely payment of bills. It allows the organization to plan for and execute tactical and operating strategies to maximize long-term goals. There will be more on budgeting later in this chapter but at this stage, the subject is part of the effort to frame the activities of financial management.

Budgeting is the activity that involves how the company plans for and allocates funds to different departments for a period of time. Most of us are familiar with budgets in our organizations. They can be seen as a spending plan (or spending constraint) but there is more to it than that. Most organizations control their budgets. They do this by looking at the rate spending occurs and by comparing actual spending to plan. This can be calculated monthly for example. A variance analysis compares actual to plan. Once the variances have been determined both in dollar terms and as a percentage, action should be taken to address any issues. Actions may include a root cause analysis of any problems (see chapters one and two) or a revising of the standards.

You can look at corporate budgeting as being very similar to household budgeting. There is household income coming in on a yearly basis and a spending plan for it. There is nothing fundamentally different in budgeting for a business. If you ever have a concern that the financial managers in your organization are magicians or speak a language that you don't understand, ask them to explain their ideas in household budgeting terms.

How is finance connected with accounting?

Finance relies on the accounting function to provide basic data on which to base decisions. They are closely related. Familiarity with basic accounting concepts (chapter fifteen) will help you understand financial activities and their impact on the organization. Accounting is generally internally oriented and keeps track of what is going on in the firm though it does cross into the external world in some reporting functions. The finance function is generally about the firm's relationship with external entities, though it has internal aspects too. Consequently, there is overlap even though the orientations of accounting and finance differ.

Awareness of the broader financial markets and external environment leads to optimal results for the organization if opportunities are identified and acted on. Taken as a whole and employing the array of concepts just discussed, financial management should now been seen as another way an organization can master its own future. It is not an isolated and arcane activity more interested in numbers than people.

As stated in our introduction, there are a wide array of concepts covered in finance and many industries treat specific activities in special ways. As a result, you should look for some differing practices of your industry (a group of similar businesses) compared to others. Performance standards such as financial ratios, for example, will differ from industry to industry. What may be an acceptable leverage ratio in the financial services industry may be a sign of trouble for a manufacturer. Some sources of industry data are listed at the end of chapter seventeen.

An understanding of the core body of financial concepts by all functional areas and even all employees is important to getting staff commitment to what financial managers try to achieve. The preceding sets the stage for a more detailed venture into finance and budgeting tools and related concepts.

How can I view the budget process as a strategic tool, not a painful task?

When you hear the words "It's time to work on the annual budget" do you shudder inwardly and groan outwardly? If so, you're not alone. For many companies, the annual budget process has become a cumbersome and expensive ordeal. The Ford Motor Company reports spending $1.2Billion on its annual budgeting and forecasting processes. Statistics suggest that the average billion-dollar company spends as many as 25,000 person days per year putting the annual budget together. Others indicate that 20-30% of senior management's time is spent on the budget. The budget journey has a lot riding on it. Wall Street is not kind to companies who fail in meeting forecasts. This failure may come from current company performance or it may relate back to a failure in the budgeting process itself. Either way, it can cost you.

In a traditional structure, the various departments each put together an annual budget that is then pushed upward and combined into a company level budget. The areas feeding numbers upward generally include the following: sales, operations, marketing, capital investments, special projects and cash flow management:

- The *sales budget* is an estimate of future sales. It is generally broken down by both unit and dollar volume. The sales budget may also be broken down by product type, geographic region, customer segment, etc., depending on the structure of the company.
- The *operations budget* is an estimate of the number of units that must be produced to meet future sales. It estimates the various costs involved in production of those units such as labor, raw materials, overhead, etc.
- Similarly cost-based, the *marketing budget* is an estimate of funds needed for promotion, marketing and public relations.
- The *capital budget* predicts what the company will spend on fixed assets such as buildings, machinery and equipment, etc. It includes the cost of acquisition of new assets as well as the maintenance and replacement of existing assets.
- A *special projects budget* will forecast costs associated with a particular upcoming company project. These costs may include materials, labor and other expenses.
- The *cash flow budget* estimates the company's future cash flows over a particular period. The cash flow budget is particularly important to help a company estimate when it

may need to use outside financing sources or tap into reserves to cover a cash shortfall in a particular period. We'll talk about the cash conversion cycle and financing options later in this chapter.

In this traditional series of activities, the finance manager generally oversees the process. It might work something like this. At the beginning of the process, senior management meets to develop business targets based on company strategy. The finance manager pulls together historical data for each area and presents each business unit manager with a package. This package may include historical financial data, a budget template, new corporate goals and objectives, and a deadline for when the budget numbers are due back to the finance department. The finance manager will collect the completed budget templates and will combine them into a master budget. This budget is presented to senior management.

And that's where the fun begins. What follows is often an exercise in negotiation as opposed to an exercise in forecasting a realistic budget. Beware of the following pitfalls in the budget negotiating process:

TIP: BUDGETING PROS AND CONS:

On the plus side—

It is a means of communicating management plans throughout the organization.

It forces managers to think about and plan for the future.

It allocates resources to where they can be used most effectively.

It establishes benchmarks and goals for use in evaluating performance.

It coordinates activities across the organization.

On the negative side—

It can be seen as a management pressure device resulting in a "meet budget at all costs" mentality.

It can cause interdepartmental conflict.

It may lead to waste, as managers develop a "use it or lose it" mentality.

Managers tend to inflate costs and build in cushions leading to waste and inefficiency.

The process is time consuming and may deflect attention from core business activities.

- Managers may know from past experience that whatever they put in their marketing budget may be cut by about half as a matter of course. So if they really want to spend $100,000 on trash and trinkets, they may actually budget $200,000 as they are anticipating a cut.
- You may be rewarding good budgeting as opposed to good performance. The manager who negotiates a 20% growth plan and brings his actual performance in at 22% might get rewarded for being above plan while the manager who forecasts 60% growth but only manages 50% may be criticized for being below plan. But really, who's had more growth?
- This same problem also discourages risk taking, especially if managers' compensation is tied to the budget. The budget/compensation link encourages managers to underestimate sales and to overestimate expenses in order to be sure of maximizing on their compensation plan goals.

- Using historical trends and applying the same ratios you've experienced in the past may mean that you end up overlooking market realities. This tendency to become overly reliant on trend analysis may invalidate your budget in times of market change.
- The budgeting process takes on a life of its own. Planning can take a backseat to a fixation on getting the numbers in. Every number in the budget should be tied to a plan. If you have money budgeted for trade shows and conferences, then you better have a list ready of trade shows and conferences you plan on having your sales people attend.

How can I make sure my budget is still timely and relevant?

The budget process can become so time consuming and cumbersome that when finally you do get the numbers you want, they will be four months out of date. Budgets are usually annual. The budget process generally starts sometime late in the year and ends sometime in the first quarter. So you are either trying to guess numbers in the future, or you are budgeting for events that have already occurred. Either way, you end up out of sync and out of date. One way to avoid the time delay problem is to move to a *continuous* or *perpetual* budget. A continuous budget, also called a rolling budget, is a twelve-month plan that rolls forward by one month as the current month ends. This structure can also work with a quarterly budget. The budget rolls forward one quarter as each quarter is completed.

To give a quick example, let's say you plan an annual budget that runs from January 2011 to December 2011. If this were a rolling budget, on Feb 1 you would add January of 2012 to the budget and January of 2011 would fall out of the budget. This type of budget is very forward-looking. It forces management to be aware of market changes and to adapt the budget accordingly. It might work well for companies that are experiencing rapid change in their marketplace. On the downside, if you practice participative budgeting, where many are involved in the budget process, you could spend a lot of management time continually revising your budget. If you chose to follow this route, assign the budget adjustment process to just one person. Software is readily available to help facilitate changes. It's important to note, that while a continuous budget may be more forward-looking, it does not necessarily result in a budget that is more achievable.

I've been asked to budget my costs for next year. Where do I get the budget numbers?

There are three main approaches to developing cost estimates for budget purposes. The first, the incremental approach, is the most common and traditional method. Using this method, the manager takes last year's costs and adds (or subtracts) from them *incrementally* to get the new numbers for this year. So how much do you add or subtract? That can be estimated based on several factors:

- You can use a proportionate ratio strategy. For example, if you are projecting that sales will be up 10%, you can also increase your marketing budget by 10%.

- You can use the rate of inflation. If inflation is estimated at 5%, then you increase your costs by 5%.
- You can use historical trends. If your costs have been increasing at a rate of 3% per year over the last several years, then you might assume they will increase again by the same amount.
- You can use industry benchmarks. If your competition is spending 20% on research and development, then you may also choose to do so.

While some feel it is outmoded, the incremental approach still has advantages. It's fairly easy and straightforward to execute. It's easy to coordinate across business units making a roll-up to a central budget quicker and less error prone. It's stable, consistent, and tends to avoid conflict. On the downside, this method may encourage a spend it or lose it attitude. Managers may build in slack or have caches of idle funds that stem from no longer relevant costs that just keep getting carried along. There is little incentive to reduce costs and it tends to encourage a status quo approach. This approach does not encourage creativity or risk taking.

An alternative to the incremental approach is zero-based budgeting. While the incremental approach starts with last year's numbers as the basis for this year's costs, zero-based budgeting starts at zero. Each cost must be individually determined and supported before it is approved for inclusion in the budget. No reference is made to prior year's spending. While this method avoids the inflationary tendencies built into incremental budgeting, it is extremely time consuming and complex.

Zero-based budgeting eliminates waste by forcing managers to think through each line item. Each cost center is forced to evaluate its missions and goals. Costs need to be justified or they risk becoming entitlements and a zero-based budget addresses this issue. Budget discussions are often more meaningful as a result of this process. Finally, it also can be used to identify areas of the business that might be candidates for outsourcing. Managers will need training to be able to successfully budget in this way. Training and the close scrutiny applied to each cost causes the process to be time consuming and fairly costly. It also just might not be necessary. You don't need a chainsaw to trim a few bushes.

While zero-based budgeting might be great for shaking up your budgeting process that may have grown stale, it does take good leadership and follow through to be effective. Don't pick and choose, reviewing some line items while allowing others to go unchanged. If you are going to review every item, make sure you do so. Otherwise, your motives may be questioned. Additionally, you may not want to apply this technique to every department every year. Maybe chose a few business units for this kind of deep analysis and leave others for next year.

> **TIP: TRADITIONAL BUDGET SHORTCOMINGS—**
>
> Traditional methods fail to identify waste.
>
> Traditional methods do not support continuous process improvement.
>
> Traditional methods do not identify cost drivers.
>
> Traditional methods lack ownership and buy-in.
>
> Benefits do not exceed time, money, and effort involved in the process.

Both incremental budgeting and zero-based budgeting are considered traditional approaches. A more contemporary approach is Activity Based Budgeting (ABB). In traditional budget practices, senior management spends time approving budget line items instead of truly looking at the allocation of resources company-wide. This narrow focus fails to maximize shareholder value as it moves energy away from strategy and more toward number crunching and guesswork. The budget ends up establishing spending limits as opposed to promoting growth. ABB seeks to change that by looking at organizational activities in the context of the products and services produced.

To get started with ABB, the company's activities (what people actually do) are identified. Costs are assigned to each activity. The activities are grouped into or assigned to products and services delivered to customers. Because of this important step, ABB is a very outwardly focused budgeting strategy in stark contrast to the inward focus of traditional methods. This method of allocating costs helps assess the profit potential of different products and services. It helps focus management attention and resources on the most profitable areas of the organization. Happily, this allows the firm to circle back to its original objective of maximizing shareholder value.

While ABB looks at result and the activities that led to these results in a constructive way, it is not without its challenges. It can be difficult to implement. Especially challenging is the allocation of costs. For example, your company develops and sells software. Your tech support group deals with outside customers. So those costs go into the budget for the product you sell. But your tech support group also supports internal customers (sales staff in this case). ABB does not have a great way to separate and allocate those costs. In addition, ABB can cause a kind of caste system to develop in your company. Since the primary focus is on activities that deal directly with the end user, support functions may feel underappreciated. Finally, ABB ignores the internal value chain. This can cause a distortion in costs as support functions may end up either under or overrepresented vis-à-vis the products they end up allocated to.

A good place to start learning about ABB is the 1997 book *Cost and Effect* in which Harvard professors Kaplan and Cooper first develop the concept. There are many accounting firms and consultants who specialize in ABB. ABB, along with Activity Based Management (ABM) can help you implement business initiatives that include reducing costs, process re-engineering, customer relationship management and supply chain management.

These three techniques focus on budgeting costs. Forecasting revenue is at least as important and has its own set of challenges. It's easy to fall into the trending trap when it comes to sales. If sales have increased 5% each year for the past three years, why not just estimate that revenues will be up again 5% this year? This is certainly the quick and easy method. It's also easy to fall into the trap of assuming a certain volume per salesperson. For example, if you generated sales of $10 million with five sales people, adding a sixth salesperson should drive an increase in revenue to $12 million.

There is of course a strong chance that your revenue growth goals will be handed to you by the finance manager as an emissary of senior management. However, with luck, senior management will have sought your input. To give them an educated answer, look at what's happening in your marketplace. Go back to the SWOT analysis you did in chapter five. What macro-environmental trends are going on and how will they affect you? Are interest rates high or low? Are they rising or falling? Is inflation high or low, rising or falling? What socio-economic trends will have an impact on your product? Are consumers spending? What's happening in your industry in terms of profitability and life cycle? What moves are your competitors making? In a perfect world, your financial controller will provide some of this analysis so that everyone is working from a consistent set of numbers. Considering all of these external factors will help establish the reality of your sales forecast.

How does the budget work with my corporate structure?

The traditional budget process was largely centralized. With the corporate pyramid firmly in your mind, you can see how this both top-down and bottom-up process followed traditional chains of command and lines of authority. In the initial top-down phase, senior management determined corporate objectives, growth targets and goals and pushed these down to managers to use in preparing their budgets. In the bottom-up segment of the process, the managers prepared numbers for their individual departments and fed them back upward. As companies become increasingly decentralized in structure, so too must the budget process.

A decentralized budget process with multilevel controls drives strategy throughout the organization. This can make your company more responsive to market changes. It will help make your budget more relevant and accurate. If you're going to put time and effort into a budgeting process, it might as well be worthwhile. In addition, further empowering employees to be responsible for control at all levels leads to better performance. While the centralization of expense management might have been a reassuring way of controlling costs during the 2007–09 recession, did you really accomplish as much as you thought?

Jeremy Hope and Robin Fraser (2003) argue that "as long as budgeting, a vestige of the old command-and-control approach to management, remains in place, the newer tools designed to decentralize strategic decision making will never achieve their full potential." Their approach is summarized in the following tool:

---

1. *Build goals based on longer-term, external benchmarks instead of negotiated annual targets.* Benchmarks may include industry best-in-class performance measures or direct competitors.
2. *Design evaluation and rewards based on relative improvement contracts.* Develop a range of performance benchmarks for the team to meet over a longer time horizon. Make performance relative to other managers.
3. *Make action planning continuous and inclusive.* Hope and Fraser recommend a five quarter rolling forecast that helps eliminate distortions caused by the drive to meet fixed performance targets for a single fiscal year.
4. *Make resources available as needed, instead of allocated in advance.* Let your managers decide what is needed when.

Adapted from Hope and Fraser (2003) *Beyond Budgeting: How Managers Can Break Free from the Annual Performance Trap.*

Tool 16.1   Budget Process Success Ideas

How do I do a better job with budgeting?

At its worst, the budget process is time-consuming and inefficient. It fails to stimulate results and provides little guidance for operational management. At its best, the company budget gives financial expression to strategy. It motivates managers to achieve commonly understood targets. It provides a framework for control, the final step in the management process. Your goal is to develop a process that reduces time spent and aligns spending with strategy.

Getting the budget right is important. Lots of decisions will be made based on the budget. Tips for getting budgeting right include:

- Practice responsibility accounting. A manager should be responsible for items that can actually be controlled. Managers should be held accountable for goals and variances between actual and plan. Drive ownership into your organization.
- Accountability does not mean punishment if goals are not met. Efforts should be made to understand the source of discrepancies and to make appropriate changes en route.
- Coordinate budgeting efforts across departments. Probably one of the best things that comes out of the budget process is the communication that happens along the way.
- Align the budget with compensation plans. Compensation plans that reward "meeting plan" may lead managers to negotiate the lowest possible numbers and to avoid taking risks. Avoid incenting your employees to favor short-term gains over the long-term health of the company.
- At all steps in the process, align budgeting with strategic planning. If they are separate functions, consider housing the two departments together. Make sure strategic planners are on the budgeting team and vice versa. The strategy should drive the budget. Too often, the budget drives the strategy.
- Find a balance between bottom-up thinking and top-down guidance. Make sure everyone is thinking long term. Use a three to five year time horizon to establish boundaries.
- Focus on allocating resources to the most profitable part of your business.

How do I figure out my capital budget?

One area that requires additional attention is the capital budget. In this discussion, the term *capital* refers to fixed assets used in production. This would include buildings, machinery and equipment, etc. Capital budgeting involves the process of analyzing projects based on their expected returns and deciding which to include in the budget within the constraints established by senior management. Capital budget decisions must be tied to the organization's strategic plan. They generally have a long-term impact on the company and should be viewed in this context. For example, the decision to purchase an asset that has a ten-year life should be tied to a ten-year sales forecast.

Forecasting demand helps establish timing, an important component of the capital budget. Many large purchases have a fairly long time horizon. So the timing coordination of bringing new capital assets on line when these resources can be productively put to use requires excellent forecasting and project management skills. More often, demand happens before resources can be allocated resulting in companies playing catch-up in terms of production. It takes skill to bring assets on line at the time when they can be effectively used.

Your goal in capital budgeting is to improve the timing and the quality of your fixed asset expansion plan. Capital investment covers the following items:

- Replacement of assets which can be further broken into two categories:
  - Replacement of worn out or damaged equipment.
  - Replacement of still serviceable equipment to modernize or reduce costs.
- Expansion plans which also fall into two categories:
  - Expansion of existing products into existing markets (via new channels or distributors for example).
  - Expansion into new products or markets.
- Compliance, which may include safety issues or other regulatory requirements that your company needs to implement.
- Other capital budgeting items which may include office buildings, parking lots, and other physical plant topics.

Determining what projects will be included in the capital budget and evaluating the viability of those projects is covered in detail in chapter seventeen. Chapter seventeen will help you understand how to calculate the payback period, the accounting rate of return, the net present value, and the internal rate of return used to evaluate asset acquisition viability. These measures are all excellent tools for understanding your capital investment options.

How do different volume levels affect my capital project decision?

Often there are choices of different project strategies that can be used to achieve similar results. However, there may be scalability differences between the different alternatives. When three projects are considered, each assuming a different volume level, a choice must be made about which project is most aligned with the firm's strategy for the period under consideration. This decision can be quantified using a crossover analysis. For example, assume project A has fixed costs of $10,000 and material costs of $10.00 per unit. Project B has fixed costs of $30,000 and material costs of $7.50 per unit. Project C has fixed costs of $50,000 and material costs of $6.47 per unit. Assume the time period is the same for all three.

Using the tools in chapter seventeen, you can evaluate each strategy separately. It may also be helpful however, to evaluate the alternatives together at different projected volume levels. A table of values at different activity levels can be created. A graph visually depicts the relationship of the various projects.

In this example, activity levels below 8,000 units will be least costly using Project A. At activity levels between 8,000 and 19,417, Project B is the least costly alternative. Above 19,417, Project C is the least costly alternative. The quantitative approach to project selection does not take into account qualitative information. Any decision should be supplemented using all available and relevant information. Issues such as independence of projects, different lives of projects, resource limitations, and owner objectives should

	Volume					
	0	5,0000	10,000	15,000	20,000	25,000
Project A	$10,000	$60,000	$110,000	$160,000	$210,000	$260,000
Project B	30,000	67,500	105,000	142,500	180,000	217,500
Project C	50,000	82,350	114,700	147,050	179,400	211,750

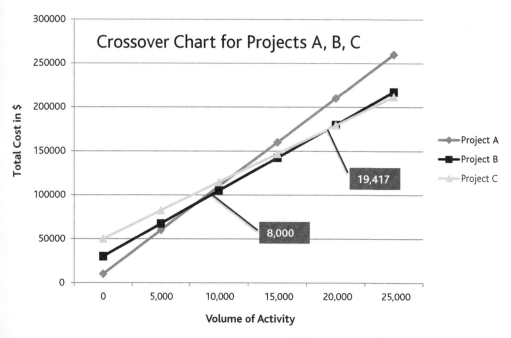

Figure 16.1 Project Cost Crossover Analysis at Different Volume Levels

be considered. Developing and maintaining competitive advantage is difficult at best. One way to keep an advantage is to have projects that are not easily replicable.

Is it better to finance by projects using debt or equity?

Once you have decided on your capital budget outflows in terms of the projects you'd like to pursue, you need to decide how to fund them. Debt, equity, and earnings are the three possible options. The pros and cons of debt versus equity are discussed in chapter seventeen. A closer look at debt financing and its potential advantages is included here.

For most smaller and some medium sized organizations, bank lending will be the primary source of debt financing while larger organizations can tap the bond market. Our analysis will focus on traditional debt. Debt financing has a unique advantage. It acts as a multiplier for earnings of the company and returns of these earnings to the owners. As an example, let's assume two companies are identical in size but Company Cautious relies solely on equity financing (contributions from the owners and earnings from

Cautious Company		Aggressive Company	
Profit before project	$100,000	Profit before project	$100,000
Equity before project	$1,000,000	Equity before project	$1,000,000
Equity financing of project	$1,000,000		
		Debt financing of project	$1,000,000
Project profit (100% equity financed)	$500,000	Project profit (100% debt financed)	$500,000
		Interest on debt	$100,000
Profit after project	$600,000	Profit after project	$500,000
Equity after project	$2,000,000	Equity after project	$1,000,000
Return on equity	30%	Return on equity	50%

Figure 16.2 The Effect of Leverage

continuing operations). Aggressive Company relies on equity for 50% of its financing and the remaining 50% is achieved through debt.

The return on equity is calculated by dividing the end profit of the project by the equity when the project is completed, $600,000/$2,000,000 = 30% for the equity financed project and $500,000/$1,000,000 = 50% for the debt financed project. While the example may be extreme, it illustrates the power of debt financing or using other people's money to maximize returns to owners. Because the use of debt is so powerful, companies may prefer to finance projects totally with debt. The effect is offset by the increased cost of debt (interest and fees) that increases as additional debt is incurred. The increase in the interest rate is to help the lender offset the risk that the borrower will default. This risk increases as the percentage of debt to equity increases. The market moderates owners' desires to use other people's money to make more money. Debt is powerful but risky.

Why are cash flows so important?

The most difficult task for many organizations is managing cash flows- incoming, and outgoing payments. Cash flow analysis addresses both cash flows for one-time projects and from ongoing operations. Let's start with the cash flow impacts from new projects. When a project is proposed, a five step process to determine the project's cash flow can be used:

1. Cost and setup data: The first step is to determine the cost and other input data for the project.
2. Depreciation schedule: The second step is to calculate depreciation (a non-cash expense, but one that affects income and other taxes).
3. Salvage: The third step is to determine the salvage value of the project assets. This is known as the residual or remaining value at the end of the asset's useful life (the asset is usually sold). Typically, the asset is fully depreciated at this point. Liquidation of the asset generates positive cash flow at the end of the project.
4. Net cash flow: The fourth step is to determine the expected cash flows from operations, the income tax effect, and finally operating cash flows for each period during the project.
5. Results: Finally the effect on the wealth of the organization is calculated. Net present value and internal rate of return may be used along with other methods to determine if the project has met the organization's standards for new projects.

How are operating cash flows different from project cash flows and how do I manage them?

Cash flows from operations are impacted by the cash conversion cycle. The cash conversion cycle (CCC) is the time it takes a firm to go through the transformation process. It starts when the firm purchases input, and it ends when the firm receives cash for its output. The ability to influence the length of the cash conversion cycle lies partly with internal policies (whether or not to take advantage of trade discounts), partly with external issues (strength of influence on customers/vendors), and the nature of the business and industry.

The major components of the cash conversion cycle are the inventory conversion period, the average receivable collection period, and the payables deferral period. These three in combination can have a significant impact on firm profitability as they affect the need to pay for financing of operations. The following formula is concerned with the length of the cycle:

CCC = Inventory Conversion period + Receivables Conversion Period – Payables Conversion Period

Inventory conversion is the time it takes from order to sale of the inventory item and is found by dividing average inventory levels by average daily sales. The average collection period is the time it takes from the creation of the collectible when the product is sold to the time cash is collected for the sale and is found by dividing the average balance of accounts receivable by average daily sales. The payable deferral period is the time it takes for customers to pay for their purchases made on credit.

Let's assume we calculate inventory conversion at thirty-six days and accounts receivable conversion at fifty-seven days. Subtract a payables deferral of twenty days. This indicates that this firm must provide for seventy-three days of cash coverage. This cash can come from operations or from short-term debt. Whether cash or debt is used will depend on availability and cost. Speeding up the cash conversion cycle flows through immediately to the firm's bottom line by saving costs. Two strategies that may help are to extend the period before payments on trade credit are made and/or to decrease the number of days receivables are outstanding. Both can often be negotiated with stakeholders.

How should the company budget its cash?

Inflows and outflows of cash are reasons to budget throughout the year. Knowing the amounts and timing of cash flows helps reduce the cost of capital while minimizing idle cash balances. Contacting your banker to explore their cash management services is a worthwhile activity. At the beginning of the chapter, development of the master budget resulted in a pro-forma income statement and balance sheet. This and other cost center budgets are used to create an overall cash budget. Items dealing with or affecting cash balances need to be included in these more detailed budgets. Cash budgeting matches the need for cash with the supply of cash, either from operations or from preplanned loans.

Failing to plan may lead to cash shortfalls. Emergency loans are expensive in terms of their transaction costs (interest and fees) and their potential cost to the reputation of the company. Financing to support cash requirements known in advance from the cash budget can be negotiated at favorable terms. Daily cash budgets can be developed along with monthly cash budgets. Daily budgeting provides for differences in timing of receipts and disbursements of cash.

Since cash is not an earning asset why would we want to hold it?

Several basic reasons for holding cash include being able to pay for transactions, allowing the company to take advantage of unexpected opportunities or to pay for unexpected obligations. Lenders may also require compensating balances against existing loans. With cash on hand you can more easily take advantage of trade discounts. If your suppliers offer you terms, the actual effective interest rate may be as high as 36%. Paying accounts payable in the ten-day grace period using either cash balances or a working capital line of credit will save the company from paying an effective 36% interest rate, well beyond normal borrowing costs for most companies.

How can a company reduce its need for cash?

Cash flows are either into or out of the company. Speeding up collections of cash or slowing payments both have the effect of reducing cash demand. Some means of speeding up cash collections include reducing the time it takes for checks to clear or speeding up the collection process. Banks often have policies where checks above certain limits must wait specified periods before the funds are available, so smaller collections made more frequently may help. If major customers use specific banks, you can speed the clearing process by opening accounts with those banks.

Collection velocity can also be improved by locating lockboxes in various geographic locations. Frequent deposits can then be made from each lockbox reducing the delaying effect of postal delivery. Even better is to enter into arrangements with customers so that payments are made electronically rather than using paper checks. This is one of the advantages available to organizations with integrated ordering and payment systems such as SAP (check the additional resources section for more on SAP.)

You can also improve your CCC by slowing the payment of your payables. Also called stretching trade accounts, this is the delay of trade payments beyond the period offered by your supplier. Many large companies (Ford for example as explained in chapter seventeen) can pay slowly as they wield considerable supplier power. As noted earlier, this can be a costly strategy in terms of the effective interest rate. However, trade credit is usually conveniently obtained, and there is generally no formal agreement. It is an on-demand source of emergency financing that should be considered in the company's overall bag of cash flow tricks.

Cash management is critical for organizations. The lack of appropriate cash management has been responsible for a large percentage of organization failures throughout time. Good cash management employs the company's assets, including cash, in the highest and best use resulting in improved profits.

Phillip Campbell, in his 2004 book *Never Run Out of Cash*, provides the following cash flow rules:

1. Never Run Out of Cash.
2. Cash is king.
3. Know the cash balance right now.
4. Do today's work today.
5. Either you do the work or have someone else do it.
6. Don't manage from the bank balance.
7. Know what you expect the cash balance to be six months from now.
8. Cash flow problems can be seen in advance.
9. You absolutely, positively must have cash flow projections.
10. Eliminate your cash flow worries so you are free to do what you do best—grow your business and make more money.

What effect does working capital management have on company profits?

Working capital is cash and short-term assets applied against short term liabilities. Like the current ratio discussed in chapter seventeen (which uses the same accounts for its calculation), it is concerned with what is happening in the short term. While the current ratio is the ratio of current assets to current liabilities, net working capital can be calculated by subtracting current liabilities from current assets. Matching cash needs with available cash provides an opportunity to enhance the company's profitability. Idle assets (cash) can provide liquidity but they detract from profits, opportunities forgone for liquidity reasons. Other than timing, working capital can be managed in the long term by adequate detailed budgeting.

Managers responsible for working with financial aspects of an organization need to know where they stand with working capital at any given time. It may be useful to calculate days of working capital on hand:

$$\text{Days of Working Capital} = \frac{\text{Receivables} + \text{Inventory} - \text{Current Payables}}{\text{Average Daily Sales}}$$

Note that the cash balance is not normally used in this calculation. Adequate working capital makes it possible for the organization to meet its short-term financial obligations. Industry averages may serve as a useful guide in determining an appropriate level of working capital. A relaxed working capital policy allows holding operating assets to cover longer periods of working capital. A tight policy closely matches working capital with the operating capital needs of the organization. In the former, working capital turnover is low and in the latter working capital turnover is high on an annualized basis. A relaxed working capital structure is less profitable than a tight policy. It is normal for inventory to be the largest component of working capital so inventory reduction efforts can improve the level of working capital.

Cash flow management, while complex, is the blood that flows through a company, pumped by its financial heart. Without enough, the company is anemic and not able to reach its potential. To understand cash flows, you must start with the budget. The budget process is the linkage between strategy and performance. It sets the stage for later evaluation of organizational performance. Budgeting needs to be as dynamic and adaptable as your market. The terms and techniques of finance help develop a common language and understanding of these life-sustaining functions.

Additional Resources

Many companies are still using Excel Spreadsheets for budgeting, but there are many more sophisticated options to help you. There are a myriad of software programs from off the shelf to custom designed. Oracle, PeopleSoft, and SAP are increasing the budgeting, planning, and forecasting capabilities of their existing enterprise planning applications. Companies such as Comshare Inc., Cognos, Inc., and Hyperion Solutions among others are all bringing budget and planning software to the market. The major accounting firms such as Deloitte & Touche and PricewaterhouseCoopers are great sources of budgeting information and ideas.

There is a wide array of resources available to companies to assist in learning about good financial management. Some of these are:

- The *Financial Times* (http://www.ft.com/home/us), which provides information about yesterday's market numbers and articles about current and future events.
- *The Economist* (http://www.economist.com/), which provides information about economic conditions and markets affected by and affecting commerce.
- There are many hundreds of other websites that provide guidance and even perform calculations for specific tasks. Loan payment calculators can determine the monthly costs of loans for land, building, and equipment.

References

Campbell, P. (2004). *Never Run Out of Cash*. Round Rock, TX: Grow and Succeed Publishing.

Ehrhardt, M. and Brigham, E. (2009). *Financial Management: Theory and Practice*, Thirteenth Edition. Mason, OH: South-Western Cengage Learning.

Friedman, T. L. (2007). *The World is Flat*. New York, NY: Picador Publishing.

Gitman, L. (2006). *Principles of Managerial Finance, 11th Ed*. Boston, MA: Pearson Education, Inc.

Helms, M. (ed.) (2005). Financial Issues for Managers. *Encyclopedia of Management*. Farmington Hills, MI: Gale Cengage.

Hope, J. and Fraser, R. (2003). *Beyond Budgeting: How Managers can Break Free from the Annual Performance Trap*. Boston, MA: Harvard Business School Press.

Kaplan, R. and Cooper, R. (1997). *Cost and Effect, Using Integrated Cost Systems to Drive Profitability and Performance*. Boston, MA: Harvard Business Press

Van Horne, J. (1986) *Financial Management and Policy*, 7th ed. Englewood Cliffs, NJ: Prentice-Hall.

17 *Organizational Preformance*

LAURA BARTHEL

In 2009 Ford Motor Company reported net income of $2.7 billion, according to the annual 10-K filing required by the Securities Exchange Commission (SEC). According to Catherine Holahan (2009), the reported income of Ford Motor fails to indicate the reasons Ford was listed by MSN Money as one of ten companies likely to go bankrupt in 2009. The bottom-line income also does not explain the fifty-eighth place ranking given by the Forbes Global 2000 list of the world's largest, most powerful companies for 2010. The views of MSN and Forbes are examples of two remarkably different perspectives over the span of a year about the performance of a single company looking at the same set of numbers.

Investment decisions of managers, owners (investors) and creditors are generally not solely based on media and published commentary such as MSN or Forbes lists. Managers, investors and creditors will refer to financial information about companies before investing or lending funds. Ford's reported income of $2.7 billion is valuable information that stakeholders (investors, creditors, customers and management) can use for decision making.

Despite the temptation to do so, the key for decision-making cannot always be drawn from the bottom lines of the financial statements such as net income. A manager should use the financial information as a tool to evaluate current performance and evaluate future investment decisions. A successful manager may be seeking additional funding for either expanding current operations, requesting funding for large purchases or making a strategic move. They should consider how investors and creditors read, use and evaluate organizational performance from the financial statements beyond the numbers reported in bold.

If numbers could talk, what would they tell stakeholders?

This question addresses the basic purpose of this chapter. To facilitate this discussion, the chapter is further broken down into the following topics:

1. How do managers use financial information to evaluate organizational performance and investment opportunities?
2. What types of funding resources should the company seek?
3. How do external stakeholders evaluate the success/failure and resources of the company?
4. How do internal decisions impact the external view and evaluation of the company?

This chapter contains a myriad of financial ratios. To help you quickly and easily find the ratios you're looking for, use reference Tool 17.1 below:

What I want to measure	Ratio Name	Formula
Profitability	Profit Percentage	Profit Percentage = Pre-tax Income / Net Sales Revenue
	Gross Profit	Gross Profit Percentage = Gross Profit / Net Sales Revenue
	Revenue Growth Percentage	(Sales this year - Sales last year)/ Sales last year
Cost-Volume-Profit	Total Cost Formula	Total Cost = (Variable Costs Per Unit × Quantity) + Fixed Cost
	Contribution Margin	Contribution Margin = Sale Revenue - Variable Cost or Contribution Margin Per Unit = Price - Variable Cost Per Unit
	Contribution Margin Ratio	Contribution Margin Ratio = Contribution Margin / Sales Revenue
	Break-Even Point in Units	Break-Even Point in Units = Fixed Cost / Contribution Margin Per Unit
	Break-Even Point in Sales Dollars	Break-Even Point in Sales Dollars = Fixed Cost / Contribution Margin Ratio
	Target Profit in Units	Target Profit Units = (Fixed Cost + Target Profit) / Contribution Margin Per Unit
Capital Investment Decisions	Payback Period	Payback Period = Investment Cost/Annual Increase in Cash flow
	Accounting Rate of Return (ARR)	ARR = Average Annual Increase in Operating Income / Average Investment Cost

Tool 17.1   Guide to Financial Ratios

	Present Value Interest Factor (PVIF)	$PVIF = 1 / (1 + r)^t$
	Net Present Value (NPV)	NPV = (Expected Future Cash Flows × PVIF) - Investment Cost
	Internal Rate of Return	IRR = Present Value of Cash Flows / Annual Cash Flow
Liquidity Ratios	Current Ratio	Current Ratio = Current Assets / Current Liabilities
	Quick Ratio	Quick Ratio = Current Assets - Inventory - Prepaid Expenses / Current Liabilities
	Creditor Days Payable	Creditor Days Payable = (Unpaid Suppliers' Bills / Sales) × 365 days
Cash Conversion Cycle	Inventory Turnover	Inventory Turnover = Cost of Goods Sold / Average Inventory
	Accounts Receivable Turnover	AR Turnover = Net Credit Sales / Average Net Accounts Receivable
	Sales Days in Receivables	Sales Days in Receivables = [(Beg. AR + End AR) / 2] / One Day's Sales
Leverage	Debt Ratio	Debt Ratio = Total Liabilities / Total Assets
	Times Interest Earned	Times Interest Earned = Income from Operations / Interest Expense
Investor Assessment	Rate of Return on Net Sales	Return on Net Sales = Net Income / Net Sales
	Rate of Return on Total Assets	Return on Net Assets = Net Income / Average Total Assets

Tool 17.1   Guide to Financial Ratios (continued)

	Rate of Return on Common Stock	Return on Common Stockholder's Equity = (Net Income - Preferred Dividends) / Average Common Stockholders' Equity
	Earnings Per Share	Earnings Per Share = (Net Income - Preferred Dividends) / Number of Common Shares Outstanding
Stock Performance	Price Per Earnings	Price per Earnings = Market Price per Share / Earnings Per Share
	Dividend Yield	Dividend Yield = Dividend per share of Common Stock / Market Price per share of Common Stock
	Book Value Per Share	Book Value per Share of Common Stock = (Total Stockholders' Equity – Preferred equity) / Number of Common Shares Outstanding

Tool 17.1   Guide to Financial Ratios (continued)

How do I use financial information to evaluate my organization's performance?

According to Paul Niven, author of *Balanced Scorecard Step-by-Step: Maximizing Performance and Maintaining Results* (2002), "If your structure is hampering employees' ability to understand and act on the firm's strategy, how can they be expected to make effective decisions that will lead to the achievement of your goals?" For maximum effectiveness, the evaluation methods should align with the overall company strategic plan and goals. If management and employees are evaluated based on performance measures that are not directly linked to the company's strategic plan and goals the focus shifts to meeting the performance measures instead of meeting long-term plans and goals.

To determine how to use financial information to evaluate organizational performance and investment opportunities consider the following questions:

1. What measures are most appropriate?
2. How can profitability be measured?
3. How can efficiency be measured?
4. How are investment opportunities evaluated?

What measures are most appropriate for me to use?

Financial information is a means of measuring organizational performance. The first step to evaluating organizational performance is to identify the measures that properly align with the company's strategic plan. Many companies use a balanced scorecard as a tool to compare company performance to its goals.

The balanced scorecard links the company's strategic plan and goals (see chapter five for more on corporate strategy) to factors critical to meeting these goals. For example, if the company has a goal of providing a quality product to consumers then a critical factor to evaluate is production quality or customer service score percentages.

After the critical factors have been determined, identify ways to measure the success of meeting the critical factors. To continue the example, a measurement for production quality may be the rate of returns of defective products. The company would use the return rate as a benchmark to measure success or failure. Other measures may include the number of reworks, cost of scrap due to quality errors, quality detection rate, results from quality audits or responses from customer satisfaction surveys. Measurements of critical factors are called key performance indicators (KPI).

The balanced scorecard can be formulated in various ways. The following example can be adapted to your company by incorporating company goals, critical factors to achieving those goals and the means of measuring the critical factors (KPIs).

Company Goals	Leader in the Industry		Increase Investor Value		Quality Product	
Critical Factors	Customer Satisfaction	Top 3	Profitability	Investor Return	Quality Production	Quality Control
Key Performance Indicator (KPI)	Return Rate	Market Share	Revenue Growth	Book to Market Value	Return Rate	Detection Rate
	Product Recommendation Rate	Revenue Growth	Profit Margin	Earnings Per Share	Scrap Cost due to Quality	Efficiency Rates

Figure 17.1 Balanced Scorecard

The balanced scorecard incorporates financial, non-financial, quantitative and qualitative key performance indicators. The identification of the KPIs based on the company's strategic plan is the first step to evaluating organizational performance.

What's the best way to measure the profitability of my area?

According to Charles W. Sawyer, US Secretary of Commerce in the Truman administration, "Profit is the ignition system to our economic engine." A common goal and strategic plan for companies is to ultimately be profitable, to continue operations and to provide a financial return to investors. Profitability is an important measure for internal and external stakeholders. Profitability calculations should include overall and continuous profitability measures.

Overall measures typically evaluate profitability at the end of an operating cycle and indicate how profitable the company was during that cycle. Other profitability measures and analysis can be conducted during the operating cycle as a means of estimating and determining continuous profit levels and then controlling factors that impact profitability.

Profitability can be measured by the following percentages:

- *Profit Percentage*—Percentage of profit from sales. The amount of profit kept as earnings for each dollar of revenue.

> Profit Percentage = Pre-tax Income / Net Sales Revenue

- *Gross Profit Percentage*—Percentage of profit earned from sales before covering operating expenses.

> Gross Profit Percentage = Gross Profit / Net Sales Revenue

- *Revenue Growth Percentage*—Percentage of increased revenue compared to the previous year(s).

> Revenue Growth Percentage =
> Sales this Year – Sales Last Year/Sales Last Year

I understand how to measure profits at a point in time, but how can I measure profit on an ongoing basis?

An analysis of the relationship between cost, volume and profit can provide information useful for estimating profits and controlling costs that impact profit. By measuring estimated profitability during the operating cycle, you can evaluate current revenue and costs and make any necessary changes as operations continue.

The relationship between cost, volume and profit can be useful. For example, if executive management has targeted a profit of $1 million to keep the value of the company stock up, then as a manager you can use cost-volume-profit analysis to determine whether you are on track to meet that target profit. Sales incentives or other short-term measures can be used if needed to make up projected shortfalls. In other words, don't wait until the end of the period to make something happen.

The cost-volume-profit analysis is a helpful tool in evaluating actual cost compared to expected cost and actual profit versus expected profit. To use this analysis, break down expenses into fixed and variable costs. Fixed costs are those that do not change due to an increase in volume. Examples of fixed costs include rent, salaries, insurance, etc. Variable costs are those costs that change with the increase in volume of even one additional item.

For example, if a company is making t-shirts and the cost for each t-shirt is $2 then for each additional shirt, variable costs increase by $2. Classification of fixed and variable costs is discussed in more detail in chapter fifteen.

To illustrate, let's assume a company knows that to run the facility no matter how many units are sold is $10. The variable cost of each unit is $5. The company can sell the units for $10. The company can analyze the expected total cost for a specific level of sales and the associated revenue at that anticipated sales level. A company with known total fixed cost and variable cost per unit can develop their cost formula as:

$$\text{Total Cost} = (\text{Variable Cost Per Unit} \times \text{\# of Units}) + \text{Total Fixed Cost}$$

The formula can be used to calculate the cost at any given level of sales. Using the example, you get:

$$\text{Total Cost} = (\$5 \times \text{\# of Units}) + \$10$$

The cost formula can be graphed to determine the estimated profit at any given sales level as shown in the Cost-Volume-Profit graph.

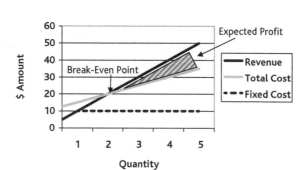

Figure 17.2 Cost-Volume-Profit Graph

The graph shows the fixed cost as a line parallel to the x-axis of the graph. Fixed cost does not change no matter how many units are sold or produced. The fixed cost plus the total variable cost equals the total cost. The revenue line represents the sales revenue received at each unit interval. In Figure 17.2, the revenue and total cost lines intersect at a unit volume of three (the break-even point).

At the break-even point, the company can determine that selling three units will provide enough revenue to cover both the fixed cost and the variable cost. One method used to determine the break-even point is called the contribution margin approach. The contribution margin is the difference between the sales price ($10 in the example), and the variable cost ($5 in the example). This difference is the amount that contributes to either fixed cost or profit. When the fixed costs are covered, the contribution margin contributes to profit. Above the break-even point the contribution margin equals the incremental increase in income.

After determining the contribution margin, the break-even point is calculated as the number of units needed to provide enough funds to cover the fixed expense. To calculate the break-even point, use the following formula:

$$\text{Break-Even Point} = \frac{\text{Fixed cost}}{\text{Contribution Margin Per Unit}}$$

This formula can also be adapted to determine the number of units necessary to earn a target profit. The contribution margin impacts fixed cost and profit. Adapting the formula to include fixed cost plus the desired profit will tell you the number of units you need to sell.

$$\text{Target Profit Point} = \frac{\text{Fixed cost} + \text{Target Profit}}{\text{Contribution Margin Per Unit}}$$

You could use this analysis as a means of measuring and controlling costs during the operating cycle by comparing the estimated fixed and variable costs with the actual total costs from invoices. If fixed costs were higher than anticipated, you could determine the amount of decrease in fixed cost needed to still meet the target profit. Start taking appropriate actions sooner rather than later.

How can I measure efficiency?

An evaluation of efficiency can help determine how to decrease fixed and variable cost from the cost-volume-profit analysis. Fixed costs are typically allocated among processes, jobs, departments or activities. These allocations help identify factors causing rises in costs within the operating cycle. The method of allocation may be determined by the type of product or service provided. A popular management theory called Activity Based Management (ABM) encourages managers to look at the activity level for specific causes of cost (drivers). ABM uses activity-based costing (ABC) to allocate costs based on activities and specific activity cost drivers. ABM allows managers to identify all key value-added activities, determine the cost drivers of each activity and make cost cutting decisions.

ABC allocates labor and overhead based on individual activity cost drivers. The analysis of each activity allows elimination of any unnecessary activities while measuring the efficiency of each activity. To measure the efficiency of an activity consider the maximum output of the activity and then compare that to current activity levels considering any constraints other than efficiency that would prevent the maximum output.

How do I evaluate investment opportunities?

Consider an opportunity to expand the company. Both that opportunity's costs and profits would impact the organization's overall performance in the long run. When faced with an investment opportunity, do a preliminary analysis to determine if the investment is worth the cost. Four methods commonly used to shed light on investment opportunities are:

1. The *payback period* calculates the number of years it would take to recover the initial investment. Use this analysis to estimate the expected annual increase in cash flows from the investment. The payback period is calculated as:

$$\text{Payback Period} = \frac{\text{Investment cost}}{\text{Annual Increase in Cash Flow}}$$

The company should determine the desired payback period and then evaluate each investment with that in mind. For example, if the company wants a payback period of four years for machine purchases. If the four-year payback period is not met the investment should not be considered further. Projects with payback periods of two years or less are probably no-brainers. Paybacks at the other end of the spectrum also make for easy decisions. A twenty-year payback is probably not something you want to undertake. The focus of the payback period is solely on cash flows and does not consider operating efficiency. The payback period also does not consider the time value of money discussed in more detail in the preceding chapter.

2. The *accounting rate of return (ARR)* is the percentage increase in operating income from the investment. The ARR is calculated as the average annual increase in operating income divided by the average investment cost.

$$\text{Accounting Rate of Return Period} = \frac{\text{Average Annual Increase in Operating Income}}{\text{Average Investment Cost}}$$

The company should determine a desired rate of return and then evaluate investment opportunities against the predetermined standard rate. For example, if the company determined that investments must have a return of at least 12%, then all investment ARRs would have to meet that standard to move forward. The ARR considers the operating income impact but does not consider the time-value-of-money.

3. *Net present value (NPV)* is also discussed in the preceding chapter. NPV compares the investment cost and the expected future cash flows over the life of the investment at the same point in time. Over a long period of time the value of money is assumed to change due to the effect of interest.

The interest difference between future value and present value is calculated by applying a discount value to the future dollar value. The incremental interest is used to discount future cash flows to the value of those cash flows in the present.

The first step of calculating the net present value is to determine the present value of future cash flows. To calculate the present value of future cash flows, multiply the future cash flow by the interest factor, also called Present Value Interest Factor (PVIF). The PVIF accounts for the interest rate and the number of periods (t) involved. Most commonly, the interest rate (r) is the organization's cost of capital or a stated interest rate. Future cash flows are discounted due to the interest impact on the value of money causing the value of money to increase over time, thus to determine present value of future cash flows they must be discounted. The interest rate is often called the discount rate when related to present value calculations. The PVIF can be determined using the Time Value of Money financial tables (published in texts and online) or financial calculators using the following formula:

$$PVIF = \frac{1}{(1 + r)^t}$$

The NPV compares the expected future cash flows with the current investment cost. To calculate the NPV, the present value of the expected future cash flow values is reduced by the investment cost already in today's dollars. If the value of the expected future cash flows is greater than the investment value today then the investment will provide a long-term return and should be considered further. Net present value is calculated as:

Net Present Value = (Expected Future Cash Flows × PVIF) − Investment Cost

If the NPV is negative, the value of the future cash flows is not as profitable as taking the cash needed for the investment and putting it in a bank at the expected interest rate. Management should not consider the investment further if the net present value is negative. The focus of the net present value calculation is cash flows and it does not consider the impact on net income.

4. *Internal Rate of Return (IRR)* is the rate of return expected for the given period of cash flows when the present value of the expected cash flows is equal to the investment cost. Therefore, the IRR is the interest rate of the PVIF when the NPV is equal to zero. To calculate IRR, set the investment cost equal to the expected cash flows multiplied

by the PVIF, and solve for the interest rate of the PVIF. To solve for the interest factor, divide the investment cost by the annual cash flow to determine the approximate PVIF. Then use the Present Value tables to match the PVIF solved for with the given number of periods to determine the interest rate (IRR).

IRR can be calculated using Tool 17.2 below:

Step 1—Solve for PVIF	Investment Cost = Annual Cash Flow × PVIF
Step 2—Determine the Interest Rate (r) of the PVIF	Using the present value tables, look up the PVIF determined from Step 1 according to the number of periods (t) provided in the problem. The table will provide a range of interest rates in which the PVIF falls for the specified number of periods. This range of interest is the range of IRR.

For example, if the investment was $1 million and the annual expected future cash flow was $200,000 for ten periods then the steps to calculate IRR would be completed as follows:

Step 1—Solve for PVIF	Investment Cost = Annual Cash Flow × PVIF 1,000,000 = 200,000 × PVIF 1,000,000 ÷ 200,000 = PVIF 5.0 = PVIF
Step 2—Determine the Interest Rate (r) of the PVIF	According to the present value tables for an annuity for ten periods (given in problem) the PVIF of 5.0 is equal to or closest to an interest rate of 15%. Therefore the present value of $200,000 over ten years would equal $1 million if the interest rate was 15% and the NPV would be zero. The IRR is 15%.

Tool 17.2   IRR Calculator

To interpret the IRR, the higher it is, the higher the return is expected to be. This analysis considers the cash flows, return, and time-value-of-money. The net present value and the internal rate of return are the most comprehensive measures of viability of an investment. After determining whether an investment is worth the capital outlay, the next step is to determine how the investment will be funded.

Advantages		Disadvantages	
Debt	**Equity**	**Debt**	**Equity**
Does not dilute ownership.	Demonstrates commitment of owners.	Decreases future financing flexibility due to financier regulations (e.g. debt covenants).	Dilutes ownership and decreases management control.
Limits lenders to interest income and not a portion of company earnings.	Lacks requirement to pledge assets as collateral.	Increases risk due to requirement to repay.	Allows owner's claim to portion of earnings.
Generates a known expense that can be planned for.	Lacks regular requirement of payment. Dividends are issued at management discretion.	Requires regular payment of interest and principal decreasing available cash flow.	Excessive equity financing demonstrates ineffective use of capital.
Generates a tax deductible interest expense.	Repayment and interest not required at specific times.	Increases break-even point due to fixed interest expense.	Does not provide a tax deduction for dividend payments.
Issue of debt is not as complicated as equity.	Generally less annual impact on cash flows.	Decreases available cash flow due to regular payments of interest and principal.	Requires compliance with state and federal regulations for issuance.
Lacks requirement of reporting and requesting vote for decisions and actions.	Leaves assets and cash flow available for debt financing.		Requires regular reporting of operations and owner vote for major decisions or actions.

Tool 17.3   Advantages and Disadvantages of Debt and Equity

How do I fund investments?

"How can we get more resources to expand?" is a common question from companies of every size. Expansion requires additional assets (e.g. resources such as cash, buildings, machinery, equipment). Assets are funded by liabilities, ownership investment or earnings. Remember the accounting equation covered in chapter fifteen. Assets always equal liabilities plus equity. To increase assets, a company has three options:

a) attract lenders/creditors;
b) attract investors;
c) generate additional profit.

The company should first consider all measures to improve internal efficiency to increase earnings. However, when earnings are not growing fast enough and additional resources are needed to operate more effectively and profitably, the company will need to seek funding from outside sources.

Creditors or owners can provide outside sources of funding, as discussed in chapter fifteen. Creditors will provide funding with the expectation of payback plus interest on the amount borrowed. Owners will provide funding in exchange for a share of ownership in the company or a claim to the net assets. They may also claim a portion of the earnings of the company. When looking to grow assets, consider the advantages and disadvantages of liabilities in the form of debt versus ownership equity. Use the tool opposite to help you evaluate alternatives.

The advantages and disadvantages of debt and equity funding should be considered in correlation with the strategic plan. Seek a balance of debt and equity and know when to acquire equity funding and when to acquire debt. This balance is reflected in the debt to equity ratio and will vary depending on your industry.

Companies generally start by acquiring funding from owners to demonstrate to lenders a commitment to the company and its strategy. As companies begin operations and begin to grow they typically seek debt financing. There are other sources of debt and equity such as venture capitalists, angel investors, and private equity firms. The following section will explain how funding decisions impact external organizational evaluation and how external creditors and investors will evaluate the company.

How will creditors look at my financial information?

The creditor will ask whether the company can repay its existing obligations plus the amount requested along with interest over the determined period. Potential creditors will pull various figures from your financial statements to answer the following:

- How well can the company pay its current liabilities?
- How effectively can the company sell inventory and collect receivables?
- Can the company pay its long-term debt?

To answer the first question, creditors will typically look at these three ratios: the current ratio, the quick ratio (also called acid-test ratio), and the creditor days payable.

1. *Current Ratio*: Lenders may look at a company that has $100,000 due for repayment next year and only has $50,000 in available cash and ask how the company will repay the $100,000? Lenders use a calculation called a current ratio to determine what current assets a company has available to cover current liabilities.

$$\text{Current Ratio} = \frac{\text{Current Assets}}{\text{Current Liabilities}}$$

The figures for the current ratio calculation are pulled from the balance sheet and notes to the financial statements covered in chapter fifteen.

The following discussion and examples are adapted from the Ford Motor Company SEC 2009 10K report displayed in the chapter fifteen of this book. Ford Motor Company did not choose to present its balance sheet in the classified format as previously discussed. A creditor however can classify some of the items as current or non-current, given the nature of the item. To get a full picture of these classifications, a creditor would need to read the notes of the financial statement to better understand the current portion of the amounts listed (especially the liabilities).

At first glance, a creditor would calculate the current assets, as illustrated from Ford's Balance Sheet at a balance of $133 million and current liabilities shown as $61 million (not including current portion of debt, deferred income taxes or liabilities of held-for-sale operations). According to the figures selected the current ratio is 2.17.

So what does this mean? The current ratio means that the company could pay its current liabilities 2.17 times with its current assets. Typically a current ratio over one is considered acceptable. A company should also consider the industry average current ratio as a benchmark. *Robert Morris Associates' Annual Statement Studies* is an excellent source for standard ratios for a variety of industries.

If the current ratio is too high, such as ten or more, it could indicate that the company is not effectively using its assets. Included in the current assets as shown in figure 15.5 is inventory. When considering the current ratio, many believe that inventory is not easily or readily convertible to cash (especially inventory that's unfinished such as work in process) and should not be considered in the current ratio because it is not readily available to repay current liabilities.

For example, if Ford Motor Company released in the news today that all Ford engines produced in the last year and a half were defective beyond repair then the inventory listed on Ford's balance sheet could not be sold. The value is not what has been listed on the balance sheet. Even if the value of inventory is stable, it still has to go through the sales cycle before it converts to cash. Therefore, when considering the current ratio the impact of inventory should be considered. To adjust for the impact of inventory, a second calculation can be used called the quick ratio or acid test ratio.

2. *Quick Ratio*: The current ratio measures the ability of a company to use current assets to cover current liabilities. The ratio assumes that all current assets can be converted to cash within the year or operating cycle. Two items included in current assets are not considered readily convertible to cash and are therefore removed from the current ratio to calculate the quick ratio. These items are inventory and pre-paid expenses. Inventory is taken out as described above and pre-paid expenses are taken out because they expire and would not result in conversion to cash. The quick ratio is the current assets less inventory and pre-paid expenses divided by the current liabilities.

$$\text{Quick Ratio} = \frac{\text{Current Assets} - \text{Inventory} - \text{Pre-Paid Expenses}}{\text{Current Liabilities}}$$

Continuing our example, according to Ford's Balance Sheet the current assets would be decreased by the inventory amount of $5.4 million. (Note: Ford did not show any pre-paid expenses to be deducted from current assets). The quick ratio, according to the figures presented on the face of the balance sheet is 2.08. The ratio indicates that Ford could pay its current liabilities approximately two times with its current assets that are available to convert to cash.

3. *Creditor Days Payable:* A creditor is interested in knowing the timeframe in which a company pays its short-term liabilities, generally suppliers. The calculation provides an estimated number of days within which the company pays its bills for supplies and inventory. The number of creditor days is calculated as the account payable (bills) at end of the period divided by the sales of the period.

$$\text{Creditor Days} = \frac{\text{Unpaid Suppliers' Bills}}{\text{Sales}} \times 365 \text{ days}$$

The number of days a company takes to pay its bills can vary greatly depending on the industry and the size of the company. While creditors will consider this number, they may not rely heavily on it. They will compare a company's figure with other companies of like size in a similar industry. Generally terms for payment are thirty days. A business with a thirty-day payment average indicates they are able to pay their bills on time.

Large companies, such as Ford, generally have large amounts of cash flow and large suppliers. They will typically attempt to extend their payable period up to sixty days (called stretching the trade) with the intention of investing the cash in the interim and earning some interest before paying the bill. Ford Motor Company's days creditor paid is calculated as the payables of $14 billion, divided by $105 billion in automotive sales, and then multiplied by 365 days. Ford Motor Company is estimated to pay its trade creditors in approximately fifty days as calculated using the formula.

What are appropriate performance measures for selling inventory and collecting receivables?

The current and quick ratios tell creditors whether the company could convert its current assets to cash in order to cover the current liabilities if the company had to pay the liability today. For a company to continue liquidating its assets to cover liabilities is unrealistic. Instead, sales of inventory or services generate income. The income would produce additional cash, and receivables that are available to convert to cash, to cover current liabilities instead of liquidating current assets.

Creditors have to consider not only how well a company can pay current liabilities but also how well the company can sell inventory and collect receivables. This section will focus on manufacturing companies and the sale of inventory rather than service companies. In order to evaluate how well a company sells inventory and collects receivables, a creditor would calculate the inventory turnover, accounts receivable turnover and days' sales in receivables.

1. *Inventory turnover*: A creditor can use figures from the Balance Sheet and the Statement of Income to determine the number of times during an operating cycle a company can sell its average level of inventory. To calculate the inventory turnover, calculate the average inventory level by adding the beginning (i.e. previous year's ending) and ending inventory balances together and dividing by two. After the average inventory is calculated the Cost of Goods Sold from the income statement is divided by the average inventory.

$$\text{Inventory Turnover} = \frac{\text{Cost of Goods Sold}}{\text{Average Inventory}}$$

$$\text{Average Inventory} = \frac{\text{Beginning Inventory} + \text{Ending Inventory}}{2}$$

According to the Ford Motor Company Statement of Income and Balance Sheet, inventory is turned over approximately sixteen times during the year. As with the other ratios, creditors would compare this figure with other companies in the automotive industry. Inventory turnover figures are generally evaluated as "bigger is better," indicating the product is in demand and the company is able to produce and deliver the product to the customer multiple times within the operating cycle.

2. *Accounts receivable turnover*: Converting receivables to cash is essential for the periodic repayments of principal and interest that creditors require. Understanding the cash cycle of the company determines how fast the company collects cash from its credit customers related to the repayment of current and future loans. To calculate accounts receivable turnover, the creditor must determine the net credit sales and the average net accounts receivable. The net credit sales may be shown on the face of the Income Statement or in a note to the financial statements. The average net accounts receivable is calculated by adding the ending net accounts receivable of the previous year (i.e. current-year-beginning) and the current year ending net accounts receivable and dividing by two.

$$\text{Accounts Receivable Turnover} = \frac{\text{Net Credit Sales}}{\text{Average Net Accounts Receivable}}$$

$$\text{Average Accounts Receivable} = \frac{\text{Beginning Accounts Rec.} + \text{Ending Accounts Rec.}}{2}$$

The turnover for accounts receivables indicates the number of times in the operating cycle the company collects its average outstanding accounts. The higher the ratio, the more times the average level of receivables is converted to cash. The faster a company collects its receivables, the better. A turnover ratio that is too high may indicate that the credit policies of the company are too strict which may be leading to missed sales opportunities.

3. *Days' Sales in Receivables*: As part of understanding the cash cycle, creditors also want to know how many days it takes for the company to collect its receivables. The days' sales in receivables calculation provides creditors with the average number of days the company takes to collect cash from a credit sale. The calculation is determined by calculating the average dollar value of one day of sales, and then calculating the average days' sales in accounts receivable.

The general rule for credit terms is thirty days as discussed in the Creditor Days Payable

Step 1

$$\text{One Day's Sales} = \frac{\text{Net Sales}}{365 \text{ days}}$$

Step 2

$$\text{Days' Sales in Average Accounts Receivable} = \frac{(\text{Beginning Accounts Receivable} + \text{Ending Accounts Receivable}/2)}{\text{One Day's Sales}}$$

section. Given the general rule of thirty days, companies should collect receivables within a close range of thirty days. The number of days may vary depending upon the industry. The days' sales in receivables figure must be compared with the industry standard.

Creditors will also consider the difference between the creditor days payable and the days' sales in receivables. For example, if a company pays creditors in approximately thirty days and collects receivables within forty days, it might indicate that the company could incur a cash flow shortfall because the company would be paying money out before it was able to collect for that period. Other factors a creditor would consider is whether the company has a high percentage of cash sales or if the company has an investment with available cash to prevent a cash flow shortage.

What do I need to know about long-term debt?

Before lending a company money to expand, a creditor will not only look at the company's ability to repay current liabilities, sell inventory and collect receivables, but also at the amount of long-term debt the company is obligated to pay. The creditor will consider the impact of that debt on the cash flow and income of the company. The accounting numbers tell creditors about a company's ability to pay long-term debt via the debt ratio and the times-interest earned ratio.

1. *Debt Ratio:* A creditor evaluating a company to lend funds will look at the financial numbers to determine if the company already has large debts to repay or if owners without an obligation to repay with interest finance the company. The debt ratio tells the creditor the proportion of assets financed by debt. The creditor will calculate the debt ratio using the total assets and total liabilities from the balance sheet.

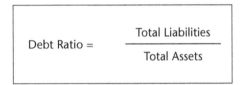

$$\text{Debt Ratio} = \frac{\text{Total Liabilities}}{\text{Total Assets}}$$

When comparing two comparable companies each requesting funding, the creditor will likely go with the company with the lower debt ratio. All else being equal, the company with a lower debt ratio is less risky than the company with a debt level in close proportion to its assets. Companies with a balanced debt ratio are more favorable because the portion funded by equity is not required to be repaid. Also, the portion funded by equity lacks preference of claim to the assets in the case of default compared to the creditors' claim to the assets. Just as with other ratio formulas and analysis discussed in this chapter, the average debt ratio for the industry should be considered in the creditor's evaluation.

2. *Times-Interest Earned:* A unique characteristic of creditors, compared to owners, is the requirement to pay interest on funds borrowed. Often creditors require periodic payment of interest and/or principal during the term of the loan. Before a new creditor will lend funds, they will evaluate whether the company can pay the amount of existing interest required by the current lender in addition to the interest payments the new creditor will require. The times-interest earned calculation determines the ease or lack thereof that a company has in paying interest. The times-interest earned ratio is calculated using the income from operations and interest expense from the income statement.

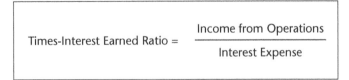

$$\text{Times-Interest Earned Ratio} = \frac{\text{Income from Operations}}{\text{Interest Expense}}$$

A high interest-earned figure tells the creditor that the burden of interest is not an issue for the company and revenue from operations more than covers the interest expense incurred. On the other hand, a low interest-earned figure would tell the creditor that the company operations do not generate enough income to handle or cover additional interest and the risk of default is higher. The evaluation of a high or low times-interest earned ratio would be based on a comparison to the industry average.

How will investors look at financial information?

While creditors earn guaranteed interest, investors purchase ownership and expect to share in earnings. When a company gets started, the original owners are investing their money with the expectation that the company will earn money. The owners will be entitled to a portion of those earnings either by the value of their share increasing or by receiving earnings in the form of distributions called dividends. Owners of stock also would hope that their stock would be valued by the market at more than the book value of the shares so that another potential investor would be willing to pay a premium to buy their shares.

These two expectations for investments shape how investors evaluate companies. A potential investor/owner looks to the financial information and market statistics (if available) to ask, "If I invest my money, will the company generate earnings that I can claim or will the value of my investment grow?" To answer these questions, a potential investor will pull various figures from a company's financial statements and market statistics to answer:

1. How profitable is the company?
2. How well is the company stock performing?

An investor provides funds for a company with the hope of claiming a portion of the earnings, which are hopefully higher than the guaranteed interest paid to creditors. The risk for investors is much higher, but their expected return is also higher. An investor evaluates the profitability of the company by determining the rate of return on net sales, the rate of return on total assets, the rate of return on common stockholders' equity, and the earnings per share of common stock.

1. *Rate of Return on Net Sales:* The investor wants to know how much of the company sales will be available to increase retained earnings and become part of the owners' claim to the assets. The rate of return on net sales calculates the rate at which sales dollars are increasing owners' claims. The rate of return on net sales is calculated from the Income Statement by dividing the net income by the net sales.

$$\text{Rate of Return on Net Sales} = \frac{\text{Net Income}}{\text{Net Sales}}$$

The rate of return on net sales is often called return on sales because it indicates the dollar value returned to the owner (via retained earnings) on each dollar of sales. For example, Ford Motor Company had net income of $2.7 billion and net sales revenue of $106 billion, so the return on sales is 0.026 indicating that for every $1 of sales the owners' claim is increased by approximately $0.03. An investor would compare this return with other returns of similar companies as well as other potential investments in different industries.

1. *Rate of Return on Total Assets:* An investor provides additional economic resources (e.g. assets) when they choose to purchase shares of ownership from the company. Therefore, before providing additional resources the investor will determine how well the company is doing with its current resources by calculating the return on total assets. The return on total assets measures the company's ability to use available economic resources to earn a profit. Return on total assets is calculated as the net income from the Income Statement, divided by the average total assets from the Balance Sheet.

$$\text{Return on Total Assets} = \frac{\text{Net Income}}{\text{Average Total Assets}}$$

$$\text{Average Total Assets} = \frac{\text{Beginning Total Assets} + \text{Ending Total Assets}}{2}$$

The return on assets, as calculated above, indicates the return to the owners from use of the available assets. The rate of return indicates the dollar value of return (increase in owners' claim) for each dollar of assets. If a company has a high return on assets, the company is effective in using the assets to earn a profit and an investor would be wise to consider or retain the investment. However, if the company has a low return on total assets as compared to the industry, the company is not effectively using the available assets. The investor is likely to question whether additional resources they might provide would aid the company in earning a profit.

2. *Rate of Return on Common Stockholders' Equity:* Return on common stockholders' equity is a measure of profitability related to the amount invested by the common stockholders. Investors want to know how well the company has performed with the resources provided by the common stockholders. If companies have a preferred stock class, common stockholders are not entitled to all the earnings because preferred stockholders are paid dividends from the net income first. Therefore, the return on common stockholders' equity is calculated as the amount available to common stockholders' (net income less preferred dividends) divided by the average common stockholders' equity (from the Balance Sheet). The preferred dividend declaration will be included in the notes to the financial statements.

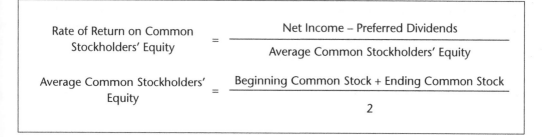

The return on common stockholders' equity determines the amount of increase to the common stockholders' claim for each dollar of sales. If the return on assets is lower than the return on common stockholders' equity, the company is considered to be leveraged by debt. The debt ratio, as discussed earlier, directly relates to the difference between return on assets and return on common stockholders' equity. A company that has more equity than debt supporting its assets means that a larger percentage of income will be returned to the owner because less is needed to pay debt. An investor may consider the debt ratio with an opposite perspective than a creditor, but will also consider the times interest earned calculation to determine the impact on income and the owners' claim.

3. *Earnings per Share of Common Stock:* Earnings per Share of Common Stock, also called earnings per share or EPS, is the most widely reviewed figure by investors. This figure is so important to investors that FASB required the EPS calculation be included on the face of the Income Statement, as shown in Figure 17.3 from a portion of Ford

NET INCOME/(LOSS) ATTRIBUTABLE TO FORD MOTOR COMPANY	2009	2008	2007
Income/(Loss) from continuing operations	$2,712	$(14,775)	$(2,836)
Income/(Loss) from discontinued operations (Note 24)	5	9	41
Net income/(loss)	$2,717	$(14,766)	$(2,795)
Average number of shares of Common and Class B Stock outstanding	2,992	2,273	1,979
AMOUNTS PER SHARE ATTRIBUTABLE TO FORD MOTOR COMPANY **COMMON AND CLASS B STOCK (Note 25)**			
Basic income/(loss)			
Income/(Loss) from continuing operations	$ 0.91	$ (6 . 50)	$(1 . 43)
Income/(Loss) from discontinued operations	—	—	0.02
Net income/(loss) [EPS]	$ 0.91	$ (6 . 50)	$(1 . 41)
Diluted income/(loss)			
Income/(Loss) from continuing operations	$ 0.86	$ (6 . 50)	$(1 . 43)
Income/(Loss) from discontinued operations	—	—	0.02
Net income/(loss) [Diluted EPS]	$ 0.86	$ (6 . 50)	$(1 . 41)

Figure 17.3 Ford Motor Company Earnings Per Share Calculation from Income Statement

Adapted from Ford Motor Company SEC 10K for YE 2009

Motor Company's Income Statement for year ended 2009. The EPS is calculated as the income available to common stockholders, divided by the number of common stock shares outstanding. To determine the income available to common stockholders subtract the preferred dividends from the net income. To determine the number of common stock shares outstanding, subtract any treasury stock shares, stock bought back by the company with the aim of reducing the number of shares outstanding, from the number of shares outstanding.

According to Figure 17.3, Ford Motor Company stockholders earned $0.91 for every share owned. An investor would evaluate this figure based on the industry standard and look favorably on Ford stock if the EPS is higher than the industry. As an owner of the company, the investor is seeking the highest return per share owned. The diluted calculation indicates to potential investors that the company has issued some classes of stock that have the ability to be converted into common stock. If those shares are converted, the earnings are divided among the current common shares plus the converted shares. When dividing earnings over more shares the earnings are diluted (i.e. decreased per share).

$$\text{Earning Per Share} = \frac{\text{Net Income} - \text{Preferred Dividends}}{\text{Number of Common Shares Outstanding}}$$

What does stock performance tell me about my organization?

Every manager should be aware of stock price and how the performance of their area affects performance of the whole. Investors choose to invest in a company because they expect the value of their stock to increase and that they will have the ability to sell the share at a higher price than they paid. The measures an investor would use to evaluate the value and performance of company shares are price per earnings, dividend yield and book value per share of common stock.

1. *Price per Earnings:* The Price per Earnings ratio measure is limited to stock that is purchased and sold on a secondary public market such as the New York Stock Exchange (NYSE). Stock not offered to the public does not have an available market to determine current value or price. For example, Ford Motor Company is a public company, so a potential investor could find the price per share at any given point in time online. The price per earnings calculation measures the amount the market is willing to pay for $1 of company earnings per share. The price per earnings is calculated as the market price per share of common stock divided by the earnings per share.

$$\text{Price per Earnings} = \frac{\text{Market Price per Share}}{\text{Earnings per Share}}$$

The price per earnings per share indicates to investors the premium or discount the market is willing to currently pay for the company stock. For example, if Ford Motor Company stock is priced at $18 per share and the earnings per share is $0.91 then the market is willing to pay 19.78 times more than the earnings received per share of stock or approximately $20 for every dollar of earnings per share. The market's willingness to pay a premium for earnings is commonly impacted by the company's longevity, market share, expectations of future growth, their exclusive rights to supreme product or service or stock performance.

2. *Dividend Yield:* Some risk-averse investors willing to accept lower return for less risk will seek companies that offer regular dividends. Investors seeking dividends and regular return of earnings will pay close attention to the dividend yield calculation. These investors are seeking to earn money via dividends on a regular basis instead of waiting for an increase in market price to sell the share for a higher return. The dividend yield tells the investor the portion of the stock market price that is annually returned in dividends. This calculation is particularly important to preferred stock holders who invest for the purpose of receiving dividend income. The dividend yield is calculated as the dividend per share of common stock, divided by the market price per share of common stock. That dividend yield is limited by the availability of the market price per share.

$$\text{Dividend Yield} \quad = \quad \frac{\text{Dividend per share of Common Stock}}{\text{Market Price per share of Common Stock}}$$

Dividend yield tells investors that for every $1 paid to purchase stock they can expect the dividend yield to be the amount returned for the $1 invested. For example, if a company's market price per share is $18 and the dividend per share of common stock is $1.20, $0.06 will be returned for every $1 spent to purchase the share. This measure provides investors with a means to determine if the investment will potentially provide earnings greater than other investments. The example provided indicates a 6% rate of return that an investor would compare to investments other than company ownership such as bank savings accounts, IRAs, bonds, etc.

3. *Book Value per Share of Common Stock:* The book value per share of common stock is the measure of the accounting dollar amount of the owners' claim to the company's total assets per share of common stock. This value represents the combination of resources provided by the owners plus the accumulated earnings not yet distributed to the owners. The book value per share of common stock is calculated as value of common stock on the Balance Sheet, total stockholders equity less preferred equity, divided among the number of common shares outstanding.

$$\text{Book Value Per Share of Common Stock} = \frac{\text{Total Stockholder's Equity} - \text{Preferred equity}}{\text{Number of Common Shares Outstanding}}$$

According to some analysts, the book value is not a good indication of value because it has no correlation with what the market is willing to pay. For example, Ford Motor Company has an equity deficit of $6.5 billion and 2.9 billion shares outstanding, indicating that the book value of the stock at the end of 2009 was negative $2.18, and the price per share was approximately $11, which does not reflect the equity deficit of the company. Other analysts say that when relating the book value per share to the market price, the closer the relationship or correlation (lower ratio) the more attractive the stock is, since the market perception is closer to reality and less risk exists of a stock plummet.

As mentioned at the beginning of this chapter, MSN Money ranked Ford as one of the ten most likely companies to go bankrupt in 2010. Ford Motor Company managed to survive 2010 without bankruptcy or government bailout, but the volatile stock price caused investors to lose money if they chose to follow the market and sell at low prices such as the $1.01 low on November 17, 2008. A year later on December 28, 2009, the stock price hit $9.89 as the daily low. In 2010, the stock price remained steady in the teens, and closely reflects the book value of the common shares.

Analysts who believe book value per share should be considered for a stock purchase decision might review the Ford stock scenario and suggest that a stock with a low ratio of market price to book value is more attractive and likely a more stable investment decision. For example, a company whose stock price is $18 and book value per share is $16 has a 1.125 ratio of price to book value. This is more attractive than the $11 to negative $2.18 ratio of negative 5.045 of Ford Motor Company because the stock is less likely to follow market supply and demand since the market price is substantiated by the book value.

How can our internal decisions impact the external view and evaluation of the company?

Management decisions often have unintended consequences. First, let's look at the impact of a special order on market perception. Assume Ford Motor Company decided to accept a large special order at the end of the year by selling excess inventory for a lower than normal price. The increased sales would be an obvious advantage but it would also have a positive impact on the inventory turnover ratio, days' sales, rate of return ratios, current ratio and long-term debt ratio. These ratios are positively impacted because the decrease in inventory cost and lower ending inventory causes a higher inventory turnover ratio. The excess income over the cost of the inventory positively impacts sales, which in turn increases ratios related to assets and sales. So based on these measures, this sale seems like a good idea. This is an example of how a company can take a flexible approach to inventory.

You also make a decision to purchase equipment with a long-term liability. This decision will cause an increase in debt but will not impact the long-term debt ratio because the assets were increased by the cost of the asset and the liability was also increased by the cost, thus a 1:1 ratio exists. The impact or change to this ratio occurs as the company earns income. Assets increase without the addition of liabilities or the value of the assets are written off as they are used through expense of depreciation, thus decreasing assets possibly faster than paying off the liability.

A third management decision with a potential unintended consequence is the issuance of stock. Issuing more stock divides the earnings among more owners, thus decreasing the earnings per share and return on stockholders' equity. However, the issuance of additional stock does improve the long-term debt ratio as assets are increased by the capital provided by owners. The percentage of assets funded by liabilities is reduced.

Lastly, think about the purchase of inventory. The purchase of inventory generally increases assets and current liabilities (accounts payable). The key ratios impacted by this type of transaction are the quick ratio and inventory turnover. The increased inventory balance causes an increased liability but is excluded as a current asset because of the assumption that inventory is not as readily convertible to cash to cover liabilities. The inventory turnover rate will likely decrease due to the increased ending inventory balance, which will increase average inventory balance compared to the cost of goods sold.

As you make daily decisions in your company, keep in mind the impact on your stakeholders. Use the ratios covered in this chapter to see the impact. Ultimately evaluation will occur from internal and external stakeholders. Keeping the methods of evaluation aligned with key strategic goals will ensure organizational success from all perspectives. Understanding how numbers talk will help you discuss your management goals with accountants, legal counsel and upper-level management.

Additional Resources

For additional information, you can research common topics such as management accounting, management evaluation methods and organizational performance. A governing body on managerial accounting is the Institute of Management Accounting and additional information can be found on their website and in their publications.

For industry ratios, Robert Morris Associates Annual Statement Studies or Dun and Bradstreet are good sources of information.

References

Business Essential Book. (2009). London, UK: A & C Black Publishers, Ltd.

Holahan, C. (2009). Ten Companies that may go Bankrupt this year. Retrieved 2/10/10 from http://articles.moneycentral.msn.com/Investing/Extra/10-companies-that-may-go-bankrupt-this-year.aspx. 4.15.2009.

Horngren, C., Harrison, W., and Oliver, M. (2009). *Financial & Managerial Accounting*. Upper Saddle River, NJ: Prentice Hall.

Niven, Paul. (2002). *Balanced Scorecard Step by Step: Maximizing Performance and Maintaining Results*. New York, NY: John Wiley & Sons, Inc.

Scott DeCarlo. Forbes. http://www.forbes.com/2010/04/21/global-2000-leading-world-business-global-2000-10_land.html?boxes=listschannelinsidelists. 4.21.2010. Retrieved 12/10/10.

Securities and Exchange Commission, (2010). *Ford Motor Company 2009 10K*.

18 *Government and Legal Issues*

TERESA ISAAC and BOBBY RICKS

Business is affected by government in various ways. Governmental legislation dictates how businesses operate. Governmental agencies regulate business by promulgating and enforcing regulation. Even a lawsuit still has governmental influence where courts interpret laws and rules and court decisions are binding on future legal proceedings. It is important for businesses to know how government works as well as knowing the laws and regulations businesses must follow.

This chapter will outline how government, courts and regulatory concerns affect business. This work covers key areas affecting mid-level managers. Knowledge of legal issues and court processes will help you understand why certain procedures are, and must be, followed in the work place. This chapter will not make you a lawyer, nor will it replace your legal counsel. Know your company policy regarding contacting legal counsel.

What's the role of government as it relates to my business?

Government seeks to partner with private business to ensure that goods and services are provided in a fair and safe manner. The ultimate goal is to allow all citizens equal opportunity for economic success. To assist, the government at the local, state and federal level regulates business enterprise. The first section of this chapter will help you stay informed about government regulation, explain which regulations affect your operation, show you how to challenge unfair regulation and assist you with educating government officials on how to improve regulation. Remember, where compliance with government regulation is concerned, you may think you don't have the time to do it right, but you may have to find the time to do it over.

How do I stay informed about government regulation?

Government regulation of business protects the health and safety of our citizens, enforces contractual obligations in a fair manner, eliminates discrimination and protects the environment. Government at the local, state and federal level provides information to the public about regulations, actively seeks input from the public about regulations and is accountable to the public for fair and impartial enforcement of those regulations.

All government agencies are required to have open meetings and to make their records available to the public through open records laws. You may attend these meetings in person, watch them on government websites with live streaming of the meetings, or read about them in the business media. This is one way to keep informed about new government regulations that may affect your business. In the United States, the Federal Register contains proposed new regulations and gives the public the opportunity to comment on the rules. State legislatures often broadcast their committee meetings on educational television and allow the public to testify at those meetings. Many local governments also televise their committee meetings and allow the public to comment on new regulations.

The Internet is another valuable tool in keeping informed about government regulation. You can locate administrative regulations, statutes and ordinances on government websites. You can also read about new government regulation in business media such as the *Wall Street Journal*, *Businessweek*, *Fortune* and *Fast Company*. Most trade associations and professional associations have journals and these publications are a wealth of information on government regulation. Your local, state and national Chamber of Commerce also has information on government regulation of business.

Which regulations affect my operation?

It may seem overwhelming at first, but you can make a checklist of local, state and federal regulations that affect your business. You are responsible for complying with the letter of the law. Each of these regulations was enacted to create a safe and fair business environment. Local government will conduct inspections before a business opens and some of these inspections may be performed by the fire department, the health department, or the building inspector. Local government will also issue a business license to operate a business within its jurisdiction. Local government has rules regarding where different types of businesses can locate and the types of signs that can be displayed at the business location.

Local government charters usually give the government the responsibility over public safety, health and welfare, public transportation, planning and zoning, streets, public housing, urban development, building codes, regulation of occupations and trades and other public works. The local building inspection office issues building permits that are required before a structure is built, moved, added to or structurally altered. They also issue demolition permits that are required before a structure is torn down. In some communities, construction-related contractors are required to register their business with the local building inspection office.

Another arm of local government is the code enforcement office. It is responsible for inspecting buildings and parking structures to see if they meet safety standards. The local environmental management office receives mandatory reports from all local businesses that transport hazardous materials. The local economic development office helps business owners find locations for their businesses and expedites any permits that may be needed. The local economic development office also helps meet workforce development needs.

The local government engineering office reviews plans to tap into existing sewer lines and issues the necessary permits. The local fire department will make an on-site visit to your business to ensure compliance with fire safety requirements of the local building code. The local planning and zoning office can advise you on local zoning regulations. They can also advise you on any procedures for granting variances and the conditions which must be met.

Local government assists businesses through the local police department which can help you with criminal history checks on employees and can help train your employees on crime prevention. Banks, gas stations, apartment complexes and fast food restaurants traditionally work closely with police on crime prevention programs. Some local police departments require you to apply for a burglar alarm permit if your business uses an alarm system.

The local purchasing department will provide you with information on bidding on government contracts and show you how to register. The local Human Rights Commission enforces local laws against employment discrimination and they have many brochures that explain the rights of employers and employees. These are just some of the local agencies to contact when making your checklist of local government regulation that could affect your operation.

At the state level of government, you will find similar agencies to those on the local level. You will also find specific statutes and administrative regulations that govern certain professions and occupations. As you make your checklist of state regulations that may affect your operation, you can review the index to your state statutes and administrative regulations for your specific business. Examples of occupations that are often regulated at the state level include doctors, chiropractors, dentists, nurses, pharmacists, funeral directors, barbers, plumbers, engineers, architects, realtors, accountants and social workers. State government also licenses and regulates those in the transportation industry and may set the rates for utility companies, which supply gas, water and electricity.

At the federal level, regulation of business tries to strike a balance between letting the free market system operate without restraint and ensuring environmental protection, consumer product safety and appropriate business oversight. Each of the federal agencies and commissions that regulate business has websites that give detailed information on how they may affect your operation. Examples of agencies at the federal level include the Environmental Protection Agency, the Equal Employment Opportunity Commission, the Federal Communication Commission, the Federal Trade Commission, the Food and Drug Administration, the National Labor Relations Board, the Occupational Safety and Health Administration, the National Transportation Safety Board, the Department of Housing and Urban Development and the Department of Transportation.

The Environmental Protection Agency (EPA), www.epa.gov, issues permits for the treatment, storage and disposal of hazardous waste. It sets limits on air pollutants from power plants, factories and chemical plants. The EPA administers laws to protect the environment and to ensure that we have clean air and water. The Toxic Substance Control Act of 1976 requires that businesses report to the EPA information on chemicals that present a substantial risk of injury to humans or the environment.

The Equal Employment Opportunity Commission, www.eeoc.gov, was established in 1965 and it is responsible for enforcing federal laws that prohibit employment discrimination. It also protects employees from retaliation once they have filed an employment discrimination complaint. The Federal Communications Commission, www.fcc.gov, oversees all radio, television, and cable communication. The Federal Trade Commission (FTC), www.ftc.gov, protects the public from false and deceptive advertising, regulates packaging and labeling of products, prohibits credit discrimination and prevents identity theft. When a company uses deceptive advertising, the FTC can require a corrective advertisement and payment of damages to consumers.

The Food and Drug Administration, www.fda.gov, requires pre-market testing of new drugs, conducts recalls of food and drugs which are hazardous to the public, and regulates the quality and safety of food. The National Labor Relations Board, www.nlrb.gov, hears cases of unfair labor practices.

The Occupational Safety and Health Administration (OSHA), www.osha.gov, ensures that workers have a safe and healthy workplace. Employers are encouraged to reduce hazards in the workplace by improving safety programs. OSHA develops and enforces mandatory job safety and health standards. OSHA can conduct workplace inspections. Employers of eleven or more staff are required to keep records of on-the-job accidents and illnesses. Employees can request an OSHA inspection.

The National Transportation Safety Board (NTSB), www.ntsb.gov, investigates transportation accidents and makes safety recommendations. The NTSB has no authority to put the recommendations into action. The Department of Housing and Urban Development (HUD), www.hud.gov, enforces the federal fair housing laws. This prevents landlords, realtors, mortgage companies, insurance companies, banks and apartment complexes from discrimination in housing-related services on the basis of race, gender, family status, religion, national origin and disability. HUD uses local fair housing offices to assist in both education and enforcement.

The Department of Transportation carries out the Interstate Commerce Act to establish safety standards for all commercial motor carriers in interstate commerce. Through the National Highway Traffic Safety Administration, it sets gas tank safety and rollover standards.

How do I challenge an unfair regulation?

While most government actions are just and fair, there will be situations where government treats its citizens unfairly. When you want to challenge a regulation, you look first to the authority of the government who made the law or rule. If there was not an appropriate delegation of power or if the authority was exceeded, you can challenge the regulation. If the rule was applied to your business in an arbitrary and capricious manner, you can also challenge the regulation. You must first exhaust your administrative remedies at the agency level with an internal appeal and then you may take your case to court.

Government agencies have a duty to deal in good faith with those they regulate and to operate on a fair and objective basis. "The goal of the administrative process must be to insure uniformity of treatment by administrative agencies to all similarly situated. Without the application of uniform rules, uniformity of treatment is difficult to achieve." Pearl vs. Marshall, 491 S.W.2d 837 (1973). Likewise the courts in Butler vs. Cerebral Palsy, 352 S.W.2d 203 (1961) and Commonwealth vs. Frost, 172 S.W.2d 905 (1943) have held that above all, administrative officers must formulate and establish reasonable and uniform regulations and apply them fairly and honestly. Further, the court in American Beauty Homes vs. Louisville, 379 S.W.2d 450 (1964) held that "no Board or officer vested with governmental authority may exercise it arbitrarily."

How do I educate government officials on ways to improve regulation?

Most government officials enact regulations for a specific purpose to try to help the general public in some way without harming the private business. If you can show the government official that the harm to your business outweighs the benefit to the public, then you may be granted some relief. If you can show the government official that the regulation does not have the intended result of helping the general public, you may be granted some relief.

When you open your business and when you celebrate awards or milestones, you should invite government officials to share in your celebrations. This is a good opportunity to take them on a tour of your business and explain your economic impact on the community. It lets the government official see your employees and learn about your business needs first hand. No government official wants to put people out of business by overregulation.

When you participate with other business owners in a meeting with government officials to discuss regulations and changes to them, make sure you have solid evidence for your claims. Be well informed before the meeting and be able to show an alternative solution to the problem the regulation was attempting to solve.

TIPS FOR RESOLVING REGULATORY ISSUES:
1. Define the problem the regulation causes your business.
2. Collect facts to demonstrate this to the elected official.
3. Generate alternative options.
4. Evaluate alternative options with the staff of the elected official.
5. Be sure to consider how many people will be affected by the old and new regulation.

Government and business are true partners in the economic success of a community. Government educates business and business educates government. While rules and regulations must be strictly complied with, there is ample opportunity for the voice of business to be heard in creating and changing business regulations. Government has the duty to enact the regulations in good faith and to apply them fairly and objectively. In this way, we are all free to enjoy life, liberty and the pursuit of happiness.

TIPS FOR MAINTAINING GOOD GOVERNMENT RELATIONS:
1. Invite government officials to share in your business celebrations.
2. Explain to the government official your economic impact on the community.
3. Use facts to support your claims when you meet with a government official.
4. Don't hide pertinent facts.

With an understanding of how government operates, and how you, as a business person, can influence the laws and regulations mandated by government organizations, we move to legal issues that occur in everyday business practices that may affect the business manager.

Organized society favors consistent and efficient practices. Some disagreements on how to conduct business are settled by governments in enacting legislation for equitable business transactions and a logical pattern of sound business practices.

What are the different types of business organizations?

Businesses are run from the simple "mom and pop" country store to conglomerates. States regulate how businesses operate to protect against inequities or illegal activities. Considering what type of business to operate helps owners decide what is best for their operations. The type of business may affect whether or not you wish to do business with that entity.

When deciding what kind of business entity to choose, you need to consider the following issues:

- Who has control of the business?
- Who owns the business?
- Who is liable if things go wrong?
- How will income be taxed?
- Who decides the vision, mission, and values of the business?
- Is the business going to be local, national, or international?
- Are the businesses' transactions enforceable?

SOLE PROPRIETORSHIPS

A sole proprietorship is the easiest form of business organization. At a minimum, even a family business should register in the city or county where they do business, which is fairly easy and inexpensive. States may also require a sole proprietor to register with the Secretary of State in order to obtain a business identification (ID) number and tax ID for a business license.

The business name is registered so people are not confused by businesses with multiple names. Also, people with unscrupulous motives cannot hide from customers or clients.

Sole proprietorships are small business entities where the owner makes all of the decisions. Generally, the owner provides start-up capital for the business. If outside financing is required, the sole proprietor borrows personally and injects that money into the business. Any profit from the business is taxed as personal income. Any liability for a business transaction is the personal liability of the sole proprietor.

GENERAL AND LIMITED PARTNERSHIPS

Other business entities begin by filing papers with the Secretary of State in the state where they are domiciled and state and federal revenue departments for income tax purposes. A registered agent is listed for the purpose of receiving legal notice for the business. If the business is carried out in more than one state, a business may also be required to register with the Secretary of State in each state where business will be conducted.

A general partnership extends the idea of a sole proprietorship to several partners who own the business and share in the decision making. The partners may provide additional funding, or may participate in business operations. Like a sole proprietorship, profits or losses from the partnership are taxed as personal income or losses divided among the partners based on their ownership percentages. Partners would be liable for business transactions jointly and severally. This means that a lawsuit against the business would be brought against the whole partnership with each partner jointly liable for the actions of all others and severally liable for the damages even if other partners cannot pay.

Other business entities, like the limited partnership, can reduce the liability of partners. A limited partnership is a business managed by general partners who make the decisions for the business. Limited partners provide capital for the business though they have no ability to make business decisions and they are not involved in day-to-day operations. Their liability is limited to their investment in the partnership. General partners would continue to be jointly and severally liable for partnership transactions. Profits or losses are taxed as personal income and are distributed based on percentage ownership.

CORPORATIONS

Corporations are more complex than partnerships, but enjoy broader limits on liability. The C-Corp type is controlled by officers and directors elected by shareholders who can participate in decision making through annual meetings. Corporate capital is raised by the sale of stock. C-Corps can be publically traded or privately held. Liability is limited to a person's investment.

A consideration of a C-Corp is double taxation. The corporation is taxed on income before profits are distributed to shareholders, who then pay tax on their profits. While this sounds like a bad idea, there can be some benefit to this system depending on the tax-bracket a person's income places them. Most major corporations are C-Corps as are many smaller businesses.

S-Corporations are corporations that in some ways are treated like a partnership, except there is generally no personal liability for business debts. S-Corp type income is taxed as personal income to the owners just like a partnership. Generally speaking, S-Corps are usually smaller companies. Limited Liability Companies, or LLCs, are like an S-Corp in that both protect your personal assets from business liability and both flow to your personal taxes. There are some noteworthy differences though:

- S-Corps can go public while LLCs cannot.
- LLCs can be owned by other companies (C-Corporations for example), while S-Corps cannot.
- Income, share distribution and ownership rules vary from S-Corps to LLCs.

A tax accountant can help you with financial decision making in determining which organization to choose. Regardless of the type chosen, disagreements between businesses and disagreements between businesses and the government often end up in court.

I have been served with a summons that my company is being sued. What do I do?

If you have been served with papers, it is likely you are being sued for a tort or breach of contract. A tort is civil, or a private wrong against the person or property of another. A breach of contract alleges that you and the plaintiff had an agreement and you did not fulfill your end of the bargain.

When you are served with notice of a lawsuit, you have a limited number of days in which to respond, typically twenty to thirty days. Immediately notify your organization's attorney and provide them with the documents served. If your company does not have in-house counsel or a law firm on retainer, start looking for an attorney who is familiar with that type of action. An attorney specializing in business and contract law would be preferred for a suit alleging breach of contract, while a product liability suit would use a lawyer with different specialties. Ask business associates who they know and who they would recommend you contact.

Notify your insurance company. They may have law firms that they recommend for the type of action filed against you. The insurance company may also be involved in settlement procedures. Lawsuits are expensive. Attorney fees, downtime from productive work to attend hearings and trials, and just the hassle of a lawsuit, not to mention the uncertainty of a trial verdict are reasons you may consider settlement. Many suits are settled for less than the amount in the complaint, and your insurance company may be willing to pay part of the settlement.

If you do go to court, begin assembling materials that may affect the suit. Make sure documents and other items that may have evidentiary value, either for or against you, don't disappear. This includes information stored electronically. Destruction of evidence may violate criminal laws affecting obstruction of justice. This includes dealing with potential witnesses. Due to the sensitivity of court proceedings, personnel with knowledge important to the case should be directed to speak only with counsel regarding the matter. Direct all inquiries to legal counsel. While this segment is addressing civil matters, the same procedures would apply if your organization was under investigation for a possible crime.

Be open and honest with your attorney. The greatest privilege in our legal system is one that exists between the attorney and client. The privilege prevents them from being a witness against you. The attorney cannot be expected to do his or her best for you if they are not aware of all matters affecting the lawsuit.

How do you get sued?

The lawsuit begins when the plaintiff files a complaint with a court having jurisdiction over the matter. See Figure 18.1 on court systems. The complaint states what the defendants allegedly did wrong, and the damages that the plaintiff claims from the wrong (usually money).

The defendant is served with a copy of the complaint and is given an opportunity to answer. The defendant admits or denies the allegations in the complaint. The parties proceed with motions in which they request the court take action on the case. Fact-finding occurs through discovery. Interrogatories are questions presented for the opposing party to answer. A request for production is asking your adversary to produce documents. Depositions are when the parties are called and questioned under oath and recorded by a court reporter. Information from discovery is used to file motions and for settlement negotiations.

Many cases are negotiated and settled. Information gathered in discovery helps you see if you should settle the case and for what amount. Trials can be expensive and you risk being held liable. If settlement cannot be reached, a trial is held.

In the US, there are state and federal courts. State courts vary from state to state, but generally follow similar formats. There are trial courts where cases would be heard, and appellate courts that hear appeals from the trial courts.

Federal courts are similar. There are 94 federal judicial districts with at least one district in each state, and other states with multiple Districts. There are Courts in the District of Columbia, Puerto Rico, Virgin Islands, Guam, and the Northern Mariana Islands. U.S. District Courts have original (trial) jurisdiction in most cases.

There are 13 Federal Circuit Courts of Appeal (11 numbered geographical circuits, the D.C. Circuit, and the Federal Circuit). The U.S. Supreme Court is the highest Federal Court and has mostly appellate jurisdiction with original jurisdiction in limited cases.

Figure 18.1 US Court System Structure

What happens if we go to trial?

A trial begins with the seating of a jury. Potential jurors are called from a pool of candidates and seated in the jury box. *Voir dire*, meaning to tell the truth, is the process used by the judge and attorneys to qualify jurors. The judge will ask preliminary questions to determine if the prospect is minimally qualified, i.e., at least eighteen years old, a resident of the judicial district, not a convicted felon, etc.

Attorneys look for a potential bias that may prejudice a juror against their case. In some courts, the attorneys present their questions to the judge who will ask the questions. After the judge and attorneys have completed the voir dire, jurors will be selected to sit for the trial.

Jurors may be stricken from the pool *for cause*, meaning an obvious bias such as being related to a party in the lawsuit, or on a peremptory challenge, meaning striking a juror without having to give a reason. There are a limited number of peremptory challenges.

After the jury is selected, the plaintiff begins with an opening statement, telling the jury about the case and what he or she will prove. The defense usually follows with an opening statement, although they may wait until after the plaintiff's case is completed to present their statement.

Following opening statements, the plaintiff begins their case. The plaintiff must prove all facts alleged in the complaint with sufficient detail to persuade the jury. Witnesses are called and evidence is presented in the form of oral statements and physical objects and documents. After a witness testifies on *direct-examination*, the opposing party can *cross-examine* the testimony in an effort to clarify or discredit the testimony presented. The calling party can do a *re-direct* examination, but only on the points raised on cross-examination.

When the plaintiff completes their case, they rest. The defense usually moves to dismiss or asks for a directed verdict. In a directed verdict, the judge decides the case as opposed to letting it be decided by the jury. These motions are generally denied though they are important for the appeals process later. The defense proceeds with their witnesses and evidence in the same manner as the plaintiff's case, then rests. Closing statements are presented, then the judge instructs the jury on how they will decide the case. After the jury deliberates, they return with a verdict. Aside from appeals and other legal processes, the case is over.

The best defense to a suit is not to get sued at all. While that may be impossible, there are some steps you can take to minimize suits:

1. Deal with reputable businesses, and be reputable yourself. If you get stuck with a bad deal, consider it experience. Do what you said you would do, regardless.
2. Next, be clear and specific about your expectations of the other business. Put it in writing. Oral contracts are valid, but written contracts are hard to deny.
3. Keep your records. The US Internal Revenue Service can go back six years on tax audits. Hold documents that long, or longer. Some federal grants recommend recipients keep certain records forever.

I'm negotiating a contract for my company. Is the company responsible for my agreement?

Companies conduct business through their people. The owners/executives of a company are principals. Principals have the authority to bind the corporation in contracts and partnership agreements. Others may also bind the organization when conducting business affairs. These people work as agents for the organization. Agency is a legal concept that one person can act for another and bind that person to an agreement. According to Reuschlein in his 1979 work, agency can occur in and out of the organization. For example, an agent may be contracted to procure goods or services for the principal organization, and need not work for the organization.

Real estate agents, stock brokers, etc. can act for others in conducting business. Agency authority can be actual, as in the case where the principal sets the parameters of the agreement for the agent to act, or authority can be apparent or implied, where an assumption of authority is necessary to conduct the activities of the organization. Universal agents have the authority to bind the organization on any matter. This is usually reserved for the executives and principals. Special agents are limited in their duties and authority to bind the organization. General agents have an amount of authority between the two.

You don't need to be concerned as much with whether your authority is universal, general or special. Focus instead on the powers given to you for your job and those that normally occur with persons in the same or similar positions.

As first laid out in Hurst Home Insurance Company vs. Ledford, 268 S.W. 1090 (1925), a principal is bound by the acts of the agent within the apparent scope of authority if the person dealing with the agent is ignorant of the limitations of authority. Where one of two parties must suffer loss through the acts of an agent, the loss should fall upon the one who authorized the agent to act rather than the innocent third party. An exception would be

> A valid ratification requires a contract, the principal must be in existence at the time of the contract, the contract provisions have been performed, and the principal must have knowledge of the contract at the time of ratification. (Reuschlein, 1979)

when the agent is acting beyond the scope of his or her apparent authority. Actions taken outside that authority are said to be *ultra vires*. If the action is outside the authority of the special agent, but within the authority of the principals or the organizational, the agreement can be *ratified*, (i.e. the principal accepts the agreement although it was made without authority).

How do I write a valid contract?

Contracts are a legal promise. They are agreements or obligations where one party becomes bound to another party to pay a sum of money or to do or not do a specific act. Though normally thought of as a written document, contracts can be oral. Written or oral, a valid contract has three main parts:

1. An offer
2. Acceptance of the offer
3. Consideration in return for the offer.

For example, a valid contract is when a company offers to sell a printer for $200 and you agree to buy it at those terms. All parties must have the legal capacity to contract. Persons, governments, corporations and other legal business entities have the capacity to contract. A person under adult age would not have the ability to agree. This is why parents are called on to agree to a minor child joining a club or buying a car.

The contract must be clear so that all parties understand the agreement. Ambiguous terms are usually interpreted in favor of the other party. If your office cleaning service agrees to "clean offices," but does not specify the meaning of the term it's implied that they will perform the necessary and usual tasks of cleaning an office. It's ambiguous as to whether cleaning includes washing windows. Express contracts specifically identify the conduct that will constitute performance. Your cleaning service provider may present a contract that shows the services they will perform: emptying trash, vacuuming floors and dusting furniture. Be specific as to what tasks will be performed so that other acts, like window washing or shampooing carpets, which are not included in the contract are not inferred.

The statute of frauds is a legal concept that certain contracts must be in writing to be enforceable. For example, Article 2-201 of the Uniform Commercial Code requires a written contract for a sale of goods over a specific value (currently $500). Oral contracts

This first paragraph identifies the parties and the offer of services.	Contract for Janitorial Services This contract is between _____, (hereafter known as the Client) and _____ (hereafter known as the Contractor). Contractor agrees to cleaning and janitorial services, more particularly described below, to be performed on the Client's facility located at _____. Therefore, the parties hereby agree as follows:
This clause sets out the consideration: Client will pay for service; service provider will perform service for pay.	1. Client shall pay Contractor $0.00 on the first of each month for services to be performed during that month.
Specific terms as to times of performance minimize disputes.	2. Contractor will have access to the facility after normal working hours, and at other mutually agreed-on times.
Specific duties make it clear and unambiguous what and how often services are to be performed.	3. Contractor will, twice weekly, vacuum carpets, sweep and mop bare floors, change entrance rugs, dust and polish furniture and decorations, clean and disinfect restroom stalls, toilets, sinks, and water fixtures, etc.
This section makes clear who will provide what supplies and equipment.	4. Client shall provide for Contractor's use the following equipment and supplies: _____ _____ Contractor is expected to provide the following equipment and supplies: _____
This shows that the contract has a definite beginning point. It also shows that the contract terms are good for the time stated. Costs rise and fall. A one year term allows both parties to negotiate for a fair price but not to get locked in for too long if prices rise.	5. This contract will begin on the date of signing and continue for one year. Either party may terminate this agreement with 30 days written notice to the other party. Any payment for services rendered owed by Client shall be due and payable at the time this agreement is terminated.
This is the acceptance of the agreement. Have two original copies with both parties signing both copies, each party keeping an original.	In witness to their agreement to these terms, the Client and Contractor affix their signatures below: _____ Client's signature, date Client's printed name Contractor's signature, date Contractor's business name
Any additional concerns should be spelled out: these may include issues of access, bonding, assignability, and bonding.	Who will do the cleaning? Since they are in the building after hours, who will have a key? Are the cleaners bonded? Is the contractor insured in the event one of the cleaners breaks something? Is this contract assignable? (Can it be sold or subcontracted to someone else?) The more clear and specific, the less likely problems will arise in the future.

Tool 18.1   Contract Basics

would be unenforceable for sales covered by the statute. As a manager, you need to know what your state has enacted regarding sales and the Statute of Frauds.

Advertisements usually do not constitute a contract because they are not a firm offer but an invitation. An offer must be clear, definite, explicit and leave nothing open for negotiation. For example, consider this ad taken from Lefkowitz vs. Great Minneapolis Surplus Store (1957), that reads "fur coats worth up to $100.00," was not clear or definite, but "black lapin stole, worth $139.50, for $1.00" was clear and definite.

How do I protect my organization in business transactions?

In addition to writing clear and specific terms into a contract, various acts of legislation work to protect both parties in a business transaction. The Uniform Commercial Code (UCC) is a set of proposed laws and rules to govern transactions in business written by the American Law Institute (ALI) and the National Conference of Commissioners of Uniform State Laws (NCCUSL). Most States enact the rules through legislation. They are often modified to reflect certain needs of the individual states. According to the ALI and NCCUSL, updates of the UCC may or may not be modified by the states. It is good for managers to know what articles of the UCC apply to their business, and to become familiar with their terms and processes.

Article 1 defines the scope of the Articles, rules of construction, definitions, and principles of interpretation. The scope of the Articles is to govern commercial transactions, permit the continued expansion of commercial practices through custom, usage and agreement of the parties.

Article 2 applies to transactions in the sale of goods. Due diligence is required to provide parties with notice, or knowledge, of transactions. Article 2 defines terms and specifies requirements such as "goods" and "security interest", and specifies the formation of sales contracts.

Article 2A applies to transactions that create a lease. Addressing issues such as who is responsible for the upkeep and maintenance of leased property. There must be conspicuous language to call the lessee's attention to the exclusion of warranties.

Article 3 applies to negotiable instruments such as a check or promissory note. A check, known as a draft, written to a specific individual requires that person's endorsement, but a note to "bearer" is paid to the person holding the instrument. Certain instruments can be transferred, and enforcement of the order to pay is governed by Article 3.

Article 4 governs bank deposits and collections. For example, the cut-off hour for handling money and making entries is determined partly by statute. This Article defines when a bank may charge a customer's account in the event of an overdraft before the date of a check.

Tool 18.2   UCC Summary (continued overleaf)

Article 4A governs funds transfers in banking. Security procedures other than comparison of an authorized specimen signature are defined as security against unauthorized payment orders is one example governed by this Article.

Article 5 applies to transactions involving letters of credit. A letter of credit, confirmation, advice, transfer, amendment, or cancellation may be issued in any form that is a record and is authenticated by signature or with the agreement of the parties or the standard practice.

Article 6 applies to a seller's inventory to prevent fraudulent bulk sales. The National Conference of Commissioners on Uniform State Laws recommended this Article be repealed as it is obsolete, but it remains law in some states.

Article 7 governs the negotiability of warehouse receipts, bills of lading, and other documents of title in the storage of goods. The Article protects the ownership of goods in storage and provides for the legal transfer of such goods.

Article 8 applies to investment securities involving ownership of a corporation, business trust, joint stock company or similar entity. The rights and responsibilities of owners, brokers and clearing corporations are defined to prevent the fraudulent transfer of securities.

Article 9 governs security interests in personal property. As a means of getting credit, debtors will promise personal property as security to a creditor. This widely-used Article is to secure an interest in property in the event of a default, and against other creditors who wish to use the property to settle their claims against the debtor. The chief concerns are the attachment of the interest to the collateral, and perfection of the interest against other creditors.

The security interest attaches to collateral when it becomes enforceable against the debtor. Such interests are "perfected" to establish priority over property against other creditors. Certain interests are perfected when they attach. Other interests are perfected when the security interest is filed in the designated office or with the Secretary of State.

Adapted from: American Law Institute and National Conference of Commissioners of Uniform State Laws, 2010.

Tool 18.2   UCC Summary (continued)

What rights do employees have?

Employees have rights established by statute, bargaining agreements, and common law. Many employees are employed "at will," meaning they can be released for almost any reason. The theory is if the employee can leave at any time, the employer can terminate the work relationship at any time. Based on the work of Muhl (2001) three exceptions to this are public policy, implied contract, and covenant of good faith:

- Public policy is where an employee is fired for an act that would violate recognized policy of the state, such as firing an injured employee because she filed a worker's compensation claim.
- Implied contract usually occurs when there is no written contract, but a company policy manual gives assurances that employees cannot be terminated except on certain terms like "just cause."
- The covenant of good faith exception implies good faith and fair dealing in all employment relationships. While 42 states recognize the Public Policy exception, only eleven states recognize a Covenant of Good Faith exception.

Wrongful termination suits generally arise when an employee claims he was fired for a reason protected by law, such as discrimination, picketing, or acting as a whistleblower. Laws against discrimination, unequal pay and work hours provide remedies for employees protected by statutes.

Title VII of the Civil Rights Act prohibits discrimination against an individual based on race, color, religion, sex or national origin. This was described more fully in chapter seven. Race is defined as having characteristics associated with a specific race: hair texture, skin color, and certain facial features. Color includes varying skin tones within a race. Religion is any set of personal beliefs of worship, and includes atheism. National origin refers to a person's national or geographical heritage. Sex discrimination includes employment issues and harassment. The victim and the harasser can be of the same sex.

The Family Medical Leave Act (FMLA) protects an employee's job and benefits when time off is taken for specific family and medical reasons. The FMLA allows eligible employees to take up to twelve work weeks in a twelve month period for the birth of a child, for a serious health condition where the employee is unable to perform the essential functions of their job, or to care for a spouse, child, or parent who has a serious health condition. Also covered is a twelve week period for adoption and for military caregiver leave and a twenty-six week period for caring for a family member who is a covered service member with a serious injury or illness.

Current regulations by the US Department of Labor define "serious health condition" as at least three consecutive, full calendar days of incapacity and two visits to a health care provider, or continuing treatment. According to the Department of Labor, the Regulations allow an employee to return to work under light duty without affecting the twelve-week leave entitlement.

The National Labor Relations Act (NLRA) gives employees the right to form or join a labor union, or assist in organizing fellow employees. While normally associated with labor unions and employee negotiations, the NLRA protects any concerted effort by an employee to improve working conditions. The key is a *concerted* effort. There must be at least two people who agree to address working conditions, although only one employee approaches management with an issue.

Improvement of working conditions includes negotiating work agreements, employee discipline, and strikes. The US Department of Labor and the National Labor Relations Board ensure both sides operate fairly when dealing with labor and management issues. Not all workers are covered by the NLRA. Independent contractors and supervisors are two classes of workers not covered by the NLRA.

The Fair Standards Labor Act (FSLA) governs minimum wage, overtime, recordkeeping and youth employment standards. The FSLA applies to businesses that have employees.

Per the US Department of Labor some exceptions are farm workers, independent contractors, salaried and commissioned employees. Employers subject to the FSLA must post notices in the workplace of the laws and regulations regarding the standards. Some states may provide greater protection than the FSLA, but cannot legislate any standard lower than the federal law.

The list of regulations and legislation goes on and not everything is covered here. As stated in the introduction, the goal of this chapter is not to make you an expert. In this chapter, we have taken some of the most common questions that you, as a mid-level manager, will likely see. Responses to the questions are not designed to take the place of legal advice, but to give you a basic understanding of legal terms and processes so that you will be aware why certain steps are taken to avoid or minimize legal trouble. The list is not all-inclusive; other governmental/legal concerns occur daily. You should become familiar with governmental and legal issues you address on a regular basis, and research the topic using some of the resources listed below.

Additional Resources

Legal information can be found easily online. Findlaw.com is a good place to start. The website has a section: *Learn About the Law* that is a good starting point for getting a basic understanding of the law. Cornell University manages the *Legal Information Institute* online at www.law.cornell.edu. The objective of the site is that everyone should be able to read and understand the laws that govern them. These sites are free, but may offer additional services for a subscription. Westlaw and LexisNexis also offer legal research on a subscription basis.

Government websites offer an array of information and services available. The US Department of Labor website: www.dol.gov, has topics on wage and hour laws and compliance assistance. The Equal Opportunity Commission site: www.eeoc.gov has information on what is covered by the EEOC and how to file a complaint. They also discuss laws and regulations on equal employment and discrimination. State government websites offer some of the same information. Search for your state's Secretary of State for information on how to incorporate your business and how to file other documents. State legislative research commissions usually post state statutes and regulations online for easy access, as does the Federal Government for federal laws and regulations.

Every county will have a law library, usually located in the courthouse. These libraries are open to the public and will have limited legal resources. Some public libraries will also have a section on law. Law schools usually have an exhaustive collection of journals, treatises, and other aids for specific legal topics. They also have librarians and sometimes eager law students who can assist you with your research. A good place to start your research is with a general treatise like American Jurisprudence or Corpus Juris Secundum. These are encyclopedias on legal topics. From these, you can move on to more specific books ranging from contract and tort law to taxation.

References

American Jurisprudence 2d ed. (1998–2011). Lawyers Cooperative Publishing American Law Institute and National Conference of Commissioners of Uniform State Laws. (2010). UCC 2010–2011 Edition.

Ayers, I., Speidel, R. (2008). *Studies in Contract Law*. Eagan, MN: West Publishing.

Eisenberg, Melvin Aron. (2005). *Cases and Materials on Corporations and Other Business Organizations*. Eagan, MN: West Publishing.

Klein, William A., Ramseyer J. Mark and Bainbridge, Stephen M. (2006). *Agency, Partnerships, and Limited Liability Entities*. Eagan, MN: West Publishing.

LexisNexis. (2010). *Ballentine's Law Dictionary*.

Muhl, C. (2001). The Employment at Will Doctrine: 3 Major Exceptions. *Monthly Labor Review*. January 2001, Vol. 124, No 1.

Murphy E., Speidel, R., Ayers, I. (2003). *Studies in Contract Law* (University Casebook). Eagan, MN: West Publishing.

Murphy, S. A. (2010). *Studies in Contract Law*. University Casebook.

NLRB, (2011). Retrieved from *www.nlrb.gov*.

Reuschlein, H. G. (1979). *Agency and Partnership*. Eagan, MN: West Publishing.

Toby, M. C. (2007). The Complete Equine Legal and Business Handbook. Lexington, KY: Blood Horse Publications.

US Department of Justice, (2005). *A Guide to Disability Rights Laws*.

US Department of Labor, (2011). Retrieved from *www.dol.gov*.

US Equal Opportunity Commission. (2011). Retrieved 2011, from http://www.eeoc.gov/eeoc/index. cfm.

19 *Websites and Information Technology*

ERIC BOLLAND

This chapter will examine the major issues and questions that managers face concerning websites and information technology (IT). In addition, there will be a section on financial evaluation of IT investments. There is very little debate that the use of technology in the workplace (including the whole spectrum of operating systems, computers, application programs, networks, and the Internet) has fundamentally reshaped all aspects of business. That transformation continues unabated making this subject an area of "where the action is" in contemporary businesses. As such, there is no wonder why IT issues are present at all levels of the organization, in all stages of planning and between and among functional units.

The role of technology in business has accelerated in many different dimensions. In communications, face-to-face meetings have been replaced by virtual meetings using communication and meeting technologies. The accuracy of business records has been dramatically improved due to the use of computer-based spreadsheets and data analysis software. A related improvement is the speed of data and information flow that helps in decision making. With more information available, decision makers can consider more possibilities, and can plan for uncertainty. The increased information, while at times more of a curse than a blessing, supports contingency planning and offers a better chance of getting it right the first time.

Additionally, easy to use technology-based presentation software has improved the communications quality and depth within and outside business organizations. Please see chapter four for a detailed discussion of presentation software and its role in communications. There is little doubt about how profoundly business has been affected by technology. Consequently, a closer look at this dimension of the organization is worthwhile for any manager.

The chapter starts with a look at the questions and issues concerning websites, then turns to the larger issues of information technology management. It then examines the matter of financing information technology projects. Starting with websites is warranted because it is a common touchpoint for all managers and it leads into larger technology issues.

The aim of the chapter is to deal with the management of these issues rather than the technical issues themselves. For most readers, this is likely to be the way they encounter information technology topics. Consider this chapter as a gateway to IT that answers your most frequent broad-based questions. The eventual solution to specific issues you may face will likely depend on your partnering with experts in your own organization or outside consultants. If you can't talk IT you'll want to be with someone who can because the concepts and jargon of the discipline often need translation. Nonetheless, at the purely conceptual level, IT ideas can be translated and understood by managers in all fields.

Do we really need a website?

Customers gravitate to an organization's website. Let's start there. The website is the boundary where the organization touches its outer environment. Today, every organization needs a website. It is the way you become known to people. They are people who will make judgments about your organization and the website is the first impression for most. Even if your first customer contact is face to face, most people will eventually look at your website. You need to have it make the right impression. First impressions are fleeting and unforgiving. If not impressed, the casual visitor will scamper away searching for something better. Customers may become frustrated if your website doesn't provide the answers they are looking for.

The actual design of a website is not at all difficult but the consequences of getting it wrong are severe. There are many website design programs available and many consulting firms willing to do it for you. Which route you take will have an impact on the viewer. Think about your own experiences. If you know nothing about a possible supplier to your organization but you need to find a supplier, how do you feel when you do an Internet search and find a possible supplier but their website is patently amateurish? Or when their homepage is reorganized from one week to another? You are likely disappointed. Such are yours and the commonly shared reactions of many. What follows are ways to ensure that this doesn't happen to you.

What should be considered in establishing a website?

Websites have become the new doorways to businesses. They are also windows to the world where anyone on the Internet can peer in. The temptation to use brick and mortar metaphors having been succumbed to for the sake of getting your attention, we should go right to the heart of this very important question. After many years of website organization and design anarchy, some general practices have emerged in establishing a website which have made the medium much more efficient.

A real challenge in developing a website is to make it attractive for the first time visitor yet also not to make it boring for repeat visitors. Change, while preserving constancy is always in juxtaposition for effective sites. Also, there has to be a balance between working graphics and graphic gimmickry. Outstanding graphics can actually reduce viewership especially if viewers have only basic Internet services. To work your way through this and make sure you are connecting with site visitors, refer to the promotion and identifying and serving customers chapters of this book (chapters eight and eleven). Advertising has many ways of putting graphics together with copy in an effectively blended manner. These should help guide your webpage design.

Who do we want to communicate with through our website?

One of the first questions to answer in the design and implementation of any website is: Who do you want to communicate with? Everyone? Not likely. That will turn your website into a clutter bucket. A website is how you inform your customers, potential customers and other important parties of your products, services, operations, organization and whatever else you want to say. You have a lot to say but you have to be efficient about how you say it. Start with the various audiences you want to communicate with. You could use chapter eleven of this book to develop audience categories. That chapter identifies important stakeholders in your organization.

> **WEBSITE TIP:**
>
> Make sure your website answers the following questions:
>
> Who are you?
>
> What do you do?
>
> What is your product or service?
>
> Why do you do what you do?
>
> How much does your product or service cost?
>
> What is unique about you?
>
> Why should customers do business with you?

One category you'll want to appeal to is current customers. Among other things, they need to know how to get answers to their questions. A frequently asked questions section (FAQs) works well for this purpose and is the convention for organizational responses. To evaluate its effectiveness, a count of question hits keeps the FAQs current. Respond promptly to new queries.

Your customers also need routes to solutions for their search for information and issues that may come up. Think about customer support and how your website can provide as much of this as possible without jamming the site with too much dense information. This is a balancing act that the customers should have input into. One way of doing that is to invite feedback from your most involved customers in the form of a listening session with your marketing and website personnel.

Another market category, perhaps the most important one to aim your website at, is prospective customers. For this, you want move a prospective browsing customer to become an actual customer. You'll want to review the chapter on identifying customers, to develop the message that will set this transition in motion. Once again, marketing considerations should drive content.

Investors also want to know about you. The section devoted to this is usually a tab labeled Investor Relations. In this section, you report financial information as you choose to publish it. You can also provide links here to webcasts of presentations to investors highlighting financial results. Webcasts can be useful not only for sharing information about the company but also for letting customers and other stakeholders put a face with a name.

You will also want to communicate with journalists and news directors. For them, and for the general public, a section such as Our Background can provide a business history and a summary of goals, mission and strategy. This section is also a good place to show the evolution or growth of your company. You can highlight geographic areas served, or special niches you target. Describe in this section how you arrived at where you are.

Sort through the rest of your stakeholders and make similar judgments. Anticipate what they may want to know about you and determine the best way to communicate that information. You might want to include suppliers, distributors, government entities, educational institutions, social organizations and potential employees, to name a few more stakeholders that may be important to you.

A good starting point for creating a website that connects with visitors is to take a look at your competitors' websites. Compile a notebook showing their homepages and other important pages. Note what strikes you as effective about their sites. Pretend you are a customer. What did you like or dislike about the site? You can prepare a checklist of what they have in audience-specific content that appears effective. Then, compare that to what you have or will have. You might find some important gaps.

Now that audience factors have been identified, you should consider the immensely important subject of content. Content should be driven by what your audience needs to know and how to make them receptive to what you have to say. With this in mind, effective websites make a departure from written communications. That said, don't forget that search engines pick up written content, not picture driven content. Don't get overly reliant on images alone.

Good websites don't necessarily use complete sentences. Concepts can be presented like a restaurant menu in which the website topics are the overview of the site. Meals are what are on the menu and courses are part of the meal. Bites are the chunks of information reduced down to the very morsels. Looking at it this way keeps irrelevant information out. The right amount of written content can be a juggling act balancing enough detail to be informative and search engine friendly, but not so much as to test the patience of the visitor.

What are some essential content elements?

The essential content is often found in themes that may be on separate pages or not. If they are not, they still need prominence at your site.

HOME PAGE

The home page is the first page your viewer encounters. It is a guide or menu to the rest of your pages. This page has to hook people and it also has to guide them to easily find what they are looking for. Tell them what you have to offer, who you are and any special offers or news.

SPECIAL OFFERS

Having special offers keeps established patrons coming back to your site. The visitor does not have to page through the site to find a special offer if you have it on the homepage. This also keeps your website lively.

CONTACT INFORMATION

Just because people got to you through the Internet doesn't mean that's how they want to contact you in the future. It is surprising just how many companies fail to provide complete contact information for visitors. This should include your physical address, postal address, phone and fax numbers as well as an email address for customer service or someone who will respond promptly to requests for information.

SEARCH FUNCTION

For larger websites, a search function that is prominently featured helps the visitor find what they are looking for. Search functions are especially useful if you have many pages on your website or if your products and services have technical names.

TITLES

For both good organization and content clarity, all of your pages should have titles. The potential customer can refer to them when contacting your sales staff with questions or to place an order.

DIRECTING TRAFFIC

One idea to consider is whether or not to direct incoming Internet visitors to a specific area. Health insurance firms, for example, like to divide their sites for policyholders, health care professionals and insurance agents based on the exclusivity of their information needs. If your customer base is clearly segmented with particular product or service needs, this is probably something you should consider.

How will our visitors evaluate our website?

As viewers, we tend to expect a lot from websites. In terms of expectations, websites come close to being a miracle media. Text, sound and video can all be delivered on your website. As rich as the website can be, viewers also want sites that download quickly. Moving parts and rich images usually don't download quickly and may not download at all for customers with slower connection speeds. This is another website balancing act.

Customers want the first page (the home page in most cases) to be easy to understand. They want navigation that works with no dead ends. Put another way, they want to know where they were, where they are, and where they are going. They want to see pages that are not crammed with content. They want readable fonts and graphics support that don't overwhelm the content.

Visitors will evaluate your website based on their perceptions of the website itself and the transactions that will occur by using it. The perceptions of the website will be the residual images of it. Their overall evaluation of the transaction will be how successful they have been in getting answers and obtaining services. Both will be used by the viewer in rating your website.

The action step for you is to constantly undertake this judgment yourself. You can get feedback from viewers as mentioned earlier and you can also look at your site statistics. You want to see hits go up as a trend and you want to see time spent exploring your site increase as well.

What goes wrong with websites?

Learning from the mistakes of others helps you avoid costs and loss of customers. Here are some of the most common mistakes in website design:

- One failing of websites is that the technical side of the business, rather than the marketing side, develops them. This can be evidenced by an overabundance of bells and whistles on the homepage. A marketing-oriented homepage talks to customers directly. It invites them into the website so it is highly advisable to have both marketing and technical staff involved in the design of the site.
- Graphics can slow page uploads. Keep the graphics simple if you want to fall inside your visitor's attention span for reasons mentioned earlier. You also reach a wider range of customers by not excluding customers with slow connections.
- Color backgrounds make text difficult to read. Try out colors against text before committing to using different combinations. Even if you are not using color backgrounds but screening in black, make sure the text stands out from the screen.
- Bad classification of information makes usage cumbersome. Information should be classified so that it is as inclusive as possible yet distinct from other classifications. Your whole classification scheme needs to consider every possible way the visitor can be served through your site. Classification should be customer centric, not company centric. Use classification titles that mean something to the visitor like "Payment Methods" not "Accounts Receivable."
- Poor navigation is shown by illogical and wandering paths to the information needed. Visitors who are navigating through your site are already headed toward becoming customers. They have stepped in your direction. The worst thing to do is to lose them around the bends. If they get to a broken link or to a page with no relevant content, you've probably lost a good prospect.

Do I need a website manager?

The short answer to this is yes. Daily management of the website keeps it alive. The amount of website maintenance depends on how complex it is. The manager does not need to be a full time person and that usually can't happen in very small businesses. The tasks of the website manager can be summarized as:

- Check all the major pages daily
- Replace old content with new
- Check for functioning links
- Review website logs to identify any technical problems and to track activity.

In addition to the person who maintains the site, you need a website editor. This may or may not be the same person. The website editor is key to maximizing website success. The editor needs to know just how your organization works and what it does. These are not technical skills. Websites that have been turned over exclusively to technical staff almost invariably become less friendly to the visitor who is in search of company products and capabilities. Marketing managers are usually good choices as editors. The editor has the final say. There may be separate content owners in areas of specific expertise but the editor needs to be able to knit it all together.

What should my website do for me?

You are going to be spending time developing and maintaining your website. It must do something valuable for you in return. Your website should be your marketing arm. It is your most prominent communications method. For smaller businesses, it constitutes the vast majority of your marketing presence. For other businesses, especially virtual businesses, it can also be your delivery platform.

As a main force to draw interest, the website is a powerful marketing tool. Organizations actively ask their marketing people to drive customers to the website, a commonly heard refrain. Once there, your website should work for you by collecting information about those who come to you. In particular, obtaining email addresses is very important. Other contact information can help your sales efforts too. You want to learn as much as you can, in as much depth as possible, about those who reach out to you.

At another level, the website can be used to prequalify customers. This can be done in brief surveys of their needs and of the resources they have available to meet those needs. Your sales people then do not have to spend time with customer prequalification and that is a distinct advantage.

Some companies help their customers along by having savings calculators embedded in the website. Others provide decision support tools that guide the customer to the right product for them. These are also prequalification devices.

You want to get feedback from visitors even if they are not customers. This was mentioned earlier but should be reinforced. Brief surveys can be used to solicit the visitor's opinions on how easy or difficult the site is to navigate, how quickly they got to what they wanted, how quickly pages loaded and how well links worked. These surveys can be compiled on a daily basis and aggregated for website redesign purposes.

How do I make sure my site comes up early and often when customers are doing a search?

Search Engine Optimization (SEO) has become one of the hot topics in website hosting and design. While it is important that your site comes up early in a search (and even more important that it comes up at all), companies who rely only on search engine traffic as a source of business are doomed to fail. Instead, search engine traffic should be an ingredient in your marketing mix. Perhaps more important is the customer who is searching specifically for your company but may not know the exact company or site name. For these customers in particular, you want your site to be search engine friendly.

As you construct your site, keeping some SEO principles in mind will make this an integrated process. Your goal here is to improve visibility organically by the design and content of your site as opposed to paying for better search engine results. In order to better understand SEO, you need to understand how search engines work, what people search for and what search terms are commonly typed in. Since this is an area requiring a fair amount of technical know-how, you may be well advised to hire a consultant for this purpose. If you're already working with a consultant on your website development, be sure this individual keeps the principles of SEO in mind.

Search engine friendly web designs have some basic elements in common. One of those core principles is using text versus pictures, graphs and other images. Remember that only text is searchable. HTML (hypertext markup language) code, the basic building block of websites, is the only thing on your website that search engines can read. Other items inserted into the site not using HTML will not be read. The search engines offer cached views that will allow you to see your website as the search engine sees it. This is a very useful step in your website development process.

Although the importance of keyword density is more of a myth than reality, repeating keywords throughout your site does help. Keywords are index terms used to retrieve documents. You might want to have a few keywords appear in bold in your site and your keyword should appear early in any title. Links help with SEO as well. Cross-linking your pages to each other and to outside websites can help move you up the search ladder. Good URL structure and design is another element in the search engine algorithm. While overly aggressive techniques designed to move your site up the search engine rankings might get you and your site banned, keeping some of these basics in mind while designing your site is probably worth doing.

Should our website be externally hosted?

Hosting means putting your website on the Internet. This can be done internally or externally. External hosting requires considerable scrutiny on your part. Because of the great turnover in hosting companies, it is critical to find a reputable company. You also want that company to know your visitors and their technical needs so that your website can deliver the right content to them rapidly. Deciding to have your site hosted internally versus externally can depend on cost, expertise and resources.

In addition to virtually every business needing a website, almost every business will have other information technology needs as well. Like everything else, IT needs to be managed. We'll now look at the role of managers in the process. IT management is a domain of the present, but just as importantly, of the future. Consequently, both aspects of IT will be addressed.

In this section, we rely on the insight of IT professionals who deal with the frequently occurring questions of IT issues. As a preface, IT professionals must understand the perspectives and sometimes the limitations that may occur when working with managers and executives in diverse functions like finance, human resource management, operations and marketing. IT professionals themselves need to communicate across their fields and connect with those who are seeking technology-based solutions.

What basic information do I need to know to make IT decisions?

To IT consultant John Higdon, an electrical engineer with thirty years experience at IBM, managers need to understand technology and how to use it. This doesn't mean understanding down to the software and hardware level but it is essential to know it at a conceptual level—what it can do and what it can't do. As Higdon (2011) puts it "Everything is tied to databases now; managers need to get access to work that is stored in these databases." Managers should move from having their own flat file spreadsheets like Excel and go to creation, storage and retrieval from more powerful database management systems.

You have probably seen how data is spread around the organization in individual nooks and crannies. A better situation is a centralized network that can be shared. "Everybody wants access; to get reports on demand that they can use to figure out how to run businesses," Higdon adds. Use of relational databases, centralization and report generation all help increase both efficiency and effectiveness. It increases throughput and reduces inventory costs, according to Higdon.

In order to understand technology and how to use it, you should explore the capabilities of potential IT solutions for your business issues. You can start with a list of decisions you think you will need to make and information you will have to collect. Then, for software, you can take steps such as reading about what a particular software program can do to help you. This is almost always available in the software manuals and in the provider website description of what functions can be performed. You don't need to plunge into features and specifications, but you do need to know the benefits for your business. Also, very importantly, you'll need to consult with your own IT people so they can identify any compatibility, capacity and support issues that may occur.

Further guidance on what information is needed to have a data management strategy is offered by Cindy Fogg, manager of IT/Business at Lexmark International. As Fogg (2011) puts it, "Having a data management strategy is needed for the organization. You may have five different systems doing different tasks for five different customer groups. You have to be consistent in the way you handle these customers so that different parts of the organization can all see them as a customer. A data management strategy is the way to cut across these different customer descriptions."

Fogg also states that the strategy focus of information technology means that IT becomes more of a core business function. "IT was looked at as a support function in the past. It needs to be looked at more as business technology and not information technology." Both Fogg and Higdon see a growing role for the technology function within the organization.

What IT issues frequently come up?

New IT systems don't just replace old systems in one fell swoop. As Higdon points out, organizations have their own legacy systems and the systems need to be worked with. Data has to be merged to provide a history. So dealing with legacy systems is likely to come up in your own expeditions in the IT world. Another issue is the matter of writing your own proprietary programs as opposed to acquiring standardized programs. The trend is definitely departing from creating customized, proprietary packages and is moving to standardized packages. Standardized packages have developed far more flexibility and customizability than in the past.

Higdon advises against customization because of the money it costs to do it and the time it takes to implement it. Fogg responds to the build-it-yourself or buy decision by saying there are three choices for businesses now, "you can build it yourself, buy from someone or go to the Internet for it." The Internet option has a lot to recommend it because you can "get a solution quickly. You can get something that is scalable for your operations. A pitfall is that it can't be customized however. You are dependent on the provider for upgrades."

Very small companies can get locked into using separate programs for narrow functions like payroll and they can't integrate these programs as they grow. This can be an important consideration if you are in this situation. When investing in any program, make sure it can grow and expand along with you or that it can be integrated with other programs.

What are some alternatives to the typical data center set-up with its investment in hardware and software?

Yet another issue is the role of networks and where information should be stored. The trend is toward networking and away from self-standing, desktop computing for many reasons. These include the power of networks; their capacity to share information and applications when needed. One especially interesting development in this area is cloud computing. So what is it and what does it do? Cloud computing transfers expertise to servers outside the organization rather than inside the organization. Imagine taking your IT department and putting it on the Internet. Your applications, programs and databases are stored centrally and they are accessible from anywhere.

Cloud computing turns IT into a service. Although Dell originally coined the term, there are now many providers for cloud computing and your "cloud" (where your data resides) can be public (shared) or private (your own cloud). As with anything, there are plusses and minuses to cloud computing which are summarized in Table 19.1.

Is cloud computing the wave of the future for IT? Only time will tell. Meanwhile, some large companies, like retailing giant Target Corporation, are embracing this concept and saving millions of dollars in the process. Target will soon have 15,000 machines in 1,750 stores running mission critical store applications with only two physical servers.

How do I manage the integration of IT into the workplace?

Fogg believes that information technology is likely to be reshaped by demographic imperatives. She notes that younger generation workers have integrated mobility into work to the point that work is no longer a place but is a connection to place. Not all the aspects of technology transformations are found on the technology side alone.

Higdon urges managers to work from an IT strategy standpoint to grapple with these issues. Identify your organization's IT strategy if it has one, and if it does not, discuss the overall direction of IT with those who are responsible for it. Having an IT strategy at least

Table 19.1 Cloud Computing Pros and Cons

Cloud Computing Pros	Cloud Computing Cons
Reduces cost: Eliminates investment in hardware and software. Replaces IT department with service provider.	Security: Your data is stored on someone else's platform.
Improves agility: Capacity can be increased as business grows without adding overhead. Users can expand software demands to anything provided in the cloud.	Security: Since many users may share a cloud (a public cloud), data may be accessible to others.
Improves reliability: Data is maintained by experts in a central location.	Privacy: Others may have access to your data and perhaps more important to your customers' data.
Reduces capital expenditures: Your in-house IT department is replaced with operating expenses.	Compliance: Cloud computing shifts the burden of regulatory compliance and legal issues to a third party.
Low barriers to entry: No initial capital outlay is needed.	Performance and control: In any service relationship the performance of the service provider can be problematic.
Device independence: Cloud programs can be accessed through the Internet from anywhere.	

puts a vector on the direction of your IT operations. Without that direction, any path will do, as the saying goes among some Native American tribes.

Managers also need to know how much they can ask of information systems. Higdon offers an example: "You might want to have a security system that electronically opens and closes the door that is tied to a video camera but you also need to explore how that camera is tied to face recognition software that decides which faces it will let into the building." In other words, knowing the objective of the IT system is not enough. You need to know about the sub issues that need to be addressed before expecting an integrated, whole scale technology solution that just needs to be plugged in and mission accomplished.

Should we hire IT consultants or do the project ourselves?

This is a question that can't be answered categorically one way or another, even though the answer is extremely consequential. There are horror stories on both sides. Companies that have used outside consultants have ended up stranded without solutions after the consultant went out of business. On the other side of the coin, companies have poured money into their own IT black hole only to realize that they never had the skills they needed to get the job done. To mitigate either extreme, the following observations and advice are offered.

In considering the practicalities of this matter, Fogg advises taking a look at something that may not be immediately considered. She advises a consideration of location and cultural issues. Smaller companies might need to have more localized help desk functions to better relate to local customers. An offshore operation will not help. On the other hand, offshore support can be available 24/7, which is a major advantage for a larger organization. Fogg also stresses the need to examine your own internal skills in comparison to the skills you would acquire by hiring an outside firm. Turnover is a problem in consulting organizations and likely in your own organization. Consequently, the importance of documentation cannot be overstated. It provides the common thread of decisions made in turnover instances.

A pitfall in all this is underestimating the need for expertise either internally or externally. If you underestimate the amount of work you will need to do and your capacity to do it, there will be blown deadlines and perhaps blown projects. For external options, the problems may come in the form of delays, re-scoped projects and failure. Sometimes even the cultural aspects are important, according to Fogg. Non-domestic consultants need to understand your requirements and you need to understand their capabilities. Testing your ability to communicate across cultures should happen early and often.

What types of IT consultants are available?

There are three basic levels of consultants:

- At the high end are professional services firms that offer a full range of IT consulting services and have a large staff which often specializes in different IT areas.
- There are also staffing firms that offer to place specialists on site at your location. They often serve to fill in on a temporary basis.
- Independent consultants, individuals who are hired guns, help with company projects.

To find these different sources of assistance in your area, performing an Internet search or asking around the local business community will help.

How can we adapt to the future of technology?

An important question in IT is "what does the future hold?" The rate of IT advancement and the breadth of it have been such that many major businesses are caught in frozen repose, the proverbial deer in the headlights. There are Fortune 500 companies that have abandoned efforts at constructing a future IT strategy because of the cascading unknowns that may be encountered. Potentially there will be revolutionary changes in operating systems, languages, computers, software and networks. These unknowns cannot be assessed so charting your IT future involves planning for considerable uncertainty. The advice of this chapter is to take on some level of futurism in your tackling of this issue, even if it is at an order of magnitude level, painted with broad strokes.

The sources for doing a technology environment assessment are internal or external. Internal assessments are done by your organization and external assessments mean going to an outside organization to get the job done. If you have internal expertise, you can form a team to raise and answer the issues. The opinions of experts are compiled from a meeting that is led by a facilitator. The facilitator solicits as many ideas as possible, gets clarification and records the ideas as the work product. This works like a brainstorming session.

You can also do your own content analysis. That's what futurists do to identify new trends. To do this, you would look at media accounts of technology topics and then quantify them in terms of how frequently the topic came up and how intensively it was reported on. Patterns will emerge and you should end up with a rank order of topics. When you look for topics, include all the media you can, from print to broadcast, cable to social networking. Outside assistance is available from consulting firms listed at the end of this chapter in the Additional Resources section.

Turning back to the internal side, one tool that can be used internally is the environmental analysis. This tool derives from chapter seven on Strategy. It is centered on an environmental analysis of technology changes. In doing this, you will want to take into account what is happening now, how significant it is and how it will affect you. These three elements can be included in a chart similar to that shown:

Table 19.2   External Environmental Evaluation

Environmental Factor	Current Factor	Significance	Consequences
IP Telephony	Shift from landlines to Internet based phone communications.	Very significant for us. Rapid shift from landlines to IP.	Reduced support for analog telephony functions. Should we abandon landlines?

This shows a single example of a factor and to make it more useful, many factors should be included. You should probably aim for ten to fifteen such factors. Beyond twenty, the tool becomes unwieldy and difficult to manage.

When you do your analysis, some of the factors that should be included are:

- Cloud computing and Software-as-Service (described above).
- Communications Convergence: The migration of voice and data systems into a single network.
- Interoperability and Standards: The ability of systems to share data and to use the data shared.
- Open Source Software Development: Collaboratively developed software that allows licensees to change (especially to improve) the software.
- Risk Management, Security and Privacy.
- Social Media and Collaboration.
- Mobility: Different ways of getting to customers and vice versa.
- Green Technology.
- New Forms of Analytics (i.e., Customer Relationship Management and Enterprise Resource Planning).

You can get more information on these factors by doing an internet search. You may also come up with your own, which would have greater relevance to you.

What are the steps in hiring a consultant for future planning or more immediate IT implementation?

Should you decide to use a consultant, there are usually a set of steps taken to ensure the project is delivered as expected:

1. The scope of the project is defined, basic costs are identified and a timeline is established. This step is a collaborative process between you and the consultant and leads to a contract for services.
2. Work is assigned to individuals and work teams are formed to undertake the project. Project managers monitor progress toward goals.
3. Work is completed.
4. Solutions are tested.
5. Problems are identified and corrected.
6. Project is completed and approved.

Working with the consulting firm, you should consider how aspects of project management, as developed in chapter fourteen, might help you successfully complete the task. Project management will aid in establishing timelines, benchmarks and responsibilities. You could also review chapter eighteen on government and legal issues to explore some of the ramifications of contracting with outside consultants.

What are some ways to analyze the financial return on technology investments?

The promise of adopting new technologies can come to nothing unless a critical consideration is taken into account. That consideration is the financial justification of the proposed investment. Technology investments are major investments by an organization. Even replacing desktop computers or purchasing new software applications adds quickly to overall information technology costs.

The decision to replace or to improve IT is something that affects the entire organization. IT departments rarely make these decisions alone. Instead, the decisions are made in a multidisciplinary fashion and the finance area of the organization is seldom excluded. This functional area evaluates organizational expenses and investments by using methods that many managers are not aware of. That is one of the reasons why it is crucial to look into the tools and practices of financial analysis to pursue substantial IT projects.

You may think it is a no-brainer to buy an enterprise-level program that integrates all your marketing databases. The financial analyst will be looking at it from the point of view of how much money do we put in, and how much do we get out compared to other investments we could make? That view departs from the advantages you foresee but is nonetheless critical for the issue of whether the new technology will be purchased or not. For that matter, the whole decision may be entirely out of your hands. This is all the more reason for you to appreciate the language and methods of financial analysis with respect to IT investments. If you can address the issues that the finance area will raise in advance of sending them your proposal, you will be in better control of the process and less likely to encounter unanticipated information needs or even outright resistance.

What are the most common financial analysis tools and how do they work?

IT investments are looked at as having a financial dimension significant enough to be considered a capital investment and not an expense. Consequently, you may very well have to justify your IT investment request. In the following discussion, three commonly used approaches are introduced which are used in IT investment decisions. In order of incurring complexity they are: payback, return on investment (ROI), and cost benefit/ cost effectiveness analysis.

Tool	When to Use	When Not to Use
Payback	As a preliminary step. When scant data is available.	If project is complex. If more sophisticated analysis is needed. When timing of cash flow is important.
Return on Investment	For simple IT projects. For comparisons with other potential projects. When scale of projects is not significant.	If project is complex. If more sophisticated analysis is needed. When timing of cash flow is important.
Cost Benefit and Cost Effectiveness Analysis	Whenever feasible. When IT investment is heavily scrutinized.	When data is not available. When IT projects are very minor.

Tool 19.1   Choosing a Financial Analysis Tool

PAYBACK ANALYSIS

This approach considers the amount of time it takes for the IT investment benefits gained to equal the initial investment. For example, if the investment costs $100,000 and the organization receives $10,000 per year in derived benefits from the investment then the payback period is ten years. This is a relatively straightforward calculation. It ignores benefits that may come in after the payback period. It also produces a result in time, not dollars. Dollar comparisons are easier to use in making decisions about possible investments.

RETURN ON INVESTMENT

ROI is calculated by dividing the annual dollar amount returned to the organization by the dollar cost of the investment. The result is a percentage. It is straightforward like payback analysis but again does not consider continued benefits that happen after the returns equal the investment. Like payback, it is well understood and quite popular. ROI has another drawback. It does not take into account the scale of the investment. A $1,000 investment and a $1,000,000 investment can have the same ROI, so it is clear that ROI in and of itself is insufficient to evaluate scale issues.

COST BENEFIT AND COST EFFECTIVENESS ANALYSIS

The last approach reviewed is cost benefit and cost effectiveness analysis. These are the recommended methods because they incorporate time-value-of-money concepts and also take into account the matter of the scale of an IT investment. The methods of cost benefit and cost effectiveness analysis are essentially the same. Cost benefit is used for yes or no decisions on single major projects. Cost effectiveness is used to compare several projects and to decide which one should be selected.

To illustrate with an analysis of a typical IT project, we will use cost effectiveness analysis. The comparison will be between purchasing a marketing database program for an initial cost of $5,000, or outsourcing this function for a cost of $1,000 per year. A five-year period is used for the comparison. For technology investments, you don't want to run much longer since new and better systems constantly enter the market. The decision is: Should we buy the program (Option A) or outsource (Option B)? For the buy option, information about the cost comes from the seller. Information about the yearly costs and benefits is calculated. Annual updates to the software are a $200 cost and benefits (annual expected benefits from efficiencies gained from an internal system) are calculated at $1,000. For the outsource option, the costs are $1,000 per year for the five years. The time value of money is now put into the analysis. The time value of money compresses future costs and benefits into the present day so the effect of time can be considered in the calculation. To do this, a discount rate is factored in. This is usually your organization's cost of capital.

The interest rate you would typically pay for borrowing money makes a good proxy for cost of capital. It should be noted that the cost of capital can be provided by your finance department. It helps to have a cooperative relationship with this department in order to to obtain this figure. In our example, the discount rate is set at 9%. Your discount rate will probably be something else entirely. Present value interest tables found in finance texts, in Internet searches, and programmed into handheld business calculators are applied to each year. For each year, the net difference between the cost and the benefit for the buy option is established and that is multiplied by each year's net of costs and benefits. Then each of the five-year results are added together. The outsource option only requires a summation of costs.

The two options can be depicted on a timeline as:

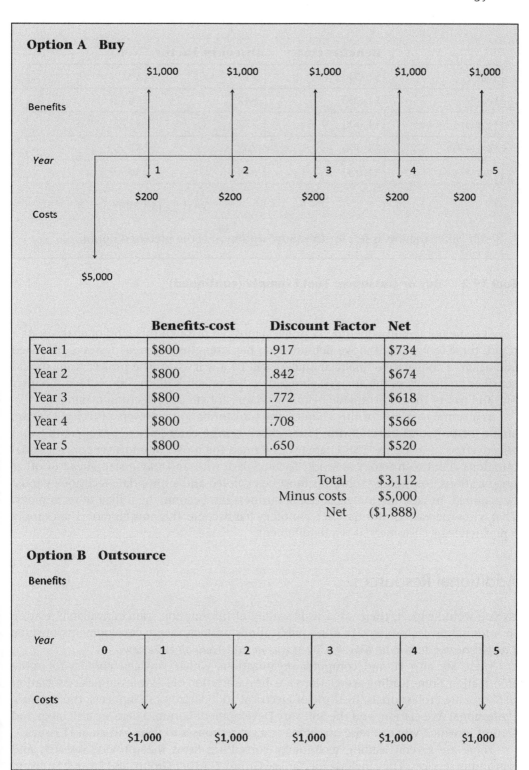

Option A   Buy

	Benefits-cost	Discount Factor	Net
Year 1	$800	.917	$734
Year 2	$800	.842	$674
Year 3	$800	.772	$618
Year 4	$800	.708	$566
Year 5	$800	.650	$520

Total $3,112
Minus costs $5,000
Net   ($1,888)

Option B   Outsource

Tool 19.2   **Buy or Outsource Tool Example (continued overleaf)**

	Benefits-cost	Discount Factor	Net
Year 1	$1,000	.917	$917
Year 2	$1,000	.842	$842
Year 3	$1,000	.772	$772
Year 4	$1,000	.708	$708
Year 5	$1,000	.650	$650

Total   ($3,889)

Result: Since the loss is less for the "Buy" option, it is the preferred option.

Tool 19.2   Buy or Outsource Tool Example (continued)

At some point, consequential IT projects must go through this kind of analysis. As a result, these tools should prove helpful. Each has strengths and weaknesses as discussed and again, a cooperative financial analyst will be a real asset. The project team should consider the results of the analysis alongside other established decision criteria. Chapter one and two of the book provide helpful guidance for effective decision making.

As a summary note for this chapter, the transformational powers of technology are abundant, profound and enduring. IT can clearly bring greater efficiency to operations and effectiveness to missions. This chapter has framed the most common yet consequential questions about technology at work. To keep pace with and stay a step ahead of other organizations, technology solutions must be explored and appropriate technology must be acquired. In fact, the milieu of doing business has become the milieu of technology. That is how pervasive information technology has become. It is now far more than simply a preference by customers; it is a requirement.

Additional Resources

As you would expect, there are a wide variety of information sources available relating to information technology. Leading publications on technology developments include: *Computerworld*, *InformationWeek*, *CIO Magazine* and *Technology Review*.

There are also IT and computer organizations which you can contact for more information. Some leading associations are the Association of IT Professionals, Association of Shareware Professionals, Institute of Electrical and Electronics Engineers, the Network Professional Association, and the Software Development Forum. There are also blogs and forums in which you can raise questions and get responses to your particular IT issues.

There are several leading technology consulting firms that provide research and consulting services. They include the Yankee Group, Gartner Group, and Frost & Sullivan. These are all very established consulting companies that have technology arms. Microsoft and Dell are both leaders in Cloud Computing solutions.

References

Bolland, E. (1988). *Cost Justifying Automation: A How to Handbook for Managers*. Fort Lee, NJ. Technical Insights.

Fogg, C. (Personal Interview). March 18, 2011.

Higdon, J. (Personal Interview). March 4, 2011.

Index

For Product Safety Concerns and Information please contact our EU
representative GPSR@taylorandfrancis.com Taylor & Francis Verlag GmbH,
Kaufingerstraße 24, 80331 München, Germany

Printed and bound by CPI Group (UK) Ltd, Croydon, CR0 4YY

08/05/2025

01864503-0002